Better Homes and Gardens.

365

comfort foods

inspiring meals for every day of the year

Houghton Mifflin Harcourt

Boston · New York · 2014

For information about permission to reproduce selections from this book, write to Permissions, Houghton Mifflin Harcourt Publishing Company, 215 Park Avenue South, New York, New York 10003.

www.hmhbooks.com

Library of Congress Cataloging-in-Publication Data:

Better homes and gardens' 365 comfort foods / [editor, Jan Miller]
    p. cm.
  Includes index.
  ISBN 978-1-118-62912-3 (pbk); 978-0-544-17836-6 (ebk)
  1. Cooking, American. 2. Comfort food. I. Miller, Jan.
  II. Better homes and gardens. III. Title: Better homes and gardens' three hundred sixty-five comfort foods. IV. Title: 365 comfort foods.
  TX715.B48584 2014
  641.5973—dc23
                      2013025650

Meredith Corporation

Editor: Jan Miller

Contributing Editors: Carrie Holcomb, Spectrum Communication Services

Recipe Development and Testing: Better Homes and Gardens Test Kitchen

Houghton Mifflin Harcourt

Publisher: Natalie Chapman

Editorial Director: Cindy Kitchel

Executive Editor: Anne Ficklen

Associate Editor: Heather Dabah

Production Editor: Jamie Selzer

Managing Editor: Marina Padakis Lowry

Art Director: Tai Blanche

Interior Design and Layout: Holly Wittenberg

Manufacturing Manager: Tom Hyland

Our seal assures you that every recipe in *365 Comfort Foods* has been tested in the Better Homes and Gardens Test Kitchen®. This means that each recipe is practical and reliable and meets our high standards of taste appeal. We guarantee your satisfaction with this book for as long as you own it.

Printed in the United States of America

DOC 10 9 8 7 6 5 4 3 2 1

Table of Contents

1 Breakfast. 5

2 Appetizers, Snacks, and Drinks 37

3 Comfort Food Classics Made Healthy . . . 69

4 Casseroles. 111

5 Soups and Stews 169

6 Slow Cooker Favorites 201

7 Main Dish Meats, Poultry, and Seafood . . . 237

8 30-Minute Meals 295

9 On the Side 331

10 Desserts 365

Index 402

Metric Information 416

Emergency Substitutions

IF YOU DON'T HAVE:	SUBSTITUTE:
Bacon, 1 slice, crisp-cooked, crumbled	1 tablespoon cooked bacon pieces
Baking powder, 1 teaspoon	½ teaspoon cream of tartar plus ¼ teaspoon baking soda
Balsamic vinegar, 1 tablespoon	1 tablespoon cider vinegar or red wine vinegar plus ½ teaspoon sugar
Bread crumbs, fine dry, ¼ cup	¾ cup soft bread crumbs, or ¼ cup cracker crumbs, or ¼ cup cornflake crumbs
Broth, beef or chicken, 1 cup	1 teaspoon or 1 cube instant beef or chicken bouillon plus 1 cup hot water
Buttermilk, 1 cup	1 tablespoon lemon juice or vinegar plus enough milk to make 1 cup (let stand 5 minutes before using) or 1 cup plain yogurt
Cornstarch, 1 tablespoon (for thickening)	2 tablespoons all-purpose flour
Egg, 1 whole	¼ cup refrigerated or frozen egg product, thawed
Garlic, 1 clove	½ teaspoon bottled minced garlic or ⅛ teaspoon garlic powder
Ginger, grated fresh, 1 teaspoon	¼ teaspoon ground ginger
Half-and-half or light cream, 1 cup	1 tablespoon melted butter or margarine plus enough whole milk to make 1 cup
Mustard, dry, 1 teaspoon	1 tablespoon prepared (in cooked mixtures)
Mustard, yellow, 1 tablespoon	½ teaspoon dry mustard plus 2 teaspoons vinegar
Onion, chopped, ½ cup	2 tablespoons dried minced onion or ½ teaspoon onion powder
Sour cream, dairy, 1 cup	1 cup plain yogurt or 1 cup light sour cream
Sugar, brown, 1 cup packed	1 cup granulated sugar plus 2 tablespoons molasses
Sugar, granulated, 1 cup	1 cup packed brown sugar or 2 cups sifted powdered sugar
Tomato juice, 1 cup	½ cup tomato sauce plus ½ cup water
Tomato sauce, 2 cups	¾ cup tomato paste plus 1 cup water
Wine, red, 1 cup	1 cup beef or chicken broth or cranberry juice in savory recipes; cranberry juice in desserts
Wine, white, 1 cup	1 cup chicken broth in savory recipes; apple juice or white grape juice in desserts

Seasonings

IF YOU DON'T HAVE:	SUBSTITUTE:
Apple pie spice, 1 teaspoon	½ teaspoon ground cinnamon plus ¼ teaspoon ground nutmeg, ⅛ teaspoon ground allspice, and pinch ground cloves or ginger
Cajun seasoning, 1 tablespoon	½ teaspoon white pepper plus ½ teaspoon garlic powder, ½ teaspoon onion powder, ½ teaspoon cayenne pepper, ½ teaspoon paprika, and ½ teaspoon black pepper
Fajita seasoning, 1 tablespoon	1½ teaspoons ground cumin plus ½ teaspoon dried oregano, crushed; ¼ teaspoon salt; ¼ teaspoon cayenne pepper; ¼ teaspoon black pepper; ⅛ teaspoon garlic powder; and ⅛ teaspoon onion powder
Herbs, snipped fresh, 1 tablespoon	½ to 1 teaspoon dried herb, crushed, or ½ teaspoon ground herb
Thai seasoning, 1 tablespoon	1 teaspoon ground coriander plus 1 teaspoon crushed red pepper, ¼ teaspoon salt, ¼ teaspoon ground ginger, ¼ teaspoon garlic powder, and ¼ teaspoon onion powder

Breakfast

Wake up with a hearty plate of biscuits and gravy, a basket of homemade muffins, or a stack of fluffy pancakes—comfort food doesn't have to come at the end of the day.

Quiche Lorraine

PREP 30 minutes BAKE 14 minutes at 450°F + 50 minutes at 325°F STAND 10 minutes MAKES 6 servings

- 1 recipe Pastry for a Single-Crust Pie
- 6 slices bacon
- ½ cup chopped onion (1 medium)
- 5 eggs, lightly beaten
- 1¼ cups half-and-half or light cream
- ¼ teaspoon salt
  Pinch ground nutmeg
- 1½ cups shredded Swiss cheese (6 ounces)
- 1 tablespoon all-purpose flour
  Chopped tomato (optional)
  Snipped fresh Italian (flat-leaf) parsley (optional)

1 Preheat oven to 450°F. Prepare Pastry for a Single-Crust Pie. On a lightly floured surface, use your hands to slightly flatten pastry. Roll pastry from center to edges into a circle about 12 inches in diameter. Wrap pastry circle around the rolling pin. Unroll into a 9-inch pie plate. Ease pastry into pie plate without stretching it. Trim pastry to ½ inch beyond edge of pie plate. Fold under extra pastry even with the plate's edge. Crimp edge as desired. Do not prick pastry.

2 Line pastry with a double thickness of foil. Bake for 8 minutes. Remove foil. Bake for 6 to 8 minutes more or until golden. Remove from oven. Reduce oven temperature to 325°F. (Pastry shell should still be hot when filling is added; do not partially bake pastry shell ahead of time.)

3 Meanwhile, in an extra-large skillet cook bacon over medium heat until crisp. Remove bacon and drain on paper towels, reserving 1 tablespoon drippings in skillet. Crumble bacon; set aside. Add onion to the reserved drippings; cook over medium heat until tender, stirring occasionally. Drain off fat.

4 In a large bowl combine eggs, half-and-half, salt, and nutmeg. Stir in crumbled bacon and onion. In a small bowl toss together cheese and flour; stir into egg mixture.

5 Pour egg mixture into the hot baked pastry shell. Bake for 50 to 55 minutes or until a knife inserted near the center comes out clean. If necessary to prevent overbrowning, cover edge of quiche with foil for the last 10 to 20 minutes of baking. Let stand for 10 minutes before serving. If desired, garnish with tomato and/or parsley.

Pastry for a Single-Crust Pie

In a medium bowl stir together 1½ cups all-purpose flour and ½ teaspoon salt. Using a pastry blender, cut in ¼ cup shortening and ¼ cup butter, cut up, until pieces are pea size. Sprinkle 1 tablespoon ice water over part of the flour mixture; toss gently with a fork. Push moistened pastry to side of bowl. Repeat moistening flour mixture, using 1 tablespoon ice water at a time, until all of the flour mixture is moistened (¼ to ⅓ cup ice water total). Gather flour mixture into a ball, kneading gently until it holds together.

NUTRITION FACTS PER SERVING:
560 cal., 39 g total fat (19 g sat. fat), 252 mg chol., 668 mg sodium, 30 g carb., 1 g fiber, 21 g pro.

Spinach and Mushroom Quiche

Prepare as directed, except omit bacon. Cook the onion and 1½ cups sliced fresh mushrooms in 1 tablespoon hot vegetable oil until tender, stirring occasionally. Stir in 3 cups lightly packed coarsely chopped fresh spinach. Stir spinach mixture into egg mixture with cheese. Continue as directed in Step 5.

Hash Brown–Crusted Quiche

PREP 35 minutes   COOK 20 minutes   BAKE 50 minutes at 325°F   STAND 10 minutes   MAKES 8 servings

1¾ pounds russet potatoes

½ teaspoon salt

⅛ teaspoon ground black pepper

1 to 2 tablespoons olive oil

1 tablespoon butter

4 slices bacon

1¼ cups coarsely shredded zucchini (1 medium)

½ cup chopped red onion (1 medium)

4 eggs, lightly beaten

1 cup half-and-half or light cream

¼ teaspoon crushed red pepper

1 cup shredded Swiss cheese (4 ounces)

1 tablespoon all-purpose flour

1 Preheat oven to 325°F. Peel and coarsely shred potatoes. Place potatoes in a large bowl; add enough water to cover potatoes. Stir well. Drain in a colander set in the sink. Repeat rinsing and draining two or three more times until water runs clear. Drain again, pressing out as much water as you can with a rubber spatula. Line a salad spinner with paper towels; add potatoes and spin.* Repeat, if necessary, until potatoes are dry. Transfer potatoes to a large bowl. Sprinkle with ¼ teaspoon of the salt and the black pepper; toss to combine.

2 In a 12-inch nonstick skillet with flared sides heat 1 tablespoon of the oil and the butter over medium-high heat until butter foams. Add potatoes, spreading into an even layer. Press gently with the back of a spatula to form a potato cake. Reduce heat to medium. Cook, without stirring, about 12 minutes or until bottom is golden and crisp.

3 Place a baking sheet or cutting board over top of skillet. Carefully invert skillet to transfer potatoes to baking sheet. If necessary, add the remaining 1 tablespoon oil to skillet. Using the baking sheet, slide potatoes back into skillet. Cook about 8 minutes more or until bottom is golden.

4 Lightly grease a 9-inch pie pan or plate. Use the baking sheet to transfer potato cake to pie pan; press potatoes into the bottom and up the sides of the pan.

5 In a large skillet cook bacon over medium heat until crisp. Remove bacon and drain on paper towels, reserving 1 tablespoon drippings in skillet. Crumble bacon; set aside. Add zucchini and onion to the reserved drippings. Cook over medium heat for 3 to 5 minutes or until tender, stirring occasionally.

6 In a large bowl combine eggs, half-and-half, crushed red pepper, and the remaining ¼ teaspoon salt. Stir in bacon and zucchini mixture. In a small bowl toss together cheese and flour; stir into egg mixture.

7 Pour egg mixture into the potato-lined pie pan. Bake, uncovered, for 50 to 55 minutes or until a knife inserted near the center comes out clean. Let stand for 10 minutes before serving.

*tip
Instead of using a salad spinner, you can dry the shredded potatoes by pressing out the water with a potato ricer or by patting them dry with paper towels.

NUTRITION FACTS PER SERVING:
324 cal., 22 g total fat (9 g sat. fat), 133 mg chol., 412 mg sodium, 20 g carb., 3 g fiber, 12 g pro.

Mushroom-Thyme Omelets

START TO FINISH 30 minutes MAKES 2 servings

Nonstick cooking spray

2 cups sliced assorted fresh mushrooms, such as button, cremini, and/or stemmed shiitake

3 tablespoons sliced green onions

1 clove garlic, minced

4 eggs, lightly beaten

1 teaspoon snipped fresh thyme

1/8 teaspoon salt

1/8 teaspoon ground black pepper

1 teaspoon olive oil

1/4 cup shredded cheddar cheese (1 ounce)

1/3 cup chopped roma tomato (1 medium)

1 tablespoon finely shredded Asiago or Parmesan cheese

Fresh thyme or parsley leaves (optional)

1 Lightly coat a 6- to 7-inch nonstick skillet with flared sides with cooking spray; heat skillet over medium heat. Add mushrooms, green onions, and garlic; cook and stir until mushrooms are tender. Using a slotted spoon, remove mushroom mixture from skillet; set aside. If necessary, drain skillet; carefully wipe out skillet with paper towels.

2 In a medium bowl combine eggs, snipped thyme, salt, and pepper.

3 Add half of the oil to the same skillet; heat skillet over medium heat. Pour half of the egg mixture into skillet. Using a wooden or plastic spatula, immediately begin stirring the eggs gently but continuously until mixture resembles small pieces of cooked egg surrounded by liquid egg. Stop stirring. Cook for 30 to 60 seconds more or until egg mixture is set.

4 Sprinkle with half of the cheddar cheese. Top with half of the mushroom mixture. Cook just until cheese begins to melt. Using the spatula, lift and fold an edge of the omelet partially over filling. Transfer to a serving plate; cover and keep warm.

5 Repeat with the remaining oil, egg mixture, cheddar cheese, and mushroom mixture. Top omelets with tomato, Asiago cheese, and, if desired, thyme leaves.

NUTRITION FACTS PER SERVING: 265 cal., 18 g total fat (7 g sat. fat), 389 mg chol., 426 mg sodium, 7 g carb., 2 g fiber, 21 g pro.

Hash Brown Omelet

START TO FINISH 25 minutes MAKES 4 servings

4 slices bacon

½ of a 20-ounce package (2 cups) refrigerated shredded hash brown potatoes

¼ cup chopped onion

¼ cup chopped green sweet pepper

4 eggs, lightly beaten

¼ cup milk

½ teaspoon salt

Pinch ground black pepper

1 cup shredded cheddar cheese (4 ounces)

Bias-sliced green onions (optional)

1 In a large skillet cook bacon over medium heat until crisp. Remove bacon and drain on paper towels, reserving 2 tablespoons drippings in skillet. Crumble bacon; set aside.

2 In a large bowl stir together potatoes, chopped onion, and sweet pepper. Add potato mixture to the reserved drippings; press gently. Cook over low heat about 7 minutes or until potatoes are brown and crisp, turning once.

3 Meanwhile, in a small bowl combine eggs, milk, salt, and black pepper. Pour egg mixture over potato mixture. Sprinkle with cheese and bacon. Cook, covered, over low heat for 5 to 7 minutes or until egg mixture is set. Loosen omelet; fold in half. Transfer to a serving plate. Cut into wedges. If desired, sprinkle with green onions.

NUTRITION FACTS PER SERVING: *382 cal., 25 g total fat (12 g sat. fat), 256 mg chol., 729 mg sodium, 20 g carb., 1 g fiber, 19 g pro.*

Baked Eggs with Cheese and Basil Sauce

PREP 15 minutes BAKE 18 minutes at 350°F MAKES 4 servings

3 tablespoons butter

2 tablespoons all-purpose flour

¼ teaspoon salt

⅛ teaspoon ground black pepper

3 tablespoons snipped fresh basil or ½ teaspoon dried basil, crushed

1 cup milk

Nonstick cooking spray

4 eggs

Salt

Ground black pepper

¼ cup shredded mozzarella cheese (1 ounce)

Snipped fresh basil (optional)

1 Preheat oven to 350°F. For sauce, in a small saucepan heat butter over medium heat until melted. Stir in flour, ¼ teaspoon salt, and ⅛ teaspoon pepper. If using, stir in dried basil. Gradually stir in milk. Cook and stir until thickened and bubbly. Cook and stir for 1 minute more. Remove from heat. If using, stir in 3 tablespoons fresh basil.

2 Lightly coat four 8- to 10-ounce round baking dishes or 6-ounce custard cups with cooking spray. To assemble, spoon about 2 tablespoons of the sauce into each prepared baking dish. Gently break an egg into the center of each dish; sprinkle with additional salt and pepper. Spoon the remaining sauce over eggs.

3 Bake for 18 to 20 minutes or until eggs are set. Sprinkle with cheese. Let stand until cheese is melted. If desired, garnish with additional fresh basil.

NUTRITION FACTS PER SERVING: *216 cal., 16 g total fat (9 g sat. fat), 245 mg chol., 419 mg sodium, 6 g carb., 0 g fiber, 10 g pro.*

Smoked Salmon Eggs Benedict

Photo on page 131

START TO FINISH **35 minutes** MAKES **4 servings**

¼ cup light sour cream

1 teaspoon lemon juice

¾ to 1 teaspoon dry mustard

3 to 4 teaspoons fat-free milk

4 eggs

4 ounces thinly sliced smoked salmon (lox-style)*

2 whole wheat English muffins, split and toasted

Finely chopped red onion (optional)

Freshly ground black pepper (optional)

1 For sauce, in a small bowl combine sour cream, lemon juice, and dry mustard. Stir in enough of the milk to reach desired consistency. Set aside.

2 Lightly grease four cups of an egg-poaching pan.** Place poaching cups into bottom pan over boiling water following the manufacturer's directions; reduce heat to simmering. Break an egg into a measuring cup. Carefully slide egg into a poaching cup. Repeat with the remaining three eggs. Cook, covered, for 4 to 6 minutes or until the whites are completely set and yolks begin to thicken but are not hard. Run a knife around edges to loosen eggs. Invert poaching cups to remove eggs.

3 Divide smoked salmon among toasted muffin halves. Top with poached eggs; spoon sauce over eggs. If desired, sprinkle with red onion and/ or pepper.

NUTRITION FACTS PER SERVING:
192 cal., 8 g total fat (3 g sat. fat), 197 mg chol., 769 mg sodium, 15 g carb., 2 g fiber, 15 g pro.

***tip**

Lox-style salmon is cured by brining and then smoking it, giving it a softer texture and brighter color. It looks almost raw, but it is fully cooked. Any smoked salmon will work in this recipe.

****tip**

If you don't have an egg-poaching pan, lightly grease a large skillet. Fill the skillet halfway with water. Bring water to boiling; reduce heat to simmering. Break an egg into a measuring cup and slip egg into the simmering water. Repeat with the remaining three eggs. Simmer, uncovered, for 3 to 5 minutes or until whites are completely set and yolks begin to thicken but are not hard. Remove eggs with a slotted spoon.

Baked Denver Strata

PREP 25 minutes BAKE 35 minutes at 350°F STAND 10 minutes MAKES 10 servings

- 6 **English muffins, split and quartered**
- 9 **eggs, lightly beaten**
- 1 **cup milk**
- 1 **4-ounce can diced green chile peppers, drained**
- ¼ **teaspoon salt**
- ¼ **teaspoon ground black pepper**
- 1 **cup diced cooked ham (about 5 ounces)**
- 1 **7-ounce jar roasted red sweet peppers, drained and cut into strips**
- ½ **cup finely chopped green onions (4)**
- 1 **2.5-ounce can sliced, pitted ripe olives, drained**
- 1½ **cups shredded provolone cheese (6 ounces)**
- ½ **cup shredded cheddar cheese (2 ounces)**

1 Preheat oven to 350°F. Grease a 3-quart rectangular baking dish. Arrange English muffin quarters in a single layer in the prepared baking dish.

2 In a large bowl combine eggs, milk, green chile peppers, salt, and black pepper. Pour egg mixture over muffin quarters. Top with ham, roasted peppers, green onions, and olives. Sprinkle with provolone cheese and cheddar cheese.

3 Bake, uncovered, about 35 minutes or until a knife inserted near the center comes out clean. Let stand for 10 minutes before serving.

NUTRITION FACTS PER SERVING:
279 cal., 14 g total fat (6 g sat. fat), 218 mg chol., 744 mg sodium, 20 g carb., 2 g fiber, 18 g pro.

Make-Ahead Directions: Prepare as directed through Step 2. Cover and chill for 2 to 24 hours. To serve, preheat oven to 350°F. Bake, uncovered, about 45 minutes or until a knife inserted near the center comes out clean. Let stand for 10 minutes before serving.

Baked Brie Strata

PREP 25 minutes CHILL 4 to 24 hours BAKE 55 minutes at 325°F STAND 10 minutes MAKES 6 servings

2 cups sliced zucchini

6 cups crusty sourdough bread torn into bite-size pieces (6 ounces)

1 4.4-ounce package Brie cheese

1 cup halved grape or cherry tomatoes

4 eggs, lightly beaten, or 1 cup refrigerated or frozen egg product, thawed

$\frac{2}{3}$ cup evaporated milk

$\frac{1}{3}$ cup sliced green onions

3 tablespoons snipped fresh dill

$\frac{1}{2}$ teaspoon salt

$\frac{1}{8}$ teaspoon ground black pepper

1 In a covered medium saucepan cook zucchini in a small amount of lightly salted boiling water for 2 to 3 minutes or just until tender; drain.

2 Grease a 2-quart rectangular baking dish. Spread 4 cups of the bread pieces in the prepared baking dish. If desired, remove and discard rind from cheese. Cut cheese into $\frac{1}{2}$-inch pieces; sprinkle evenly over bread in baking dish. Top with zucchini and tomatoes. Sprinkle with the remaining 2 cups bread pieces.

3 In a medium bowl combine eggs, evaporated milk, green onions, dill, salt, and pepper. Pour evenly over layers in dish. Press down gently with the back of a large spoon to moisten all of the ingredients. Cover with plastic wrap and chill for 4 to 24 hours.

4 Preheat oven to 325°F. Remove plastic wrap; cover dish with foil. Bake for 30 minutes. Bake, uncovered, for 25 to 30 minutes more or until a knife inserted near the center comes out clean. Let stand for 10 minutes before serving.

NUTRITION FACTS PER SERVING:
251 cal., 12 g total fat (6 g sat. fat), 170 mg chol., 592 mg sodium, 22 g carb., 2 g fiber, 15 g pro.

Potato-Ham Bake

PREP 25 minutes BAKE 30 minutes at 400°F STAND 5 minutes MAKES 4 servings

1   pound Yukon gold potatoes, sliced

1   8-ounce tub light cream cheese spread with chive and onion

¾   cup milk

¼   cup finely shredded Parmesan cheese (1 ounce)

¼   teaspoon ground black pepper

1   tablespoon snipped fresh tarragon or ½ teaspoon dried tarragon, crushed

8   ounces cooked ham, cut into bite-size pieces

1   pound fresh asparagus, trimmed and cut into 2- to 3-inch pieces

Ground black pepper (optional)

Fresh tarragon sprigs (optional)

1 Preheat oven to 400°F. Lightly grease a 1½-quart shallow baking dish; set aside. In a covered medium saucepan cook potatoes in enough lightly salted boiling water to cover for 5 to 7 minutes or just until tender; drain. Transfer potatoes to a medium bowl; set aside.

2 For sauce, in the same saucepan combine cream cheese spread, milk, 2 tablespoons of the Parmesan cheese, and the ¼ teaspoon pepper. Cook and stir over medium heat until Parmesan cheese is melted and mixture is smooth. Remove from heat; stir in snipped fresh or dried tarragon.

3 Layer half of the potatoes, half of the ham, half of the asparagus, and half of the sauce in the prepared baking dish. Repeat layers. Bake, covered, for 20 minutes. Sprinkle with the remaining 2 tablespoons Parmesan cheese. Bake, uncovered, for 10 to 12 minutes more or until heated through. Let stand for 5 minutes before serving. If desired, sprinkle with additional pepper and garnish with tarragon sprigs.

NUTRITION FACTS PER SERVING:
346 cal., 16 g total fat (9 g sat. fat), 67 mg chol., 1162 mg sodium, 30 g carb., 5 g fiber, 22 g pro.

Easy Hash Brown Bake

Photo on page 140

PREP **30 minutes**   BAKE **45 minutes at 350°F**   MAKES **12 servings**

- ¼ cup vegetable oil
- 1 32-ounce package frozen diced hash brown potatoes
- ½ cup chopped onion (1 medium)
- 1 10.75-ounce can condensed cream of chicken soup
- 1 16-ounce carton light sour cream
- 2 cups diced cooked ham (about 10 ounces)
- 8 ounces American cheese, cubed*
- ¼ teaspoon ground black pepper
- 2 cups crushed cornflakes
- ¼ cup butter, melted

1 Preheat oven to 350°F. In a large skillet heat oil over medium-high heat. Add hash brown potatoes; cook for 7 minutes, stirring occasionally. Stir in onion; cook about 3 minutes more or until some of the potatoes are light brown. Stir in soup. Stir in sour cream, ham, cheese, and pepper. Transfer mixture to an ungreased 3-quart shallow baking dish.

2 In a medium bowl stir together cornflakes and melted butter; sprinkle over potato mixture. Bake, uncovered, for 45 to 50 minutes or until bubbly.

NUTRITION FACTS PER SERVING:
366 cal., 22 g total fat (10 g sat. fat), 58 mg chol., 1002 mg sodium, 29 g carb., 2 g fiber, 13 g pro.

Make-Ahead Directions: Prepare as directed in Step 1. Cover and chill for 8 to 24 hours. To serve, continue as directed in Step 2, except bake, uncovered, for 50 to 55 minutes or until bubbly.

*tip
Buy a chunk of American cheese from a deli or look for the American cheese slices that have not been individually wrapped.

Asparagus, Zucchini, and Yellow Pepper Frittata with Fontina

PREP 30 minutes BAKE 35 minutes at 350°F STAND 10 minutes MAKES 8 servings

1½ pounds fresh asparagus or two 9- or 10-ounce packages frozen cut asparagus

1 medium yellow sweet pepper, seeded and cut into ¼-inch strips*

⅓ cup chopped onion (1 small)

1 small zucchini, halved lengthwise and cut into ¼-inch slices

10 eggs, lightly beaten

1 cup half-and-half, light cream, or milk

2 tablespoons snipped fresh Italian (flat-leaf) parsley

1¼ teaspoons salt

¼ to ½ teaspoon ground black pepper

½ cup shredded fontina cheese (2 ounces)

1 Preheat oven to 350°F. Grease a 2-quart rectangular baking dish; set aside.

2 If using fresh asparagus, snap off and discard woody bases. If desired, scrape off scales. Cut asparagus into 1-inch pieces.

3 In a medium saucepan bring about 1 inch water to boiling. Add fresh or frozen asparagus, sweet pepper, and onion. Return just to boiling; reduce heat. Boil gently, covered, about 1 minute or until vegetables are crisp-tender; drain. Set aside a few asparagus tips for garnish. Spread the asparagus-pepper mixture evenly in the prepared baking dish. Layer with zucchini slices.

4 In a large bowl combine eggs, half-and-half, parsley, salt, and black pepper. Pour evenly over vegetables in dish. Sprinkle with cheese. Bake, uncovered, about 35 minutes or until a knife inserted near the center comes out clean. Let stand for 10 minutes before serving. Garnish with the reserved asparagus tips.

NUTRITION FACTS PER SERVING:
186 cal., 12 g total fat (6 g sat. fat), 253 mg chol., 541 mg sodium, 6 g carb., 2 g fiber, 13 g pro.

*tip
For even more color, use red and orange sweet peppers in addition to the yellow. Just be sure your total measurement of pepper strips is about 1 cup.

Fried Egg, Avocado, and Bacon Breakfast Sandwiches

Photo on page 131

START TO FINISH **25 minutes**   MAKES **4 servings**

- 1   **large ripe avocado**
- 2   **tablespoons light mayonnaise or salad dressing**
- 1   **teaspoon lemon juice**
- 1   **clove garlic, minced**
- 2   **teaspoons butter**
- 4   **eggs**
      Salt (optional)
      Ground black pepper (optional)
- 8   **slices whole wheat bread, toasted**
- 4   **slices cheddar cheese (optional)**
- 8   **slices bacon, crisp-cooked, drained, and halved crosswise**

1 Halve, pit, and peel avocado. Place one avocado half in a small bowl; mash with a fork or the back of a wooden spoon. Stir in mayonnaise, lemon juice, and garlic. Thinly slice the remaining avocado half. Set aside.

2 In a large skillet heat butter over medium heat until melted. Break eggs into skillet. If desired, sprinkle with salt and pepper. Reduce heat to low; cook eggs for 3 to 4 minutes or until whites are completely set and yolks start to thicken.

3 For fried eggs over easy or over hard, when the whites are completely set and the yolks start to thicken, turn the eggs and cook for 30 seconds more (over easy) or 1 minute more (over hard).

4 Layer four of the bread slices with cheese, if desired, avocado slices, bacon, and fried eggs. Spread the remaining four bread slices with mayonnaise mixture; place on sandwiches, spread sides down.

NUTRITION FACTS PER SERVING:
257 cal., 14 g total fat (2 g sat. fat), 10 mg chol., 432 mg sodium, 27 g carb., 7 g fiber, 9 g pro.

Bacon-Biscuit Egg Sandwiches

PREP 30 minutes BAKE 16 minutes at 450°F MAKES 6 servings

- 3 **cups all-purpose flour**
- 1 **tablespoon sugar**
- 1 **tablespoon baking powder**
- 1 **teaspoon cracked black pepper**
- ¾ **teaspoon cream of tartar**
- ½ **teaspoon salt**
- ¾ **cup butter**
- 1¼ **cups buttermilk or sour milk***
- 6 **slices bacon, crisp-cooked, drained, and crumbled**
- ¼ **cup shredded cheddar cheese (1 ounce)**
- 1 **recipe Cheese-and-Onion Scrambled Eggs**
  Mayonnaise (optional)
- 1 **ripe avocado, pitted, peeled, and sliced**

1 Preheat oven to 450°F. In a large bowl stir together flour, sugar, baking powder, pepper, cream of tartar, and salt. Using a pastry blender, cut in butter until mixture resembles coarse crumbs. Make a well in the center of flour mixture. Add buttermilk and 4 slices of the bacon all at once. Using a fork, stir just until mixture is moistened.

2 Turn dough out onto a lightly floured surface. Knead dough by folding and gently pressing it just until dough holds together. Pat or lightly roll dough until 1 inch thick. Cut dough with a floured 3-inch round cutter. Dip cutter into flour between cuts and reroll scraps as necessary. Place dough rounds 1 inch apart on an ungreased baking sheet.

3 Sprinkle biscuits with cheese and remaining 2 slices crumbled bacon. Bake for 16 to 18 minutes or until golden. (You will only need six biscuits for this recipe. Store any remaining biscuits to use later.**) Prepare Cheese-and-Onion Scrambled Eggs.

4 Split the six biscuits. If desired, spread mayonnaise on cut sides of biscuits. Fill biscuits with avocado slices and scrambled eggs.

NUTRITION FACTS PER SERVING:
633 cal., 39 g total fat (20 g sat. fat), 270 mg chol., 1012 mg sodium, 49 g carb., 3 g fiber, 21 g pro.

*tip

To make 1¼ cups sour milk, place 4 teaspoons lemon juice or vinegar in a glass measuring cup. Add enough milk to make 1¼ cups total liquid; stir. Let stand for 5 minutes before using.

**tip

Place any remaining biscuits in an airtight container; cover. Store in the refrigerator for up to 2 days or freeze for up to 2 months.

Cheese-and-Onion Scrambled Eggs

In a medium bowl whisk together 6 eggs; ⅓ cup milk, half-and-half, or light cream; ¼ teaspoon salt; and pinch ground black pepper. In a large skillet heat 1 tablespoon butter over medium heat until melted. Add 2 tablespoons sliced green onion (1); cook and stir for 30 seconds. Pour in egg mixture. Cook over medium heat, without stirring, until mixture begins to set on the bottom and around edges. Using a spatula or large spoon, lift and fold the partially cooked egg mixture so the uncooked portion flows underneath. Fold in ½ cup shredded cheddar, mozzarella, or Monterey Jack cheese with jalapeño peppers (2 ounces). Continue cooking over medium heat for 2 to 3 minutes or until egg mixture is cooked through but is still glossy and moist. Immediately remove from heat.

Black Bean and Corn Breakfast Burritos

START TO FINISH **30 minutes**   MAKES **6 servings**

2   **teaspoons olive oil**

2   **medium fresh poblano chile peppers, seeded and chopped***

¾   **cup canned black beans, rinsed and drained**

¾   **cup frozen whole kernel corn, thawed**

⅓   **cup red or green salsa**

½   **teaspoon ground cumin**

½   **teaspoon chili powder**

6   **eggs, lightly beaten**

Pinch salt

Pinch ground black pepper

6   **8-inch whole grain flour tortillas, warmed according to package directions**

¾   **cup crumbled queso fresco or shredded reduced-fat Monterey Jack cheese (3 ounces)**

¼   **cup snipped fresh cilantro**

½   **cup red or green salsa (optional)**

1 In a large skillet heat 1 teaspoon of the oil over medium heat. Add poblano peppers; cook about 3 minutes or just until tender, stirring occasionally. Stir in beans, corn, ⅓ cup salsa, cumin, and chili powder. Cook and stir about 2 minutes or until heated through. Remove vegetable mixture from skillet and set aside.

2 In a medium bowl combine eggs, salt, and black pepper. In the same skillet heat the remaining 1 teaspoon oil over medium heat. Pour in egg mixture. Cook, without stirring, until mixture begins to set on the bottom and around the edges. Using a spatula or a large spoon, lift and fold the partially cooked egg mixture so the uncooked portion flows underneath. Continue cooking over medium heat for 2 to 3 minutes or until egg mixture is cooked through but is still glossy and moist. Immediately remove from heat. Gently fold in vegetable mixture.

3 Spoon about ⅔ cup of the egg mixture onto each tortilla just below the center. Top with cheese and cilantro. Fold bottom edge of each tortilla up and over filling. Fold in opposite sides; roll up from the bottom. Cut in half before serving. If desired, serve with ½ cup salsa.

NUTRITION FACTS PER SERVING:
297 cal., 12 g total fat (4 g sat. fat), 216 mg chol., 602 mg sodium, 29 g carb., 12 g fiber, 20 g pro.

***tip**

Because chile peppers contain volatile oils that can burn your skin and eyes, avoid direct contact with them as much as possible. When working with chile peppers, wear plastic or rubber gloves. If your bare hands do touch the peppers, wash your hands and nails well with soap and warm water.

Breakfast

Flaky Buttermilk Biscuits with Sausage Gravy

PREP 30 minutes BAKE 15 minutes at 450°F MAKES 6 servings

- 3 cups all-purpose flour
- 1 tablespoon baking powder
- 1 tablespoon sugar
- 1 teaspoon salt
- ¾ teaspoon cream of tartar
- ¾ cup butter or ½ cup butter and ¼ cup shortening
- 1¼ cups buttermilk or sour milk,* or 1 cup milk
- 1 recipe Sausage Gravy

  Snipped fresh chives (optional)

1 Preheat oven to 450°F. In a large bowl stir together flour, baking powder, sugar, salt, and cream of tartar. Using a pastry blender, cut in butter until mixture resembles coarse crumbs. Make a well in the center of flour mixture. Add buttermilk all at once. Using a fork, stir just until moistened.

2 Turn dough out onto a lightly floured surface. Knead dough by folding and gently pressing it just until dough holds together. Pat or lightly roll dough until 1¼ inches thick. Cut dough with a floured 2½-inch round cutter. Dip cutter into flour between cuts and reroll scraps as necessary.

3 Place dough rounds 1 inch apart on an ungreased baking sheet. Bake for 15 to 18 minutes or until golden. Remove biscuits from baking sheet. Cool slightly.

4 To serve, split warm biscuits and place on serving plates. Spoon Sausage Gravy over split biscuits. If desired, sprinkle with chives.

NUTRITION FACTS PER SERVING:
897 cal., 57 g total fat (26 g sat. fat), 155 mg chol., 1704 mg sodium, 65 g carb., 2 g fiber, 30 g pro.

Sausage Gravy

In an extra-large skillet cook 1½ pounds bulk pork sausage and 1 cup chopped onion (1 large) over medium-high heat until meat is brown and onion is tender, using a wooden spoon to break up meat as it cooks. Do not drain. Sprinkle ¼ cup all-purpose flour over meat mixture; stir to combine. Cook and stir over medium heat for 1 minute. Gradually stir in 3 cups milk. Cook and stir until thickened and bubbly. Cook and stir for 1 minute more. Season to taste with salt and ground black pepper. If desired, stir in 2 teaspoons snipped fresh thyme.

Make-Ahead Directions: Prepare biscuits as directed; cool completely. Place biscuits in a resealable plastic freezer bag; seal, label, and freeze for up to 2 months. Prepare Sausage Gravy as directed. Place in an airtight container; cover and chill for up to 48 hours. To serve, thaw biscuits at room temperature (allow about 2 hours). Preheat oven to 350°F. Place biscuits on a baking sheet. Bake about 5 minutes or until warm. In a medium saucepan reheat gravy over medium-low heat for 5 to 10 minutes or until heated through. If necessary, stir in additional milk to reach desired consistency.

*tip

To make 1¼ cups sour milk, place 4 teaspoons lemon juice or vinegar in a glass measuring cup. Add enough milk to make 1¼ cups total liquid; stir. Let stand for 5 minutes before using.

Cornflake Chicken 'n' Waffles

PREP 30 minutes MARINATE 30 minutes to 24 hours BAKE 25 minutes at 375°F MAKES 6 servings

- ⅓ **cup buttermilk or sour milk***
- 1 **teaspoon salt**
- ½ **teaspoon garlic powder or onion powder**
- ¼ **teaspoon cayenne pepper**
- 1½ **pounds skinless, boneless chicken breast halves, cut into 2-inch pieces**
  Nonstick cooking spray
- 3 **cups cornflakes, finely crushed****
- 1½ **teaspoons poultry seasoning**
- 3 **tablespoons butter, melted**
- 4 **slices bacon, finely chopped**
  Melted butter (optional)
- ¼ **cup all-purpose flour**
- 3 **cups milk**
- 1½ **teaspoons snipped fresh thyme**
- ¼ **teaspoon ground black pepper**
- 6 **frozen waffles, toasted, or other favorite baked waffles**
  Maple syrup (optional)

1 In a resealable plastic bag set in a bowl combine buttermilk, ½ teaspoon of the salt, the garlic powder, and cayenne pepper. Add chicken. Seal bag; turn to coat chicken. Marinate in the refrigerator for at least 30 minutes or up to 24 hours.

2 Preheat oven to 375°F. Coat a baking sheet with cooking spray; set aside.

3 In a shallow dish combine cornflakes, poultry seasoning, and ¼ teaspoon of the salt. Stir in 3 tablespoons melted butter. Remove chicken pieces, one at a time, from buttermilk mixture and roll in cornflake mixture to coat. Arrange on the prepared baking sheet, making sure pieces do not touch. Sprinkle chicken with any remaining cornflake mixture.

4 Bake, uncovered, for 25 to 30 minutes or until chicken is no longer pink (170°F). Do not turn pieces while baking.

5 Meanwhile, for gravy, in a large skillet cook bacon over medium heat until brown. Measure bacon drippings; add as much additional melted butter as needed to measure ¼ cup total mixture. Stir in flour until combined; gradually stir in milk. Bring to simmering; stir in thyme, black pepper, and the remaining ¼ teaspoon salt. Cook and stir for 2 to 3 minutes or until thickened and bubbly.

6 To serve, divide waffles among serving plates. Top with chicken pieces and some of the gravy. If desired, drizzle with maple syrup. Serve with the remaining gravy.

NUTRITION FACTS PER SERVING:
630 cal., 34 g total fat (11 g sat. fat), 150 mg chol., 1105 mg sodium, 42 g carb., 1 g fiber, 38 g pro.

*tip
To make ⅓ cup sour milk, place 1 teaspoon lemon juice or vinegar in a glass measuring cup. Add enough milk to make ⅓ cup total liquid; stir. Let stand for 5 minutes before using.

**tip
To crush the cornflakes, place half of them in a resealable plastic bag, let out some of the air, and seal the bag. Roll a rolling pin over the top of the bag several times. Flip the bag over and repeat until the cornflakes are crumbled into small pieces. Repeat with the remaining cornflakes.

Breakfast

Overnight Three-Grain Waffles   *Photo on page 130*

PREP 25 minutes   CHILL Overnight   BAKE Per manufacturer's directions   MAKES 4 servings

1¼   cups all-purpose flour

1   cup yellow cornmeal

½   cup oat bran

3   tablespoons sugar

1   package active dry yeast

½   teaspoon salt

2   cups milk

2   eggs

⅓   cup vegetable oil

1   recipe Praline Sauce
     or maple syrup

1 In a large mixing bowl stir together flour, cornmeal, oat bran, sugar, yeast, and salt. Add milk, eggs, and oil. Beat with an electric mixer on medium speed about 1 minute or until combined. Cover batter loosely with plastic wrap and chill overnight.

2 To bake waffles, stir batter. Add batter to a preheated, lightly greased waffle baker according to the manufacturer's directions. Close lid quickly; do not open until done. Bake according to the manufacturer's directions. When done, use a fork to lift waffle off grid. Repeat with the remaining batter. Serve warm with Praline Sauce.

NUTRITION FACTS PER SERVING: *515 cal., 19 g total fat (5 g sat. fat), 67 mg chol., 212 mg sodium, 81 g carb., 3 g fiber, 9 g pro.*

Praline Sauce

In a small saucepan heat 3 tablespoons butter over medium heat until melted. Stir in 3 tablespoons packed brown sugar and 2 tablespoons whipping cream. Bring to boiling, stirring constantly; reduce heat. Boil gently, uncovered, for 3 minutes, stirring occasionally. Stir in 1 teaspoon vanilla; cool.

Oven-Puffed Pancake with Caramelized Plums

PREP 30 minutes BAKE 15 minutes at 450°F MAKES 4 servings

¼ cup butter

2 to 3 firm ripe plums, pitted and cut into 1-inch wedges

3 eggs, lightly beaten

½ cup all-purpose flour

½ cup milk

1 teaspoon vanilla

½ teaspoon kosher salt

½ cup packed brown sugar

2 teaspoons ground cinnamon

¼ cup butter, melted

3 tablespoons lemon juice

1 Preheat oven to 450°F. In a 10-inch cast-iron or oven-going skillet heat ¼ cup butter over medium-high heat until melted. Add plums; cook about 5 minutes or until softened and golden, stirring occasionally. Keep warm.

2 In a medium bowl combine eggs, flour, milk, vanilla, and salt. Pour egg mixture over plums. Transfer skillet to oven. Bake for 10 to 12 minutes or until puffed and brown. Remove from oven.

3 In a small bowl combine brown sugar and cinnamon. Pour ¼ cup melted butter over pancake; sprinkle with brown sugar mixture. Bake about 5 minutes more or until brown sugar is melted and dark brown. Remove from oven. Drizzle with lemon juice.

4 Serve pancake from skillet or slide out onto a serving plate. Cut into wedges and serve immediately.

NUTRITION FACTS PER SERVING:
458 cal., 27 g total fat (16 g sat. fat), 203 mg chol., 525 mg sodium, 46 g carb., 2 g fiber, 8 g pro.

Blueberry Pancakes *Photo on page 131*

START TO FINISH **30 minutes** MAKES **20 to 24 servings**

- 2½ cups all-purpose flour
- 1 cup whole wheat pastry flour
- ¼ cup sugar
- 4 teaspoons baking powder
- 1 teaspoon baking soda
- ½ teaspoon salt
- 2 eggs, lightly beaten
- 4 cups buttermilk or sour milk*
- ⅓ cup vegetable oil
- 1 cup fresh or frozen blueberries**
- Maple syrup (optional)

1 In a large bowl stir together all-purpose flour, whole wheat flour, sugar, baking powder, baking soda, and salt. In another large bowl combine eggs, buttermilk, and oil. Add egg mixture all at once to flour mixture. Stir just until moistened (batter should be slightly lumpy). Gently stir in blueberries.

2 For each pancake, pour a scant ⅓ cup batter onto a hot, lightly greased griddle or heavy skillet. Cook over medium heat for 2 to 3 minutes on each side or until pancakes are golden. Turn over when surfaces are bubbly and edges are slightly dry. Serve warm. If desired, serve with maple syrup.

NUTRITION FACTS PER SERVING:
152 cal., 5 g total fat (1 g sat. fat), 21 mg chol., 253 mg sodium, 23 g carb., 1 g fiber, 5 g pro.

*tip
To make 4 cups sour milk, place ¼ cup lemon juice or vinegar in a glass measuring cup. Add enough milk to make 4 cups total liquid; stir. Let stand for 5 minutes before using.

**tip
If you like, replace the blueberries with one of the following dried fruit options: chopped apple, raisins, dates, cranberries, cherries, or mixed fruit.

Pumpkin Pancakes

START TO FINISH **30 minutes** MAKES **16 servings**

2 **cups all-purpose flour**

3 **tablespoons packed brown sugar**

1 **tablespoon baking powder**

½ **teaspoon salt**

½ **teaspoon pumpkin pie spice or ground cinnamon (optional)**

3 **eggs, lightly beaten**

1¾ **cups milk**

¾ **cup canned pumpkin**

¼ **cup vegetable oil**

Maple syrup (optional)

1 In a large bowl stir together flour, brown sugar, baking powder, salt, and, if desired, pumpkin pie spice. In a medium bowl combine eggs, milk, pumpkin, and oil. Add egg mixture all at once to flour mixture. Stir just until moistened (batter should be slightly lumpy).

2 For each pancake, pour about ¼ cup batter onto a hot, lightly greased griddle or heavy skillet. Spread batter, if necessary. Cook over medium heat for 1 to 2 minutes on each side or until pancakes are golden. Turn over when surfaces are bubbly and edges are slightly dry. Serve warm. If desired, serve with maple syrup.

NUTRITION FACTS PER SERVING:
128 cal., 5 g total fat (1 g sat. fat), 42 mg chol., 167 mg sodium, 17 g carb., 1 g fiber, 4 g pro.

tips

Keep pancakes warm while cooking the remaining batter by placing the cooked pancakes on an ovenproof plate in a 200°F oven.

Pancakes are ready to turn when the tops are bubbly all over with a few broken bubbles. Edges will be slightly dry. Be sure you turn pancakes only once.

Breakfast

Baked French Toast

PREP 30 minutes CHILL 2 to 24 hours BAKE 35 minutes at 375°F MAKES 6 servings

- 5 **eggs, lightly beaten**
- 1 **cup milk**
- ⅓ **cup granulated sugar**
- ⅓ **cup whipping cream**
- 1 **teaspoon vanilla**
- ¼ **teaspoon ground cinnamon**
   Pinch salt
- 6 **1-inch slices dry challah or brioche***
- 1 **tablespoon granulated sugar**
   Powdered sugar
- 1 **recipe Spiced Maple Syrup**

1 Grease a 3-quart rectangular baking dish; set aside. In a large shallow dish combine eggs, milk, ⅓ cup granulated sugar, whipping cream, vanilla, cinnamon, and salt, stirring until sugar is dissolved.

2 Dip bread slices, one at a time, into egg mixture, turning to coat both sides. Arrange in the prepared baking dish. Cover and chill for 2 to 24 hours.

3 Preheat oven to 375°F. Sprinkle bread slices with 1 tablespoon granulated sugar. Bake, uncovered, about 35 minutes or until bread is golden and puffed. Sprinkle with powdered sugar and serve with Spiced Maple Syrup.

NUTRITION FACTS PER SERVING:
477 cal., 24 g total fat (11 g sat. fat), 274 mg chol., 281 mg sodium, 55 g carb., 1 g fiber, 11 g pro.

Spiced Maple Syrup

In a small saucepan combine ½ cup maple syrup, 3 inches stick cinnamon, and 2 whole cloves. Bring to boiling; remove from heat. Let stand for 20 minutes. Using a slotted spoon, remove cinnamon and cloves.

tip

French toast was created as a way to use up day-old bread, and it's delicious with many varieties of breads. Try it with sliced croissants, challah, sourdough, or even a hearty multigrain bread.

*tip

To dry bread slices, preheat oven to 300°F. Place bread slices on a large baking sheet. Bake, uncovered, for 5 minutes; cool. Or place bread slices on a wire rack; cover loosely and let stand overnight.

Ham-and-Cheese Stuffed French Toast

PREP 20 minutes COOK 6 minutes per batch MAKES 6 servings

2 eggs, lightly beaten

1 cup half-and-half, light cream, or milk

1 teaspoon vanilla

$\frac{1}{2}$ teaspoon ground cinnamon

12 slices firm-texture white, wheat, or rye bread

6 ounces sliced Gruyère or Swiss cheese

8 ounces very thinly sliced cooked ham

Butter

1 carambola (star fruit), sliced (optional)

1 kiwifruit, peeled and sliced (optional)

1 In a shallow dish combine eggs, half-and-half, vanilla, and cinnamon; set aside.

2 Layer six of the bread slices with cheese and ham. Top with the remaining six bread slices. Dip sandwiches, one at a time, into egg mixture, turning to coat both sides.

3 Cook sandwiches, half at a time if necessary, on a hot buttered griddle or nonstick skillet over medium heat for 6 to 8 minutes or until golden, turning once. Cut each sandwich in half diagonally. Serve warm. If desired, garnish with carambola and/or kiwifruit.

NUTRITION FACTS PER SERVING:
449 cal., 28 g total fat (14 g sat. fat), 153 mg chol., 968 mg sodium, 29 g carb., 0 g fiber, 23 g pro.

Overnight Coffee Cake

PREP 25 minutes CHILL Overnight BAKE 35 minutes at 350°F MAKES 15 servings

- 3 cups all-purpose flour
- 1½ teaspoons baking powder
- 1½ teaspoons baking soda
- 1 teaspoon salt
- 1 cup butter, softened
- 1¼ cups granulated sugar
- 3 eggs
- 1 15-ounce carton ricotta cheese
- ¾ cup chopped pecans or walnuts
- ½ cup packed dark brown sugar
- 2 tablespoons toasted wheat germ
- 1 tablespoon ground cinnamon
- 1 teaspoon ground nutmeg

1 Lightly grease the bottom and ½ inch up the sides of a 13×9×2-inch baking pan. In a large bowl stir together flour, baking powder, baking soda, and salt. Set aside.

2 In a large mixing bowl beat butter with an electric mixer on medium to high speed for 30 seconds. Add granulated sugar. Beat until combined, scraping sides of bowl occasionally. Add eggs, one at a time, beating well after each addition. Beat in ricotta cheese until combined. Beat in as much of the flour mixture as you can with the mixer. Using a wooden spoon, stir in any remaining flour mixture. Pour batter into the prepared baking pan, spreading evenly.

3 In a small bowl combine nuts, brown sugar, wheat germ, cinnamon, and nutmeg. Sprinkle mixture evenly over batter. Cover and chill overnight.

4 Preheat oven to 350°F. Bake for 35 to 40 minutes or until a wooden toothpick inserted near the center comes out clean. Serve warm.

NUTRITION FACTS PER SERVING:
397 cal., 22 g total fat (10 g sat. fat), 91 mg chol., 438 mg sodium, 43 g carb., 1 g fiber, 8 g pro.

Banana Bread

PREP 25 minutes BAKE 55 minutes at 350°F COOL 10 minutes MAKES 16 servings

2	cups all-purpose flour
1½	teaspoons baking powder
½	teaspoon baking soda
½	teaspoon ground cinnamon
¼	teaspoon salt
¼	teaspoon ground nutmeg
⅛	teaspoon ground ginger
2	eggs, lightly beaten
1½	cups mashed bananas (4 to 5 medium)
1	cup sugar
½	cup vegetable oil or melted butter
¼	cup chopped walnuts
1	recipe Streusel-Nut Topping (optional)

1 Preheat oven to 350°F. Grease the bottom(s) and ½ inch up the sides of one 9×5×3-inch or two 7½×3½×2-inch loaf pan(s); set aside. In a large bowl stir together flour, baking powder, baking soda, cinnamon, salt, nutmeg, and ginger. Make a well in the center of flour mixture; set aside.

2 In a medium bowl combine eggs, mashed bananas, sugar, and oil. Add egg mixture all at once to flour mixture. Stir just until moistened (batter should be lumpy). Fold in walnuts. Spoon batter into the prepared loaf pan(s). If desired, sprinkle with Streusel-Nut Topping.

3 Bake for 55 to 60 minutes for 9x5-inch pan, 40 to 45 minutes for 7½×3½-inch pans, or until a wooden toothpick inserted near the center(s) comes out clean. If necessary to prevent overbrowning, cover loosely with foil for the last 15 minutes of baking.

4 Cool in pan(s) on a wire rack for 10 minutes. Remove from pan(s). Cool completely on wire rack. Wrap and store overnight before slicing.

NUTRITION FACTS PER SERVING:
213 cal., 9 g total fat (1 g sat. fat), 26 mg chol., 108 mg sodium, 32 g carb., 1 g fiber, 3 g pro.

Streusel-Nut Topping

In a small bowl combine ¼ cup packed brown sugar and 3 tablespoons all-purpose flour. Using a pastry blender, cut in 2 tablespoons butter until mixture resembles coarse crumbs. Stir in ⅓ cup chopped walnuts.

Orange-Raisin Brunch Bread

PREP 35 minutes   RISE 1 hour 40 minutes   BAKE 25 minutes at 350°F   MAKES 8 servings

2¾ | to 3 cups all-purpose flour
1 | package active dry yeast
½ | cup butter
¼ | cup milk
¼ | cup water
2 | tablespoons sugar
½ | teaspoon salt
2 | eggs
1 | tablespoon finely shredded orange peel
¾ | cup golden raisins
 | Milk
 | Apricot jam

1 In a large mixing bowl stir together 1½ cups of the flour and the yeast; set aside. In a medium saucepan heat and stir butter, ¼ cup milk, the water, sugar, and salt just until warm (120°F to 130°F) and butter is almost melted. Add butter mixture to flour mixture; add eggs and orange peel. Beat with an electric mixer on low to medium speed for 30 seconds, scraping sides of bowl constantly. Beat on high speed for 3 minutes. Using a wooden spoon, stir in raisins and as much of the remaining flour as you can.

2 Turn dough out on a lightly floured surface. Knead in enough of the remaining flour to make a moderately soft dough that is smooth and elastic (3 to 5 minutes total). Shape dough into a ball. Place in a lightly greased bowl, turning once to grease surface of dough. Cover and let rise in a warm place until double in size (1 to 1¼ hours). Meanwhile, grease a large baking sheet; set aside.

3 Punch dough down. Turn dough out onto a lightly floured surface. Divide dough into thirds. Cover and let rest for 5 minutes. Roll each portion into a 26-inch-long rope. To shape, line up the ropes, 1 inch apart, on the prepared baking sheet. Starting in the middle, loosely braid by bringing the left rope under the center rope. Bring the right rope under the new center rope. Repeat to end. On the other end, braid by bringing the outside ropes alternately over the center rope to center. Press ends together. Shape braid into a ring. Moisten ends with water; pinch together to seal ring. Cover and let rise in a warm place for 40 minutes (dough will rise slightly).

4 Preheat oven to 350°F. Lightly brush ring with additional milk. Place a foil ball or oven-going glass measuring cup or jar in center of ring to preserve its shape. Bake for 25 to 30 minutes or until golden and bread sounds hollow when lightly tapped. Remove from baking sheet and cool on a wire rack. Serve with jam.

NUTRITION FACTS PER SERVING: *343 cal., 13 g total fat (8 g sat. fat), 84 mg chol., 252 mg sodium, 49 g carb., 2 g fiber, 4 g pro.*

Ooey-Gooey Monkey Bread

PREP 20 minutes BAKE 30 minutes at 350°F STAND 10 minutes MAKES 10 servings

1   cup sugar

2   teaspoons ground cinnamon

½   cup butter, melted

2   12-ounce cans (20 biscuits total) refrigerated buttermilk biscuits

⅓   cup caramel-flavor ice cream topping

2   tablespoons maple syrup

1 Preheat oven to 350°F. Generously grease a 10-inch fluted tube pan or regular tube pan; set aside.

2 In a medium bowl stir together sugar and cinnamon; set aside. Place melted butter in another medium bowl. Using kitchen scissors, cut each biscuit into fourths. Toss biscuit pieces, several at a time, in melted butter, then in cinnamon-sugar to coat. Layer biscuit pieces in the prepared tube pan; press lightly. Sprinkle with any remaining cinnamon-sugar and drizzle with any remaining melted butter.

3 In a small bowl combine caramel topping and maple syrup. Drizzle mixture over biscuits.

4 Bake about 30 minutes or until golden and a wooden toothpick inserted near the center comes out clean. Let stand in pan for 10 minutes. Invert onto a large serving platter. Serve warm.

NUTRITION FACTS PER SERVING:
298 cal., 11 g total fat (6 g sat. fat), 25 mg chol., 500 mg sodium, 50 g carb., 1 g fiber, 3 g pro.

Breakfast

Apple Cider Doughnuts

PREP 45 minutes RISE 2 hours 15 minutes COOK 2 minutes per batch MAKES 16 to 18 servings

$3\frac{1}{4}$ to $3\frac{3}{4}$ cups all-purpose flour
2 packages active dry yeast
1 teaspoon apple pie spice
$\frac{1}{2}$ cup sugar
$\frac{1}{2}$ cup apple cider or apple juice
$\frac{1}{4}$ cup milk
$\frac{1}{4}$ cup butter
1 teaspoon salt
2 eggs
Vegetable oil for deep-fat frying
1 recipe Spiced Glaze

1 In a large mixing bowl combine $1\frac{1}{2}$ cups of the flour, the yeast, and apple pie spice; set aside. In a medium saucepan heat and stir sugar, cider, milk, butter, and salt just until warm (120°F to 130°F) and butter is almost melted. Add cider mixture to flour mixture; add eggs. Beat with an electric mixer on low to medium speed for 30 seconds, scraping sides of bowl constantly. Beat on high speed for 3 minutes. Using a wooden spoon, stir in as much of the remaining flour as you can.

2 Turn dough out onto a lightly floured surface. Knead in enough of the remaining flour to make a moderately soft dough that is smooth and elastic (3 to 5 minutes total). Shape dough into a ball. Place in a lightly greased bowl, turning once to grease surface of dough. Cover and let rise in a warm place until double in size (about $1\frac{1}{2}$ hours).

3 Punch dough down. Turn out onto a lightly floured surface. Divide in half. Cover and let rest for 10 minutes. Meanwhile, line a large baking sheet with waxed paper. Lightly flour the waxed paper; set baking sheet aside.

4 Roll each dough half until $\frac{1}{2}$ inch thick. Cut dough with a floured $2\frac{1}{2}$-inch doughnut cutter. Dip cutter into flour between cuts and reroll scraps as necessary. Place cutouts on the prepared baking sheet. Cover and let rise in a warm place until very light (45 to 60 minutes).

5 In a deep-fat fryer or large heavy saucepan heat 1 inch oil to 365°F. Fry two or three doughnuts in hot oil about 2 minutes or until golden, turning once. Remove with a slotted spoon and drain on paper towels. Repeat with the remaining doughnuts and doughnut holes.

6 Dip tops of cooled doughnuts in Spiced Glaze. Drizzle or dip doughnut holes in any remaining glaze. Let stand until set.

NUTRITION FACTS PER SERVING:
260 cal., 8 g total fat (2 g sat. fat), 31 mg chol., 184 mg sodium, 42 g carb., 1 g fiber, 4 g pro.

Spiced Glaze

In a small bowl combine 2 cups powdered sugar and $\frac{1}{4}$ teaspoon apple pie spice. Stir in enough milk (2 to 3 tablespoons) to reach thin icing consistency.

Cinnamon Rolls

Photo on page 129

PREP 50 minutes RISE 2 hours BAKE 30 minutes at 375°F COOL 5 minutes MAKES 12 servings

$4\frac{1}{2}$ to 5 cups all-purpose flour

1 package active dry yeast

1 cup milk

$\frac{1}{3}$ cup butter

$\frac{1}{3}$ cup granulated sugar

$\frac{1}{2}$ teaspoon salt

3 eggs

$\frac{3}{4}$ cup packed brown sugar

$\frac{1}{4}$ cup all-purpose flour

1 tablespoon ground cinnamon or apple pie spice

$\frac{1}{2}$ cup butter

$1\frac{1}{4}$ cups finely chopped peeled apples, $\frac{1}{2}$ cup raisins, or $\frac{1}{2}$ cup semisweet chocolate pieces

1 recipe Vanilla Frosting

Make-Ahead Directions:

Prepare as directed through Step 5, except do not let rise after arranging in pan. Cover loosely with oiled waxed paper, then with plastic wrap. Chill for 2 to 24 hours. Before baking, let chilled rolls stand, covered, at room temperature for 30 minutes. Uncover and bake as directed. Or prepare, bake, and cool rolls as directed. Do not frost. Wrap in plastic wrap, then overwrap in foil. Freeze for up to 2 months. To serve, thaw at room temperature. Spread or drizzle with Vanilla Frosting.

1 In a large mixing bowl combine $2\frac{1}{4}$ cups of the flour and the yeast; set aside. In a small saucepan heat and stir milk, $\frac{1}{3}$ cup butter, granulated sugar, and salt just until warm (120°F to 130°F) and butter is almost melted. Add milk mixture to flour mixture; add eggs. Beat with an electric mixer on low to medium speed for 30 seconds, scraping sides of bowl constantly. Beat on high speed for 3 minutes. Using a wooden spoon, stir in as much of the remaining $2\frac{1}{4}$ to $2\frac{3}{4}$ cups flour as you can.

2 Turn dough out onto a lightly floured surface. Knead in enough of the remaining flour to make a moderately soft dough that is smooth and elastic (3 to 5 minutes total). Shape dough into a ball. Place in a lightly greased bowl, turning once to grease surface of dough. Cover and let rise in a warm place until double in size ($1\frac{1}{4}$ to $1\frac{1}{2}$ hours).

3 Punch dough down. Turn out onto a lightly floured surface. Cover and let rest for 10 minutes. Meanwhile, lightly grease a 13×9×2-inch baking pan; set aside.

Vanilla Frosting

In a medium bowl beat 1 cup powdered sugar, 2 tablespoons softened butter, 2 tablespoons milk, and 1 teaspoon vanilla with a wooden spoon until smooth. Gradually beat in 2 cups additional powdered sugar. If necessary, beat in additional milk, 1 teaspoon at a time, to reach spreading or drizzling consistency.

4 For filling, in a medium bowl stir together brown sugar, $\frac{1}{4}$ cup flour, and cinnamon. Using a pastry blender, cut in $\frac{1}{2}$ cup butter until crumbly.

5 Roll dough into an 18×12-inch rectangle. Sprinkle with filling, leaving about 1 inch unfilled along one of the long sides. Top with apples. Roll up rectangle, starting from the filled long side; pinch dough to seal seam. Slice rolled rectangle into 12 slices. Arrange in the prepared baking pan. Cover and let rise in a warm place until nearly double in size (about 45 minutes).

6 Preheat oven to 375°F. Bake about 30 minutes or until golden, covering loosely with foil for the last 10 minutes of baking. Cool in pan on a wire rack for 5 minutes. Invert onto another wire rack; cool slightly. Invert again onto a serving platter. Spread or drizzle with Vanilla Frosting. Serve warm.

NUTRITION FACTS PER SERVING:
545 cal., 17 g total fat (10 g sat. fat), 94 mg chol., 234 mg sodium, 91 g carb., 2 g fiber, 8 g pro.

Peanut Butter–Streusel Muffins

Photo on page 131

PREP 30 minutes BAKE 22 minutes at 375°F COOL 5 minutes MAKES 12 servings

1¼ **cups all-purpose flour**
¾ **cup packed brown sugar**
3 **tablespoons butter**
2 **tablespoons peanut butter**
¼ **cup chopped peanuts**
½ **cup miniature semisweet chocolate pieces**
¼ **cup peanut butter**
½ **cup milk**
1 **egg**
1 **teaspoon baking powder**
¼ **teaspoon baking soda**
¼ **teaspoon salt**

1 Preheat oven to 375°F. Line twelve 2½-inch muffin cups with paper bake cups; set aside. For streusel topping, in a small bowl stir together ¼ cup of the flour and ¼ cup of the brown sugar. Using a pastry blender, cut in 1 tablespoon of the butter and the 2 tablespoons peanut butter until mixture resembles coarse crumbs. Stir in peanuts and ¼ cup of the chocolate pieces. Set aside.

2 In a large bowl combine the remaining 2 tablespoons butter and ¼ cup peanut butter. Beat with an electric mixer on medium to high speed about 30 seconds or until combined. Add about ½ cup of the remaining flour, the remaining ½ cup brown sugar, half of the milk, the egg, baking powder, baking soda, and salt. Beat on low speed until combined, scraping sides of bowl constantly. Add the remaining flour and the remaining milk. Beat on low to medium speed just until combined. Stir in the remaining ¼ cup chocolate pieces.

3 Spoon batter into the prepared muffin cups, filling each about two-thirds full. Sprinkle with streusel topping. Bake for 22 to 25 minutes or until a wooden toothpick inserted near the centers comes out clean.

4 Cool in muffin cups on a wire rack for 5 minutes. Remove from muffin cups. Serve warm.

NUTRITION FACTS PER SERVING:
255 cal., 12 g total fat (5 g sat. fat), 26 mg chol., 191 mg sodium, 33 g carb., 1 g fiber, 6 g pro.

Make-Ahead Directions: Prepare and bake as directed; cool completely. Layer muffins between sheets of waxed paper in an airtight container; cover. Freeze for up to 3 months. To serve, preheat oven to 350°F. Wrap frozen muffins in foil. Bake for 20 to 25 minutes or until warm.

PREP 20 minutes BAKE 25 minutes at 350°F COOL 5 minutes MAKES 16 servings

- **2** cups all-purpose flour
- **2** teaspoons baking powder
- **$\frac{1}{2}$** teaspoon salt
- **$\frac{1}{2}$** cup butter, softened
- **1** cup sugar
- **2** eggs
- **$\frac{1}{2}$** cup milk
- **1** teaspoon vanilla
- **2** to $2\frac{1}{2}$ cups fresh or frozen blueberries
- **1** tablespoon sugar
- **$\frac{1}{4}$** teaspoon ground cinnamon

1 Preheat oven to 350°F. Line sixteen $2\frac{1}{2}$-inch (standard) or six $3\frac{1}{2}$-inch (jumbo) muffin cups with paper bake cups; set aside. In a medium bowl stir together flour, baking powder, and salt; set aside.

2 In a large mixing bowl beat butter with an electric mixer on medium to high speed for 30 seconds. Add 1 cup sugar. Beat until combined, scraping sides of bowl occasionally. Beat in eggs, milk, and vanilla (mixture will look slightly curdled). Stir in flour mixture just until moistened (batter should be lumpy). Gently stir in blueberries.

3 Spoon batter into the prepared muffin cups, filling each nearly full. In a small bowl combine 1 tablespoon sugar and cinnamon. Sprinkle cinnamon-sugar over batter.

4 Bake for 25 to 30 minutes for $2\frac{1}{2}$-inch muffins, 35 to 40 minutes for $3\frac{1}{2}$-inch muffins, or until golden and a wooden toothpick inserted in the centers comes out clean. Cool in muffin cups on a wire rack for 5 minutes. Remove from muffin cups. Serve warm.

NUTRITION FACTS PER SERVING: *184 cal., 7 g total fat (4 g sat. fat), 42 mg chol., 171 mg sodium, 29 g carb., 1 g fiber, 3 g pro.*

tip

For perfect texture, don't overmix muffin batter. After adding the liquids to the flour mixture, stir just until the dry ingredients are moist. The batter will still look lumpy with little bits of flour.

Fruit-and-Nut Baked Oatmeal

PREP 15 minutes BAKE 20 minutes at 350°F MAKES 4 servings

1¾ cups milk

2 tablespoons butter

1 cup regular rolled oats

⅓ cup snipped dried apricots

⅓ cup dried tart cherries

⅓ cup golden raisins

5 tablespoons packed brown sugar

½ teaspoon vanilla

¼ teaspoon salt

½ cup coarsely chopped walnuts or pecans

Snipped dried apricots and/or dried tart cherries (optional)

Milk (optional)

1 Preheat oven to 350°F. Lightly grease four 6-ounce au gratin dishes or one 1½-quart casserole; set aside.

2 In a medium saucepan combine 1¾ cups milk and butter. Bring to boiling. Gradually stir in oats. Stir in ⅓ cup dried apricots, ⅓ cup dried cherries, raisins, 3 tablespoons of the brown sugar, the vanilla, and salt. Cook and stir for 1 minute. Transfer mixture to the prepared au gratin dishes or casserole. If using au gratin dishes, place in a 15×10×1-inch baking pan.

3 Bake, uncovered, for 15 minutes. Sprinkle with the remaining 2 tablespoons brown sugar and nuts. Bake, uncovered, about 5 minutes more or until bubbly. Cool slightly. If desired, serve warm oatmeal with additional dried fruit and additional milk.

NUTRITION FACTS PER SERVING:
446 cal., 19 g total fat (6 g sat. fat), 24 mg chol., 242 mg sodium, 63 g carb., 5 g fiber, 9 g pro.

2

Appetizers, Snacks, and Drinks

Some foods bring comfort by simply sharing them with friends and family. You'll find something for every occasion in this cozy collection of nibbles, noshes, and sips.

Creamy Marshmallow Dip for Fruit

PREP 15 minutes CHILL 1 hour MAKES 8 servings

- 1 **8-ounce package cream cheese, softened***
- 1 **8-ounce carton sour cream or one 6-ounce carton plain yogurt**
- 1 **7-ounce jar marshmallow crème**
- 1 **teaspoon vanilla**
- 2 **to 3 tablespoons milk**
- ½ **teaspoon ground cinnamon, pumpkin pie spice, or apple pie spice (optional)**

   Assorted fruit dippers, such as strawberries, raspberries, grapes, cantaloupe chunks, and/or pineapple chunks

1 In a medium mixing bowl beat cream cheese with an electric mixer on low speed until smooth. Gradually add sour cream, beating until combined. Add marshmallow crème and vanilla; beat just until combined. Stir in enough of the milk to reach dipping consistency. If desired, stir in cinnamon.

2 Cover and chill for at least 1 hour before serving. Serve with fruit dippers.

NUTRITION FACTS PER SERVING:
234 cal., 15 g total fat (9 g sat. fat), 46 mg chol., 135 mg sodium, 22 g carb., 0 g fiber, 3 g pro.

Lightened-Up Marshmallow Dip

Prepare as directed, except substitute reduced-fat cream cheese (Neufchâtel) and light sour cream for the regular cream cheese and sour cream.

NUTRITION FACTS PER SERVING: *137 cal., 9 g total fat (5 g sat. fat), 30 mg chol., 117 mg sodium, 10 g carb., 0 g fiber, 5 g pro.*

*tip
The quickest way to soften cream cheese is in the microwave. In a microwave-safe bowl, heat unwrapped cream cheese, uncovered, on 100 percent power (high). Allow 10 to 20 seconds for 3 ounces and 30 to 60 seconds for 8 ounces. Let it stand for 5 minutes before using.

Bacon-Cheddar Cheese Ball

PREP 40 minutes STAND 45 minutes CHILL 2 to 24 hours MAKES 4 servings

8 ounces extra sharp cheddar cheese, finely shredded (2 cups)

1 8-ounce package reduced-fat cream cheese (Neufchâtel)

½ of a 2-ounce jar sliced pimientos, rinsed, drained, patted dry, and chopped

2 tablespoons apricot preserves

1 tablespoon milk

1½ teaspoons Worcestershire sauce

⅛ teaspoon bottled hot pepper sauce

15 slices bacon, crisp-cooked and drained

¼ cup pistachio nuts, chopped
   Celery sticks, cucumber slices, apricot halves, crackers, and/or toasted baguette-style French bread slices

1 In a large mixing bowl let cheddar cheese and cream cheese stand at room temperature for 30 minutes. Add pimientos, preserves, milk, Worcestershire sauce, and hot pepper sauce. Crumble 10 of the bacon slices and add to mixture. Beat with an electric mixer on medium speed until almost smooth.

2 Crumble the remaining 5 bacon slices. Cover and chill cheese mixture and the remaining bacon separately for 2 to 24 hours.

3 Shape cheese mixture into a ball; roll in remaining bacon and pistachios. Let stand for 15 minutes. Serve with celery, cucumber, apricots, crackers, and/or toasted bread.

NUTRITION FACTS PER SERVING: *218 cal., 17 g total fat (5 g sat. fat), 49 mg chol., 361 mg sodium, 6 g carb., 1 g fiber, 11 g pro.*

Cheesy Artichoke and Spinach Dip

PREP 25 minutes BAKE 30 minutes at 350°F MAKES 22 servings

½ cup chopped onion
(1 medium)

½ cup chopped red sweet
pepper (1 small)

2 cloves garlic, minced

1 tablespoon olive oil

2 8-ounce packages reduced-fat
cream cheese (Neufchâtel),
softened

1½ cups finely shredded
Parmesan or Romano cheese
(6 ounces)

¼ cup milk

¼ cup mayonnaise

¼ cup light sour cream

4 cups chopped fresh spinach
leaves

1 14-ounce can artichoke
hearts, drained and chopped

Bagel chips, corn tortilla
chips, and/or toasted
baguette-style French bread
slices

1 Preheat oven to 350°F. In a large skillet cook onion, sweet pepper, and garlic in hot oil over medium heat until tender, stirring occasionally; cool.

2 In a large bowl stir together cream cheese, Parmesan cheese, milk, mayonnaise, and sour cream. Stir in onion mixture, spinach, and artichoke hearts. Spread mixture in a deep 9-inch pie plate or a 1½-quart shallow baking dish.

3 Bake, uncovered, about 30 minutes or until bubbly around the edges. Serve with bagel chips, tortilla chips, and/or toasted bread.

NUTRITION FACTS PER SERVING:
113 cal., 9 g total fat (4 g sat. fat), 21 mg chol., 243 mg sodium, 3 g carb., 1 g fiber, 5 g pro.

Make-Ahead Directions: Prepare as directed through Step 2. Cover and chill for up to 24 hours. To serve, preheat oven to 350°F. Bake, uncovered, about 40 minutes or until bubbly around the edges.

Roasted Corn and Crab Dip *Photo on page 134*

PREP 25 minutes   ROAST 20 minutes at 425°F   BAKE 20 minutes at 375°F   MAKES 10 servings

Nonstick cooking spray

1 cup frozen whole kernel corn, thawed

1 cup chopped red sweet pepper (1 large)

2 teaspoons olive oil

1 cup cooked crabmeat, cartilage removed, or one 6 ounce can crabmeat, drained, flaked, and cartilage removed

1 cup shredded Monterey Jack cheese with jalapeño peppers (4 ounces)

⅓ cup mayonnaise

¼ cup sour cream

¼ cup sliced green onions (2)

¼ teaspoon ground black pepper

Broken tostada shells, toasted baguette-style French bread slices, and/or crackers

1 Preheat oven to 425°F. Lightly coat a 1-quart quiche dish or shallow baking dish with cooking spray; set aside. In a shallow baking pan combine corn and sweet pepper. Drizzle with oil; toss to coat. Roast, uncovered, about 20 minutes or until vegetables start to brown, stirring occasionally. Remove from oven; cool. Reduce oven temperature to 375°F.

2 Meanwhile, in a medium bowl stir together crabmeat, cheese, mayonnaise, sour cream, green onions, and black pepper. Stir in roasted vegetables. Transfer mixture to the prepared quiche dish.

3 Bake, uncovered, about 20 minutes or until bubbly around the edges. Serve with broken tostada shells, toasted bread, and/or crackers.

NUTRITION FACTS PER SERVING:
151 cal., 12 g total fat (4 g sat. fat), 29 mg chol., 180 mg sodium, 5 g carb., 1 g fiber, 7 g pro.

Make-Ahead Directions: Prepare as directed through Step 2. Cover and chill for up to 24 hours. To serve, preheat oven to 425°F. Bake as directed.

tip

If you have time to shell some fresh crab, the meat from snow crab legs or king crab legs is especially tasty in this dip.

Appetizers, Snacks, and Drinks

Dill Dip

PREP 10 minutes CHILL 1 to 24 hours MAKES 32 servings

1 8-ounce package cream cheese, softened

1 8-ounce carton sour cream

2 tablespoons finely chopped green onion (1)

2 tablespoons snipped fresh dill or 2 teaspoons dried dill

½ teaspoon seasoned salt or salt

Milk (optional)

Assorted vegetable dippers, crackers, and/or chips

In a medium mixing bowl beat cream cheese, sour cream, green onion, dill, and seasoned salt with an electric mixer on low speed until fluffy. Cover and chill for 1 to 24 hours. If dip thickens after chilling, stir in 1 to 2 tablespoons milk. Serve with vegetable dippers, crackers, and/or chips.

NUTRITION FACTS PER TABLESPOON:
38 cal., 4 g total fat (2 g sat. fat), 11 mg chol., 52 mg sodium, 1 g carb., 0 g fiber, 0 g pro.

Creamy Blue Cheese Dip

Prepare as directed, except omit dill and seasoned salt or salt. Stir ½ cup crumbled blue cheese (2 ounces) and ⅓ cup finely chopped toasted walnuts into the beaten cream cheese mixture. Makes 44 (1-tablespoon) servings.

Spinach-Dill Dip

Prepare as directed, except stir half of a 10-ounce package frozen chopped spinach, thawed and well drained, into the beaten cream cheese mixture. Makes 40 (1-tablespoon) servings.

Mexican Seven-Layer Dip

PREP 20 minutes   CHILL 4 to 24 hours   MAKES 16 servings

- 1   16-ounce can refried beans
- ½   cup salsa
- 1   7-ounce package refrigerated avocado dip (guacamole)
- 1   8-ounce carton sour cream
- 1   cup shredded cheddar or taco cheese (4 ounces)
- ¼   cup sliced green onions (2)
- ¼   cup sliced, pitted ripe olives
- 1   cup chopped, seeded tomatoes (2 medium)
- 8   cups tortilla chips or crackers

1 In a medium bowl combine refried beans and salsa; spread onto a 12-inch platter or in a 2-quart rectangular baking dish. Carefully layer avocado dip and sour cream over bean mixture. Top with cheese, green onions, and olives. Cover and chill for 4 to 24 hours.

2 Before serving, sprinkle with chopped tomatoes. Serve with tortilla chips or crackers.

NUTRITION FACTS PER SERVING:
179 cal., 11 g total fat (4 g sat. fat), 15 mg chol., 340 mg sodium, 16 g carb., 3 g fiber, 5 g pro.

Guacamole

START TO FINISH **15 minutes** MAKES **20 servings**

2 **ripe avocados,* seeded, peeled, and coarsely mashed****

2 **tablespoons sour cream**

2 **tablespoons snipped fresh cilantro**

1 **tablespoon lime juice**

¼ **teaspoon salt**

Several drops bottled hot pepper sauce (optional)

Sliced green onions

Chopped tomatoes

Tortilla chips

1 In a medium bowl combine avocados, sour cream, cilantro, lime juice, salt, and, if desired, hot pepper sauce. Cover surface with plastic wrap; chill until ready to serve (up to 8 hours).

2 To serve, transfer guacamole to a serving bowl. Sprinkle with green onions and tomatoes. Serve with tortilla chips.

NUTRITION FACTS PER SERVING:
25 cal., 2 g total fat (0 g sat. fat), 1 mg chol., 17 mg sodium, 1 g carb., 1 g fiber, 0 g pro.

Toasted Cumin Guacamole

In a small dry skillet heat 2 teaspoons cumin seeds over medium-high heat for 1 to 2 minutes or until lightly toasted, shaking skillet occasionally. Remove seeds from skillet; cool. Coarsely crush cumin seeds; stir into avocado mixture.

*tip

Ripe avocados feel soft under gentle palm pressure. (Don't press them with your finger or they'll bruise.) To speed ripening, place avocados in a closed paper bag at room temperature. Ripe ones can be refrigerated for several days.

**tip

If you prefer, do not mash avocados. Place avocado halves, sour cream, cilantro, lime juice, salt, and, if desired, hot pepper sauce in a heavy resealable plastic bag. Seal bag. Knead bag with your hands to combine ingredients. Chill until ready to serve (up to 8 hours). To serve, arrange chips on a serving platter. Snip a hole in one corner of the bag. Pipe guacamole onto chips. Sprinkle with green onions and tomatoes.

Chili con Queso

½ cup finely chopped onion (1 medium)

1 tablespoon butter

1⅓ cups chopped, seeded tomatoes (about 2 medium)

1 4-ounce can diced green chile peppers, undrained

½ teaspoon ground cumin

2 ounces Monterey Jack cheese with jalapeño peppers, shredded (½ cup)

1 teaspoon cornstarch

1 8-ounce package cream cheese, cubed

Tortilla chips or corn chips

1 In a medium saucepan cook onion in butter until tender. Stir in tomatoes, chile peppers, and cumin. Bring to boiling; reduce heat. Simmer, uncovered, for 10 minutes, stirring occasionally.

2 Toss shredded Monterey Jack cheese with cornstarch. Gradually add cheese mixture to saucepan, stirring until cheese is melted. Gradually add the cream cheese, stirring until cheese is melted and smooth. Heat through. Serve with chips.

NUTRITION FACTS PER SERVING: *58 cal., 5 g total fat (3 g sat. fat), 16 mg chol., 79 mg sodium, 5 g carb., 0 g fiber, 2 g pro.*

Slow Cooker Directions: Prepare as above. Transfer mixture to a 1½- or 2-quart slow cooker. Keep warm on low-heat setting, if available, up to 2 hours, stirring occasionally.

Roasted Poblano Chili con Queso

Preheat oven to 425°F. Line a baking sheet with foil; set aside. Quarter 2 fresh poblano chile peppers lengthwise; remove stems, seeds, and membranes.* Place pepper pieces, cut sides down, on the prepared baking sheet. Bake for 20 to 25 minutes or until skins are blistered and dark. Bring foil up around peppers to enclose. Let stand about 15 minutes or until cool. Using a sharp knife, loosen edges of the skins; gently pull off the skin in strips and discard. Finely chop peppers. Prepare Chili Con Queso as above, except substitute the finely chopped poblano peppers for the canned diced green chile peppers.

*tip

Because chile peppers contain volatile oils that can burn your skin and eyes, avoid direct contact with chiles as much as possible. When working with chile peppers, wear plastic or rubber gloves. If your bare hands do touch the chile peppers, wash your hands well with soap and warm water.

Sweet Potato Fritters
with Yogurt-Chive Dipping Sauce *Photo on page 135*

PREP 25 minutes COOK 2 minutes per batch MAKES 6 servings

- 1 **pound sweet potatoes, peeled and cut into ½-inch pieces (2½ cups)**
- 1 **egg**
- ¼ **cup packed brown sugar**
- 2 **tablespoons butter**
- 1 **cup all-purpose flour**
- ⅓ **cup fine dry bread crumbs**
- 2 **teaspoons baking powder**
- ¼ **teaspoon salt**
- **Vegetable oil for deep-fat frying**
- 1 **recipe Yogurt-Chive Dipping Sauce**

1 In a covered large saucepan cook sweet potatoes in enough boiling water to cover for 12 to 15 minutes or until very tender. Drain and cool slightly. In a food processor combine sweet potatoes, egg, brown sugar, and butter. Cover and process until smooth. In a small bowl stir together flour, bread crumbs, baking powder, and salt. Add flour mixture to sweet potato mixture. Cover and process just until combined.

2 In a deep-fat fryer or large heavy saucepan heat 1 inch oil to 350°F. For each fritter, drop 1 tablespoon of the batter into hot oil. Fry, a few at a time, about 2 minutes or until fritters are golden, turning once. Remove with a slotted spoon and drain on paper towels. Serve warm with Yogurt-Chive Dipping Sauce.

NUTRITION FACTS PER SERVING:
53 cal., 2 g total fat (1 g sat. fat), 8 mg chol., 65 mg sodium, 7 g carb., 0 g fiber, 1 g pro.

Yogurt-Chive Dipping Sauce

In a small bowl combine one 6-ounce carton plain low-fat yogurt, 1 tablespoon snipped fresh chives, and 1 clove garlic, minced. Season to taste with salt and ground black pepper.

Sweet-and-Savory Potato Chips

PREP 25 minutes SOAK 10 minutes COOK 3 minutes per batch MAKES 12 servings

3   **medium sweet potatoes
(about 1 pound total)**

3   **medium baking potatoes
(about 1 pound total)**

**Peanut oil or vegetable oil
for deep-fat drying**

Coarse salt

1 Peel potatoes; cut into very thin slices (about $\frac{1}{16}$ inch thick).* Place potato slices in a large bowl of ice water; soak for 10 minutes. Drain potato slices; pat dry with paper towels.

2 Preheat oven to 300°F. In a deep-fat fryer or large heavy saucepan heat 1 inch oil to 350°F. Fry half of the potato slices in hot oil for 3 to 5 minutes or until golden and crisp. Remove with a slotted spoon and drain on wire racks.

3 Transfer chips to a shallow baking pan. Sprinkle with salt. Keep chips warm in the oven while frying the remaining potato slices. If desired, store in an airtight container at room temperature for up to 2 days.

NUTRITION FACTS PER SERVING:
53 cal., 2 g total fat (1 g sat. fat), 8 mg chol., 65 mg sodium, 7 g carb., 0 g fiber, 1 g pro.

*tip

A mandoline, a special slicing tool, makes quick work of slicing thin, even potato slices. Look for a mandoline at a kitchen specialty shop.

Soft Pretzels *Photo on page 133*

PREP 45 minutes   RISE 1 hour 15 minutes   BAKE 4 minutes at 475°F + 18 to 20 minutes at 350°F   MAKES 20 servings

$2\frac{1}{2}$ **to 3 cups all-purpose flour**

1 **package active dry yeast**

$1\frac{1}{2}$ **cups fat-free milk**

$\frac{1}{4}$ **cup sugar**

2 **tablespoons vegetable oil**

1 **teaspoon salt**

$1\frac{1}{2}$ **cups whole wheat flour**

3 **quarts water**

2 **tablespoons salt**

1 **egg white, lightly beaten**

1 **tablespoon water**

Sesame seeds, poppy seeds, or coarse salt

To Store: Place cooled pretzels in a freezer bag. Seal, label, and freeze for up to 3 months. Thaw at room temperature. If desired, warm pretzels in a toaster before serving.

*tip

To shape each pretzel, cross one end over the other about 4 inches from each end of a strip. Twist once at the crossover point. Fold ends up and over the edge of circle. Moisten ends with water; tuck them under bottom edge of circle. Press to seal.

1 In a large mixing bowl stir together $1\frac{1}{2}$ cups of the all-purpose flour and the yeast; set aside. In a medium saucepan heat and stir milk, sugar, oil, and 1 teaspoon salt just until warm (120°F to 130°F). Add milk mixture to flour mixture. Beat with an electric mixer on low to medium speed for 30 seconds, scraping sides of bowl constantly. Beat on high speed for 3 minutes. Using a wooden spoon, stir in whole wheat flour and as much of the remaining all-purpose flour as you can.

2 Turn dough out onto a lightly floured surface. Knead in enough of the remaining all-purpose flour to make a moderately stiff dough that is smooth and elastic (6 to 8 minutes total). Shape dough into a ball. Place in a lightly greased bowl, turning once to grease surface of dough. Cover and let rise in a warm place until double in size (about $1\frac{1}{4}$ hours).

3 Punch dough down. Turn dough out onto a lightly floured surface. Cover and let rest for 10 minutes. Meanwhile, lightly grease two large baking sheets.

4 Preheat oven to 475°F. Roll dough into a 12×10-inch rectangle. Cut into twenty 12×$\frac{1}{2}$-inch strips. Shape each strip into a pretzel.*

5 Carefully place pretzels on the prepared baking sheets. Bake for 4 minutes. Remove from oven. Reduce oven temperature to 350°F. Generously grease two large baking sheets; set aside.

6 In a Dutch oven bring the 3 quarts water to boiling; add 2 tablespoons salt, stirring until dissolved. Lower pretzels, three or four at a time, into boiling water. Boil for 2 minutes, turning once. Using a slotted spoon, remove pretzels from water; drain on paper towels. Let stand for a few seconds. Place about $\frac{1}{2}$ inch apart on the generously greased baking sheets.

7 In a small bowl combine egg white and the 1 tablespoon water. Brush pretzels with egg white mixture. Sprinkle lightly with sesame seeds. Bake for 18 to 20 minutes or until golden. Immediately remove from baking sheets. Cool on wire racks.

NUTRITION FACTS PER SERVING:
126 cal., 2 g total fat (0 g sat. fat), 0 mg chol., 245 mg sodium, 22 g carb., 2 g fiber, 4 g pro.

Potato Skins

PREP 20 minutes BAKE 50 minutes at 425°F MAKES 12 servings

6   large baking potatoes
    (about 8 ounces each)

1   tablespoon vegetable oil

1   to 1½ teaspoons chili powder

    Several drops bottled hot
    pepper sauce

    Salt

8   slices bacon, crisp-cooked,
    drained, and crumbled

⅔   cup finely chopped tomato

2   tablespoons finely chopped
    green onion (1)

1   cup shredded cheddar cheese
    (4 ounces)

½   cup sour cream

1 Preheat oven to 425°F. Scrub potatoes thoroughly with a brush; pat dry. Prick potatoes several times with a fork. Bake for 40 to 45 minutes or until tender; cool slightly.

2 Cut each potato lengthwise into four wedges. Carefully scoop out potato pulp, leaving ¼-inch shells. Cover and chill potato pulp for another use.

3 Line an extra-large baking sheet with foil; set aside. In a small bowl combine oil, chili powder, and hot pepper sauce. Using a pastry brush, brush insides of potato wedges with oil mixture. Sprinkle with salt. Place potato wedges in a single layer on the prepared baking sheet. Sprinkle with bacon, tomato, and green onion; top with cheese.

4 Bake, uncovered, about 10 minutes more or until potato wedges are heated through and cheese is melted. Serve with sour cream.

NUTRITION FACTS PER SERVING:
64 cal., 4 g total fat (2 g sat. fat), 10 mg chol., 146 mg sodium, 4 g carb., 1 g fiber, 3 g pro.

Make-Ahead Directions: Prepare as directed through Step 3. Cover and chill potato wedges for up to 24 hours. To serve, preheat oven to 425°F. Bake as directed.

Fried Ravioli with Marinara Sauce *Photo on page 132*

PREP 30 minutes COOK 2 minutes per batch MAKES 12 servings

Vegetable oil for deep-fat frying

3 cups frozen mini cheese-filled ravioli

1¼ cups panko (Japanese-style bread crumbs)

¼ teaspoon salt

¼ teaspoon ground black pepper

1 egg, lightly beaten

⅓ cup milk

1 tablespoon snipped fresh Italian (flat-leaf) parsley

1 cup marinara sauce, warmed

1 In a 4- to 5-quart Dutch oven heat 1 inch oil to 350°F. Preheat oven to 200°F. Line a 15×10×1-inch baking pan with paper towels; set aside.

2 Meanwhile, cook ravioli according to package directions; drain. Rinse with cold water; drain again.

3 In a shallow bowl combine panko,* salt, and pepper. In another shallow bowl combine egg and milk. Dip about ½ cup of the cooked ravioli into egg mixture, allowing excess to drip off. Dip into panko mixture, turning to coat.

4 Fry the ½ cup ravioli in hot oil about 2 minutes or until golden and crisp. Remove with a slotted spoon and drain on wire racks. Transfer to the prepared baking pan and keep warm in the oven while coating and frying the remaining ravioli.

5 Sprinkle ravioli with parsley and serve with marinara sauce.

NUTRITION FACTS PER SERVING: *196 cal., 12 g total fat (2 g sat. fat), 30 mg chol., 257 mg sodium, 16 g carb., 1 g fiber, 5 g pro.*

*tip

Add half of the panko to begin dipping ravioli, then gradually add additional panko as needed to keep the bread crumbs crisp for coating.

Stuffed Mushrooms

PREP 40 minutes   BAKE 27 minutes at 400°F   MAKES 10 servings

- 2 pounds fresh cremini or button mushrooms (about 32), each 1½ to 2 inches in diameter
- 3 tablespoons olive oil
- ⅛ teaspoon salt
- 3 tablespoons finely chopped onion
- 1 teaspoon snipped fresh thyme or ½ teaspoon dried thyme, crushed
- 1 teaspoon snipped fresh oregano or ½ teaspoon dried oregano, crushed
- 1 clove garlic, minced
- 4 large green Swiss chard leaves, stemmed and chopped
- ½ cup shredded ricotta salata or crumbled feta cheese (2 ounces)
- ½ cup soft bread crumbs (from 1 slice bread)
- ⅛ to ¼ teaspoon ground black pepper
- 3 tablespoons grated Parmesan cheese

1 Preheat oven to 400°F. Remove stems from mushrooms; set stems aside. In an extra-large bowl combine mushroom caps, 1 tablespoon of the oil, and the salt; toss gently to coat. Arrange mushroom caps, stemmed sides down, in a 15×10×1-inch baking pan. Bake about 15 minutes or just until mushrooms are tender but not shriveled, and have released some juices. Carefully drain well; cool slightly. Turn mushrooms stemmed sides up; gently pat dry with paper towels.

2 Meanwhile, chop the reserved mushroom stems. In a large skillet heat the remaining 2 tablespoons oil over medium-high heat. Add chopped mushroom stems and onion; cook about 5 minutes or until onion is tender and most of the juices have evaporated, stirring occasionally. Stir in thyme, oregano, and garlic; cook and stir until fragrant. Stir in Swiss chard; cook until wilted, stirring occasionally. Remove from heat; cool. Stir in ricotta salata, bread crumbs, and pepper.

3 Spoon chard mixture into mushroom caps. If desired, cover and chill for up to 24 hours. Sprinkle stuffed mushrooms with Parmesan cheese. Bake, uncovered, for 12 to 15 minutes or until heated through.

NUTRITION FACTS PER SERVING:
87 cal., 6 g total fat (2 g sat. fat), 6 mg chol., 150 mg sodium, 6 g carb., 1 g fiber, 4 g pro.

Appetizers, Snacks, and Drinks

Olive Medley Pinwheels

PREP 25 minutes   CHILL 2 to 4 hours   MAKES 10 servings

- 1   8-ounce package cream cheese, softened
- ½   cup pitted green olives, chopped
- ½   cup pitted ripe olives, chopped
- ½   cup pitted kalamata olives, chopped
- 1   teaspoon finely shredded lemon peel
- ¼   teaspoon garlic powder
- ¼   teaspoon ground black pepper
- 4   8-inch flour tortillas, warmed
- 8   fresh basil leaves
- ½   cup bottled roasted red sweet peppers, well-drained and cut into strips

1 In a medium mixing bowl beat cream cheese with an electric mixer on medium speed until smooth. Stir in olives, lemon peel, garlic powder, and black pepper.

2 Spread olive mixture on one side of tortillas. Arrange basil leaves and roasted pepper strips horizontally along centers; roll up tortillas from the bottoms. Wrap in plastic wrap and chill for 2 to 4 hours. To serve, trim ends. Cut tortilla rolls into about ½-inch slices.

NUTRITION FACTS PER SERVING:
161 cal., 12 g total fat (6 g sat. fat), 25 mg chol., 435 mg sodium, 11 g carb., 1 g fiber, 3 g pro.

Avocado Deviled Eggs

START TO FINISH **45 minutes**   MAKES **24 servings**

12 eggs

½ cup mayonnaise

1 tablespoon country Dijon-style mustard

1 teaspoon caper juice or sweet or dill pickle juice

⅛ teaspoon freshly ground black pepper

Dash bottled hot pepper sauce

1 ripe but firm avocado

1 teaspoon lemon juice

Snipped fresh chives (optional)

1 Place eggs in a single layer in a large Dutch oven. Add enough cold water to cover the eggs by 1 inch. Bring to a rapid boil over high heat (water will have large rapidly breaking bubbles). Remove from heat. Cover and let stand for 15 minutes; drain. Run cold water over eggs or place them in ice water until cool enough to handle; drain. Peel eggs and cut in half lengthwise. Remove yolks and place in a large bowl. Set whites aside.

2 Mash egg yolks with a fork. Stir in mayonnaise, mustard, caper juice, black pepper, and hot pepper sauce.

3 Pit and peel avocado; cut into ½-inch pieces. Drizzle with lemon juice; toss gently to coat. Spoon or pipe egg yolk mixture into egg white halves. Top with avocado and, if desired, chives. Cover and chill until serving time (up to 4 hours).

NUTRITION FACTS PER SERVING:
79 cal., 7 g total fat (1 g sat. fat), 95 mg chol., 73 mg sodium, 1 g carb., 0 g fiber, 3 g pro.

Saucy Spiced Apricot Meatballs

PREP 25 minutes BAKE 15 minutes at 350°F MAKES 12 servings

½ **cup soft bread crumbs (from 1 slice bread)**

2 **tablespoons fat-free milk**

1 **egg white**

¼ **cup finely chopped onion**

¼ **cup finely snipped dried apricots**

1 **clove garlic, minced**

½ **teaspoon salt**

¼ **teaspoon ground ancho chile pepper or chili powder**

6 **ounces lean ground pork**

6 **ounces uncooked ground turkey breast**

1 **recipe Spiced Apricot Sauce**

1 Preheat oven to 350°F. Line a 15×10×1-inch baking pan with foil. Lightly grease foil; set pan aside. In a medium bowl combine bread crumbs and milk. Let stand for 5 minutes. Stir in egg white, onion, dried apricots, garlic, salt, and ground ancho pepper. Add ground pork and ground turkey; mix well.

2 Shape meat mixture into 24 meatballs. Place meatballs in the prepared baking pan. Bake for 15 to 20 minutes or until meatballs are no longer pink (165°F). If necessary, drain meatballs on paper towels.

3 Place meatballs in a 1½-quart slow cooker. Add Spiced Apricot Sauce; toss gently to coat. Turn cooker to warm setting or low-heat setting; keep warm for up to 2 hours. Use short skewers or toothpicks to serve meatballs.

NUTRITION FACTS PER SERVING:
89 cal., 3 g total fat (1 g sat. fat), 16 mg chol., 203 mg sodium, 9 g carb., 1 g fiber, 7 g pro.

Spiced Apricot Sauce

In a small saucepan combine ½ cup apricot nectar, 1 teaspoon cornstarch, ¼ teaspoon ground ancho chile pepper or chili powder, ⅛ teaspoon salt, and ⅛ teaspoon ground nutmeg. Cook and stir over medium heat until thickened and bubbly. Cook and stir for 1 minute more.

Sugared Bacon-Wrapped Smokies

Photo on page 134

PREP 35 minutes   BAKE 30 minutes at 350°F   MAKES 45 servings

Nonstick cooking spray

1   1-pound package small, cooked smoked sausage links

15   slices bacon, each cut crosswise into thirds

¾   cup packed brown sugar

1 Preheat oven to 350°F. Line a 15×10×1-inch baking pan with foil. Lightly coat foil with cooking spray; set pan aside.

2 Wrap each sausage link with a bacon piece, overlapping bacon at the ends. Press ends to seal or secure with a wooden toothpick.

3 Place brown sugar in a large plastic bag. Add bacon-wrapped sausages, several at a time, shaking gently to coat. Place sausages in the prepared baking pan. If desired, cover and chill for up to 24 hours.

4 Bake, uncovered, about 30 minutes or until bacon is brown.

NUTRITION FACTS PER SERVING:
102 cal., 8 g total fat (3 g sat. fat), 15 mg chol., 210 mg sodium, 4 g carb., 0 g fiber, 3 g pro.

Hot Wings

PREP 25 minutes MARINATE 30 minutes BROIL 20 minutes MAKES 12 servings

12 chicken wings (about
    2½ pounds total)

 3 tablespoons bottled hot
    pepper sauce

 2 tablespoons butter, melted

1½ teaspoons paprika

 ¼ teaspoon salt

 ¼ teaspoon cayenne pepper

    Desired dipping sauce

    Celery sticks (optional)

1 Cut off and discard tips of chicken wings. Cut wings at joints to form 24 pieces. Place chicken wing pieces in a resealable plastic bag set in a shallow dish.

2 For marinade, in a small bowl combine hot pepper sauce, melted butter, paprika, salt, and cayenne pepper. Pour marinade over chicken wings. Seal bag; turn to coat chicken. Marinate at room temperature for 30 minutes.

3 Preheat broiler. Drain chicken wings, discarding marinade. Place chicken on the unheated rack of a broiler pan. Broil 4 to 5 inches from the heat about 10 minutes or until light brown. Turn chicken wings. Broil for 10 to 15 minutes more or until chicken is no longer pink.

4 Serve chicken wings with dipping sauce and, if desired, celery sticks.

NUTRITION FACTS PER SERVING:
197 cal., 17 g total fat (5 g sat. fat), 49 mg chol., 271 mg sodium, 1 g carb., 0 g fiber, 10 g pro.

Ragin' Cajun Wings

Prepare as directed, except reduce bottled hot pepper sauce to 1 tablespoon and omit paprika and cayenne pepper. Stir 2 tablespoons chili sauce, 1½ teaspoons Cajun seasoning, and ½ teaspoon vinegar into marinade.

Fiery Chipotle Wings

Prepare as directed, except use bottled hot chipotle pepper sauce in place of bottled hot pepper sauce and use ground chipotle chile pepper in place of cayenne pepper.

Florida Crab Cakes

PREP 35 minutes COOK 6 minutes MAKES 12 servings

- 1 **egg, lightly beaten**
- ¼ **cup fine dry bread crumbs**
- ¼ **cup finely chopped green onions (2)**
- 2 **tablespoons mayonnaise**
- 1 **tablespoon snipped fresh parsley**
- 2 **teaspoons snipped fresh thyme or ½ teaspoon dried thyme, crushed**
- 2 **teaspoons Dijon-style mustard**
- ½ **teaspoon Worcestershire sauce**
- ⅛ **teaspoon salt**
- 1 **cup cooked lump crabmeat, cartilage removed, or one 6-ounce can crabmeat, drained, flaked, and cartilage removed**
- 3 **tablespoons fine dry bread crumbs**
- 3 **tablespoons yellow cornmeal**
- 2 **tablespoons vegetable oil**
- 1 **recipe Tropical Salsa**

1 In a medium bowl combine egg, ¼ cup bread crumbs, green onions, mayonnaise, parsley, thyme, mustard, Worcestershire sauce, and salt. Add crabmeat; mix well. Using moistened hands, shape crab mixture into twelve ½-inch-thick patties.

2 In a small bowl combine 3 tablespoons bread crumbs and cornmeal. Dip patties into cornmeal mixture, turning to coat.

3 In an extra-large skillet heat oil over medium heat. Add crab patties. Cook about 6 minutes or until heated through and golden, turning once. If patties brown too quickly, reduce heat to medium-low. Serve crab cakes with Tropical Salsa.

NUTRITION FACTS PER SERVING:
100 cal., 5 g total fat (1 g sat. fat), 26 mg chol., 275 mg sodium, 9 g carb., 1 g fiber, 4 g pro.

Tropical Salsa

In a small bowl combine 1 small papaya, seeded, peeled, and chopped; 1 medium carambola (star fruit), seeded and chopped; 2 tablespoons finely chopped red onion; 1 tablespoon lime juice; 1 tablespoon honey; ⅛ teaspoon salt; and ⅛ teaspoon cayenne pepper.

Marinated Shrimp Scampi

PREP 35 minutes MARINATE 1 hour BROIL 4 minutes MAKES 10 servings

- 2 **pounds fresh or frozen extra-jumbo shrimp in shells (30 to 40)**
- ¼ **cup olive oil**
- ¼ **cup dry white wine**
- 6 **cloves garlic, minced**
- 2 **teaspoons finely shredded lemon peel**
- ½ **teaspoon salt**
- ½ **teaspoon crushed red pepper**
- 2 **tablespoons snipped fresh Italian (flat-leaf) parsley**
  Lemon wedges

1 Thaw shrimp, if frozen. Peel and devein shrimp, leaving tails intact.* Rinse shrimp; pat dry with paper towels. Place shrimp in a resealable plastic bag set in a shallow dish.

2 For marinade, in a small bowl combine oil, wine, garlic, lemon peel, salt, and crushed red pepper. Pour marinade over shrimp. Seal bag; turn to coat shrimp. Marinate in the refrigerator for 1 hour.

3 Preheat broiler. Drain shrimp, reserving marinade. Arrange shrimp on the unheated rack of a broiler pan. Broil 4 to 5 inches from the heat for 2 minutes. Turn shrimp over and brush with the reserved marinade. Broil for 2 to 4 minutes more or until shrimp are opaque.

4 To serve, mound shrimp on a serving platter. Sprinkle with parsley and squeeze lemon wedges over shrimp.

NUTRITION FACTS PER SERVING: *126 cal., 4 g total fat (1 g sat. fat), 138 mg chol., 193 mg sodium, 2 g carb., 1 g fiber, 19 g pro.*

*tip
To peel shrimp, use your fingers to open the shell lengthwise down the body's underside. Starting at the head end, peel the shell back from the body. Then gently pull on the tail portion of the shell and remove it. To devein shrimp, use a sharp knife to make a shallow slit along the shrimp's back from the head end to the tail. Rinse under cold running water to remove the vein, using the tip of a knife, if necessary.

Rosemary-Roasted Nuts

PREP 15 minutes BAKE 12 minutes at 375°F MAKES 30 servings

- 3 cups whole unblanched almonds
- 1½ cups walnuts
- 1 cup raw pumpkin seeds (pepitas)
- 2 tablespoons finely snipped fresh rosemary
- 2 teaspoons packed brown sugar
- 1 teaspoon sea salt
- ½ teaspoon cayenne pepper
- 2 tablespoons butter, melted

1 Preheat oven to 375°F. In a 15×10×1-inch baking pan combine almonds, walnuts, and pumpkin seeds. Bake about 12 minutes or until toasted, stirring once.

2 In a small bowl combine rosemary, brown sugar, salt, and cayenne pepper. Stir in melted butter. Drizzle butter mixture over warm nuts; toss gently to coat. Serve warm or cooled to room temperature. Store in an airtight container at room temperature for up to 3 days.

NUTRITION FACTS PER SERVING:
177 cal., 15 g total fat (2 g sat. fat), 2 mg chol., 60 mg sodium, 5 g carb., 2 g fiber, 6 g pro.

Appetizers, Snacks, and Drinks

Chili Nuts

Photo on page 134

- **3 cups peanuts, cashews, or almonds**
- **1 tablespoon olive oil or vegetable oil**
- **2 teaspoons chili powder**
- **½ teaspoon garlic powder**
- **½ teaspoon ground cumin**
- **¼ teaspoon celery salt**
- **¼ teaspoon cayenne pepper**
- **¼ teaspoon ground cinnamon**

1 Preheat oven to 325°F. In a medium bowl combine nuts and oil; stir to coat nuts evenly. In a small bowl stir together chili powder, garlic powder, cumin, celery salt, cayenne pepper, and cinnamon. Sprinkle over nut mixture; toss to coat nuts evenly.

2 Spread nuts in a single layer in a 15×10×1-inch baking pan. Bake for 15 minutes, stirring twice; cool. Store in an airtight container at room temperature for up to 2 weeks.

NUTRITION FACTS PER SERVING:
226 cal., 19 g total fat (3 g sat. fat), 0 mg chol., 43 mg sodium, 8 g carb., 3 g fiber, 9 g pro.

Homemade Kettle-Style Corn

PREP 20 minutes   BAKE 30 minutes at 300°F   MAKES 16 servings

16 cups popped popcorn
    (about ⅔ cup unpopped)

¼   cup light-color corn syrup

¼   cup butter

    Salt

1 Preheat oven to 300°F. Place popcorn in a large roasting pan. In a small saucepan heat and stir corn syrup and butter over medium heat until butter is melted. Pour butter mixture over popcorn; toss gently to coat. Sprinkle lightly with salt; toss gently to coat.

2 Bake for 30 minutes, stirring every 10 minutes. Cool mixture in pan. Break up any clusters before serving. Store in an airtight container at room temperature for up to 1 week.

NUTRITION FACTS PER SERVING:
64 cal., 3 g total fat (2 g sat. fat), 8 mg chol., 59 mg sodium, 8 g carb., 1 g fiber, 1 g pro.

Shirley Temple

START TO FINISH 5 minutes   MAKES 1 serving

Ice cubes

2 tablespoons maraschino
   cherry juice

Ginger ale or lemon-lime
carbonated beverage, chilled

1 red maraschino cherry
   with stem

½ of an orange slice

Fill a glass with ice cubes. Pour cherry juice over ice. Add enough ginger ale to fill glass. Garnish with maraschino cherry and orange slice half.

NUTRITION FACTS PER SERVING: *204 cal., 0 g total fat (0 g sat. fat), 0 mg chol., 35 mg sodium, 54 g carb., 0 g fiber, 0 g pro.*

Watermelon and Strawberry Lemonade

PREP 30 minutes CHILL 4 to 24 hours MAKES 10 servings

6 cups cubed, seeded
   watermelon

2 cups quartered strawberries

⅓ cup agave nectar

1 cup lemon juice

1 2-liter bottle club soda
   or sparkling water, chilled

   Ice cubes

   Watermelon wedges
   (optional)

   Whole strawberries
   (optional)

1 In a food processor or blender combine half of the cubed watermelon, half of the quartered strawberries, and half of the agave nectar. Cover and process or blend until smooth. Transfer to a pitcher. Repeat with the remaining cubed watermelon, quartered strawberries, and agave nectar.

2 Add lemon juice to mixture in pitcher. Chill for 4 to 24 hours or until very cold.

3 To serve, in an extra-large pitcher or punch bowl combine fruit juice mixture and chilled club soda. Serve in glasses over ice cubes. If desired, garnish with watermelon wedges and whole strawberries.

NUTRITION FACTS PER SERVING:
74 cal., 0 g total fat (0 g sat. fat), 0 mg chol., 43 mg sodium, 19 g carb., 2 g fiber, 1 g pro.

Apricot Green Tea

START TO FINISH **15 minutes** MAKES **8 servings**

8	cups water
12	dried apricot halves
½	cup apricot nectar
¼	cup packed brown sugar or turbinado (raw) sugar
4	green tea bags
¼	teaspoon ground ginger
8	cinnamon sticks

1 In a 4-quart Dutch oven combine the water, dried apricots, apricot nectar, brown sugar, green tea bags, and ginger. Bring to boiling; reduce heat. Simmer, covered, for 10 minutes.

2 Place a cinnamon stick in each mug. Strain tea mixture; pour into the prepared mugs.

NUTRITION FACTS PER SERVING: *64 cal., 0 g total fat (0 g sat. fat), 0 mg chol., 10 mg sodium, 16 g carb., 1 g fiber, 0 g pro.*

tip
To make a refreshing iced version, prepare tea as directed in step 1 above, then remove the tea bags and let it cool at room temperature for at least 2 hours. Serve over ice in glasses rimmed with cinnamon-sugar.

Hot Apple Cider

PREP 10 minutes COOK 10 minutes MAKES 12 servings

1 small orange, halved
1 teaspoon whole cloves
8 cups apple cider or apple juice
4 cups cranberry juice
1 tablespoon honey
6 inches stick cinnamon

1 Stud orange halves with cloves by pushing tip of cloves into orange peel.

2 In a 4- to 6-quart Dutch oven combine cider, cranberry juice, and honey. Add clove-studded orange halves and stick cinnamon. Bring to boiling; reduce heat. Simmer, covered, for 10 minutes. Discard orange halves and stick cinnamon before serving.

NUTRITION FACTS PER SERVING: *118 cal., 0 g total fat (0 g sat. fat), 0 mg chol., 2 mg sodium, 16 g carb., 0 g fiber, 0 g pro.*

tip
Serving Hot Apple Cider from a slow cooker set on low is nice for a party because you won't have to worry about maintaining the temperature.

Appetizers, Snacks, and Drinks

Peppermint Hot Chocolate

START TO FINISH 15 minutes MAKES 2 servings

1½ cups whole milk

¼ cup chopped semisweet chocolate bar or pieces

6 tablespoons peppermint schnapps*

Whipped cream (optional)

Crushed peppermint candy **

1 In a small saucepan heat ½ cup of the milk over low heat just until bubbles appear around the edges. Whisking constantly, add chocolate and heat until chocolate is melted. Add the remaining 1 cup milk, whisking until combined and heated through.

2 Spoon half of the schnapps into mugs; add hot chocolate mixture. Top with whipped cream (if desired) and sprinkle with crushed candy.

NUTRITION FACTS PER SERVING:
377 cal., 12 g total fat (7 g sat. fat), 18 mg chol., 81 mg sodium, 48 g carb., 1 g fiber, 7 g pro.

*tip
For a nonalcoholic version, use ¼ to ½ teaspoon peppermint extract in place of the schnapps.

**tip
To crush peppermint candy, break a candy cane or peppermint stick into 1-inch pieces; place in a food processor. Cover and process until crushed. Or place candy pieces in a heavy resealable plastic bag. Cover with a towel; use a meat mallet or rolling pin to crush the candy.

Chai

1 cup water

2 black tea bags, such as orange pekoe, English Breakfast, Lapsang Souchong, or Darjeeling

3 inches stick cinnamon

1 cup milk

2 tablespoons turbinado (raw) sugar, granulated sugar, or honey

1 teaspoon vanilla

¼ teaspoon ground ginger

⅛ teaspoon ground cardamom

1 In a small saucepan combine the water, tea bags, and stick cinnamon. Bring to boiling. Remove from heat. Cover and let stand for 5 minutes. Remove and discard tea bags and stick cinnamon.

2 Whisk the milk, sugar, vanilla, ginger, and cardamom into the tea. Heat and stir over medium heat just until mixture is heated through (do not boil). Serve in warm mugs.

NUTRITION FACTS PER SERVING:
122 cal., 2 g total fat (2 g sat. fat), 10 mg chol., 55 mg sodium, 20 g carb., 1 g fiber, 4 g pro.

Vanilla Café Latte

START TO FINISH **5 minutes** MAKES **1 serving**

¼ **cup hot espresso or strong coffee**

2 **teaspoons vanilla-flavor syrup or 1 teaspoon sugar and ¼ teaspoon vanilla**

2 **to 3 tablespoons steamed milk**

2 **tablespoons frothed milk***

Ground cinnamon or grated chocolate

Pour the espresso or coffee into a 6-ounce cup. Stir in vanilla syrup. Add steamed milk and top with frothed milk. Sprinkle with cinnamon.

NUTRITION FACTS PER SERVING:
55 cal., 1 g total fat (1 g sat. fat), 5 mg chol., 26 mg sodium, 9 g carb., 0 g fiber, 0 g pro.

*tip
To make frothed milk, use the steam wand on your espresso machine to steam and froth the milk. Or place hot, but not boiling, milk in a blender. Cover and blend until froth forms on top of the milk. Or place the hot milk in a deep bowl and use an immersion blender to blend the milk until froth forms on top.

Comfort Food Classics Made Healthy

3

Comfort on your plate doesn't have to mean disaster for your waistline. Check out these lightened-up versions of your comfort food favorites.

Spiced Pot Roast with Root Vegetables

PREP 30 minutes   COOK 1 hour 40 minutes   MAKES 10 servings

- 1 **pound boneless beef chuck pot roast**
- 3½ **teaspoons garam masala***
- ½ **teaspoon salt**
- 1 **tablespoon vegetable oil**
- 1 **cup beef broth**
- ¼ **cup dry red wine or beef broth**
- 30 **carrots with tops (about 12 ounces) or 2 cups packaged peeled baby carrots**
- 1 **pound round red potatoes, quartered**
- 2 **parsnips, peeled and cut into ½-inch slices**
- 1 **rutabaga, peeled and cut into 1-inch pieces**
- 1 **red onion, cut into wedges**
- 2 **tablespoons cornstarch**
- 2 **tablespoons cold water**
- 1 **8-ounce carton plain low-fat yogurt**
- **Salt**
- **Ground black pepper**

1 Trim fat from roast. For rub, in a small bowl stir together 2½ teaspoons of the garam masala and the ½ teaspoon salt. Sprinkle rub evenly over meat; rub in with your fingers. In a 4-quart Dutch oven heat oil over medium-high heat. Brown roast on all sides in hot oil. Drain off fat.

2 Pour broth and wine over roast. Bring to boiling; reduce heat. Simmer, covered, for 1¼ hours.

3 Add carrots, potatoes, parsnips, rutabaga, and onion to beef mixture. Return to boiling; reduce heat. Simmer, covered, for 25 to 30 minutes or until beef and vegetables are tender. Using a slotted spoon, transfer beef and vegetable mixture to a platter; keep warm.

4 Skim and discard fat from cooking liquid. For sauce, strain cooking liquid. Return 1½ cups of the cooking liquid to the Dutch oven. Discard remaining cooking liquid. In a small bowl stir together cornstarch, the cold water, and the remaining 1 teaspoon garam masala; add to liquid in Dutch oven. Cook and stir over medium heat until thickened and bubbly. Cook and stir for 2 minutes more. Stir in yogurt; heat through (do not boil). Season to taste with additional salt and pepper. Serve sauce with meat and vegetables.

NUTRITION FACTS PER SERVING: *274 cal., 7 g total fat (2 g sat. fat), 82 mg chol., 381 mg sodium, 18 g carb., 3 g fiber, 32 g pro.*

Slow Cooker Directions: Trim fat from roast. In a small bowl, combine the 2½ teaspoons garam masala and the ½ teaspoon salt; rub the mixture onto the meat. Omit browning step. Place meat in a 5- to 6-quart slow cooker. Top with the 1 cup broth, the wine, carrots, potatoes, parsnips, rutabaga, and onion. Cover and cook on low-heat setting for 10 to 12 hours or on high-heat setting for 5 to 6 hours. Transfer meat and vegetables to a serving platter. Skim and discard fat from cooking liquid. For sauce, strain cooking liquid. Pour 1½ cups of the cooking liquid into a medium saucepan. Discard remaining liquid. In a small bowl, stir together cornstarch, the water, and the 1 teaspoon garam masala. Add to liquid in saucepan. Cook and stir over medium heat until thickened and bubbly. Cook and stir for 2 minutes more. Stir in yogurt; heat through (do not boil). Season to taste with additional salt and pepper. Serve sauce with meat and vegetables.

*tip

Garam masala, an Indian spice blend used in this pot roast, usually contains white and/or black pepper, cumin, cardamom, cinnamon, and cloves.

Flat-Iron Steak with BBQ Beans

Photo on page 138

START TO FINISH **20 minutes**   MAKES **4 servings**

- **2**   **boneless beef shoulder top blade (flat-iron) steaks, halved (1 to 1¼ pounds total)**
- **2**   **teaspoons fajita seasoning**
- **1**   **15-ounce can black beans, rinsed and drained**
- **⅓**   **cup barbecue sauce**
- **2**   **tomatoes, sliced**
-     **Corn bread (optional)**
-     **Pickled jalapeño chile peppers (optional)**

1 Grease a grill pan. Preheat grill pan over medium-high heat. Sprinkle steaks on all sides with fajita seasoning. Place steaks on hot grill pan; cook for 8 to 13 minutes for medium rare (145°F) or for 12 to 15 minutes for medium (160°F), turning steaks twice.

2 Meanwhile, in a medium microwave-safe bowl stir together beans and barbecue sauce. Cover loosely with plastic wrap. Microwave on 100 percent power (high) for 3 minutes, stirring once.

3 Serve steaks with bean mixture, tomatoes, and, if desired, corn bread. If desired, garnish with jalapeño peppers.

NUTRITION FACTS PER SERVING:
272 cal., 8 g total fat (2 g sat. fat), 67 mg chol., 667 mg sodium, 25 g carb., 6 g fiber, 29 g pro.

Baked Penne with Meat Sauce

PREP 30 minutes BAKE 20 minutes at 375°F MAKES 6 servings

- 8   ounces dried penne pasta
- 1   14-ounce can whole Italian-style tomatoes, undrained
- ½   of a 6-ounce can (⅓ cup) tomato paste with Italian seasonings
- ¼   cup dry red wine or tomato juice
- ½   teaspoon sugar
- 2   teaspoons snipped fresh oregano or ½ teaspoon dried oregano, crushed
- ¼   teaspoon ground black pepper
- 1   pound lean ground beef
- ½   cup chopped onion (1 medium)
- ¼   cup sliced, pitted ripe olives
- ½   cup shredded reduced-fat mozzarella cheese (2 ounces)

1. Cook pasta according to package directions; drain and set aside.

2. Meanwhile, in a food processor or blender combine tomatoes, tomato paste, wine, sugar, dried oregano (if using), and pepper. Cover and process or blend until smooth. Set aside.

3. Preheat oven to 375°F. In a large skillet cook ground beef and onion over medium heat until meat is brown, using a wooden spoon to break up meat as it cooks. Drain off fat. Stir tomato mixture into meat mixture in skillet. Bring to boiling; reduce heat. Simmer, covered, for 10 minutes. Stir in pasta, fresh oregano (if using), and olives. Divide the pasta mixture among six 10- to 12-ounce individual casseroles or spoon all of the pasta mixture into a 2-quart casserole. Cover with foil or lid(s).

4. Bake individual casseroles for 15 minutes or 2-quart casserole for 30 minutes. Sprinkle with cheese. Bake, uncovered, about 5 minutes more or until cheese melts.

NUTRITION FACTS PER SERVING:
339 cal., 11 g total fat (4 g sat. fat), 59 mg chol., 349 mg sodium, 33 g carb., 3 g fiber, 24 g pro.

Lasagna Panini

START TO FINISH 25 minutes   MAKES 4 servings

- 8   ounces lean ground beef
- 1   8-ounce can pizza sauce
- 4   2-ounce whole grain ciabatta rolls
- ¼   cup finely shredded Parmesan cheese
- 1   cup fresh spinach leaves
- ½   cup sliced fresh mushrooms
- ¼   cup chopped yellow or green sweet pepper
- ½   cup shredded part-skim mozzarella cheese (2 ounces)

     Nonstick cooking spray

1 In a medium skillet cook ground beef over medium heat until meat is brown, using a wooden spoon to break up meat as it cooks. Drain off fat. Set aside 2 tablespoons of the pizza sauce. Stir the remaining pizza sauce into the cooked meat.

2 Cut a thin slice from the top of each roll; hollow out rolls (use for bread crumbs in other recipes). Brush cut sides of top roll slices with the reserved 2 tablespoons pizza sauce; set aside. Divide meat mixture among the rolls. Sprinkle with Parmesan cheese. Divide spinach, mushrooms, sweet pepper, and mozzarella cheese among the sandwiches, mounding slightly if necessary. Add top roll slices, pressing down as needed.

3 Coat sandwiches lightly with cooking spray. Preheat a covered indoor grill, panini press, grill pan, or large skillet. Place sandwiches, half at a time if necessary, in grill or panini press. Cover and cook about 5 minutes or until golden brown and cheese is melted. (If using a grill pan or skillet, place sandwiches on grill pan or skillet. Weigh sandwiches down with a heavy skillet [add food cans for more weight] and cook for 2 to 3 minutes. Turn sandwiches over. Weigh down and cook about 2 minutes more or until golden brown and cheese is melted.)

NUTRITION FACTS PER SERVING: *345 cal., 11 g total fat (5 g sat. fat), 51 mg chol., 645 mg sodium, 36 g carb., 4 g fiber, 23 g pro.*

tip

If you like it spicy, replace half or all of the ground beef with Italian sausage. Ground turkey sausage works well, too.

Comfort Food Classics Made Healthy

Beef–Sweet Pepper Calzones   *Photo on page 138*

74

- 8   ounces extra-lean ground beef (95% lean)
- 1/3   cup chopped red sweet pepper
- 1/3   cup chopped green sweet pepper
- 1/4   teaspoon dried Italian seasoning, crushed
- 1/4   teaspoon dried oregano, crushed
- Nonstick cooking spray
- 1   13.8-ounce can refrigerated pizza dough
- 3/4   cup shredded mozzarella cheese (3 ounces)
- 1   cup reduced-sodium tomato-base pasta sauce, warmed

1 In a large nonstick skillet cook ground beef over medium heat until brown, using a wooden spoon to break up meat as it cooks. Drain off fat. Add sweet peppers, Italian seasoning, and oregano to meat in skillet; cook over medium heat about 3 minutes or until sweet peppers are tender. Set aside.

2 Preheat oven to 450°F. Line a large baking sheet with foil; lightly coat the foil with cooking spray. On a lightly floured surface, gently shape pizza dough into a 12-inch square, using a rolling pin as needed. Cut dough into four 6-inch squares. Divide meat mixture among dough squares, spooning meat mixture into center of each square. Sprinkle meat mixture with 1/2 cup of the cheese.

3 Lifting a corner of a square, stretch dough over filling to opposite corner to make a triangle. Press edges with the tines of a fork to seal. Place on prepared baking sheet. Repeat with the remaining squares to make four triangles total.

4 Bake for 12 to 14 minutes or until lightly browned. Sprinkle with the remaining 1/4 cup cheese. Let stand for 5 minutes before serving. Serve with warmed pasta sauce.

NUTRITION FACTS PER SERVING:
431 cal., 12 g total fat (4 g sat. fat), 49 mg chol., 852 mg sodium, 53 g carb., 3 g fiber, 27 g pro.

Our Best Meat Loaf

PREP 20 minutes BAKE 1 hour 10 minutes at 350°F STAND 10 minutes MAKES 8 servings

2 eggs

¾ cup milk

⅔ cup fine dry bread crumbs
   or 2 cups soft bread crumbs
   (about 3 slices bread)

¼ cup finely chopped onion

2 tablespoons snipped fresh
   parsley

1 teaspoon salt

½ teaspoon dried sage, basil,
   or oregano, crushed

⅛ teaspoon ground black pepper

1½ pounds ground beef, lamb,
   or pork

¼ cup ketchup

2 tablespoons packed brown
   sugar

1 teaspoon dry mustard

1 Preheat oven to 350°F. In a large bowl use a fork to beat together eggs and milk; stir in bread crumbs, onion, parsley, salt, sage, and pepper. Add ground meat; mix well. Lightly pat mixture into an 8×4×2-inch loaf pan.

2 Bake for 1 to 1¼ hours or until an instant-read thermometer inserted in center registers 160°F.* Spoon off fat. In a small bowl combine ketchup, brown sugar, and dry mustard; spread over meat loaf. Bake for 10 minutes more. Let stand for 10 minutes before serving.

NUTRITION FACTS PER SERVING:
243 cal., 13 g total fat (5 g sat. fat), 108 mg chol., 631 mg sodium, 12 g carb., 1 g fiber, 20 g pro.

75

*tip
The internal color of meat loaf is not a reliable doneness indicator. A beef, lamb, or pork loaf cooked to 160°F is safe, regardless of color. To measure the doneness of a meat loaf, insert an instant-read thermometer into the center of the loaf to a depth of 2 to 3 inches.

Beef and Noodles

PREP 35 minutes COOK 1 hour 40 minutes MAKES 4 servings

- 1 **pound boneless beef round steak or chuck roast**
- ¼ **cup all-purpose flour**
- 1 **tablespoon vegetable oil**
- ½ **cup chopped onion (1 medium)**
- 2 **cloves garlic, minced**
- 3 **cups beef broth**
- 1 **teaspoon dried marjoram or basil, crushed**
- ¼ **teaspoon ground black pepper**
- 8 **ounces frozen noodles**
- 2 **tablespoons snipped fresh parsley**

1 Trim fat from meat. Cut meat into ¾-inch cubes. Put flour in a resealable plastic bag. Add meat cubes, a few at a time, shaking to coat. In a large saucepan heat oil over medium-high heat. Cook half of the meat in hot oil until brown. Remove from saucepan. Add the remaining meat, the onion, and garlic to the saucepan; cook until meat is brown, adding more oil if necessary. Drain off fat. Return all meat to the saucepan.

2 Stir in broth, marjoram, and pepper. Bring to boiling; reduce heat. Simmer, covered, for 1¼ to 1½ hours or until meat is tender.

3 Stir frozen noodles into broth mixture. Bring to boiling; reduce heat. Cook, uncovered, for 25 to 30 minutes or until noodles are tender. Sprinkle with parsley.

NUTRITION FACTS PER SERVING:
351 cal., 12 g total fat (3 g sat. fat), 94 mg chol., 677 mg sodium, 29 g carb., 1 g fiber, 31 g pro.

Tomato-Topped Lamb Chops and Rice

START TO FINISH **20 minutes**   MAKES **4 servings**

8   lamb loin chops, cut 1 inch
     thick

     Salt

     Ground black pepper

1   8.8-ounce pouch cooked long
     grain rice

4   roma tomatoes, cut up

4   green onions, cut into 1-inch
     pieces

1   tablespoon snipped fresh
     oregano

1   tablespoon balsamic vinegar

1 Trim fat from chops. Sprinkle chops with salt and pepper. For a charcoal or gas grill, grill chops on the rack of a covered grill directly over medium heat for 12 to 14 minutes for medium-rare (145°F) or 15 to 17 minutes for medium (160°F), turning once halfway through grilling time.

2 Meanwhile, heat rice in the microwave oven according to package directions. In a food processor combine tomatoes, green onions, and oregano. Cover and process with on/off pulses until coarsely chopped. Transfer to a small bowl; stir in vinegar. Season to taste with additional salt and pepper.

3 Divide rice among four dinner plates; top with chops. Serve with tomato mixture.

NUTRITION FACTS PER SERVING:
273 cal., 7 g total fat (2 g sat. fat), 70 mg chol., 153 mg sodium, 26 g carb., 3 g fiber, 25 g pro.

Mama's Spicy Meatballs with Fresh Tomato Sauce *Photo on page 136*

PREP 20 minutes BAKE 20 minutes at 350°F COOK 20 minutes (sauce) MAKES 6 servings

Nonstick cooking spray

¼ cup chili sauce

¼ cup seasoned fine dry bread crumbs

2 tablespoons finely chopped onion

1 tablespoon grated Parmesan or Romano cheese

1 tablespoon finely chopped, drained pepperoncini salad pepper

1½ teaspoons fennel seeds, crushed

1 pound extra-lean ground pork

1 recipe Fresh Tomato Sauce

3 cups hot cooked broken lasagna noodles

1 Preheat oven to 350°F. Lightly coat a 15×10×1-inch baking pan with cooking spray; set aside. In a large bowl combine chili sauce, bread crumbs, onion, cheese, pepperoncini pepper, and fennel seeds. Add ground pork. Mix well. Shape into 36 meatballs. Place in prepared pan.

2 Bake, uncovered, for 20 to 25 minutes or until browned and cooked through. Remove from oven; drain off fat.

3 Add baked meatballs to warm Fresh Tomato Sauce; heat through. Serve over hot cooked lasagna noodles.

NUTRITION FACTS PER SERVING: *304 cal., 7 g total fat (2 g sat. fat), 45 mg chol., 520 mg sodium, 36 g carb., 4 g fiber, 23 g pro.*

Fresh Tomato Sauce

In a large saucepan heat 1 tablespoon vegetable oil over medium heat. Add ⅓ cup finely chopped onion (1 small) and 4 cloves garlic, minced; cook for 3 to 5 minutes or until onion is tender, stirring occasionally. Stir in 3 cups peeled, seeded, and chopped roma tomatoes or one 28-ounce can whole peeled roma tomatoes, drained and chopped. Stir in ½ cup red wine, 1 to 2 teaspoons balsamic vinegar, ½ teaspoon salt, and ½ teaspoon ground black pepper. Bring to boiling; reduce heat. Simmer, uncovered, for 20 to 25 minutes or until sauce is slightly thickened, stirring occasionally.

Skillet-Roasted Potatoes with Pork

PREP 25 minutes ROAST 25 minutes at 425°F STAND 10 minutes MAKES 4 servings

1 teaspoon dried rosemary, crushed

½ teaspoon salt

¼ teaspoon ground black pepper

1 12- to 16-ounce pork tenderloin

12 ounces 2- to 3-inch Yukon gold potatoes, quartered

2 tablespoons olive oil

2 cloves garlic, thinly sliced

1 teaspoon finely shredded lemon peel

¼ teaspoon smoked paprika or regular paprika

8 cups arugula, tough stems removed, or fresh baby spinach (about 6 ounces)

1 Preheat oven to 425°F. In a small bowl combine rosemary, ¼ teaspoon of the salt, and the pepper. Trim fat from meat. Place meat on a rack in a shallow roasting pan. Sprinkle all over with the rosemary mixture. Roast for 25 to 35 minutes or until an instant-read thermometer inserted in center registers 150°F. Remove from oven. Cover with foil; let stand for 10 minutes. Temperature of meat after standing should be 155°F.

2 Meanwhile, in a covered large nonstick skillet cook potatoes in a small amount of boiling lightly salted water about 15 minutes or just until potatoes are tender, stirring occasionally. Drain water from skillet.

3 Add 1 tablespoon of the oil and the garlic to potatoes in skillet. Cook over medium-high heat for 5 to 10 minutes or until potatoes are browned, stirring occasionally. Sprinkle with lemon peel, the remaining ¼ teaspoon salt, and the paprika. Toss to coat. Transfer potatoes to a bowl. Cover and keep warm.

4 In the same skillet heat the remaining 1 tablespoon oil over medium heat. Add arugula, in batches if necessary. Cook and toss for 30 to 60 seconds or just until arugula is wilted.

5 To serve, divide arugula among four serving plates. Top with potatoes. Thinly slice pork crosswise; arrange on plates.

NUTRITION FACTS PER SERVING:
232 cal., 9 g total fat (2 g sat. fat), 55 mg chol., 352 mg sodium, 17 g carb., 3 g fiber, 21 g pro.

Southwest Pork Chops

START TO FINISH **30 minutes** MAKES **6 servings**

6   bone-in pork rib chops,
    cut ¾ inch thick (about
    2½ pounds total)

    Nonstick cooking spray

1   15-ounce can Mexican-style
    or Tex-Mex-style chili beans

1   cup salsa

1   cup frozen whole kernel corn

3   cups hot cooked rice

    Snipped fresh cilantro
    (optional)

1 Trim fat from chops. Coat a 12-inch nonstick skillet with cooking spray. Heat skillet over medium-high heat. Add chops, half at a time if necessary, to hot skillet; cook about 4 minutes or until brown, turning once halfway through cooking time. Remove chops from skillet.

2 Add chili beans, salsa, and corn to skillet; stir to combine. Place chops on top of bean mixture. Bring to boiling; reduce heat. Simmer, covered, for 15 to 20 minutes or until chops are slightly pink in centers and juices run clear (155°F). Serve over hot cooked rice. If desired, sprinkle with cilantro.

NUTRITION FACTS PER SERVING:
379 cal., 10 g total fat (3 g sat. fat), 71 mg chol., 490 mg sodium, 38 g carb., 5 g fiber, 33 g pro.

Teriyaki Pork Lo Mein

START TO FINISH **35 minutes** MAKES **6 servings**

12   ounces boneless pork loin

10   ounces dried multigrain spaghetti, angel hair pasta (capellini), or soba (buckwheat noodles)

¼   cup oyster sauce

¼   cup reduced-sodium teriyaki sauce

¼   cup dry sherry, sweet rice wine (mirin), sake, or chicken broth

2   teaspoons canola oil

2   teaspoons toasted sesame oil

1   tablespoon grated fresh ginger

1   medium red onion, halved and thinly sliced

3   cups sliced fresh mushrooms (8 ounces)

2   cups fresh sugar snap peas, halved

1 If desired, partially freeze meat for easier slicing. Trim fat from meat. Thinly slice meat across the grain into bite-size strips. Set aside.

2 Cook spaghetti according to package directions; drain. Rinse with cold water; drain again. For sauce, in a small bowl combine oyster sauce, teriyaki sauce, and sherry. Set aside.

3 Pour canola oil and sesame oil into a wok or 12-inch nonstick skillet; heat wok over medium-high heat. (Add more canola oil as necessary during cooking.) Add ginger; cook and stir for 15 seconds. Add onion; cook and stir for 2 minutes. Add mushrooms; cook and stir for 2 minutes. Add sugar snap peas; cook and stir about 1 minute more or until vegetables are crisp-tender. Remove vegetables from wok; cover and keep warm.

4 Add meat to wok. Cook and stir for 2 to 3 minutes or until meat is slightly pink in center. Add cooked spaghetti, vegetables, and sauce. Using two spatulas or wooden spoons, gently toss mixture while cooking for 3 to 4 minutes more or until heated through.

NUTRITION FACTS PER SERVING:
331 cal., 7 g total fat (1 g sat. fat), 31 mg chol., 634 mg sodium, 41 g carb., 5 g fiber, 24 g pro.

Pork and Ale Ragout

PREP 25 minutes   COOK 35 minutes   MAKES 6 servings

2	tablespoons all-purpose flour
$\frac{1}{2}$	teaspoon crushed red pepper
1	pound boneless pork sirloin, cut into $\frac{3}{4}$-inch cubes
1	tablespoon vegetable oil
2	cloves garlic, minced
3	cups vegetable broth
1	12-ounce can beer or $1\frac{1}{2}$ cups vegetable broth
3	parsnips, peeled and cut into $\frac{3}{4}$-inch slices
2	sweet potatoes, peeled and cut into 1-inch cubes
1	onion, cut into thin wedges
2	tablespoons snipped fresh thyme or $1\frac{1}{2}$ teaspoons dried thyme, crushed
1	tablespoon packed brown sugar
1	tablespoon Dijon-style mustard
4	tomatoes, coarsely chopped
2	green apples, cored and cut into wedges

1 In a resealable plastic bag combine flour and crushed red pepper. Add meat cubes, a few at a time, shaking to coat.

2 In a 4-quart Dutch oven heat oil over medium-high heat. Add meat and garlic, half at a time, to hot oil; cook and stir until meat is brown. Return all meat and garlic to Dutch oven. Add broth, beer, parsnips, sweet potatoes, onion, dried thyme (if using), brown sugar, and mustard.

3 Bring to boiling; reduce heat. Simmer, covered, for 30 minutes. Stir in tomatoes, apples, and fresh thyme (if using). Return to boiling; reduce heat. Simmer, covered, about 5 minutes more or until meat, vegetables, and apples are tender.

NUTRITION FACTS PER SERVING:
288 cal., 7 g total fat (2 g sat. fat), 48 mg chol., 571 mg sodium, 36 g carb., 6 g fiber, 20 g pro.

Pizza Stew with Biscuits

PREP 20 minutes   SLOW COOK 3 hours (low) + 45 to 60 minutes (high)   MAKES 5 servings

8 ounces fresh cremini mushrooms, quartered or sliced

¾ cup chopped green sweet pepper (1 medium)

⅓ cup finely chopped onion (1 small)

1 teaspoon dried Italian seasoning, crushed

¼ teaspoon salt

¼ teaspoon ground black pepper

2 cups marinara sauce

1¼ pounds uncooked ground turkey breast

¾ cup biscuit mix

⅓ cup grated Parmesan cheese

¼ teaspoon dried oregano, crushed

¼ cup fat-free milk

½ cup shredded part-skim mozzarella cheese (2 ounces) (optional)

1 In a 3½- or 4-quart slow cooker combine mushrooms, sweet pepper, onion, Italian seasoning, salt, and black pepper. Pour marinara sauce over all. Using a wooden spoon, break ground turkey into bite-size pieces. Add to cooker, stirring to combine.

2 Cover and cook on low-heat setting for 3 hours.

3 In a small bowl combine biscuit mix, Parmesan cheese, and oregano. Add milk; stir with a fork until combined.

4 Turn cooker to high-heat setting. Drop Parmesan cheese mixture by tablespoons into five mounds onto mixture in cooker, spacing mounds evenly.

5 Cover and cook for 45 to 60 minutes more or until a wooden toothpick inserted into the centers of dumplings comes out clean.

6 To serve, if desired, sprinkle each serving with mozzarella cheese.

NUTRITION FACTS PER SERVING:
323 cal., 7 g total fat (2 g sat. fat), 62 mg chol., 851 mg sodium, 32 g carb., 4 g fiber, 33 g pro.

Chicken Piccata

START TO FINISH 25 minutes MAKES 4 servings

- 2   8-ounce skinless, boneless chicken breast halves, cut in half horizontally
- ¼   teaspoon salt
- ¼   teaspoon ground black pepper
- 1   tablespoon butter
- 2   cloves garlic, minced
- ½   cup reduced-sodium chicken broth
- 1   medium lemon, thinly sliced
- 2   tablespoons capers, rinsed and drained
- 1   tablespoon snipped fresh parsley

1 Place each chicken breast portion between two pieces of plastic wrap. Using the flat side of a meat mallet, pound each chicken portion lightly until about ¼ inch thick. Remove plastic wrap. Sprinkle chicken with salt and pepper.

2 In a large skillet melt butter over medium-high heat. Add chicken; cook for 6 to 8 minutes or until browned and no longer pink in center, turning once halfway through cooking. Remove chicken from skillet; set aside.

3 Add garlic to the hot skillet; cook for 30 seconds to 1 minute or until lightly browned. Add broth to skillet, scraping up any browned bits from the bottom of the skillet. Bring to boiling. Add lemon slices and capers. Cover; reduce heat to low. Cook for 4 to 5 minutes or until lemon slices are softened and releasing their juice. Return chicken to skillet; heat through.

4 To serve, spoon caper mixture over chicken. Sprinkle with parsley.

NUTRITION FACTS PER SERVING: *161 cal., 4 g total fat (2 g sat. fat), 73 mg chol., 440 mg sodium, 4 g carb., 2 g fiber, 27 g pro.*

Chicken with Marsala Risotto

START TO FINISH **50 minutes** MAKES **4 servings**

- 2 cups thinly sliced fresh cremini mushrooms (about 6 ounces)
- ½ of a large sweet onion, thinly sliced
- 1 tablespoon olive oil
- ¾ cup uncooked Arborio rice
- 3 cloves garlic, minced
- ⅓ cup dry Marsala
- 2½ to 3 cups reduced-sodium chicken broth
- 1 tablespoon snipped fresh thyme or 1 teaspoon dried thyme, crushed
- 2 teaspoons snipped fresh rosemary or ½ teaspoon dried rosemary, crushed
- ½ teaspoon ground black pepper
- ¼ teaspoon salt
- 14 to 16 ounces chicken breast tenderloins
- Nonstick cooking spray
- ½ cup finely shredded Asiago or Parmesan cheese (2 ounces)
- 2 cups coarsely chopped fresh spinach

1 In a large saucepan cook mushrooms and onion in hot oil over medium heat about 10 minutes or until tender and light brown, stirring occasionally. Add rice and 1 clove of the garlic. Cook and stir for 2 to 3 minutes or until rice begins to brown. Remove from heat. Carefully add Marsala; return to heat. Cook and stir until Marsala is absorbed.

2 Meanwhile, in a medium saucepan bring broth to boiling; reduce heat until simmering. Slowly add ½ cup of the hot broth to rice mixture, stirring constantly. Continue to cook and stir over medium heat until broth is absorbed. Add the remaining broth, ½ cup at a time, stirring constantly until broth is absorbed. (This should take 15 to 20 minutes.)

3 In a small bowl combine thyme, rosemary, ¼ teaspoon of the pepper, and the salt. Rub the remaining 2 cloves garlic over chicken; sprinkle with thyme mixture. Lightly coat both sides of chicken with cooking spray.

4 Heat a grill pan over medium-high heat. Add chicken; cook for 8 to 10 minutes or until chicken is no longer pink (170°F), turning once halfway through cooking time. If chicken browns too quickly, reduce heat to medium.

5 Add cheese and the remaining ¼ teaspoon pepper to rice mixture, stirring until cheese is melted. Stir in spinach. Spoon rice mixture onto serving plates. Top with chicken.

NUTRITION FACTS PER SERVING: *375 cal., 11 g total fat (4 g sat. fat), 78 mg chol., 772 mg sodium, 34 g carb., 2 g fiber, 31 g pro.*

Sweet Herbed Oven-Fried Chicken

Photo on page 137

PREP 20 minutes BAKE 22 minutes at 375°F MAKES 4 servings

1   egg, beaten

2   tablespoons milk

1   cup Kashi GoLean® cereal,
     original flavor, crushed

1   cup cornflakes, crushed

¼   cup snipped fresh basil

¼   teaspoon salt

⅛   teaspoon ground black pepper

4   skinless, boneless chicken
     breast halves (about
     1½ pounds total)

     Honey

1 Preheat oven to 375°F. Grease a 15×10×1-inch baking pan; set aside. In a shallow dish combine egg and milk. In a second shallow dish combine crushed cereals, basil, salt, and pepper. Dip chicken pieces, one at a time, into egg mixture; dip into cereal mixture, turning to coat.

2 Arrange chicken in the prepared baking pan, making sure the pieces do not touch. Sprinkle chicken pieces with any remaining cereal mixture so they are generously coated.

3 Bake for 22 to 25 minutes or until chicken is no longer pink (170°F). Do not turn chicken pieces while baking. Serve with honey.

NUTRITION FACTS PER SERVING:
343 cal., 6 g total fat (2 g sat. fat), 156 mg chol., 438 mg sodium, 32 g carb., 3 g fiber, 42 g pro.

Chicken and Noodles

PREP **25 minutes**   COOK **20 minutes**   MAKES **8 servings**

1   **12-ounce package frozen noodles (about 3 cups)***

3   **cups reduced-sodium chicken broth**

2   **cups sliced carrots (4 medium)**

1   **cup chopped onion (1 large)**

½   **cup sliced celery (1 stalk)**

2   **cups milk**

1   **cup frozen peas**

3   **tablespoons all-purpose flour**

½   **teaspoon salt**

⅛   **teaspoon ground black pepper**

2   **cups chopped cooked chicken**

Coarsely ground black pepper (optional)

1 In 4-quart Dutch oven combine noodles, broth, carrots, onion, and celery. Bring to boiling; reduce heat. Simmer, covered, about 20 minutes or until noodles and vegetables are tender. Stir in 1½ cups of the milk and the peas.

2 In a small bowl stir together the remaining ½ cup milk, the flour, salt, and the ⅛ teaspoon pepper. Whisk until smooth; stir into noodle mixture. Stir in chicken. Cook and stir until thickened and bubbly. Cook and stir for 1 minute more. If desired, sprinkle with coarsely ground pepper.

NUTRITION FACTS PER SERVING:
269 cal., 5 g total fat (2 g sat. fat), 86 mg chol., 468 mg sodium, 36 g carb., 3 g fiber, 19 g pro.

***tip**
Save time with frozen noodles. They have the thick texture and eggy flavor reminiscent of homemade noodles without all of the work.

Comfort Food Classics Made Healthy

Chicken and Rice–Stuffed Peppers

START TO FINISH **30 minutes** MAKES **4 servings**

4   small or 2 large red and/or
    yellow sweet peppers

Salt

Ground black pepper

1   cup 1-inch pieces fresh
    asparagus or broccoli florets

1   8.8-ounce pouch cooked long
    grain rice

1   cup cubed cooked chicken

½   cup finely shredded Parmesan
    or Romano cheese (2 ounces)

¼   cup milk

½   to 1 teaspoon dried oregano,
    crushed

¼   teaspoon salt

⅛   teaspoon ground black pepper

¼   cup broken walnuts, toasted if
    desired

Shaved or shredded Parmesan
or Romano cheese (optional)

1 Cut sweet peppers in half lengthwise. Remove seeds and membranes. If necessary, cut a thin slice from the bottom of each sweet pepper half so it stays upright. In a Dutch oven cook sweet peppers in enough boiling water to cover for 3 minutes; drain well. Place on a serving platter, cut sides up. Sprinkle lightly with salt and black pepper; set aside.

2 Meanwhile, for filling, in a covered medium saucepan cook asparagus in a small amount of boiling water for 1 to 2 minutes or just until tender. Drain; return to hot saucepan. Stir in rice, chicken, the ½ cup cheese, the milk, oregano, the ¼ teaspoon salt, and the ⅛ teaspoon black pepper. Cook and stir over medium heat until heated through. Stir in walnuts.

3 Divide filling among sweet pepper halves. If desired, top with additional cheese.

NUTRITION FACTS PER SERVING:
321 cal., 13 g total fat (4 g sat. fat), 43 mg chol., 581 mg sodium, 32 g carb., 5 g fiber, 21 g pro.

Skillet Chicken, Macaroni, and Cheese

START TO FINISH **35 minutes** MAKES **5 servings**

1½ cups dried multigrain or regular elbow macaroni (6 ounces)

Nonstick cooking spray

12 ounces skinless, boneless chicken breast halves, cut into 1-inch pieces

¼ cup finely chopped onion

1 6.5-ounce package light semisoft cheese with garlic and herbs

1⅔ cups fat-free milk

1 tablespoon all-purpose flour

¾ cup shredded reduced-fat cheddar cheese (3 ounces)

2 cups baby spinach

1 cup cherry tomatoes, quartered

1 In a medium saucepan cook macaroni according to package directions, except do not add any salt to the water; drain.

2 Meanwhile, coat a large nonstick skillet with cooking spray; heat skillet over medium-high heat. Add chicken and onion to hot skillet. Cook for 4 to 6 minutes or until chicken is no longer pink and onion is tender, stirring frequently. (If onion browns too quickly, reduce heat to medium.) Remove skillet from heat. Add semisoft cheese; stir until melted.

3 In a medium bowl whisk together milk and flour until smooth. Add all at once to chicken mixture. Cook and stir over medium heat until thickened and bubbly. Reduce heat to low. Add cheddar cheese, stirring until melted. Add cooked macaroni; cook and stir for 1 to 2 minutes or until heated through. Stir in spinach. Top with cherry tomatoes. Serve immediately.

NUTRITION FACTS PER SERVING:
369 cal., 12 g total fat (7 g sat. fat), 85 mg chol., 393 mg sodium, 33 g carb., 4 g fiber, 33 g pro.

tip

An easy makeover for many pasta dishes can be achieved by simply switching to whole grain or multigrain pasta and loading up on the vegetables.

Turkey and Stuffing Bake

PREP 25 minutes   BAKE 35 minutes at 350°F   STAND 5 minutes   MAKES 8 servings

- 3   cups water
- 1   cup chopped red sweet pepper (1 large)
- ½   cup uncooked long grain white rice
- ½   cup chopped onion (1 medium)
- 1   8-ounce package herb-seasoned stuffing mix
- 3   eggs, lightly beaten
- 4   cups chopped cooked turkey or chicken
- 1   10.75-ounce can condensed cream of chicken soup
- ½   cup sour cream
- ¼   cup milk
- 2   teaspoons dry sherry

1 Preheat oven to 350°F. Grease a 3-quart baking dish; set aside. In a medium saucepan bring 1 cup of the water to boiling. Stir in sweet pepper, rice, and onion. Reduce heat to low. Cook, covered, for 15 to 18 minutes or until rice and vegetables are tender.

2 Meanwhile, in a large bowl combine stuffing mix and the remaining 2 cups water. Stir in eggs, turkey, and half of the soup. Stir in cooked rice mixture. Transfer mixture to the prepared baking dish. Bake, uncovered, for 35 to 40 minutes or until heated through.

3 Meanwhile, for sauce, in a small saucepan combine the remaining soup, the sour cream, and milk. Cook over low heat until heated through. Stir in sherry.

4 Let casserole stand for 5 minutes before serving. Spoon sauce over top.

NUTRITION FACTS PER SERVING:
383 cal., 12 g total fat (4 g sat. fat), 142 mg chol., 765 mg sodium, 38 g carb., 3 g fiber, 29 g pro.

Roasted Salmon and Tomatoes

PREP 15 minutes BAKE 12 minutes at 450°F MAKES 4 servings

4   4-ounce fresh or frozen
     skinless salmon fillets,
     about 1 inch thick

¼   teaspoon kosher salt or salt

     Nonstick cooking spray

1   pound roma tomatoes, seeded
     and chopped

1   tablespoon Worcestershire
     sauce for chicken

¼   teaspoon coarsely ground
     black pepper

     Fresh marjoram or oregano
     sprigs (optional)

     Dijon-style mustard

1 Preheat oven to 450°F. Thaw salmon, if frozen. Rinse salmon; pat dry with paper towels. Sprinkle with ⅛ teaspoon of the salt.

2 Lightly coat a 13×9×2-inch baking pan with cooking spray. Place salmon in the prepared baking pan, tucking under any thin edges. Arrange tomatoes around salmon. Sprinkle tomatoes with Worcestershire sauce, pepper, and the remaining ⅛ teaspoon salt.

3 Bake for 12 to 16 minutes or until salmon flakes easily when tested with a fork. If desired, garnish with marjoram. Serve with mustard.

NUTRITION FACTS PER SERVING:
283 cal., 15 g total fat (3 g sat. fat), 83 mg chol., 359 mg sodium, 6 g carb., 1 g fiber, 30 g pro.

Cajun-Flavored Catfish

PREP 15 minutes BAKE 15 minutes at 350°F MAKES 4 servings

1 pound fresh or frozen skinless catfish fillets, about ½ inch thick

1 tablespoon ground black pepper

1 tablespoon dried oregano, crushed

2 teaspoons seasoned salt

2 teaspoons onion powder

1 teaspoon crushed red pepper

¾ teaspoon chili powder

½ teaspoon ground cumin

1 Thaw fish, if frozen. Rinse fish; pat dry with paper towels.

2 Preheat oven to 350°F. Grease a 3-quart rectangular baking dish; set aside. For Cajun seasoning, stir together black pepper, oregano, seasoned salt, onion powder, crushed red pepper, chili powder, and cumin. Set aside 1 tablespoon of the seasoning. (Store remaining seasoning in an airtight container at room temperature for up to 1 month; use on fish or pork.)

3 Coat all sides of the fish fillets with the reserved 1 tablespoon Cajun seasoning. Arrange fish in a single layer in the prepared baking dish.

4 Bake for 15 to 18 minutes or until fish flakes easily when tested with a fork, turning once halfway through baking time.

NUTRITION FACTS PER SERVING:
233 cal., 13 g total fat (3 g sat. fat), 79 mg chol., 283 mg sodium, 1 g carb., 0 g fiber, 27 g pro.

tip
The Cajun seasoning that flavors this dish also tastes delicious on chicken or pork. Turn up the heat even more by adding ¼ to ½ teaspoon cayenne pepper to the blend.

Crispy Fish and Peppers

PREP 15 minutes   COOK 4 to 6 minutes per ½-inch thickness   MAKES 4 servings

- 1 **pound fresh or frozen small fish fillets, such as grouper, catfish, or tilapia**
- ¾ **cup buttermilk**
- 1 **egg**
- 1 **teaspoon Cajun seasoning**
- 1 **cup all-purpose flour**
- 3 **to 4 tablespoons vegetable oil**
- 1 **cup sliced and/or chopped miniature sweet peppers**
- 1 **lemon, cut up**

1 Thaw fish, if frozen. Rinse fish; pat dry with paper towels. Measure thickness of fish.

2 In a shallow dish whisk together buttermilk, egg, and Cajun seasoning. Place flour in another shallow dish. Dip fish in buttermilk, then in flour, turning to coat. Repeat to coat fish twice.

3 In a large heavy skillet heat 3 tablespoons of the oil over medium-high heat. Carefully add fish to hot oil (working in batches, if necessary). Cook for 4 to 6 minutes per ½-inch thickness or until golden brown, turning once halfway through cooking time. (Add additional oil during cooking, if needed.) Drain on paper towels.

4 Drain oil from skillet; wipe out skillet with paper towel. Add sweet peppers to skillet; cook about 2 minutes or until crisp-tender.

5 Serve fish with sweet peppers and lemon wedges.

NUTRITION FACTS PER SERVING:
251 cal., 13 g total fat (2 g sat. fat), 97 mg chol., 188 mg sodium, 8 g carb., 2 g fiber, 26 g pro.

93

Pacific Northwest Paella

START TO FINISH 45 minutes　MAKES 6 servings

1¼　pounds fresh or frozen skinless salmon fillets, about 1 inch thick

4　slices apple wood-smoked bacon

3　cups sliced fresh cremini or button mushrooms (8 ounces)

1　cup chopped onion (1 large)

2　cloves garlic, minced

2½　cups chicken broth

1　cup uncooked long grain white rice

2　teaspoons snipped fresh thyme or ½ teaspoon dried thyme, crushed

¼　teaspoon cracked black pepper

1　pound fresh asparagus, trimmed and cut into 1-inch pieces, or one 10-ounce package frozen cut asparagus, thawed

⅓　cup chopped roma tomato (1)

1 Thaw fish, if frozen. In a large deep skillet or paella pan cook bacon over medium heat until crisp. Drain bacon on paper towels, reserving drippings in skillet. Crumble bacon; set aside.

2 Add mushrooms, onion, and garlic to the reserved drippings. Cook about 5 minutes or until onion is tender. Stir in broth, rice, and thyme. Bring to boiling; reduce heat. Simmer, covered, for 10 minutes.

3 Meanwhile, rinse fish; pat dry with paper towels. Cut fish into 1-inch pieces. Sprinkle with pepper; toss gently.

4 Place fish and asparagus on top of rice mixture. Simmer, covered, for 10 to 12 minutes more or until fish flakes easily when tested with a fork and asparagus is crisp-tender. Sprinkle with tomato and crumbled bacon.

NUTRITION FACTS PER SERVING:
320 cal., 10 g total fat (3 g sat. fat), 56 mg chol., 569 mg sodium, 31 g carb., 2 g fiber, 27 g pro.

Creole-Style Shrimp and Grits

START TO FINISH 35 minutes MAKES 4 servings

1   pound fresh or frozen
    medium shrimp
1   cup yellow grits
12 ounces fresh asparagus,
    trimmed and bias-sliced into
    2-inch pieces
1   medium red sweet pepper,
    seeded and cut into ½-inch
    squares
½   cup chopped onion
    (1 medium)
2   cloves garlic, minced
1   tablespoon olive oil
2   tablespoons all-purpose flour
2   teaspoons salt-free Creole
    seasoning
¾   cup reduced-sodium chicken
    broth
¼   teaspoon salt
¼   teaspoon ground black pepper

1 Thaw shrimp, if frozen. Peel and devein shrimp, leaving tails intact, if desired. Rinse shrimp; pat dry with paper towels. Prepare grits according to package directions. Cover and keep warm.

2 Meanwhile, in a large skillet cook asparagus, sweet pepper, onion, and garlic in hot oil over medium heat for 4 to 5 minutes or just until vegetables are tender.

3 Stir flour and Creole seasoning into vegetable mixture. Add broth, salt, and black pepper. Cook and stir just until bubbly; reduce heat. Stir in shrimp. Cover and cook for 1 to 3 minutes or until shrimp are opaque, stirring once. Serve over cooked grits.

NUTRITION FACTS PER SERVING:
308 cal., 5 g total fat (1 g sat. fat), 143 mg chol., 899 mg sodium, 43 g carb., 4 g fiber, 21 g pro.

95

Comfort Food Classics Made Healthy

Spicy Shrimp Pasta

START TO FINISH **30 minutes** MAKES **4 servings**

12 **ounces fresh or frozen large shrimp in shells**

8 **ounces dried linguine or fettuccine**

2 **tablespoons olive oil or vegetable oil**

1 **or 2 fresh jalapeño chile peppers, stemmed, seeded, and finely chopped***

2 **cloves garlic, minced**

½ **teaspoon salt**

¼ **teaspoon ground black pepper**

2 **cups cherry tomatoes, halved**

Finely shredded Parmesan cheese (optional)

1 Thaw shrimp, if frozen. Peel and devein shrimp, leaving tails intact if desired. Rinse shrimp; pat dry with paper towels. In a large saucepan cook linguine according to package directions; drain. Return linguine to hot saucepan; cover and keep warm.

2 Meanwhile, in a large skillet heat oil over medium-high heat. Add jalapeño peppers, garlic, salt, and black pepper; cook and stir for 1 minute. Add shrimp; cook and stir about 3 minutes or until shrimp are opaque. Stir in tomatoes; heat through.

3 Add shrimp mixture to cooked linguine; gently toss to combine. If desired, serve with cheese.

NUTRITION FACTS PER SERVING:
363 cal., 9 g total fat (1 g sat. fat), 97 mg chol., 396 mg sodium, 48 g carb., 3 g fiber, 21 g pro.

*tip

Because chile peppers contain volatile oils that can burn your skin and eyes, avoid direct contact with them as much as possible. When working with chile peppers, wear plastic or rubber gloves. If your bare hands do touch the peppers, wash your hands and nails well with soap and warm water.

Greek Vegetable and Feta Cheese Pie

PREP 35 minutes   BAKE 40 minutes at 375°F   STAND 15 minutes   MAKES 6 servings

- 1 **tablespoon olive oil**
- 1 **cup chopped onion (1 large)**
- ¾ **cup chopped red sweet pepper (1 medium)**
- 2½ **cups thinly sliced zucchini (2 medium)**
- 1 **10-ounce package frozen chopped spinach, thawed and well drained**
- 2 **cloves garlic, minced**
- ½ **teaspoon salt**
- 1½ **cups evaporated low-fat milk**
- 2 **eggs, lightly beaten**
- ¼ **teaspoon ground black pepper**
- ⅛ **teaspoon ground nutmeg**
- **Nonstick cooking spray**
- 10 **sheets frozen phyllo dough (14×9-inch rectangles), thawed**
- ½ **cup crumbled reduced-fat feta cheese (2 ounces)**

1 Preheat oven to 375°F. In a large nonstick skillet heat oil over medium-high heat. Add onion and sweet pepper; cook about 4 minutes or just until vegetables are tender. Add zucchini; cook about 4 minutes more or just until zucchini begins to brown. Add spinach, garlic, and ¼ teaspoon of the salt; cook for 2 minutes more.

2 In a small bowl combine evaporated milk, eggs, the remaining ¼ teaspoon salt, the black pepper, and nutmeg.

3 Coat a 9-inch pie plate with cooking spray. Unfold phyllo dough; remove one sheet of the phyllo dough. (As you work, cover the remaining phyllo dough with plastic wrap to prevent it from drying out.) Place phyllo dough sheet in prepared pie plate; lightly coat with cooking spray, gently pressing into bottom and up sides of pie plate and letting ends of phyllo sheet hang over edges of pie plate. Repeat with the remaining 9 phyllo sheets, placing sheets in a crisscross pattern. Spoon vegetable mixture evenly over phyllo; sprinkle with cheese. Pour egg mixture over all. Fold overlapping ends of phyllo toward center of pie plate. Coat the top of the phyllo with cooking spray; gently press to hold shape.

4 Bake about 40 minutes or until a knife inserted near the center comes out clean. Let stand for 15 minutes on a wire rack. Cut into wedges and serve warm.

NUTRITION FACTS PER SERVING:
252 cal., 9 g total fat (2 g sat. fat), 83 mg chol., 576 mg sodium, 31 g carb., 4 g fiber, 13 g pro.

tip
When working with phyllo, be sure to keep it covered with a moist towel. Exposing the phyllo sheets to air eventually dries them out and causes cracking. The towel shouldn't be too wet or the sheets in the stack will stick together. Don't worry if the phyllo rips or tears when you remove it from the stack. Other sheets will cover up any imperfections.

Vegetable-Polenta Lasagna

PREP 20 minutes CHILL 30 minutes BAKE 40 minutes at 350°F MAKES 8 servings

4 **cups water**

1½ **cups yellow cornmeal**

1¼ **teaspoons salt**

1 **small onion, thinly sliced**

1 **tablespoon olive oil**

4 **cups fresh mushrooms, halved**

¼ **teaspoon ground black pepper**

2 **12-ounce jars roasted red sweet peppers, drained and cut into thin strips**

1¼ **cups marinara pasta sauce**

1 **cup shredded mozzarella cheese (4 ounces)**

Snipped fresh Italian (flat-leaf) parsley (optional)

1 For polenta, in a medium saucepan bring 2½ cups of the water to boiling. Meanwhile, in a small bowl combine cornmeal, the remaining 1½ cups water, and 1 teaspoon of the salt. Slowly add cornmeal mixture to the boiling water, stirring constantly. Cook and stir until mixture returns to boiling. Reduce heat to low. Cook, uncovered, for 10 to 15 minutes or until very thick, stirring frequently. Spread evenly in an ungreased 3-quart rectangular baking dish; cool. Cover and chill about 30 minutes or until firm.

2 Preheat oven to 350°F. In a large nonstick skillet cook onion in hot oil over medium heat for 3 to 4 minutes or until tender. Add mushrooms, the remaining ¼ teaspoon salt, and the black pepper. Cook and stir about 5 minutes or until mushrooms are tender. Remove from heat. Stir in roasted peppers.

3 Spread marinara sauce over chilled polenta. Top with vegetable mixture; sprinkle with cheese.

4 Bake, covered, for 30 minutes. Uncover and bake for 10 to 15 minutes more or until edges are bubbly. If desired, sprinkle with parsley.

NUTRITION FACTS PER SERVING:
188 cal., 7 g total fat (2 g sat. fat), 8 mg chol., 649 mg sodium, 27 g carb., 4 g fiber, 8 g pro.

Baked Eggplant Parmesan

PREP 30 minutes STAND 30 minutes BAKE 24 minutes at 375°F + 8 minutes at 400°F MAKES 4 servings

Nonstick cooking spray

1	1½-pound eggplant
1	teaspoon salt
2	egg whites, lightly beaten
1½	cups whole wheat panko (Japanese-style bread crumbs)
3	tablespoons grated Parmesan cheese
1	teaspoon garlic powder
1	teaspoon dried basil, crushed
1	teaspoon dried oregano, crushed
1	cup tomato-and-basil pasta sauce
¾	cup shredded Italian cheese blend (4 ounces)

1 Preheat oven to 375°F. Line a large baking sheet with parchment paper; coat paper with cooking spray. Set aside. Cut eggplant crosswise into eight ¾-inch-thick slices, discarding small ends. Place slices on a double layer of paper towels. Sprinkle all sides of eggplant with salt. Let stand about 30 minutes or until liquid is visible on the surface. Rinse salt and liquid off eggplant slices; pat dry with paper towels.

2 Place egg whites in a shallow dish. In another shallow dish combine panko, Parmesan cheese, garlic powder, basil, and oregano.

3 Dip eggplant slices in egg whites, then in panko mixture, turning to coat both sides of each slice. Place coated slices on the prepared baking sheet. Sprinkle eggplant slices with any remaining panko mixture. Lightly coat tops of coated eggplant slices with cooking spray.

4 Bake for 12 to 15 minutes or until tops are lightly browned. Carefully turn eggplant slices. Bake for 12 to 15 minutes more or until lightly browned and eggplant is tender.

5 Remove from oven. Increase oven temperature to 400°F. Spoon 2 tablespoons of the pasta sauce onto each eggplant slice. Divide cheese evenly among eggplant slices. Bake for 8 to 10 minutes more or until cheese is lightly browned.

NUTRITION FACTS PER SERVING:
279 cal., 8 g total fat (4 g sat. fat), 18 mg chol., 513 mg sodium, 36 g carb., 9 g fiber, 16 g pro.

Veggie Burgers

PREP 25 minutes COOK 8 minutes MAKES 4 servings

1	19-ounce can cannellini beans (white kidney beans), rinsed and drained
1½	cups soft bread crumbs (from about 2 slices bread)
¼	cup shredded carrot
¼	cup finely chopped onion
1	egg
3	tablespoons olive oil
2	tablespoons snipped fresh parsley
¼	teaspoon salt
¼	teaspoon ground black pepper
4	slices Italian bread, toasted
1	cup packed fresh baby spinach
¼	cup Easy Tomato Sauce

1 In a medium bowl mash beans with a fork or potato masher. Stir in half of the bread crumbs, the carrot, onion, egg, 1 tablespoon of the oil, half of the parsley, the salt, and pepper. Shape bean mixture into four patties (mixture will be soft).

2 In a shallow dish combine the remaining bread crumbs and the remaining parsley. Dip patties in bread crumb mixture, turning to coat.

3 In a large skillet heat the remaining 2 tablespoons oil over medium heat. Add patties. Cook about 8 minutes or until well browned, turning once.

4 Layer bread slices with spinach and burgers. Top with Easy Tomato Sauce.

NUTRITION FACTS PER SERVING:
353 cal., 13 g total fat (2 g sat. fat), 53 mg chol., 873 mg sodium, 48 g carb., 9 g fiber, 15 g pro.

Easy Tomato Sauce

Place one 14.5-ounce can diced tomatoes, undrained, in a blender or food processor. Cover and blend or process to desired consistency. Pour into a bowl and stir in 2 tablespoons snipped fresh basil. Season to taste with salt and ground black pepper. Makes about 1½ cups.

Fresh Taco Salad

START TO FINISH **30 minutes** MAKES **6 servings**

4 cups mixed salad greens

1 15-ounce can black beans*, rinsed and drained

2 ears of corn, husks and silks removed and kernels cut off the cobs

¾ cup matchstick-size pieces peeled jicama

½ cup chopped tomato

1 medium avocado, pitted, peeled, and sliced

1 fresh jalapeño chile pepper, stemmed, seeded, and thinly sliced**

2 cups multigrain tortilla chips with flaxseeds

½ cup refrigerated fresh salsa

½ cup crumbled queso fresco (2 ounces)

1 recipe Cilantro Ranch Dressing

Line a large serving platter with salad greens. In a medium bowl combine beans, corn, jicama, and tomato. Spoon mixture over greens. Arrange avocado and jalapeño pepper slices over bean mixture. Top with chips, salsa, and cheese. Drizzle with Cilantro Ranch Dressing.

NUTRITION FACTS PER SERVING:
214 cal., 9 g total fat (3 g sat. fat), 11 mg chol., 447 mg sodium, 29 g carb., 8 g fiber, 10 g pro.

Cilantro Ranch Dressing

In a small bowl whisk together ⅓ cup light sour cream; ¼ cup buttermilk; 2 tablespoons snipped fresh cilantro; 1 tablespoon snipped fresh chives; 1 tablespoon lime juice; 2 cloves garlic, minced; and 1 teaspoon chili powder. Makes about ½ cup.

Black beans, also called turtle beans, are a tasty way to add fiber to your diet. With rich flavor and a velvety texture, they also deliver a big dose of health-enhancing folate.

Because chile peppers contain volatile oils that can burn your skin and eyes, avoid direct contact with them as much as possible. When working with chile peppers, wear plastic or rubber gloves. If your bare hands do touch the peppers, wash your hands and nails well with soap and warm water.

Crispy Chipotle Bean Burritos

PREP 30 minutes BAKE 20 minutes at 400°F MAKES 6 servings

- 2 teaspoons canola oil
- ½ cup thinly sliced green onions (4)
- 3 cloves garlic, minced
- 1 15-ounce can pinto beans, rinsed and drained
- 1 cup frozen whole kernel corn, thawed
- 1 cup cooked brown rice
- 1 cup chopped, seeded tomatoes (2 medium)
- 3 ounces Cotija or queso fresco cheese, crumbled, or reduced-fat Monterey Jack cheese, shredded (¾ cup)
- 1 to 1½ teaspoons finely chopped canned chipotle chile peppers in adobo sauce*
- 12 sheets frozen phyllo dough (14×9-inch rectangles), thawed
- Butter-flavor nonstick cooking spray
- ⅓ cup light sour cream
- Sliced green onions (optional)

1 Preheat oven to 400°F. In a medium saucepan heat oil over medium heat. Add the ½ cup green onions and the garlic; cook about 3 minutes or just until green onions are tender, stirring occasionally. Remove from heat. Stir in beans, corn, rice, ½ cup of the tomatoes, the cheese, and chipotle peppers. Set aside.

2 Unroll phyllo dough; remove one sheet of the phyllo dough and place on a flat surface. (As you work, cover the remaining phyllo dough with plastic wrap to prevent it from drying out.) Lightly coat the phyllo sheet with cooking spray. Lay another sheet of phyllo dough on top of the first sheet and lightly coat with cooking spray. Repeat with two more sheets to make a stack of four sheets. Repeat with the remaining phyllo sheets to make two more stacks. Cut each phyllo stack in half crosswise to make six stacks total (each 9×7 inches).

3 To assemble burritos, spoon about ⅔ cup of the bean mixture along one long side of each phyllo stack, leaving about 1½ inches of space on each end. Fold short sides up and over filling; roll up phyllo around filling, starting at the long side. Place burritos, seam side down, on a large baking sheet. Coat tops of burritos with cooking spray.

4 Bake about 20 minutes or until tops are golden brown and filling is heated through. Serve with the remaining ½ cup tomatoes and the sour cream. If desired, sprinkle with additional green onions.

NUTRITION FACTS PER SERVING:
323 cal., 11 g total fat (2 g sat. fat), 18 mg chol., 429 mg sodium, 47 g carb., 6 g fiber, 14 g pro.

tip
Because chile peppers contain volatile oils that can burn your skin and eyes, avoid direct contact with them as much as possible. When working with chile peppers, wear plastic or rubber gloves. If your bare hands do touch the peppers, wash your hands and nails well with soap and warm water.

Baked Apples

PREP 15 minutes BAKE 40 minutes at 350°F MAKES 4 servings

4 cooking apples

½ cup raisins, snipped pitted whole dates, or mixed dried fruit bits

2 tablespoons packed brown sugar

½ teaspoon ground cinnamon

¼ teaspoon ground nutmeg

⅓ cup apple juice, apple cider, or water

Vanilla ice cream or half-and-half (optional)

1 Preheat oven to 350°F. Core apples; peel a strip from the top of each apple. Place apples in a 2-quart casserole. In a small bowl combine raisins, brown sugar, cinnamon, and nutmeg; spoon into centers of apples. Pour apple juice around apples in casserole.

2 Bake for 40 to 45 minutes or until the apples are tender, basting occasionally with liquid from casserole. Serve warm. If desired, serve with ice cream.

NUTRITION FACTS PER SERVING:
164 cal., 1 g total fat (0 g sat. fat), 0 mg chol., 5 mg sodium, 42 g carb., 5 g fiber, 1 g pro.

tip
When baking whole apples, choose varieties that will hold their shape and not turn to mush in the oven. Rome Beauty, Jonathan, McIntosh, and Granny Smith are good options.

Comfort Food Classics Made Healthy

Pear-Cranberry Deep-Dish Pie

Photo on page 138

PREP **40 minutes**   BAKE **55 minutes at 375°F**   COOL **30 minutes**   MAKES **10 servings**

⅓ **cup granulated sugar**

2 **tablespoons all-purpose flour**

¼ **teaspoon ground nutmeg**

¼ **teaspoon ground ginger**

6 **ripe, yet still firm, pears, cored and sliced (2 to 2½ pounds total)**

1 **cup fresh or thawed frozen cranberries**

1 **recipe Pastry**

1 **tablespoon fat-free milk**

Demerara sugar or turbinado (raw) sugar (optional)

1 Preheat oven to 375°F. In a very large bowl combine the granulated sugar, flour, nutmeg, and ginger. Add pear slices and cranberries; toss gently to coat. Transfer to an ungreased 2-quart round baking dish or casserole.

2 Prepare Pastry. On a lightly floured surface, use your hands to slightly flatten pastry. Roll pastry from center to edges into a circle about 1 inch wider than the top of the baking dish or casserole. Using cookie cutters, cut a few small shapes from center of the pastry. Set shapes aside. Wrap pastry circle around the rolling pin. Unroll on top of the fruit mixture. Trim pastry to ½ inch beyond edge of baking dish or casserole. Fold under extra pastry even with the dish's edge. Crimp edge as desired. Brush top of pastry and dough cutouts with milk. Place dough cutouts on the pastry, leaving openings for air to vent.

3 Place baking dish or casserole on a foil-lined baking sheet. If desired, sprinkle with demerara sugar. Bake for 55 to 60 minutes or until pear mixture is bubbly. Cool pie about 30 minutes on a wire rack. Serve warm. (Or, cool completely before serving.)

NUTRITION FACTS PER SERVING:
169 cal., 4 g total fat (1 g sat. fat), 0 mg chol., 96 mg sodium, 34 g carb., 4 g fiber, 2 g pro.

Pastry

In a medium bowl stir together ¾ cup cake flour, ¼ cup whole wheat flour, and ¼ teaspoon salt. Using a pastry blender, cut in ¼ cup cold butter until pieces are peasize. Sprinkle 1 tablespoon cold water over part of the flour mixture; gently toss with a fork. Push moistened dough to the side of the bowl. Repeat moistening flour mixture, using 1 tablespoon cold water at a time, until all of the flour mixture is moistened (3 to 4 tablespoons cold water total). Shape dough into a ball.

Strawberry Cream Pie

PREP **25 minutes** CHILL **2 hours + 2 to 24 hours** MAKES **10 servings**

$2\frac{1}{3}$ cups fresh **strawberries,** hulled

$\frac{1}{4}$ cup sugar

1 envelope unflavored gelatin

2 tablespoons frozen limeade concentrate or frozen lemonade concentrate, thawed

3 egg whites

1 tablespoon tequila or orange juice

1 3-ounce package ladyfingers, split

2 tablespoons orange juice

$\frac{1}{2}$ of an 8-ounce container frozen light whipped dessert topping, thawed

Sliced strawberries (optional)

Fresh mint (optional)

1 Place the $2\frac{1}{2}$ cups strawberries in a blender or food processor. Cover and blend or process until nearly smooth. (You should have about $1\frac{1}{2}$ cups.)

2 In a medium saucepan stir together sugar and gelatin. Stir in blended strawberries and the limeade concentrate. Cook and stir over medium heat until mixture bubbles and gelatin is dissolved. In a medium bowl lightly beat egg whites with a fork. Gradually stir about half of the gelatin mixture into the egg whites. Return egg white mixture to saucepan. Cook and stir over low heat about 3 minutes or until mixture is slightly thickened. (Do not boil.) Pour into a medium bowl; stir in tequila. Chill about 2 hours or until mixture mounds when spooned, stirring occasionally.

3 Cut half of the split ladyfingers in half crosswise; stand on end around the outside edge of a 9-inch tart pan with a removable bottom or a 9-inch springform pan. Arrange the remaining split ladyfingers in the bottom of the pan. Drizzle the orange juice over the ladyfingers.

4 Fold whipped topping into chilled strawberry mixture. Spoon into prepared pan. Cover and chill for 2 to 24 hours. If desired, garnish with additional sliced strawberries and fresh mint.

NUTRITION FACTS PER SERVING:
113 cal., 2 g total fat (2 g sat. fat), 31 mg chol., 35 mg sodium, 18 g carb., 1 g fiber, 5 g pro.

tip
Make this pie the day before a big event for a dessert that's ready when your guests arrive.

Comfort Food Classics Made Healthy

Upside-Down Pineapple-Ginger Carrot Cake

PREP 25 minutes BAKE 35 minutes at 350°F COOL 35 minutes MAKES 9 servings

Nonstick cooking spray

2 tablespoons butter, melted

3 tablespoons packed brown sugar

4 thin slices fresh pineapple

1 tablespoon finely chopped crystallized ginger

1 cup white whole wheat flour

¾ cup granulated sugar

1½ teaspoons apple pie spice

½ teaspoon baking powder

½ teaspoon baking soda

⅛ teaspoon salt

1 cup finely shredded carrots (2 medium)

⅓ cup canola oil

¼ cup fat-free milk

3 egg whites

Powdered sugar (optional)

1 Preheat oven to 350°F. Lightly coat an 8×8×2-inch baking pan with cooking spray. Drizzle bottom of pan with the melted butter; sprinkle with brown sugar. Arrange pineapple slices in pan; sprinkle with crystallized ginger.

2 In a large bowl stir together flour, granulated sugar, apple pie spice, baking powder, baking soda, and salt. Add carrots, oil, and milk, stirring until moistened. In a medium mixing bowl beat egg whites with an electric mixer on medium speed until stiff peaks form (tips stand straight). Fold beaten egg whites into carrot mixture. Pour batter into pan over pineapple slices, spreading evenly.

3 Bake for 35 to 40 minutes or until a wooden toothpick inserted near the center comes out clean. Cool in pan on a wire rack for 5 minutes. Loosen sides of cake; invert onto a serving platter. Cool for 30 minutes. If desired, sprinkle lightly with powdered sugar. Serve warm.

NUTRITION FACTS PER SERVING:
192 cal., 8 g total fat (2 g sat. fat), 5 mg chol., 130 mg sodium, 29 g carb., 1 g fiber, 3 g pro.

Baked Pumpkin Pudding

PREP 20 minutes BAKE 40 minutes at 350°F COOL 15 minutes MAKES 4 servings

Nonstick cooking spray

1 cup canned pumpkin

½ cup milk

⅓ cup packed brown sugar

2 egg whites, lightly beaten

½ teaspoon pumpkin pie spice

2 tablespoons quick-cooking rolled oats

1 tablespoon toasted pumpkin seeds (pepitas) or coarsely chopped pecans or pistachios

2 teaspoons packed brown sugar

1 teaspoon butter, softened

Toasted pumpkin seeds (pepitas) (optional)

1 Preheat oven to 350°F. Lightly coat four 6-ounce ramekins or custard cups with cooking spray. Place ramekins in a 13×9×2-inch baking pan; set aside. In a medium bowl stir together pumpkin, milk, the ⅓ cup brown sugar, the egg whites, and pumpkin pie spice. Divide pumpkin mixture evenly among ramekins.

2 In a small bowl combine oats, the 1 tablespoon pumpkin seeds, the 2 teaspoons brown sugar, and the butter, stirring with a fork until crumbly. Sprinkle oat mixture evenly over pumpkin mixture in ramekins.

3 Place baking dish on oven rack. Pour enough boiling water into the baking dish around ramekins to a depth of 1 inch. Bake for 40 to 45 minutes or until a knife inserted near the center of each pudding comes out clean. Carefully remove ramekins from water. Cool on a wire rack for 15 minutes before serving. (Or, after cooling for up to 1 hour, cover and chill for up to 24 hours before serving.) If desired, garnish with additional pumpkin seeds.

NUTRITION FACTS PER SERVING:
148 cal., 2 g total fat (10 g sat. fat), 3 mg chol., 59 mg sodium, 29 g carb., 2 g fiber, 4 g pro.

Cinnamon and Brown Sugar Custards

PREP 20 minutes COOK 20 minutes BAKE 30 minutes at 350°F MAKES 4 servings

108

1½ cups diced carrots (3 medium)
2 eggs, lightly beaten
⅓ to ½ cup packed brown sugar
¼ cup fat-free milk
½ teaspoon ground cinnamon
  Whipped cream (optional)

1 Preheat oven to 350°F. Lightly grease four 6- to 8-ounce ramekins or custard cups. Place ramekins in a 13×9×2-inch baking pan; set aside.

2 Meanwhile, place carrots in a medium saucepan; cover with 2 inches of water. Bring to boiling; reduce heat. Simmer, covered, for 20 to 25 minutes or until very tender. Drain; rinse with cold water and drain again.

3 Place carrots in a food processor. Cover and process about 20 seconds or until smooth. Add eggs, brown sugar, milk, and cinnamon to carrots in food processor; cover and process until smooth.

4 Divide carrot mixture evenly among prepared ramekins. Place baking pan on oven rack. Pour enough hot water into the baking pan around ramekins to reach halfway up sides of ramekins. Bake for 30 to 35 minutes or until a knife inserted near the center comes out clean. Cool on a wire rack. If desired, serve with whipped cream. Chill within 2 hours.

NUTRITION FACTS PER SERVING:
130 cal., 3 g total fat (1 g sat. fat), 93 mg chol., 79 mg sodium, 24 g carb., 1 g fiber, 4 g pro.

Brownie Raspberry Tart

PREP **25 minutes** BAKE **10 minutes at 350°F** MAKES **10 servings**

Nonstick cooking spray

½ cup granulated sugar or sugar substitute blend equivalent to ½ cup granulated sugar*

3 tablespoons canola oil

2 egg whites

⅔ cup all-purpose flour

½ cup unsweetened cocoa powder

¼ teaspoon salt

¼ cup water

½ cup tub-style light cream cheese

3 tablespoons powdered sugar

1 tablespoon light chocolate-flavor syrup

¼ cup sliced almonds, toasted

1 to 1½ cups fresh red raspberries

1 For brownie crust, preheat oven to 350°F. Coat a 12-inch pizza pan with cooking spray; set aside. In a medium mixing bowl combine the granulated sugar and the oil. Beat with an electric mixer on medium speed until well mixed. Add egg whites, one at a time, beating well after each addition. In a small bowl stir together flour, cocoa powder, and salt. Add flour mixture and the water to the beaten mixture. Beat just until combined. Spread in the prepared pan. Bake for 10 minutes. Cool completely in pan on a wire rack.

2 Just before serving, stir together cream cheese, the powdered sugar, and chocolate-flavor syrup until well mixed. Spread evenly over the brownie crust. Sprinkle almonds over. Top with raspberries.

NUTRITION FACTS PER SERVING:
175 cal., 8 g total fat (2 g sat. fat), 6 mg chol., 132 mg sodium, 25 g carb., 3 g fiber, 4 g pro.

109

***tip**
You can substitute Splenda Sugar Blend for Baking. Follow package directions to use the product amount equivalent to ½ cup granulated sugar.

Marbled Angel Food Cake

PREP 20 minutes BAKE per package directions MAKES 12 servings

- 1   16-ounce package angel food cake mix
- ¼   cup unsweetened cocoa powder
- 2   cups powdered sugar
- 2   tablespoons unsweetened cocoa powder
- 3   to 4 tablespoons milk

1 Prepare cake mix according to package directions. Transfer 4 cups of the batter to a large bowl; sift the ¼ cup cocoa powder over batter and fold in until combined. Alternately pour white and chocolate batters into an ungreased 10-inch tube pan; cut through batter with a knife or spatula to marble. Bake and cool as directed on package.

2 In a medium bowl stir together powdered sugar and the 2 tablespoons cocoa powder. Stir in enough milk to make drizzling consistency. Drizzle over top and down sides of cake.

NUTRITION FACTS PER SERVING:
219 cal., 1 g total fat (0 g sat. fat), 0 mg chol., 256 mg sodium, 51 g carb., 0 g fiber, 4 g pro.

Casseroles

4

Nothing says comfort quite like one of these bubbly one-dish meals.

Cheeseburger and Fries Casserole   *Photo on page 141*

PREP 20 minutes   BAKE 40 minutes at 350°F   MAKES 6 servings

1½   pounds lean ground beef
¾   cup chopped green sweet pepper (1 medium)
½   cup chopped onion (1 medium)
2   cloves garlic, minced
1   14.5-ounce can diced tomatoes, undrained
1   6-ounce can tomato paste
1   10.75-ounce can condensed cheddar cheese soup
½   cup light sour cream
4   cups frozen French-fried shoestring potatoes
1   teaspoon seasoned salt (optional)
    Assorted toppers, such as ketchup, pickle slices, yellow mustard, and/or chopped tomato (optional)*

1 Preheat oven to 350°F. In a 12-inch skillet cook ground beef, sweet pepper, onion, and garlic over medium-high heat until meat is brown and vegetables are tender, using a wooden spoon to break up meat as it cooks. Drain off fat. Stir in tomatoes and tomato paste. Bring to boiling; reduce heat. Simmer, uncovered, for 5 minutes.

2 Transfer mixture to an ungreased 2-quart rectangular baking dish. In a medium bowl stir together soup and sour cream; spread over meat mixture. Sprinkle with shoestring potatoes and, if desired, seasoned salt.

3 Bake, uncovered, for 40 to 45 minutes or until heated through and potatoes are golden. If desired, serve with assorted toppers.

NUTRITION FACTS PER SERVING:
493 cal., 26 g total fat (10 g sat. fat), 87 mg chol., 1319 mg sodium, 46 g carb., 5 g fiber, 28 g pro.

*tip
Any topping that you like on a cheeseburger will taste good on this casserole. Try chopped onion, diced avocado, shredded cheese, bacon, or jalapeño peppers.

Double-Crust Pizza Casserole

PREP 25 minutes   BAKE 25 minutes at 425°F   STAND 5 minutes   MAKES 12 servings

3   cups all-purpose flour

3   cups packaged instant mashed potato flakes

2   cups milk

⅓   cup olive oil

1   pound lean ground beef

12   ounces bulk Italian sausage

1   cup coarsely chopped onion (1 large)

1   8-ounce can tomato sauce

1   6-ounce can tomato paste with garlic, basil, and oregano

1   2.25-ounce can sliced, pitted ripe olives, drained (optional)

½   of a 1.3-ounce envelope (about 2 tablespoons) sloppy joe seasoning mix

1   cup shredded mozzarella cheese (4 ounces)

1   tablespoon yellow cornmeal

1 Preheat oven to 425°F. In a large bowl combine flour, potato flakes, milk, and oil; set aside. (Dough will stiffen slightly as it stands.)

2 For filling, in a large skillet cook ground beef, sausage, and onion over medium-high heat until meat is brown and onion is tender, using a wooden spoon to break up meat as it cooks. Drain off fat. Stir in tomato sauce, tomato paste, olives (if desired), and seasoning mix.

3 Using floured fingers, press half of the dough onto the bottom and about 1½ inches up the sides of an ungreased 3-quart rectangular baking dish. Spread filling over crust; sprinkle with cheese.

4 Place the remaining dough on a lightly floured sheet of waxed paper. Sprinkle dough lightly with flour; top with another sheet of waxed paper. Roll dough into a 15×11-inch rectangle; remove top paper. Invert dough onto filling; remove paper. Trim edges as necessary. Fold under edges of top crust and seal to bottom crust. Sprinkle with cornmeal.

5 Bake, uncovered, for 25 to 30 minutes or until filling is heated through and crust is golden. Let stand for 5 minutes before serving.

NUTRITION FACTS PER SERVING: *458 cal., 21 g total fat (8 g sat. fat), 52 mg chol., 738 mg sodium, 43 g carb., 1 g fiber, 22 g pro.*

Beef Stroganoff Casserole

PREP 35 minutes   BAKE 30 minutes at 350°F   MAKES 6 servings

12 ounces dried campanelle or penne pasta

1 17-ounce package refrigerated cooked beef roast au jus

2 large fresh portobello mushrooms

2 tablespoons butter

1 medium sweet onion, cut into thin wedges

2 cloves garlic, minced

3 tablespoons all-purpose flour

2 tablespoons tomato paste

1 14.5-ounce can beef broth

1 tablespoon Worcestershire sauce

1 teaspoon smoked paprika or Spanish paprika

¼ teaspoon salt

¼ teaspoon ground black pepper

Snipped fresh parsley (optional)

½ cup sour cream

1 tablespoon prepared horseradish

1 teaspoon snipped fresh dill or ¼ teaspoon dried dill

1 Preheat oven to 350°F. Cook pasta according to package directions; drain. Meanwhile, place roast on a cutting board; reserve juices. Using two forks, pull meat apart into bite-size pieces; set aside.

2 Remove and discard stems and gills from mushrooms; coarsely chop mushroom caps (you should have about 4 cups). In a 12-inch skillet heat butter over medium heat until melted. Add mushrooms, onion, and garlic; cook for 4 to 5 minutes or until onion is tender, stirring occasionally. Stir in flour and tomato paste. Add broth, Worcestershire sauce, paprika, salt, pepper, and the reserved meat juices. Cook and stir until thickened and bubbly. Remove from heat. Stir in pasta and meat.

3 Transfer mixture to an ungreased 3-quart casserole or rectangular baking dish. Bake, covered, about 30 minutes or until heated through. If desired, sprinkle with parsley.

4 Meanwhile, in a small bowl combine sour cream, horseradish, and dill. Spoon sour cream mixture over each serving.

NUTRITION FACTS PER SERVING:
450 cal., 14 g total fat (7 g sat. fat), 61 mg chol., 770 mg sodium, 57 g carb., 4 g fiber, 26 g pro.

Easy Shepherd's Pie

PREP 30 minutes BAKE 25 minutes at 425°F MAKES 8 servings

2 pounds ground beef
1¼ cups all-purpose flour
1 envelope (half of a 2-ounce package) onion soup mix
1 10.75-ounce can condensed cream of mushroom soup
1 8-ounce carton sour cream
2¼ cups water
1 tablespoon ketchup
¼ cup butter
½ teaspoon salt
2 cups packaged instant mashed potato flakes
½ cup milk
2 eggs, lightly beaten
2 teaspoons baking powder

1 Preheat oven to 425°F. In an extra-large skillet cook ground beef over medium-high heat until brown, using a wooden spoon to break up meat as it cooks. Drain off fat. Stir in ¼ cup of the flour and the onion soup mix. Stir in mushroom soup, sour cream, ¾ cup of the water, and the ketchup. Cook until heated through, stirring occasionally.

2 Meanwhile, in a medium saucepan combine the remaining 1½ cups water, the butter, and salt. Bring to boiling; remove from heat. Add potato flakes and milk, stirring until combined. Stir in eggs, the remaining 1 cup flour, and the baking powder.

3 Transfer meat mixture to an ungreased 3-quart rectangular baking dish. Drop potato mixture into mounds on top of meat mixture.

4 Bake, uncovered, about 25 minutes or until tops of potatoes are golden.

NUTRITION FACTS PER SERVING:
465 cal., 24 g total fat (11 g sat. fat), 143 mg chol., 911 mg sodium, 32 g carb., 1 g fiber, 24 g pro.

115

Classic Lasagna

PREP 30 minutes COOK 15 minutes BAKE 30 minutes at 375°F STAND 10 minutes MAKES 12 servings

9	dried lasagna noodles
1	pound bulk Italian or pork sausage, or ground beef
1	cup chopped onion (1 large)
2	cloves garlic, minced
1	14.5-ounce can diced tomatoes, undrained
1	8-ounce can tomato sauce
1	tablespoon dried Italian seasoning, crushed
1	teaspoon fennel seeds, crushed (optional)
¼	teaspoon ground black pepper
1	egg, lightly beaten
1	15-ounce carton ricotta cheese or 2 cups cream-style cottage cheese, drained
¼	cup grated Parmesan cheese
2	cups shredded mozzarella cheese (8 ounces)
	Grated Parmesan cheese (optional)

1 Preheat oven to 375°F. Cook lasagna noodles according to package directions; drain. Rinse with cold water; drain again. Place lasagna noodles in a single layer on a sheet of foil; set aside.

2 For sauce, in a large skillet cook sausage, onion, and garlic over medium-high heat until meat is brown, using a wooden spoon to break up meat as it cooks. Drain off fat. Stir in tomatoes, tomato sauce, Italian seasoning, fennel seeds (if desired), and pepper. Bring to boiling; reduce heat. Simmer, covered, for 15 minutes, stirring occasionally.

3 For filling, in a medium bowl combine egg, ricotta cheese, and ¼ cup Parmesan cheese; set aside.

4 Spread about ¼ cup of the sauce in the bottom of an ungreased 3-quart rectangular baking dish. Arrange 3 of the cooked noodles over sauce in dish. Spread with one-third of the filling. Top with one-third of the remaining sauce and one-third of the mozzarella cheese. Repeat layers two more times, starting with noodles and ending with mozzarella cheese (make sure the top layer of noodles is completely covered with sauce). If desired, sprinkle with additional Parmesan cheese.

5 Bake, uncovered, for 30 to 35 minutes or until heated through. Let stand for 10 minutes before serving.

NUTRITION FACTS PER SERVING: *335 cal., 21 g total fat (10 g sat. fat), 78 mg chol., 623 mg sodium, 19 g carb., 2 g fiber, 18 g pro.*

Make-Ahead Directions: Prepare as directed through Step 4. Cover with plastic wrap and chill for 2 to 24 hours. To serve, preheat oven to 375°F. Remove plastic wrap; cover with foil. Bake for 40 minutes. Bake, uncovered, about 20 minutes more or until heated through. Let stand for 10 minutes before serving.

Baked Beef Ravioli

PREP 20 minutes BAKE 20 minutes at 375°F MAKES 8 servings

2 9-ounce packages refrigerated cheese-filled ravioli

1½ pounds ground beef

1 cup chopped onion (1 large)

6 cloves garlic, minced

1 14.5-ounce can diced tomatoes, undrained

1 10.75-ounce can condensed tomato soup

1 teaspoon dried basil, crushed

1 teaspoon dried oregano, crushed

1½ cups shredded mozzarella cheese (6 ounces)

½ cup finely shredded Parmesan cheese (2 ounces)

1 Preheat oven to 375°F. Cook ravioli according to package directions; drain and set aside.

2 Meanwhile, in a large skillet cook ground beef, onion, and garlic over medium-high heat until meat is brown and onion is tender, using a wooden spoon to break up meat as it cooks. Drain off fat. Stir in tomatoes, soup, basil, and oregano. Gently stir in cooked ravioli.

3 Transfer mixture to an ungreased 3-quart shallow baking dish. Sprinkle with mozzarella cheese and Parmesan cheese. Bake, uncovered, about 20 minutes or until heated through.

NUTRITION FACTS PER SERVING:
503 cal., 20 g total fat (9 g sat. fat), 113 mg chol., 854 mg sodium, 40 g carb., 3 g fiber, 40 g pro.

Mexican Biscuit Casserole

PREP 30 minutes BAKE 20 minutes at 350°F STAND 5 minutes MAKES 6 servings

- 1½ pounds lean ground beef
- 1 15-ounce can red kidney beans, undrained
- 1 11-ounce can whole kernel corn with sweet peppers, drained
- ¾ cup water
- 1 1.25-ounce envelope taco seasoning mix
- 2 cups packaged biscuit mix
- ⅔ cup milk
- 1 cup shredded cheddar cheese (4 ounces)

1 Preheat oven to 350°F. In a large skillet cook ground beef over medium-high heat until brown, using a wooden spoon to break up meat as it cooks. Drain off fat. Stir in beans, corn, water, and taco seasoning mix. Bring to boiling.

2 Meanwhile, in a medium bowl combine biscuit mix and milk; stir just until moistened.

3 Transfer meat mixture to an ungreased 2-quart rectangular baking dish. Sprinkle with cheese. Drop biscuit mixture into mounds on top of hot meat mixture.

4 Bake, uncovered, about 20 minutes or until a wooden toothpick inserted in the centers of biscuits comes out clean. Let stand for 5 minutes before serving.

NUTRITION FACTS PER SERVING:
554 cal., 24 g total fat (10 g sat. fat), 93 mg chol., 1736 mg sodium, 52 g carb., 6 g fiber, 34 g pro.

Bean-and-Beef Tortilla Casserole

PREP 25 minutes   BAKE 35 minutes at 350°F   MAKES 6 servings

8   ounces ground beef

½   cup chopped onion
    (1 medium)

1   teaspoon chili powder

½   teaspoon ground cumin

1   15-ounce can pinto beans,
    rinsed and drained

1   4-ounce can diced green chile
    peppers, undrained

1   8-ounce carton sour cream
    or light sour cream

2   tablespoons all-purpose flour

¼   teaspoon garlic powder

8   6-inch corn tortillas

1   10-ounce can enchilada sauce

1   cup shredded cheddar cheese
    (4 ounces)

1 Preheat oven to 350°F. Lightly grease a 2-quart rectangular baking dish; set aside. In a large skillet cook ground beef and onion over medium-high heat until meat is brown and onion is tender, using a wooden spoon to break up meat as it cooks. Drain off fat. Stir in chili powder and cumin. Stir in beans and green chile peppers; set aside.

2 In a small bowl stir together sour cream, flour, and garlic powder.

3 Arrange half of the tortillas to cover the bottom of the prepared baking dish, cutting to fit if necessary. Top with half of the meat mixture, half of the sour cream mixture, and half of the enchilada sauce. Repeat layers.

4 Bake, covered, about 30 minutes or until heated through. Sprinkle with cheese. Bake, uncovered, about 5 minutes more or until cheese is melted.

NUTRITION FACTS PER SERVING:
408 cal., 22 g total fat (11 g sat. fat), 65 mg chol., 668 mg sodium, 34 g carb., 6 g fiber, 19 g pro.

119

Make-Ahead Directions: Prepare as directed through Step 3. Cover with plastic wrap and chill for 2 to 24 hours. To serve, preheat oven to 350°F. Remove plastic wrap; cover with foil. Bake about 35 minutes or until heated through. Sprinkle with cheese. Bake, uncovered, about 5 minutes more or until cheese is melted.

Cincinnati-Style Chili Casserole

PREP 25 minutes BAKE 1 hour at 350°F MAKES 16 servings

- 2 **pounds lean ground beef**
- 2 **cups chopped onions (2 large)**
- 1 **26-ounce jar tomato and garlic pasta sauce**
- 1 **15-ounce can red kidney beans, rinsed and drained**
- ½ **cup water**
- 2 **tablespoons chili powder**
- 2 **tablespoons semisweet chocolate pieces**
- 1 **tablespoon cider vinegar**
- 1 **teaspoon ground cinnamon**
- ¼ **teaspoon cayenne pepper**
- ¼ **teaspoon ground allspice**
- 1 **pound dried ziti or gemelli pasta**
- **Shredded cheddar cheese (optional)**
- **Chopped onion (optional)**

1 Preheat oven to 350°F. In an oven-going 4- to 5-quart Dutch oven cook ground beef and 2 cups onions over medium-high heat until meat is brown and onions are tender, using a wooden spoon to break up meat as it cooks. Drain off fat.

2 Stir in pasta sauce, beans, water, chili powder, chocolate, vinegar, cinnamon, cayenne pepper, and allspice. Transfer Dutch oven to oven. Bake, covered, for 1 hour, stirring once halfway through baking.

3 To serve, cook pasta according to package directions; drain. Serve chili over hot cooked pasta. If desired, sprinkle with cheese and onion.

NUTRITION FACTS PER SERVING:
257 cal., 7 g total fat (2 g sat. fat), 36 mg chol., 277 mg sodium, 33 g carb., 4 g fiber, 17 g pro.

Moussaka

PREP 50 minutes   BAKE 35 minutes at 325°F   STAND 10 minutes   MAKES 4 servings

2 tablespoons vegetable oil

1 eggplant (1 pound), peeled and cut into ½-inch slices

1 pound ground lamb or ground beef

½ cup chopped onion (1 medium)

1 clove garlic, minced

1 8-ounce can tomato sauce

¼ cup dry red wine or beef broth

½ teaspoon salt

¼ teaspoon dried oregano, crushed

⅛ teaspoon ground cinnamon

1 egg, lightly beaten

2 tablespoons butter

2 tablespoons all-purpose flour
   Pinch ground black pepper

1 cup milk

1 egg

¼ cup shredded Parmesan cheese (1 ounce)

1 In a large skillet heat oil over medium-high heat. Add half of the eggplant slices; cook about 4 minutes or until brown, turning once. Using a slotted spatula, remove from skillet. Repeat with the remaining eggplant slices, adding more oil if necessary.

2 In the same skillet cook ground lamb, onion, and garlic over medium-high heat until meat is brown, using a wooden spoon to break up meat as it cooks. Drain off fat. Stir in tomato sauce, wine, ¼ teaspoon of the salt, the oregano, and cinnamon. Bring to boiling; reduce heat. Simmer, uncovered, about 10 minutes or until most of the liquid is absorbed. Cool mixture slightly. Gradually stir about ½ cup of the hot meat mixture into the 1 beaten egg. Return egg mixture to skillet.

3 Meanwhile, in a medium saucepan heat butter over medium heat until melted. Stir in flour, pepper, and the remaining ¼ teaspoon salt. Gradually stir in milk. Cook and stir until thickened and bubbly. In a medium bowl lightly beat 1 egg with a fork. Gradually stir hot milk mixture into beaten egg.

4 Preheat oven to 325°F. Arrange half of the eggplant slices in an ungreased 2-quart rectangular baking dish. Spread meat mixture over eggplant in dish; top with the remaining eggplant slices. Pour the hot milk mixture over layers in dish. Sprinkle with cheese.

5 Bake, uncovered, for 35 to 40 minutes or until edges are bubbly. Let stand for 10 minutes before serving.

NUTRITION FACTS PER SERVING:
499 cal., 34 g total fat (13 g sat. fat), 207 mg chol., 801 mg sodium, 18 g carb., 5 g fiber, 29 g pro.

Pork Chop Casserole

PREP 25 minutes   BAKE 30 minutes at 350°F   MAKES 8 servings

- 6 ounces dried medium egg noodles
- 8 boneless pork loin chops, cut about ¾ inch thick
- ⅓ cup all-purpose flour
- ¼ teaspoon salt
- ¼ teaspoon ground black pepper
- 2 tablespoons vegetable oil
- 1 10.75-ounce can condensed cream of mushroom soup
- ⅔ cup chicken broth
- ½ cup sour cream
- ½ teaspoon ground ginger
- ½ teaspoon dried rosemary, crushed
- 1 2.8-ounce can French-fried onions

1 Preheat oven to 350°F. Cook noodles according to package directions; drain and set aside.

2 Meanwhile, trim fat from chops. In a shallow dish stir together flour, salt, and pepper. Dip chops into flour mixture, shaking off excess.

3 In a large skillet heat oil over medium-high heat. Add chops, half at a time, and cook until brown on both sides. Remove from heat.

4 For sauce, in a medium bowl stir together soup, broth, sour cream, ginger, and rosemary. Gently stir in cooked noodles and half of the French-fried onions. Transfer mixture to an ungreased 3-quart rectangular baking dish. Top with chops.

5 Bake, covered, for 25 minutes. Sprinkle with the remaining French-fried onions. Bake, uncovered, for 5 to 10 minutes more or until chops are tender and juices run clear (160°F).

NUTRITION FACTS PER SERVING:
411 cal., 19 g total fat (5 g sat. fat), 95 mg chol., 536 mg sodium, 31 g carb., 1 g fiber, 28 g pro.

One-Step Ham Casserole

Photo on page 141

PREP 15 minutes BAKE 50 minutes at 375°F STAND 10 minutes MAKES 4 servings

1½ cups milk

1 10.75-ounce can condensed cream of celery soup

2 cups diced cooked ham (about 10 ounces)

1 cup dried elbow macaroni

1 4-ounce can (drained weight) sliced mushrooms, drained

2 tablespoons diced pimiento

1 tablespoon dried minced onion or ½ cup chopped onion (1 medium)

½ cup shredded American cheese (2 ounces)

1 Preheat oven to 375°F. In an ungreased 2-quart casserole gradually stir milk into soup. Stir in ham, macaroni, mushrooms, pimiento, and onion.

2 Bake, covered, about 40 minutes or until macaroni is tender. Sprinkle with cheese. Bake, uncovered, about 10 minutes more or until cheese is melted. Let stand for 10 minutes before serving.

NUTRITION FACTS PER SERVING:
341 cal., 12 g total fat (6 g sat. fat), 61 mg chol., 2042 mg sodium, 33 g carb., 2 g fiber, 26 g pro.

Baked Risotto with Sausage and Artichokes

PREP 30 minutes BAKE 1 hour 10 minutes at 350°F STAND 5 minutes MAKES 6 servings

- 1 pound bulk Italian sausage
- 1 cup chopped fennel (1 medium bulb)
- ½ cup chopped onion (1 medium)
- 2 cloves garlic, minced
- ¾ cup uncooked Arborio or long grain white rice
- 2 14-ounce cans quartered artichoke hearts, drained
- 1 cup shredded carrots (2 medium)
- 2 teaspoons snipped fresh thyme
- ½ teaspoon ground black pepper
- 2 cups chicken broth
- ⅓ cup dry white wine or chicken broth
- ½ cup panko (Japanese-style bread crumbs)
- ¼ cup finely shredded Asiago or Parmesan cheese (1 ounce)
- ½ teaspoon finely shredded lemon peel
- 1 tablespoon butter, melted

1 Preheat oven to 350°F. In an extra-large skillet cook sausage, fennel, onion, and garlic over medium-high heat until sausage is brown and vegetables are tender, using a wooden spoon to break up meat as it cooks. Drain off fat. Add rice; cook and stir for 1 minute.

2 Stir in artichoke hearts, carrots, thyme, and pepper. Stir in broth and wine. Bring just to boiling.

3 Transfer mixture to an ungreased 2½-quart casserole. Bake, covered, about 1 hour or until rice is tender, stirring once halfway through baking.

4 Meanwhile, in a small bowl combine panko, cheese, and lemon peel; stir in melted butter. Sprinkle panko mixture over sausage mixture. Bake, uncovered, about 10 minutes more or until heated through and crumbs are light brown. Let stand for 5 minutes before serving.

NUTRITION FACTS PER SERVING:
473 cal., 28 g total fat (11 g sat. fat), 68 mg chol., 1429 mg sodium, 36 g carb., 7 g fiber, 18 g pro.

Corn Bread–Topped Sausage Bake

PREP 25 minutes BAKE 20 minutes at 425°F MAKES 6 servings

- 1 8.5-ounce package corn muffin mix
- 2 tablespoons vegetable oil
- ½ cup chopped carrot (1 medium)
- ¼ cup chopped onion
- ¼ cup chopped green sweet pepper
- ¼ cup chopped celery
- 1 11.5-ounce can condensed bean with bacon soup
- ¾ cup milk
- 2 teaspoons yellow mustard
- 1 pound cooked smoked Polish sausage, sliced

   Shredded cheddar cheese (optional)

1 Preheat oven to 425°F. For corn bread batter, prepare muffin mix according to package directions (do not bake); set aside.

2 In a medium saucepan heat oil over medium heat. Add carrot, onion, sweet pepper, and celery; cook until tender, stirring occasionally. Stir in soup, milk, and mustard; stir in sausage. Cook and stir until bubbly. Transfer mixture to an ungreased 2-quart rectangular baking dish. Pour corn bread batter over hot sausage mixture, spreading evenly.

3 Bake, uncovered, for 20 to 25 minutes or until a wooden toothpick inserted in the corn bread topper comes out clean. If desired, sprinkle each serving with cheese.

NUTRITION FACTS PER SERVING:
562 cal., 34 g total fat (11 g sat. fat), 94 mg chol., 1566 mg sodium, 43 g carb., 6 g fiber, 20 g pro.

tip
Any cooked sausage, such as turkey kielbasa, smoked bratwurst, or andouille, will bake up beautifully in this casserole.

Saucy Bow-Tie Pasta Casserole

PREP 35 minutes BAKE 30 minutes at 350°F + 5 minutes at 400°F STAND 5 minutes MAKES 8 servings

- 8 ounces dried bow-tie, penne, or ziti pasta
- 1 tablespoon butter
- 2 red onions, cut into thin wedges, or 5 medium leeks, sliced
- 2 cloves garlic, minced
- 1 24 to 26-ounce jar any flavor tomato pasta sauce
- 1 10-ounce package frozen chopped spinach, thawed and well drained
- 1½ cups cubed cooked ham
- 1 cup seeded and chopped tomatoes (2 medium)
- 1 8-ounce can tomato sauce
- ⅓ cup grated Parmesan cheese
- 2 cups shredded mozzarella or Muenster cheese (8 ounces)

  Grated Parmesan cheese (optional)

  Fresh Italian (flat-leaf) parsley sprigs (optional)

1 Preheat oven to 350°F. In a Dutch oven cook pasta according to package directions; drain. Rinse with cold water; drain again and set aside.

2 In the same Dutch oven heat butter over medium heat until melted. Add onions and garlic; cook, covered, for 8 to 10 minutes or until onions are tender, stirring occasionally. Stir in cooked pasta, pasta sauce, spinach, ham, tomatoes, tomato sauce, and ⅓ cup Parmesan cheese. Transfer mixture to an ungreased 3-quart rectangular baking dish.

3 Bake, covered, about 30 minutes or until heated through. Increase oven temperature to 400°F. Top with mozzarella cheese and, if desired, additional Parmesan cheese. Bake, uncovered, about 5 minutes more or until cheeses are melted. Let stand for 5 minutes before serving. If desired, garnish with parsley sprigs.

NUTRITION FACTS PER SERVING:
291 cal., 11 g total fat (6 g sat. fat), 34 mg chol., 1046 mg sodium, 32 g carb., 5 g fiber, 19 g pro.

Chicken and Wild Rice Casserole

PREP 30 minutes BAKE 35 minutes at 350°F MAKES 4 servings

1   6-ounce package long grain and wild rice mix

2   tablespoons butter

½   cup chopped onion (1 medium)

½   cup chopped celery (1 stalk)

1   10.5- or 10.75-ounce can condensed chicken with white and wild rice soup or cream of chicken soup

½   cup sour cream

⅓   cup dry white wine or chicken broth

2   tablespoons snipped fresh basil or ½ teaspoon dried basil, crushed

2   cups shredded cooked chicken or turkey (about 10 ounces)

⅓   cup finely shredded Parmesan cheese

1 Prepare rice mix according to package directions and set aside. Meanwhile, preheat oven to 350°F.

2 In a large skillet heat butter over medium heat until melted. Add onion and celery; cook until tender, stirring occasionally. Stir in soup, sour cream, wine, and basil. Stir in cooked rice and chicken.

3 Transfer mixture to an ungreased 2-quart shallow baking dish. Sprinkle with cheese. Bake, uncovered, about 35 minutes or until heated through.

NUTRITION FACTS PER SERVING:
479 cal., 20 g total fat (10 g sat. fat), 101 mg chol., 1559 mg sodium, 42 g carb., 2 g fiber, 30 g pro.

tip

If you don't have any leftover chicken, use about half of a 2- to 2½-pound purchased roasted chicken from the deli, then skin, bone, and chop the meat. Or, cook your own chicken. In a large skillet, combine 12 ounces skinless, boneless chicken breast halves and 1½ cups water. Bring to boiling; reduce heat. Simmer, covered, for 12 to 14 minutes or until chicken is no longer pink (170°F). Drain and chop.

Creamy Chicken–Broccoli Bake

PREP 30 minutes BAKE 45 minutes at 350°F MAKES 6 servings

Nonstick cooking spray

6 ounces dried medium egg noodles

12 ounces skinless, boneless chicken breast halves, cut into bite-size pieces

1 tablespoon vegetable oil (optional)

1½ cups sliced fresh mushrooms (4 ounces)

½ cup sliced green onions (4)

½ cup chopped red sweet pepper (1 small)

1 10.75-ounce can condensed cream of broccoli soup

1 8-ounce carton sour cream

¼ cup chicken broth

1 teaspoon dry mustard

⅛ teaspoon ground black pepper

1 10-ounce package frozen chopped broccoli, thawed and drained

¼ cup fine dry bread crumbs

1 tablespoon butter, melted

1 Preheat oven to 350°F. Lightly coat a 2-quart square baking dish with cooking spray; set aside. Cook noodles according to package directions; drain and set aside.

2 Meanwhile, coat a large skillet with cooking spray; heat skillet over medium heat. Add chicken; cook and stir about 3 minutes or until chicken is no longer pink. Transfer chicken to a large bowl.

3 If needed, add oil to skillet. Add mushrooms, green onions, and sweet pepper; cook over medium heat until vegetables are tender, stirring occasionally. Transfer vegetables to bowl with chicken. Stir in soup, sour cream, broth, dry mustard, and black pepper. Gently stir in cooked noodles and broccoli.

4 Transfer chicken mixture to the prepared baking dish. In a small bowl combine bread crumbs and melted butter; sprinkle over chicken mixture. Bake, covered, for 30 minutes. Bake, uncovered, about 15 minutes more or until heated through.

NUTRITION FACTS PER SERVING:
354 cal., 16 g total fat (8 g sat. fat), 83 mg chol., 545 mg sodium, 33 g carb., 3 g fiber, 22 g pro.

Cinnamon Rolls
page 33

Overnight Three-
Grain Waffles

page 22

130

Peanut Butter Streusel Muffins
page 34

Fried Egg, Avocado, and Bacon Breakfast Sandwiches page 17

Blueberry Pancakes
page 24

Smoked Salmon Eggs Benedict
page 11

131

Fried Ravioli
with Marinara Sauce
page 50

132

Soft Pretzels
page 48

Roasted Corn
and Crab Dip
page 41

Chili Nuts page 60

Sugared Bacon-Wrapped
Smokies page 55

Sweet Potato Fritters
with Yogurt-Chive
Dipping Sauce
page 46

Mama's Spicy Meatballs
with Fresh Tomato Sauce
page 78

Sweet Herbed
Oven-Fried Chicken
page 86

137

Pear-Cranberry
Deep Dish Pie
page 104

Flat Iron Steak
with BBQ Beans page 71

Beef-Sweet Pepper
Calzones page 74

Chicken
Enchilada
Casserole
page 148

139

Easy Hash Brown Bake
page 15

140

Tuna Noodle Casserole page 153

Herbed Root Vegetable Cobbler page 165

One-Step Ham Casserole page 123

Cheeseburger and Fries Casserole page 112

Baked Potato Soup
page 183

142

Chicken Posole Soup
page 188

143

Clam Chowder page 192

144

Meatball Tortilla Soup page 174

Creamy and Comforting
Corn Chowder page 198

Kansas City Steak Soup
page 170

Baked Chicken Cordon Bleu

PREP 50 minutes BAKE 40 minutes at 350°F MAKES 6 servings

- 3   6-ounce packages long grain and wild rice mix
- 2   tablespoons butter
- 2   cups sliced fresh mushrooms (5½ ounces)
- ¼   cup sliced green onions (2)
- 2   cloves garlic, minced
- 2   tablespoons all-purpose flour
- 2   cups half-and-half or light cream
- ½   cup shredded Gruyère cheese (2 ounces)
- 2   tablespoons dry sherry (optional)
- 6   skinless, boneless chicken breast halves (about 2½ pounds total)
- 3   ounces Gruyère cheese, cut into six 3×½×½-inch sticks
- 6   very thin slices Black Forest or country-style ham (about 6 ounces)
- ½   teaspoon salt
- ¼   teaspoon ground black pepper
- ⅓   cup all-purpose flour
- 2   eggs, lightly beaten
- 2   tablespoons water
- 1½ cups panko (Japanese-style bread crumbs)
- ¼   cup vegetable oil

1 Preheat oven to 350°F. Prepare rice mix according to package directions. Spread cooked rice in the bottom of an ungreased 3-quart shallow baking dish.

2 Meanwhile, for sauce, in a medium saucepan heat butter over medium heat until melted. Add mushrooms, green onions, and garlic; cook until tender, stirring occasionally. Stir in 2 tablespoons flour. Gradually stir in half-and-half. Cook and stir until thickened and bubbly. Add shredded cheese, stirring until melted. If desired, stir in sherry. Spoon sauce over rice; cover and keep warm.

3 Starting from the thickest side of each chicken breast half, cut a horizontal slit to, but not through, the other side. Wrap each stick of cheese in a slice of ham and insert into a slit. Secure with toothpicks. Sprinkle chicken with salt and pepper.

4 Place ⅓ cup flour in a shallow dish. In a second shallow dish combine eggs and water. Place panko in a third shallow dish. Dip chicken into flour, shaking off excess. Dip into egg mixture, then into panko, turning to coat.

5 In an extra-large skillet heat 2 tablespoons of the oil over medium heat. Add half of the chicken; cook about 4 minutes or until brown on both sides. Place chicken on top of sauce. Repeat with the remaining 2 tablespoons oil and the remaining chicken. Remove toothpicks.

6 Bake, covered, for 40 to 45 minutes or until chicken is no longer pink (170°F).

NUTRITION FACTS PER SERVING:
862 cal., 36 g total fat (15 g sat. fat), 256 mg chol., 1586 mg sodium, 66 g carb., 3 g fiber, 68 g pro.

Potluck Chicken Tetrazzini

PREP 30 minutes BAKE 15 minutes at 350°F STAND 5 minutes MAKES 10 servings

1 2- to 2½-pound purchased roasted chicken

8 ounces dried spaghetti or linguine, broken in half

12 ounces fresh asparagus, trimmed and cut into 1-inch pieces

2 tablespoons butter

8 ounces small whole fresh button mushrooms

3 medium red and/or yellow sweet peppers, seeded and cut into 1-inch pieces

¼ cup all-purpose flour

⅛ teaspoon ground black pepper

1 14.5-ounce can chicken broth

¾ cup milk

½ cup shredded Swiss cheese (2 ounces)

2 to 3 teaspoons finely shredded lemon peel

1½ cups cubed sourdough bread

1 tablespoon olive oil

2 tablespoons snipped fresh parsley

1 Remove and discard skin from chicken. Pull meat from bones, discarding bones. Cut meat into chunks; measure 3 cups chicken. Save the remaining chicken for another use.

2 Cook spaghetti according to package directions, adding asparagus for the last 1 minute of cooking; drain. Return spaghetti mixture to pan.

3 Meanwhile, preheat oven to 350°F. In a large skillet heat butter over medium heat until melted. Add mushrooms and sweet peppers; cook for 8 to 10 minutes or until mushrooms are tender, stirring occasionally. Stir in flour and black pepper. Gradually stir in broth and milk. Cook and stir until thickened and bubbly.

4 Add chicken, mushroom mixture, cheese, and half of the lemon peel to spaghetti mixture; toss gently to coat. Transfer mixture to an ungreased 3-quart rectangular baking dish.

5 In a medium bowl toss together bread cubes, oil, and the remaining lemon peel. Sprinkle bread mixture over spaghetti mixture. Bake, uncovered, about 15 minutes or until heated through. Let stand for 5 minutes before serving. Sprinkle with parsley.

NUTRITION FACTS PER SERVING:
282 cal., 10 g total fat (4 g sat. fat), 48 mg chol., 258 mg sodium, 28 g carb., 2 g fiber, 20 g pro.

146

To Store: Most casseroles freeze beautifully (except those that contain a lot of dairy, such as sour cream). To freeze, prepare casseroles in a foil-lined dish. Freeze overnight in the dish; remove from the dish. Wrap foil carefully over the top of the casserole or place the frozen casserole in a large zipping freezer bag.

Three-Cheese Ziti and Smoked Chicken Casserole

PREP 25 minutes BAKE 25 minutes at 375°F STAND 10 minutes MAKES 6 servings

- 12 ounces dried ziti pasta
- 3 tablespoons butter
- 2 cloves garlic, minced
- 3 tablespoons all-purpose flour
- ¼ teaspoon salt
- ¼ teaspoon ground white pepper
- 3½ cups milk
- 1½ cups finely shredded Asiago or Parmesan cheese (6 ounces)
- 1 cup finely shredded fontina cheese (4 ounces)
- ½ cup crumbled blue cheese (2 ounces)
- 2 cups chopped smoked chicken or shredded purchased roasted chicken (about 10 ounces)
- ⅓ cup panko (Japanese-style bread crumbs) or fine dry bread crumbs
- 2 teaspoons truffle-flavor oil or melted butter

1 Preheat oven to 375°F. Grease a 2-quart casserole; set aside. Cook pasta according to package directions; drain. Return pasta to pan.

2 Meanwhile, in a medium saucepan heat butter over medium heat until melted. Add garlic; cook and stir for 30 seconds. Stir in flour, salt, and pepper. Gradually stir in milk. Cook and stir until thickened and bubbly. Gradually add Asiago cheese, fontina cheese, and blue cheese, stirring until melted. Stir in chicken. Stir chicken mixture into cooked pasta.

3 Transfer mixture to the prepared casserole. In a small bowl combine panko and truffle oil; sprinkle over pasta mixture. Bake, uncovered, about 25 minutes or until heated through and crumbs are light brown. Let stand for 10 minutes before serving.

147

NUTRITION FACTS PER SERVING:
753 cal., 39 g total fat (22 g sat. fat), 141 mg chol., 953 mg sodium, 56 g carb., 2 g fiber, 43 g pro.

Chicken Enchilada Casserole

Photo on page 139

PREP 30 minutes BAKE 40 minutes at 350°F MAKES 6 servings

- 2 tablespoons butter
- ¼ cup slivered almonds, toasted
- ¼ cup chopped onion
- 1 or 2 medium fresh jalapeño chile peppers, seeded and chopped* (optional)
- 1 4-ounce can diced green chile peppers, drained
- 1 3-ounce package cream cheese, softened
- 1 tablespoon milk
- 1 teaspoon ground cumin
- 3 cups chopped cooked chicken
- 12 7-inch flour tortillas or 6-inch corn tortillas
- 1 10.75-ounce can condensed cream of chicken or cream of mushroom soup
- 1 8-ounce carton sour cream
- 1 cup milk
- ¾ cup shredded Monterey Jack or cheddar cheese (3 ounces)
- 2 tablespoons slivered almonds, toasted

1 Preheat oven to 350°F. Grease a 3-quart rectangular baking dish; set aside. In a medium skillet heat butter over medium heat until melted. Add ¼ cup almonds, onion, and jalapeño peppers, if desired; cook until onion is tender, stirring occasionally. Remove from heat. Stir in 1 tablespoon of the canned chile peppers; reserve the remaining peppers for sauce.

2 In a medium bowl combine cream cheese, 1 tablespoon milk, and cumin. Stir in onion mixture and chicken. Spoon about ¼ cup of the chicken mixture onto each tortilla near an edge; roll up tortilla. Place filled tortillas, seam side down, in the prepared baking dish.

3 For sauce, in a medium bowl combine soup, sour cream, 1 cup milk, and the remaining canned chile peppers. Pour evenly over tortilla rolls.

4 Bake, covered, about 35 minutes or until heated through. Sprinkle enchiladas with cheese and 2 tablespoons almonds. Bake, uncovered, about 5 minutes more or until cheese is melted.

NUTRITION FACTS PER SERVING: *660 cal., 38 g total fat (16 g sat. fat), 127 mg chol., 1140 mg sodium, 44 g carb., 3 g fiber, 35 g pro.*

*tip
Because chile peppers contain volatile oils that can burn your skin and eyes, avoid direct contact with them as much as possible. When working with chile peppers, wear plastic or rubber gloves. If your bare hands do touch the peppers, wash your hands and nails well with soap and warm water.

tip
If you prefer a red sauce on your enchiladas, omit the soup, sour cream, 1 cup milk, and 2 tablespoons almonds. Stir the reserved canned chile peppers into two 10-ounce cans enchilada sauce. Bake as directed.

Lightened-Up Chicken Enchiladas

Prepare as directed, except use 4 ounces fat-free or light cream cheese (Neufchâtel), reduced-sodium condensed soup, fat-free or light sour cream, fat-free milk, and reduced-fat Monterey Jack cheese. Omit the 2 tablespoons almonds. Top the baked enchiladas with ½ cup chopped tomato (1 medium).

NUTRITION FACTS PER SERVING: *546 cal., 21 g total fat (8 g sat. fat), 91 mg chol., 1,058 mg sodium, 51 g carb., 4 g fiber, 37 g pro.*

Deep-Dish Chicken Potpie

PREP 50 minutes BAKE 35 minutes at 400°F STAND 20 minutes MAKES 9 servings

- 3 tablespoons butter
- 1½ cups chopped leeks or onions (4 to 5 leeks)
- 1½ cups sliced fresh mushrooms (4 ounces)
- 1¼ cups sliced celery (about 2 stalks)
- ¾ cup chopped red sweet pepper (1 medium)
- ½ cup all-purpose flour
- 1½ teaspoons poultry seasoning
- ¼ teaspoon salt
- ¼ teaspoon ground black pepper
- 2¼ cups chicken broth
- 1½ cups half-and-half, light cream, or milk
- 3¾ cups chopped cooked chicken (about 1¼ pounds)
- 1½ cups frozen peas or frozen peas and carrots
- 1 recipe Pastry Topper
- 1 egg, lightly beaten

1 Preheat oven to 400°F. In a large saucepan heat butter over medium heat until melted. Add leeks, mushrooms, celery, and sweet pepper. Cook and stir for 5 to 8 minutes or until vegetables are tender. Stir in flour, poultry seasoning, salt, and black pepper. Gradually stir in broth and half-and-half. Cook and stir until thickened and bubbly. Stir in chicken and peas. Cover chicken mixture and keep warm.

2 Prepare Pastry Topper. On a lightly floured surface, use your hands to slightly flatten pastry. Roll pastry from center to edges into a 14×10-inch rectangle. Cut slits in pastry to allow steam to escape or use a small cookie cutter to make cutouts in pastry.

3 Transfer hot chicken mixture to an ungreased 13×9×2-inch baking pan. Wrap pastry rectangle around the rolling pin. Unroll pastry on top of chicken mixture. Fold under extra pastry even with the edges of baking pan. Press pastry along edges to seal. Brush pastry with egg.

4 Bake, uncovered, for 35 to 40 minutes or until filling is bubbly and pastry is golden. Let stand for 20 minutes before serving.

NUTRITION FACTS PER SERVING:
520 cal., 30 g total fat (11 g sat. fat), 101 mg chol., 644 mg sodium, 38 g carb., 3 g fiber, 22 g pro.

Pastry Topper

In a large bowl stir together 2¼ cups all-purpose flour and ¾ teaspoon salt. Using a pastry blender, cut in ⅔ cup shortening until pieces are pea size. Sprinkle 1 tablespoon ice water over part of the flour mixture; toss gently with a fork. Push moistened pastry to side of bowl. Repeat moistening flour mixture, using 1 tablespoon ice water at a time, until all of the flour mixture is moistened (7 to 9 tablespoons ice water total). Gather flour mixture into a ball, kneading gently until it holds together.

Turkey Manicotti

PREP 30 minutes   COOK 30 minutes   BAKE 25 minutes at 350°F   STAND 10 minutes   MAKES 6 servings

- 12 dried manicotti shells*
- 2 tablespoons olive oil
- ½ cup chopped onion (1 medium)
- 4 cloves garlic, minced
- 2 14.5-ounce cans diced fire-roasted tomatoes, undrained
- ⅓ cup dry red wine
- 2 tablespoons tomato paste
- 2 cups chopped cooked turkey (about 10 ounces)
- 1 cup shredded mozzarella cheese (4 ounces)
- ¾ cup ricotta cheese
- ½ of an 8-ounce tub cream cheese spread with chive and onion
- ¼ cup grated Parmesan cheese
- 1 teaspoon dried basil, crushed
- ½ teaspoon dried oregano, crushed
- ¼ teaspoon salt
- ¼ teaspoon ground black pepper

1 Cook manicotti according to package directions; drain. Rinse with cold water; drain again and set aside. Meanwhile, for sauce, in a medium saucepan heat oil over medium-high heat. Add onion and garlic; cook until onion is tender, stirring occasionally. Stir in tomatoes, wine, and tomato paste. Bring to boiling; reduce heat. Simmer, covered, for 30 minutes.

2 Preheat oven to 350°F. For filling, in a large bowl combine turkey, ½ cup of the mozzarella cheese, the ricotta cheese, cream cheese spread, Parmesan cheese, basil, oregano, salt, and pepper. Using a small spoon, carefully fill each manicotti shell with about ¼ cup of the filling. Arrange filled shells in an ungreased 3-quart rectangular baking dish. Pour sauce over shells. Sprinkle with the remaining ½ cup mozzarella cheese.

3 Bake, covered, for 25 to 30 minutes or until heated through. Let stand, covered, for 10 minutes before serving.

NUTRITION FACTS PER SERVING:
503 cal., 22 g total fat (11 g sat. fat), 83 mg chol., 777 mg sodium, 42 g carb., 2 g fiber, 30 g pro.

*tip
Cook a few extra manicotti shells to allow for any that break.

Nacho Turkey Casserole

PREP 20 minutes BAKE 30 minutes at 350°F MAKES 8 servings

5 cups slightly crushed tortilla chips

4 cups cubed cooked turkey or chicken (about 1¼ pounds)

2 16-ounce jars salsa

1 10-ounce package frozen whole kernel corn

½ cup sour cream

2 tablespoons all-purpose flour

1 cup shredded Monterey Jack cheese with jalapeño peppers or mozzarella cheese (4 ounces)

1 fresh jalapeño chile pepper, thinly sliced* (optional)

1 Preheat oven to 350°F. Grease a 3-quart rectangular baking dish. Spread 3 cups of the tortilla chips in the bottom of the prepared baking dish. In a large bowl combine turkey, salsa, corn, sour cream, and flour. Spoon turkey mixture over tortilla chips in dish.

2 Bake, uncovered, for 25 minutes. Sprinkle with the remaining 2 cups tortilla chips and the cheese. Bake, uncovered, for 5 to 10 minutes more or until heated through. If desired, garnish with jalapeño pepper.

NUTRITION FACTS PER SERVING:
444 cal., 17 g total fat (7 g sat. fat), 74 mg chol., 1127 mg sodium, 46 g carb., 4 g fiber, 29 g pro.

151

 **tip**

Because chile peppers contain volatile oils that can burn your skin and eyes, avoid direct contact with them as much as possible. When working with chile peppers, wear plastic or rubber gloves. If your bare hands do touch the peppers, wash your hands and nails well with soap and warm water.

One-Dish Turkey and Biscuits

PREP 30 minutes BAKE 20 minutes at 425°F MAKES 4 servings

- 1 cup chicken broth
- ½ cup finely chopped onion (1 medium)
- ½ cup finely chopped celery (1 stalk)
- 1½ cups frozen peas and carrots
- 1¼ cups packaged biscuit mix
- 1½ cups milk
- 2 teaspoons dried parsley flakes
- 3 tablespoons all-purpose flour
- 2 cups cubed cooked turkey breast (about 10 ounces)
- ½ teaspoon dried sage, crushed
- ⅛ teaspoon ground black pepper

1 Preheat oven to 425°F. In a medium saucepan combine broth, onion, and celery. Bring to boiling; reduce heat. Simmer, covered, for 5 minutes. Add peas and carrots; return to boiling.

2 Meanwhile, in a small bowl combine biscuit mix, ½ cup of the milk, and the parsley; stir just until moistened.

3 In a small bowl gradually stir the remaining 1 cup milk into the flour; stir into vegetable mixture in saucepan. Cook and stir over medium heat until thickened and bubbly. Stir in turkey, sage, and pepper. Transfer mixture to an ungreased 2-quart casserole.

4 Drop biscuit mixture into eight mounds on top of hot turkey mixture. Bake, uncovered, for 20 to 25 minutes or until biscuits are golden.

NUTRITION FACTS PER SERVING:
356 cal., 8 g total fat (3 g sat. fat), 67 mg chol., 844 mg sodium, 41 g carb., 3 g fiber, 30 g pro.

152

Tuna Noodle Casserole

Photo on page 141

PREP 25 minutes BAKE 20 minutes at 375°F STAND 5 minutes MAKES 8 servings

4 cups dried wide egg noodles
¼ cup butter or vegetable oil
1 cup chopped celery (2 stalks)
¾ cup chopped onion
¼ cup all-purpose flour
3 tablespoons Dijon-style mustard
½ teaspoon ground black pepper
¼ teaspoon salt
3 cups milk
2 12-ounce cans chunk light tuna, drained
⅔ cup chopped roma tomatoes (2 medium)
1 cup whole or crushed potato chips (optional)

1 Preheat oven to 375°F. Lightly grease a 3-quart rectangular baking dish; set aside. Cook noodles according to package directions; drain. Return noodles to pan.

2 Meanwhile, for sauce, in a large saucepan heat butter over medium heat until melted. Add celery and onion; cook until vegetables are tender, stirring occasionally. Stir in flour, mustard, pepper, and salt. Gradually stir in milk. Cook and stir until thickened and bubbly.

3 Gently fold sauce, tuna, and tomatoes into cooked noodles. Transfer mixture to the prepared baking dish. If desired, top with potato chips.

4 Bake, uncovered, about 20 minutes or until heated through. Let stand for 5 minutes before serving.

NUTRITION FACTS PER SERVING:
403 cal., 18 g total fat (7 g sat. fat), 91 mg chol., 679 mg sodium, 30 g carb., 2 g fiber, 27 g pro.

153

Smoky Salmon Casserole

PREP 30 minutes BAKE 25 minutes at 350°F STAND 10 minutes MAKES 6 servings

154

- 8 ounces dried bow-tie or penne pasta
- 2 tablespoons butter
- 1 cup chopped red sweet pepper (1 medium)
- ½ cup chopped green onions (4)
- 2 tablespoons all-purpose flour
- ¼ teaspoon ground black pepper
- 2½ cups milk
- 1½ cups shredded smoked Gouda cheese (6 ounces)
- ½ teaspoon finely shredded lemon peel
- 1 tablespoon lemon juice
- 1 4.5-ounce piece smoked salmon, flaked, skin and bones removed
- 1 14-ounce can artichoke hearts, drained and quartered
- 1 cup soft bread crumbs (from 2 slices bread) or panko (Japanese-style bread crumbs)
- ¼ cup pine nuts
  Ground black pepper

1 Preheat oven to 350°F. Cook pasta according to package directions; drain and set aside.

2 Meanwhile, for cheese sauce, in a large skillet heat butter over medium heat until melted. Add sweet pepper and green onions; cook and stir about 3 minutes or until tender. Stir in flour and ¼ teaspoon black pepper. Gradually stir in milk. Cook and stir until slightly thickened and bubbly. Gradually add cheese, stirring until melted. Stir in lemon peel and lemon juice (mixture may appear curdled).

3 In a large bowl combine cooked pasta, cheese sauce, smoked salmon, and artichoke hearts. Transfer mixture to an ungreased 2-quart square or rectangular baking dish.

4 Sprinkle with bread crumbs, pine nuts, and additional black pepper. Bake, uncovered, for 25 to 30 minutes or until heated through and topping is golden. Let stand for 10 minutes before serving.

NUTRITION FACTS PER SERVING:
470 cal., 19 g total fat (10 g sat. fat), 74 mg chol., 780 mg sodium, 45 g carb., 4 g fiber, 30 g pro.

Make-Ahead Directions: Prepare as directed through Step 3. Cover and chill for 2 to 24 hours. To serve, preheat oven to 350°F. Continue as directed in Step 4, except bake, uncovered, for 45 to 50 minutes.

Cajun Shrimp and Corn Bread Casserole

PREP 35 minutes BAKE 15 minutes at 400°F STAND 5 minutes MAKES 6 servings

- 1 **pound fresh or frozen large shrimp in shells**
- 1 **teaspoon Cajun seasoning**
- 1 **tablespoon canola oil**
- 1½ **cups coarsely chopped green and/or red sweet peppers (2 medium)**
- 1 **cup sliced celery (2 stalks)**
- ½ **cup chopped onion (1 medium)**
- 2 **cloves garlic, minced**
- 1 **15-ounce can black-eyed peas, rinsed and drained**
- 1 **14.5-ounce can no-salt-added stewed tomatoes, undrained and cut up**
- 1 **recipe Corn Bread Dumplings**
  Snipped fresh parsley (optional)

1 Thaw shrimp, if frozen. Preheat oven to 400°F. Peel and devein shrimp, leaving tails intact (if desired). Rinse shrimp; pat dry with paper towels. In a large bowl combine shrimp and ½ teaspoon of the Cajun seasoning; toss gently to coat. Set aside.

2 In a 10-inch cast-iron skillet or large oven-going skillet heat oil over medium-high heat. Add sweet peppers, celery, and onion; cook for 5 to 7 minutes or until vegetables are tender, stirring occasionally. Add shrimp and garlic; cook and stir for 2 to 3 minutes or until shrimp are opaque.

3 Stir in black-eyed peas, tomatoes, and the remaining ½ teaspoon Cajun seasoning. Drop Corn Bread Dumplings dough into eight mounds on top of shrimp mixture.

4 Bake, uncovered, for 15 to 18 minutes or until a wooden toothpick inserted near the centers of dumplings comes out clean. Let stand for 5 minutes before serving. If desired, sprinkle with parsley.

NUTRITION FACTS PER SERVING:
336 cal., 10 g total fat (1 g sat. fat), 122 mg chol., 496 mg sodium, 42 g carb., 6 g fiber, 21 g pro.

Corn Bread Dumplings

In a medium bowl stir together ¾ cup all-purpose flour, ⅓ cup yellow cornmeal, 1 tablespoon sugar, 1¼ teaspoons baking powder, and ¼ teaspoon salt. In a small bowl combine 1 lightly beaten egg, ¼ cup fat-free milk, and 2 tablespoons canola oil. Add egg mixture all at once to flour mixture. Stir just until moistened.

tip

When buying fresh shrimp, look for firm meat, translucent and moist shells with no black spots, and a fresh scent. With large shrimp, you'll get 31 to 40 per pound.

Crab and Spinach Pasta with Fontina

PREP 25 minutes BAKE 30 minutes at 375°F STAND 10 minutes MAKES 6 servings

8   ounces dried bow-tie pasta

1   26-ounce jar any flavor
     tomato-base pasta sauce

2   6-ounce cans crabmeat,
     drained, flaked, and cartilage
     removed

1   10-ounce package frozen
     chopped spinach, thawed and
     well drained

1½   cups shredded fontina cheese
     (6 ounces)

1 Preheat oven to 375°F. Lightly grease a 2-quart square baking dish; set aside. Cook pasta according to package directions; drain and set aside.

2 Meanwhile, in a large bowl combine pasta sauce, crabmeat, spinach, and ¾ cup of the cheese. Add cooked pasta; toss gently to combine. Transfer mixture to the prepared baking dish. Sprinkle with the remaining ¾ cup cheese.

3 Bake, uncovered, for 30 to 35 minutes or until mixture is bubbly around the edges and cheese is light brown. Let stand for 10 minutes before serving.

NUTRITION FACTS PER SERVING:
359 cal., 11 g total fat (6 g sat. fat), 105 mg chol., 912 mg sodium, 39 g carb., 4 g fiber, 26 g pro.

Cheese and Vegetable Rice Casserole

PREP 20 minutes BAKE 35 minutes at 350°F STAND 10 minutes MAKES 6 servings

- 1 16-ounce package frozen broccoli, cauliflower, and carrots, thawed
- 4 cups cooked rice
- 1 15-ounce can black beans, rinsed and drained
- 1 12-ounce jar roasted red sweet peppers, drained and coarsely chopped
- 1 cup frozen whole kernel corn, thawed
- 2 4-ounce cans diced green chile peppers, drained
- 2 cups shredded cheddar cheese (8 ounces)
- 1¼ cups chicken broth
- ½ cup seasoned fine dry bread crumbs
- 2 tablespoons butter, melted

1 Preheat oven to 350°F. Lightly grease a 3-quart rectangular baking dish; set aside.

2 In a large bowl stir together vegetable mix, rice, beans, roasted peppers, corn, and chile peppers. Stir in 1 cup of the cheese and the broth. Transfer mixture to the prepared baking dish. Sprinkle with the remaining 1 cup cheese.

3 In a small bowl combine bread crumbs and melted butter. Sprinkle over vegetable mixture.

4 Bake, uncovered, for 35 to 40 minutes or until mixture is heated through and crumbs are golden. Let stand for 10 minutes before serving.

NUTRITION FACTS PER SERVING: *471 cal., 18 g total fat (10 g sat. fat), 50 mg chol., 1423 mg sodium, 60 g carb., 8 g fiber, 21 g pro.*

157

Casserole-Style Chiles Rellenos

PREP 25 minutes BAKE 15 minutes at 450°F MAKES 8 servings

4 poblano chile peppers or green sweet peppers

6 eggs, lightly beaten

½ cup milk

½ teaspoon salt

1 tablespoon vegetable oil

½ cup chopped red sweet pepper (1 small)

½ cup chopped green onions (4)

1 tablespoon seeded and finely chopped fresh jalapeño chile pepper*

2 cloves garlic, minced

1 cup shredded cheddar cheese (4 ounces)

1 cup picante sauce

½ cup sour cream

1 Preheat oven to 450°F. Generously grease a 3-quart rectangular baking dish; set aside. Cut poblano peppers in half lengthwise, leaving stems intact; remove seeds and membranes. Cook peppers in boiling water for 3 minutes. Invert onto paper towels to drain. Place pepper halves, cut sides up, in the prepared baking dish.

2 In a medium bowl combine eggs, milk, and salt; set aside. In a large skillet heat oil over medium heat. Add sweet pepper, green onions, jalapeño pepper, and garlic; cook just until sweet pepper is tender, stirring occasionally. Remove vegetables from skillet.

3 Pour egg mixture into the same skillet. Cook over medium heat, without stirring, until mixture starts to set on the bottom and around the edges. Using a spatula or large spoon, lift and fold the partially cooked egg mixture so the uncooked portion flows underneath. Continue cooking over medium heat for 2 to 3 minutes or until egg mixture is cooked through but is still glossy and moist. Remove from heat. Fold in vegetable mixture and ½ cup of the cheese.

4 Fill pepper halves with egg mixture. Sprinkle with the remaining ½ cup cheese. Bake, uncovered, about 15 minutes or until heated through. Serve with picante sauce and sour cream.

NUTRITION FACTS PER SERVING:
197 cal., 13 g total fat (6 g sat. fat), 181 mg chol., 516 mg sodium, 9 g carb., 1 g fiber, 10 g pro.

*tip
Because chile peppers contain volatile oils that can burn your skin and eyes, avoid direct contact with them as much as possible. When working with chile peppers, wear plastic or rubber gloves. If your bare hands do touch the peppers, wash your hands and nails well with soap and warm water.

Baked Ziti with Three Cheeses

PREP 30 minutes BAKE 30 minutes at 425°F MAKES 6 servings

12 ounces dried ziti or penne pasta

1 14.5-ounce can fire-roasted crushed tomatoes or one 14.5-ounce can diced tomatoes, undrained

2 tablespoons olive oil

1 cup chopped onion (1 large)

12 cloves garlic, minced (2 tablespoons)

½ cup dry white wine

2 cups whipping cream

1 cup shredded Parmesan cheese (4 ounces)

¾ cup crumbled Gorgonzola or other blue cheese (3 ounces)

½ cup shredded fontina cheese (2 ounces)

¾ teaspoon salt

¼ teaspoon ground black pepper

Snipped fresh Italian (flat-leaf) parsley (optional)

1 Preheat oven to 425°F. Cook pasta according to package directions; drain and set aside. Transfer to an ungreased 3-quart rectangular baking dish; stir in tomatoes.

2 Meanwhile, in a large saucepan heat oil over medium heat. Add onion and garlic; cook just until tender, stirring occasionally. Carefully stir in wine; cook about 3 minutes or until liquid is reduced by half. Add whipping cream. Bring to boiling; reduce heat. Boil gently, uncovered, about 5 minutes or until mixture is slightly thickened, stirring frequently. Remove from heat. Stir in Parmesan cheese, Gorgonzola cheese, fontina cheese, salt, and pepper.

3 Pour cheese mixture over pasta mixture. Bake, covered, for 30 to 35 minutes or until sauce is bubbly. Stir pasta to coat. If desired, sprinkle with parsley.

NUTRITION FACTS PER SERVING:
741 cal., 48 g total fat (28 g sat. fat), 141 mg chol., 970 mg sodium, 53 g carb., 3 g fiber, 24 g pro.

159

Loaded Macaroni and Cheese

PREP 25 minutes BAKE 30 minutes at 375°F STAND 10 minutes MAKES 6 servings

- 2 cups dried macaroni
- 1 cup cottage cheese
- 4 ounces cream cheese, softened
- 1 tablespoon yellow mustard
- ½ teaspoon salt
- ½ teaspoon ground black pepper
- Dash bottled hot pepper sauce
- 2 cups cooked broccoli florets
- 1 cup sliced fresh mushrooms
- ½ cup finely chopped onion (1 medium)
- 1 cup shredded mozzarella cheese (4 ounces)
- 1 cup shredded cheddar cheese (4 ounces)
- ¼ cup grated Parmesan cheese

1 Preheat oven to 375°F. Grease a 2-quart square baking dish; set aside. Cook macaroni according to package directions; drain and set aside.

2 Meanwhile, in a large bowl combine cottage cheese, cream cheese, mustard, salt, black pepper, and hot pepper sauce. Stir in broccoli, mushrooms, and onion. Stir in mozzarella cheese and ¼ cup of the cheddar cheese. Gently stir in cooked macaroni. Transfer mixture to the prepared baking dish.

3 Bake, covered, for 20 minutes. Sprinkle with the remaining ¾ cup cheddar cheese and the Parmesan cheese. Bake, uncovered, about 10 minutes more or until cheeses are melted. Let stand for 10 minutes before serving.

NUTRITION FACTS PER SERVING:
400 cal., 18 g total fat (11 g sat. fat), 59 mg chol., 730 mg sodium, 35 g carb., 3 g fiber, 24 g pro.

Tortellini-Vegetable Bake

PREP 30 minutes BAKE 30 minutes at 350°F MAKES 8 servings

2 9-ounce packages refrigerated cheese-filled tortellini

1½ cups sugar snap peas, trimmed and halved crosswise

½ cup thinly sliced carrot (1 medium)

1 tablespoon butter

1 cup sliced fresh mushrooms

⅓ cup vegetable broth

2 teaspoons all-purpose flour

1½ teaspoons dried oregano, crushed

½ teaspoon garlic salt

½ teaspoon ground black pepper

1 cup milk

1 8-ounce package cream cheese, cubed and softened

1 tablespoon lemon juice

1 cup quartered cherry tomatoes

½ cup coarsely chopped red or green sweet pepper (1 small)

2 tablespoons grated Parmesan cheese

1 Preheat oven to 350°F. Cook tortellini according to package directions, adding sugar snap peas and carrot for the last 1 minute of cooking; drain and set aside.

2 Meanwhile, in a 12-inch skillet heat butter over medium heat until melted. Add mushrooms; cook about 5 minutes or until tender, stirring occasionally. Remove from skillet and set aside.

3 In a screw-top jar combine broth, flour, oregano, garlic salt, and black pepper. Cover and shake until smooth. Add to the same skillet; add milk. Cook and stir over medium heat until thickened and bubbly. Add cream cheese; cook and stir until smooth. Remove from heat; stir in lemon juice.

4 Stir tortellini mixture, cooked mushrooms, tomatoes, and sweet pepper into cream cheese mixture. Transfer to an ungreased 3-quart rectangular baking dish. Bake, covered, about 30 minutes or until heated through. Sprinkle with Parmesan cheese.

NUTRITION FACTS PER SERVING:
353 cal., 17 g total fat (9 g sat. fat), 69 mg chol., 468 mg sodium, 37 g carb., 1 g fiber, 15 g pro.

161

Creamy Artichoke Lasagna Bake

PREP 50 minutes BAKE 35 minutes at 350°F STAND 15 minutes MAKES 12 servings

- 9 dried lasagna noodles
- 3 tablespoons olive oil
- 2 9-ounce packages frozen artichoke hearts, thawed and halved lengthwise
- ½ cup pine nuts
- 4 cloves garlic, minced
- 1 15-ounce carton ricotta cheese
- 1 cup finely shredded Parmesan cheese (4 ounces)
- 1 cup snipped fresh basil
- 1 egg
- ¾ teaspoon salt
- 1 cup chicken broth or vegetable broth
- ¼ cup all-purpose flour
- 2 cups half-and-half or light cream
- 1 cup shredded mozzarella cheese (4 ounces)

1 Preheat oven to 350°F. Cook lasagna noodles according to package directions; drain. Rinse with cold water; drain again. Place lasagna noodles in a single layer on a sheet of foil; set aside.

2 In a large saucepan heat 2 tablespoons of the oil over medium heat. Add artichokes, pine nuts, and half of the garlic. Cook for 2 to 3 minutes or until artichokes are tender, stirring frequently. Transfer to a large bowl. Stir in ricotta cheese, ½ cup of the Parmesan cheese, ½ cup of the basil, the egg, and salt.

3 For sauce, in a small bowl combine broth and flour. In the same saucepan heat the remaining 1 tablespoon oil over medium heat. Add the remaining garlic; cook and stir for 30 seconds. Stir in flour mixture and half-and-half. Cook and stir until thickened and bubbly. Remove from heat. Stir in the remaining ½ cup basil.

4 In a small bowl combine mozzarella cheese and the remaining ½ cup Parmesan cheese.

5 Spread about 1 cup of the sauce in the bottom of an ungreased 3-quart shallow baking dish or 13×9×2-inch baking pan. Arrange 3 of the cooked lasagna noodles over sauce in dish. Spread with one-third of the artichoke mixture and one-third of the remaining sauce. Sprinkle with ½ cup of the mozzarella mixture. Repeat layers two more times, starting with noodles and ending with mozzarella mixture.

6 Bake, uncovered, for 35 to 40 minutes or until edges are bubbly and top is light brown. Let stand for 15 minutes before serving.

NUTRITION FACTS PER SERVING:
350 cal., 21 g total fat (10 g sat. fat), 64 mg chol., 470 mg sodium, 25 g carb., 3 g fiber, 16 g pro.

tip Allowing a casserole to stand for several minutes after it comes out of the oven improves texture and flavor, and allows the food to firm up and hold a cut edge. This is especially true for layered casseroles and hot, cheesy dishes.

Green Bean Casserole with Crispy Shallots

PREP 45 minutes   BAKE 20 minutes at 375°F   MAKES 8 servings

1½   pounds haricots verts or thin green beans, trimmed

¼   cup butter

12   ounces fresh button mushrooms, sliced

12   ounces fresh shiitake mushrooms, stems discarded and caps sliced

6   cloves garlic, minced

1   tablespoon snipped fresh thyme or 1 teaspoon dried thyme, crushed

¼   teaspoon salt

¼   teaspoon ground black pepper

2   tablespoons all-purpose flour

2   cups half-and-half or light cream

½   cup finely shredded Parmesan cheese (2 ounces)

⅛   teaspoon salt

⅛   teaspoon ground black pepper

⅓   cup pine nuts, toasted

½   cup olive oil

4   shallots, thinly sliced crosswise, or 1 cup thinly sliced sweet onion (1 large)

1 Preheat oven to 375°F. Grease a 2-quart casserole; set aside. In an extra-large skillet cook haricots verts in lightly salted boiling water about 3 minutes or until crisp-tender; drain. Transfer to a bowl of ice water to stop cooking; drain again and set aside.

2 In the same skillet heat 2 tablespoons of the butter over medium-high heat until melted. Add button and shiitake mushrooms, garlic, and thyme. Cook until mushrooms are tender and liquid is evaporated, stirring occasionally. Stir in ¼ teaspoon salt and ¼ teaspoon pepper. Gently stir in cooked haricots verts.

3 For sauce, in a small saucepan heat the remaining 2 tablespoons butter over medium heat until melted. Stir in flour. Gradually stir in half-and-half. Cook and stir until thickened and bubbly. Cook and stir for 1 minute more. Stir in cheese, ⅛ teaspoon salt, and ⅛ teaspoon pepper. Pour sauce over bean mixture, stirring gently just until combined.

4 Transfer bean mixture to the prepared casserole. Bake, uncovered, about 20 minutes or until bubbly. Sprinkle with pine nuts.

5 Meanwhile, rinse and dry saucepan. In the saucepan heat oil over medium-high heat. Working in batches, cook shallots in hot oil about 1½ minutes or until golden and slightly crisp. Remove with a slotted spoon and drain on paper towels. Before serving, top casserole with fried shallots.

NUTRITION FACTS PER SERVING:
385 cal., 32 g total fat (11 g sat. fat), 41 mg chol., 270 mg sodium, 21 g carb., 4 g fiber, 9 g pro.

163

Make-Ahead Directions: Prepare as directed through Step 3. Cover and chill for up to 24 hours. Cook shallots as directed in Step 5. Transfer to an airtight container. Cover and chill for up to 24 hours. To serve, let casserole stand at room temperature for 30 minutes. Bake as directed in Step 4. Top with pine nuts and fried shallots.

Broccoli-Cauliflower Bake

PREP 25 minutes BAKE 20 minutes at 375°F MAKES 8 servings

4   cups broccoli florets*
3   cups cauliflower florets*
1   tablespoon butter
½   cup chopped onion
    (1 medium)
1   10.75-ounce can condensed
    cream of mushroom soup
    or cream of chicken soup
3   ounces American cheese,
    cubed, or process Swiss
    cheese, torn
¼   cup milk
½   teaspoon dried basil, thyme,
    or marjoram, crushed
¾   cup soft bread crumbs**
    (from about 2 slices bread)
1   tablespoon butter, melted**

1 Preheat oven to 375°F. In a covered large saucepan cook broccoli and cauliflower in a small amount of lightly salted boiling water for 6 to 8 minutes or until vegetables are crisp-tender; drain in a colander and set aside.

2 In the same saucepan heat 1 tablespoon butter over medium heat until melted. Add onion; cook until tender, stirring occasionally. Stir in soup, cheese, milk, and basil. Cook and stir over medium-low heat until cheese is melted. Stir in cooked broccoli and cauliflower. Transfer mixture to an ungreased 1½-quart casserole.

3 In a small bowl combine bread crumbs and 1 tablespoon melted butter; toss to coat. Sprinkle crumb mixture over vegetable mixture. Bake, uncovered, about 20 minutes or until heated through.

NUTRITION FACTS PER SERVING:
137 cal., 9 g total fat (5 g sat. fat), 20 mg chol., 497 mg sodium, 11 g carb., 3 g fiber, 5 g pro.

*tip
If you like, substitute 8 cups frozen broccoli and cauliflower, thawed, for the fresh broccoli and cauliflower florets. Prepare as directed, except omit Step 1 and bake, uncovered, about 35 minutes or until heated through.

**tip
For a different topper, omit the bread crumbs and 1 tablespoon melted butter. In a small bowl combine ⅔ cup crushed stone-ground wheat crackers, ⅓ cup finely chopped walnuts, and ¼ cup finely shredded Parmesan cheese (1 ounce). Drizzle with 2 tablespoons melted butter; toss to coat.

Herbed Root Vegetable Cobbler

Photo on page 141

PREP 45 minutes BAKE 1 hour 12 minutes at 400°F STAND 20 minutes MAKES 12 servings

- 1 pound Yukon gold potatoes, cut into 1-inch pieces
- 1 pound rutabaga, peeled and cut into 1-inch pieces
- 4 medium carrots, cut into 1-inch pieces
- 2 medium parsnips, peeled and cut into 1-inch pieces
- 1 red onion, cut into thin wedges
- 2 cloves garlic, minced
- 1 cup chicken broth
- 1½ teaspoons dried fines herbes, herbes de Provence, or Italian seasoning, crushed
- ½ teaspoon salt
- ¼ teaspoon ground black pepper
- 1 4-ounce container semisoft cheese with garlic and fines herbes
- 1 recipe Herbed Parmesan Dumplings

1 Preheat oven to 400°F. In an ungreased 3-quart shallow baking dish combine potatoes, rutabaga, carrots, parsnips, onion, and garlic.

2 In a small bowl combine broth, fines herbes, salt, and pepper. Pour broth mixture over vegetables, stirring to coat. Bake, covered, about 1 hour or until vegetables are nearly tender. Uncover vegetables;* stir in cheese.

3 Drop Herbed Parmesan Dumplings batter into 12 mounds on top of hot vegetables. Bake, uncovered, for 12 to 15 minutes more or until a wooden toothpick inserted in the centers of dumplings comes out clean. Let stand for 20 minutes before serving.

NUTRITION FACTS PER SERVING:
235 cal., 11 g total fat (6 g sat. fat), 61 mg chol., 424 mg sodium, 29 g carb., 4 g fiber, 6 g pro.

165

Herbed Parmesan Dumplings

In a medium bowl stir together 1½ cups all-purpose flour; 2 teaspoons baking powder; 1½ teaspoons dried fines herbes, herbes de Provence, or Italian seasoning, crushed; and ½ teaspoon salt. Using a pastry blender, cut in 6 tablespoons butter until mixture resembles coarse crumbs. Stir in ¼ cup finely shredded Parmesan cheese (1 ounce). In a small bowl combine 2 lightly beaten eggs and ⅓ cup milk. Add egg mixture all at once to flour mixture. Stir just until moistened.

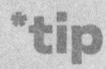
*tip

Be sure to uncover the vegetables so the steam escapes away from you.

Creamed Corn Casserole

PREP 15 minutes BAKE 50 minutes at 375°F MAKES 12 servings

Nonstick cooking spray

2 16-ounce packages frozen
   whole kernel corn

1 tablespoon butter

2 cups chopped red and/or
   green sweet peppers
   (2 medium)

1 cup chopped onion (1 large)

¼ teaspoon ground black pepper

1 10.75-ounce can condensed
   cream of celery soup

1 8-ounce tub cream cheese
   spread with chive and onion
   or cream cheese spread with
   garden vegetables

¼ cup milk

1 Preheat oven to 375°F. Lightly coat a 2-quart casserole with cooking spray; set aside. Place corn in a colander. Run cool water over corn to thaw; drain and set aside.

2 In a large saucepan heat butter over medium heat until melted. Add sweet peppers and onion; cook until tender, stirring occasionally. Stir in thawed corn and black pepper. In a medium bowl combine soup, cream cheese spread, and milk. Stir soup mixture into corn mixture. Transfer to the prepared casserole.

3 Bake, covered, for 50 to 55 minutes or until heated through, stirring once.

NUTRITION FACTS PER SERVING:
169 cal., 9 g total fat (4 g sat. fat), 26 mg chol., 270 mg sodium, 21 g carb., 3 g fiber, 5 g pro.

166

Slow Cooker Directions: Prepare as directed, except do not thaw the corn and omit the nonstick cooking spray and butter. In a 3½- or 4-quart slow cooker combine frozen corn, sweet peppers, onion, and black pepper. In a medium bowl combine soup, cream cheese spread, and milk. Pour soup mixture over corn mixture in cooker. Cover and cook on low-heat setting for 8 to 10 hours or on high-heat setting for 4 to 5 hours. Stir before serving.

New Potato Bake

PREP 25 minutes   BAKE 25 minutes at 375°F   STAND 10 minutes   MAKES 6 servings

1½   pounds tiny new potatoes,
      quartered
1   6-ounce package fresh baby
      spinach (about 5 cups)
1   tablespoon butter
½   cup chopped green onions (4)
1   tablespoon all-purpose flour
¼   teaspoon salt
⅛   teaspoon cayenne pepper
      Pinch ground nutmeg
1   cup milk
1   cup shredded Swiss cheese
      (4 ounces)

1 Preheat oven to 375°F. Lightly grease a 2-quart square baking dish; set aside. In a covered large saucepan cook potatoes in enough lightly salted boiling water to cover for 8 minutes. Stir in spinach; drain well. Return potato mixture to pan.

2 Meanwhile, for sauce, in a small saucepan heat butter over medium heat until melted. Add green onions; cook about 3 minutes or until softened. Stir in flour, salt, cayenne pepper, and nutmeg. Gradually stir in milk. Cook and stir until thickened and bubbly. Stir in ½ cup of the cheese until melted.

3 Pour sauce over potato mixture; stir gently to combine. Transfer mixture to the prepared baking dish. Sprinkle with the remaining ½ cup cheese.

4 Bake, uncovered, for 25 to 30 minutes or until potatoes are tender. Let stand for 10 minutes before serving.

NUTRITION FACTS PER SERVING:
210 cal., 8 g total fat (5 g sat. fat), 26 mg chol., 192 mg sodium, 25 g carb., 3 g fiber, 10 g pro.

167

tip
If you're cooking for a crowd, double the ingredients and bake this side dish in a 3-quart rectangular baking dish.

Cheesy Potluck Potatoes

PREP 20 minutes BAKE 30 minutes at 350°F MAKES 10 servings

2   to 2¼ pounds small red potatoes, coarsely chopped (about 6 cups)

1   cup chopped onion (1 large)

1   8-ounce carton sour cream

1   cup shredded Monterey Jack cheese (4 ounces)

1   cup shredded sharp cheddar cheese (4 ounces)

½   teaspoon salt

¼   to ½ teaspoon cayenne pepper

1   14.5-ounce can diced tomatoes, drained

1 Preheat oven to 350°F. In a covered large saucepan cook potatoes and onion in enough lightly salted boiling water to cover for 10 to 12 minutes or until potatoes are tender; drain. Stir in sour cream, Monterey Jack cheese, cheddar cheese, salt, and cayenne pepper. Stir in tomatoes.

2 Transfer mixture to an ungreased 2-quart rectangular baking dish. Bake, uncovered, about 30 minutes or until heated through.

NUTRITION FACTS PER SERVING: *214 cal., 12 g total fat (8 g sat. fat), 32 mg chol., 268 mg sodium, 19 g carb., 2 g fiber, 9 g pro.*

Soups and Stews

A steaming hot bowl of soup is the
epitome of comfort food, and these
simmering favorites will fill your
stomach and satisfy the soul.

5

Kansas City Steak Soup

Photo on page 144

PREP 20 minutes COOK 20 minutes MAKES 6 servings

1½ pounds lean ground beef
1 cup chopped onion (1 large)
1 cup sliced celery (2 stalks)
2 14.5-ounce cans lower-sodium beef broth
1 28-ounce can diced tomatoes, undrained
1 10-ounce package frozen mixed vegetables
2 tablespoons bottled steak sauce
2 teaspoons Worcestershire sauce
¼ teaspoon salt
¼ teaspoon ground black pepper
¼ cup all-purpose flour
   Steak sauce (optional)

1 In a large Dutch oven cook ground beef, onion, and celery over medium-high heat until meat is brown and vegetables are tender, using a wooden spoon to break up meat as it cooks. Drain off fat.

2 Stir in 1 can of the broth, the tomatoes, frozen vegetables, steak sauce, Worcestershire sauce, salt, and pepper. Bring to boiling; reduce heat. Simmer, covered, for 20 minutes.

3 In a medium bowl whisk together the remaining can of broth and flour; stir into mixture in Dutch oven. Cook until thickened and bubbly. Cook and stir for 1 minute more. Serve with additional steak sauce, if desired.

NUTRITION FACTS PER SERVING:
306 cal., 12 g total fat (5 g sat. fat), 74 mg chol., 747 mg sodium, 21 g carb., 4 g fiber, 27 g pro.

170

Easy Beef and Noodle Soup

START TO FINISH **25 minutes** MAKES **4 servings**

1 pound lean ground beef

2½ cups water

1 10.75-ounce can condensed cream of onion soup

1 10.5-ounce can condensed beef broth

1½ cups dried medium egg noodles

2 tablespoons dried parsley flakes

Finely shredded Parmesan cheese (optional)

1 In a large saucepan or skillet cook ground beef over medium-high heat until brown, using a wooden spoon to break up meat as it cooks. Drain off fat. Stir in water, soup, broth, noodles, and parsley.

2 Bring to boiling; reduce heat. Simmer, covered, about 5 minutes or until noodles are tender, stirring occasionally. If desired, sprinkle each serving with cheese.

NUTRITION FACTS PER SERVING:
357 cal., 19 g total fat (7 g sat. fat), 98 mg chol., 1218 mg sodium, 19 g carb., 1 g fiber, 27 g pro.

All-American Cheeseburger Soup

START TO FINISH 40 minutes MAKES 6 servings

- 1 pound ground beef
- ½ cup chopped onion (1 medium)
- ½ cup chopped celery (1 stalk)
- 2 cloves garlic, minced
- 2 tablespoons all-purpose flour
- 2 14.5-ounce cans lower-sodium beef broth
- 2 cups coarsely chopped potatoes (2 medium)
- 2 cups shredded cheddar and American cheese blend (8 ounces)
- 1 14.5-ounce can diced tomatoes, drained
- 1 6-ounce can tomato paste
- ¼ cup ketchup
- 2 tablespoons Dijon-style mustard
- 1 cup whole milk
- 3 cocktail buns or brown-and-serve rolls, split and toasted* (optional)

  Cheeseburger toppings, such as pickles, onions, lettuce, Dijon-style mustard, and/or ketchup (optional)

1 In a 4-quart Dutch oven cook ground beef, onion, celery, and garlic over medium-high heat until meat is brown and vegetables are tender, using a wooden spoon to break up meat as it cooks. Drain off fat.

2 Sprinkle meat mixture with flour; cook and stir for 2 minutes. Stir in broth and potatoes. Bring to boiling, stirring occasionally; reduce heat. Simmer, covered, about 10 minutes or until potatoes are tender.

3 Stir in cheese, tomatoes, tomato paste, ¼ cup ketchup, and 2 tablespoons mustard. Cook and stir until cheese is melted and mixture just comes to a gentle boil. Stir in milk; heat through. If desired, serve with toasted buns and cheeseburger toppings.

NUTRITION FACTS PER SERVING:
477 cal., 27 g total fat (13 g sat. fat), 93 mg chol., 1309 mg sodium, 28 g carb., 4 g fiber, 29 g pro.

172

*tip
To toast buns, preheat broiler. Place split buns, cut sides up, on a baking sheet. Brush lightly with 1 tablespoon melted butter or olive oil. Broil 3 to 4 inches from the heat about 1 minute or until toasted. Or using a grill pan, brush buns as directed and cook buns, cut sides down, over medium-high heat for 1 to 2 minutes or until toasted.

Goulash

PREP 35 minutes   COOK 1 hour 15 minutes   MAKES 6 servings

1 pound boneless beef top round steak

2 tablespoons vegetable oil

½ cup chopped onion (1 medium)

2 tablespoons all-purpose flour

1 tablespoon Hungarian paprika

2 cloves garlic, minced

3 14.5-ounce cans chicken broth

1 14.5-ounce can diced tomatoes, undrained

1½ cups sliced carrots (3 medium)

2 tablespoons tomato paste

1 bay leaf

½ teaspoon dried marjoram, crushed

½ teaspoon caraway seeds, crushed

½ teaspoon ground black pepper

2 cups cubed, peeled potatoes (2 medium)

Sour cream (optional)

1 Trim fat from meat. Cut meat into ½-inch pieces. In a 4- to 5-quart Dutch oven heat oil over medium-high heat. Add meat and onion; cook about 5 minutes or until meat is brown.

2 Sprinkle meat mixture with flour, paprika, and garlic; cook and stir for 3 minutes. Gradually stir in broth, tomatoes, carrots, tomato paste, bay leaf, marjoram, caraway seeds, and pepper. Bring to boiling; reduce heat. Simmer, covered, for 50 minutes, stirring occasionally.

3 Stir in potatoes. Simmer, covered, for 25 to 30 minutes more or until meat and potatoes are tender. Remove and discard bay leaf. If desired, top each serving with sour cream.

NUTRITION FACTS PER SERVING:
235 cal., 7 g total fat (1 g sat. fat), 39 mg chol., 1074 mg sodium, 22 g carb., 3 g fiber, 21 g pro.

Meatball Tortilla Soup

Photo on page 144

PREP 30 minutes BAKE 15 minutes (meatballs) at 350°F COOK 20 minutes MAKES 6 servings

2 tablespoons vegetable oil

3 6- to 7-inch corn or flour tortillas, cut into strips

1 recipe Tex-Mex Meatballs

2 14.5-ounce cans Mexican-style stewed tomatoes, undrained and cut up

2 14.5-ounce cans chicken broth

1 15-ounce can black beans, rinsed and drained

1 cup frozen whole kernel corn

2 teaspoons chili powder

Snipped fresh cilantro (optional)

1 In a large skillet heat oil over medium-high heat. Add tortilla strips; cook and stir for 3 to 4 minutes or until crisp. Using a slotted spoon, remove tortilla strips and drain on paper towels.

2 In a large saucepan combine Tex-Mex Meatballs, tomatoes, broth, beans, corn, and chili powder. Bring to boiling; reduce heat. Simmer, covered, for 20 minutes.

3 Ladle soup into bowls; top with fried tortilla strips. If desired, sprinkle with cilantro.

NUTRITION FACTS PER SERVING:
393 cal., 18 g total fat (5 g sat. fat), 88 mg chol., 1485 mg sodium, 36 g carb., 8 g fiber, 24 g pro.

Tex-Mex Meatballs

Preheat oven to 350°F. In a large bowl combine 1 lightly beaten egg, $\frac{1}{3}$ cup canned diced green chile peppers, $\frac{1}{4}$ cup fine dry bread crumbs, $\frac{1}{4}$ cup finely chopped onion, and half of a 1.25-ounce envelope taco seasoning mix. Add 1 pound lean ground beef; mix well. On a cutting board, pat mixture into a 6×4-inch rectangle. Cut into twenty-four 1-inch squares. Shape each square into a meatball. Arrange meatballs in a 15×10×1-inch baking pan. Bake for 15 to 20 minutes or until done (160°F), rotating pan once. Drain off fat.

Chili

PREP **15 minutes** COOK **20 minutes** MAKES **4 servings**

1 **pound ground beef**

½ **cup chopped green sweet pepper (1 small)**

½ **cup chopped onion (1 medium)**

4 **cloves garlic, minced**

1 **15-ounce can tomato sauce**

1 **15-ounce can red kidney beans, rinsed and drained**

1 **14.5-ounce can diced tomatoes, undrained**

2 **to 3 teaspoons chili powder**

½ **teaspoon salt**

½ **teaspoon dried basil, crushed, or ground cumin**

¼ **teaspoon ground black pepper**

Shredded cheddar cheese (optional)

Sour cream (optional)

Chopped green onions (optional)

Bottled hot pepper sauce (optional)

1 In a large saucepan or Dutch oven cook ground beef, sweet pepper, ½ cup onion, and garlic over medium-high heat until meat is brown and onion is tender, using a wooden spoon to break up meat as it cooks. Drain off fat.

2 Stir in tomato sauce, beans, tomatoes, chili powder, salt, basil, and black pepper. Bring to boiling; reduce heat. Simmer, covered, for 20 minutes.

3 If desired, top each serving with cheese, sour cream, and/or green onions, and serve with hot pepper sauce.

NUTRITION FACTS PER SERVING:
381 cal., 15 g total fat (6 g sat. fat), 71 mg chol., 1265 mg sodium, 35 g carb., 9 g fiber, 32 g pro.

tip

Set up a buffet of tasty toppers for your chili. In addition to cheese and sliced green onions, try these flavor boosters:

• Combine one 9-ounce carton sour cream and ¼ cup snipped fresh cilantro. If desired, add a squeeze of fresh lime juice.

• Combine 1 firm, ripe avocado, pitted, peeled, and chopped; 2 cups cherry tomatoes, quartered; 1 tablespoon lime juice; and 1 fresh jalapeño chile pepper, seeded and chopped.

Soups and Stews

Mustard-Herb Beef Stew

PREP 30 minutes COOK 1 hour MAKES 6 servings

$\frac{1}{3}$ cup all-purpose flour

1 tablespoon snipped fresh Italian (flat-leaf) parsley

1 teaspoon snipped fresh thyme or $\frac{1}{2}$ teaspoon dried thyme, crushed

1 teaspoon ground black pepper

$\frac{1}{2}$ teaspoon salt

$1\frac{1}{2}$ pounds boneless beef chuck roast

2 tablespoons olive oil

4 medium carrots, cut into 1-inch pieces

8 tiny Yukon gold potatoes, halved

8 to 10 ounces cipollini onions, peeled, or 1 medium onion, cut into wedges

8 ounces fresh cremini mushrooms, halved if large

3 tablespoons tomato paste

2 tablespoons spicy brown mustard

1 14.5-ounce can beef broth

1 12-ounce bottle dark porter beer or nonalcoholic beer

1 bay leaf

1 In a large bowl stir together flour, parsley, thyme, pepper, and salt. Trim fat from meat. Cut meat into 1- to $1\frac{1}{2}$-inch pieces. Add meat, a few pieces at a time, to flour mixture, stirring to coat. Reserve leftover flour mixture.

2 In a 6-quart Dutch oven cook meat in hot oil over medium-high heat until brown. Stir in carrots, potatoes, onions, and mushrooms. Cook and stir for 3 minutes. Stir in tomato paste, mustard, and the reserved flour mixture. Add broth, beer, and bay leaf. Bring to boiling; reduce heat. Simmer, covered, for 1 to $1\frac{1}{4}$ hours or until meat is tender. Remove and discard bay leaf.

NUTRITION FACTS PER SERVING:
426 cal., 11 g total fat (3 g sat. fat), 50 mg chol., 880 mg sodium, 43 g carb., 5 g fiber, 33 g pro.

176

Luck o' the Irish Stew

PREP 25 minutes COOK 1 hour 15 minutes MAKES 6 servings

- 1 pound boneless lamb or beef chuck roast
- 4 cups beef broth
- 2 medium onions, cut into wedges
- 1 bay leaf
- ¼ teaspoon ground black pepper
- 4 medium potatoes (about 1½ pounds), peeled and quartered
- 6 medium carrots, cut into ½-inch pieces
- ½ teaspoon dried thyme, crushed
- ¼ teaspoon dried basil, crushed
- ½ cup cold water
- ¼ cup all-purpose flour
- Salt
- Ground black pepper
- Fresh thyme sprigs (optional)

1 Trim fat from meat. Cut meat into ¾-inch pieces. In a large saucepan combine meat, broth, onions, bay leaf, and ¼ teaspoon pepper. Bring to boiling; reduce heat. Simmer, covered, for 45 minutes. Skim off fat.

2 Add potatoes, carrots, dried thyme, and basil. Return to boiling; reduce heat. Simmer, covered, for 30 to 35 minutes more or until vegetables are tender. Remove and discard bay leaf.

3 In a small bowl combine the water and flour; stir into meat mixture. Cook and stir until thickened and bubbly. Cook and stir for 1 minute more. Season to taste with salt and additional pepper. If desired, garnish with fresh thyme sprigs.

NUTRITION FACTS PER SERVING:
230 cal., 3 g total fat (1 g sat. fat), 48 mg chol., 649 mg sodium, 30 g carb., 4 g fiber, 20 g pro.

177

Vegetable-Pork Oven Stew

PREP 30 minutes BAKE 2 hours at 325°F MAKES 6 servings

1½ **pounds boneless pork shoulder roast or pork stew meat**

1 **tablespoon vegetable oil**

1½ **cups coarsely chopped onions (3 medium)**

2 **14.5-ounce cans reduced-sodium chicken or vegetable broth**

1 **teaspoon dried thyme, crushed**

1 **teaspoon dried oregano, crushed**

1 **teaspoon lemon-pepper seasoning**

½ **teaspoon salt**

¼ **cup all-purpose flour**

1 **16-ounce package frozen whole kernel corn**

1 **pound tiny new potatoes, halved**

2 **cups fresh green beans cut into 2-inch pieces, or frozen cut green beans**

1 Preheat oven to 325°F. Trim fat from meat. Cut meat into ¾-inch pieces. In a 4-quart oven-going Dutch oven cook half of the meat in hot oil over medium-high heat until brown. Using a slotted spoon, remove meat from Dutch oven. Add the remaining meat and onions; cook until meat is brown. Drain off fat. Return all of the meat to Dutch oven.

2 Reserve ½ cup of the broth and set aside. Stir the remaining broth, thyme, oregano, lemon-pepper seasoning, and salt into meat mixture. Bring to boiling. Cover tightly; transfer Dutch oven to oven. Bake for 1 hour.

3 In a small bowl combine the reserved ½ cup broth and the flour; stir into meat mixture. Stir in corn, potatoes, and green beans. Bake, covered, about 1 hour more or until meat and vegetables are tender and mixture is slightly thickened.

NUTRITION FACTS PER SERVING:
308 cal., 8 g total fat (2 g sat. fat), 46 mg chol., 625 mg sodium, 41 g carb., 6 g fiber, 20 g pro.

Brazilian Pork and Black Bean Stew

PREP 1 hour 15 minutes   STAND 1 hour   COOK 2 hours 45 minutes   MAKES 10 servings

- 1 pound dried black beans
- 2 pounds boneless pork shoulder roast
- 3 tablespoons vegetable oil
- 1½ pounds meaty smoked pork hocks or meaty ham bone
- 2 cups chopped onions (2 large)
- 6 cloves garlic, minced
- 1 teaspoon cayenne pepper
- 1 14.5-ounce can diced tomatoes, undrained
- 8 ounces cooked link sausage flavored with garlic or kielbasa, sliced ½ inch thick
- ½ cup snipped fresh parsley
- ½ teaspoon salt
- 5 cups hot cooked rice
  Hot cooked collard greens (optional)
  Orange wedges

1 Rinse beans; drain. In a 4-quart Dutch oven combine beans and 8 cups water. Bring to boiling; reduce heat. Simmer, uncovered, for 2 minutes. Remove from heat. Cover and let stand for 1 hour. (Or place beans in water in Dutch oven. Cover and let soak in a cool place for 6 to 8 hours or overnight.) Drain and rinse beans.

2 Trim fat from pork roast. Cut roast into 1½-inch pieces. In the same Dutch oven heat 2 tablespoons of the oil over medium-high heat. Add roast, half at a time, and cook until brown. Drain off fat. Return all of the roast to Dutch oven. Add beans, pork hocks, and 4 cups fresh water. Bring to boiling; reduce heat. Simmer, covered, for 2 hours. Remove pork hocks from Dutch oven. When cool enough to handle, remove meat from bones; discard bones. Using two forks, pull meat apart into shreds. Return shredded meat to Dutch oven.

3 Meanwhile, in a large skillet heat the remaining 1 tablespoon oil over medium-high heat. Add onions; cook for 5 minutes, stirring occasionally. Add garlic and cayenne pepper; cook and stir for 30 seconds. Add tomatoes; cook for 10 minutes more, stirring occasionally. Stir tomato mixture, sausage, parsley, and salt into bean mixture. Simmer, uncovered, for 30 minutes. Serve with rice and, if desired, collard greens. Squeeze an orange wedge over each serving.

NUTRITION FACTS PER SERVING:
726 cal., 33 g total fat (11 g sat. fat), 110 mg chol., 1017 mg sodium, 64 g carb., 10 g fiber, 43 g pro.

Pea Soup

PREP 20 minutes   COOK 45 minutes   MAKES 4 servings

1   bay leaf
2   whole cloves
1   sprig fresh thyme
¼   cup butter
1   cup chopped celery (2 stalks)
½   cup chopped onion
    (1 medium)
1   clove garlic, minced
2   14.5-ounce cans reduced-
    sodium chicken broth
1   pound meaty smoked pork
    hocks or meaty ham bone
1   cup dried split peas, rinsed
    and drained
¼   cup shredded carrot
⅛   teaspoon ground black pepper
½   cup milk
    Bottled hot pepper sauce
    Finely shredded Parmesan
    cheese (optional)

1   Place bay leaf, cloves, and thyme sprig in the center of a double-thick, 6-inch square of 100-percent-cotton cheesecloth. Bring up corners; tie closed with clean kitchen string. Set aside.

2   In a large saucepan or 4-quart Dutch oven heat butter over medium heat until melted. Add celery, onion, and garlic; cook about 5 minutes or until tender, stirring occasionally. Add cheesecloth bag, broth, pork hocks, split peas, carrot, and pepper. Bring to boiling; reduce heat. Simmer, covered, for 45 to 55 minutes or until split peas are tender, stirring occasionally.

3   Remove and discard cheesecloth bag. Remove pork hocks from Dutch oven. When cool enough to handle, remove meat from bones; discard bones. Chop meat. Return meat to Dutch oven. Stir in milk and hot pepper sauce; heat through. If desired, sprinkle each serving with cheese.

NUTRITION FACTS PER SERVING:
352 cal., 16 g total fat (9 g sat. fat), 47 mg chol., 987 mg sodium, 35 g carb., 13 g fiber, 20 g pro.

Ham and Bean Soup

PREP **45 minutes** STAND **1 hour** COOK **1 hour** MAKES **4 servings**

1   **cup dried navy beans**

1   **tablespoon butter**

1   **to 1½ pounds meaty smoked pork hocks or meaty ham bone**

1½   **cups sliced celery (3 stalks)**

1½   **cups chopped onions (3 medium)**

1   **bay leaf**

¾   **teaspoon dried thyme, crushed**

¼   **teaspoon salt**

¼   **teaspoon ground black pepper**

    Salt

    Ground black pepper

1 Rinse beans, drain. In a large Dutch oven combine beans and 4 cups water. Bring to boiling; reduce heat. Simmer, uncovered, for 2 minutes. Remove from heat. Cover and let stand for 1 hour. (Or place beans in water in Dutch oven. Cover and let soak in a cool place for 6 to 8 hours or overnight.) Drain and rinse beans; set aside.

2 In the same Dutch oven heat butter over medium-high heat until melted. Add pork hocks; cook until brown on all sides. Add celery and onions; cook until tender, stirring occasionally. Add beans, 4 cups fresh water, bay leaf, thyme, ¼ teaspoon salt, and ¼ teaspoon pepper. Bring to boiling; reduce heat. Simmer, covered, for 1 to 1½ hours or until beans are tender.

3 Remove pork hocks from Dutch oven. When cool enough to handle, remove meat from bones; coarsely chop meat. Discard bones and bay leaf. Using a potato masher, slightly mash beans in Dutch oven. Stir in chopped meat; heat through. Season to taste with additional salt and pepper.

Slow Cooker Directions: Rinse beans; drain. In a large saucepan combine beans and enough water to cover beans by 2 inches. Bring to boiling; reduce heat. Simmer, uncovered, for 10 minutes. Remove from heat. Cover and let stand for 1 hour. Drain and rinse beans. In a 3½- or 4-quart slow cooker combine pork hocks, celery, onions, bay leaf, thyme, ¼ teaspoon salt, and ¼ teaspoon pepper. Omit butter. Stir in beans and 4 cups fresh water. Cover and cook on low-heat setting for 8 to 10 hours or on high-heat setting for 4 to 5 hours. Remove pork hocks. When cool enough to handle, remove meat from bones; coarsely chop meat. Discard bones and bay leaf. Slightly mash beans in slow cooker. Stir in chopped meat. Season to taste with additional salt and pepper.

Easy Ham and Bean Soup

Prepare as directed, except omit dried navy beans, pork hocks, water, and salt. Cook celery and onions in butter as directed in Step 2. Add 4 cups chicken broth; two 15-ounce cans navy beans, rinsed and drained; and 1 cup cubed cooked ham (5 ounces) with bay leaf, thyme, and ¼ teaspoon pepper. Bring to boiling; reduce heat. Simmer, uncovered, about 20 minutes or until heated through. Remove bay leaf. Slightly mash beans in Dutch oven. Makes 4 servings.

NUTRITION FACTS PER SERVING:
267 cal., 5 g total fat (3 g sat. fat), 26 mg chol., 750 mg sodium, 37 g carb., 14 g fiber, 18 g pro.

Three-Cheese Beer Soup

START TO FINISH 45 minutes   MAKES 10 servings

1½ cups shredded sharp cheddar
    cheese (6 ounces)

1¼ cups shredded white cheddar
    cheese (5 ounces)

¼   cup butter

½   cup finely chopped onion
    (1 medium)

½   cup finely chopped carrot
    (1 medium)

¼   cup thinly sliced green
    onions (2)

2   cloves garlic, minced

½   cup all-purpose flour

½   teaspoon dry mustard

5   cups chicken broth

1   12-ounce bottle beer

1   cup whipping cream

1½ cups frozen diced hash brown
    potatoes

1½ cups small broccoli florets

10 slices bacon, crisp-cooked,
    drained, and chopped

⅓   cup grated Parmesan or
    Romano cheese

½   teaspoon bottled hot pepper
    sauce

½   teaspoon Worcestershire
    sauce

1 Allow cheddar cheeses to stand at room temperature for 30 minutes. Meanwhile, in a 4-quart Dutch oven heat butter over medium heat until melted. Add ½ cup onion, carrot, green onions, and garlic. Cook for 8 to 10 minutes or until vegetables are tender, stirring occasionally.

2 Stir in flour and dry mustard (mixture will be thick). Gradually stir in broth. Cook and stir until bubbly. Add beer and whipping cream; stir in hash brown potatoes and broccoli. Bring to boiling; reduce heat. Simmer, uncovered, for 5 minutes, stirring occasionally.

3 Gradually add cheddar cheeses, stirring after each addition until cheeses are melted. Stir in bacon, Parmesan cheese, hot pepper sauce, and Worcestershire sauce.

NUTRITION FACTS PER SERVING:
390 cal., 29 g total fat (17 g sat. fat), 90 mg chol., 964 mg sodium, 16 g carb., 1 g fiber, 15 g pro.

Baked Potato Soup

Photo on page 142

PREP 35 minutes BAKE 40 minutes at 425°F MAKES 5 servings

- 2 large baking potatoes (about 8 ounces each)
- 3 tablespoons butter
- 6 tablespoons thinly sliced green onions (3)
- 3 tablespoons all-purpose flour
- 2 teaspoons snipped fresh dill or chives or ¼ teaspoon dried dill
- ¼ teaspoon salt
- ¼ teaspoon ground black pepper
- 4 cups milk
- 1¼ cups shredded American cheese (5 ounces)
- 4 slices bacon, crisp-cooked, drained, and crumbled

1 Preheat oven to 425°F. Scrub potatoes thoroughly with a brush; pat dry. Prick potatoes several times with a fork. Bake for 40 to 60 minutes or until tender; cool slightly. Cut potatoes in half lengthwise. Gently scoop out pulp, breaking up any large pieces. Discard potato skins.

2 In a large saucepan heat butter over medium heat until melted. Add half of the green onions; cook and stir until tender. Stir in flour, dill, salt, and pepper. Gradually stir in milk. Cook and stir for 12 to 15 minutes or until thickened and bubbly. Add potato pulp and 1 cup of the cheese, stirring until cheese is melted.

3 Ladle soup into bowls. Top with the remaining ¼ cup cheese, the remaining green onions, and the bacon.

NUTRITION FACTS PER SERVING:
377 cal., 23 g total fat (14 g sat. fat), 67 mg chol., 801 mg sodium, 26 g carb., 1 g fiber, 17 g pro.

183

Pasta Fagioli

PREP 20 minutes   COOK 20 minutes   MAKES 6 servings

1	tablespoon olive oil
1	cup chopped onion (1 large)
3	ounces pancetta or bacon, chopped
3	cloves garlic, thinly sliced
¾	cup dry red wine
2	15- to 19-ounce cans cannellini beans (white kidney beans), rinsed and drained
2	14.5-ounce cans chicken broth
1	28-ounce can crushed tomatoes
1	teaspoon salt
¼	teaspoon crushed red pepper
1½	cups dried ditali pasta
¼	cup snipped fresh basil
1	tablespoon snipped fresh oregano
	Shaved Parmesan cheese (optional)
	Fresh oregano leaves (optional)

1 In a 4-quart Dutch oven heat oil over medium heat. Add onion, pancetta, and garlic; cook about 5 minutes or until onion is tender, stirring occasionally. Remove from heat. Add wine; return to heat. Stir to scrape up any crusty brown bits.

2 Stir in beans, broth, tomatoes, salt, and crushed red pepper. Bring to boiling; reduce heat. Simmer, covered, for 20 minutes.

3 Meanwhile, cook pasta according to package directions; drain. Stir cooked pasta, basil, and snipped oregano into bean mixture. If desired, garnish each serving with cheese and oregano leaves.

NUTRITION FACTS PER SERVING:
415 cal., 9 g total fat (2 g sat. fat), 11 mg chol., 1577 mg sodium, 68 g carb., 11 g fiber, 19 g pro.

tip
You can use elbow macaroni if you are unable to find ditali pasta.

Chicken and Wild Rice Soup

PREP 30 minutes   COOK 50 minutes   MAKES 4 servings

1 tablespoon butter

½ cup finely chopped carrot (1 medium)

½ cup finely chopped onion (1 medium)

½ cup finely chopped celery (1 stalk)

4 cups chicken broth

¾ cup uncooked wild rice, rinsed and drained

12 ounces skinless, boneless chicken breast halves, cut into ¾-inch pieces

2 tablespoons all-purpose flour

2 tablespoons butter, softened

2 cups half-and-half or light cream

Salt

Ground black pepper

1 In a Dutch oven heat 1 tablespoon butter over medium heat until melted. Add carrot, onion, and celery; cook about 5 minutes or until tender, stirring occasionally. Add broth and rice. Bring to boiling; reduce heat. Simmer, covered, for 30 minutes. Stir in chicken. Simmer, covered, for 20 to 25 minutes more or until rice is tender.

2 In a small bowl combine flour and 2 tablespoons softened butter to make a smooth paste. Stir flour mixture into rice mixture. Cook and stir until thickened and bubbly. Cook and stir for 1 minute more. Add half-and-half. Cook and stir over medium heat until heated through. Season to taste with salt and pepper.

NUTRITION FACTS PER SERVING: *479 cal., 24 g total fat (14 g sat. fat), 119 mg chol., 1213 mg sodium, 36 g carb., 3 g fiber, 30 g pro.*

185

Chicken Soup with Chive Dumplings

PREP 45 minutes COOK 35 minutes MAKES 6 servings

1 **pound skinless, boneless chicken breast halves**

Salt

Ground black pepper

2 **tablespoons olive oil**

1 **cup chopped carrots (2 medium)**

1 **cup chopped celery (2 stalks)**

⅓ **cup chopped leek (1 medium)**

6 **cups chicken broth**

4 **sprigs fresh thyme**

1 **bay leaf**

1½ **cups all-purpose flour**

1 **tablespoon snipped fresh chives**

2 **teaspoons baking powder**

1 **teaspoon salt**

3 **tablespoons butter**

¾ **cup milk**

¼ **cup snipped fresh Italian (flat-leaf) parsley**

1 Sprinkle chicken with salt and pepper. In a large Dutch oven cook chicken in hot oil over medium-high heat until brown on both sides. Reduce heat to medium. Cook, covered, for 7 to 9 minutes or until chicken is no longer pink (170°F). Remove chicken; cool.

2 Add carrots, celery, and leek to Dutch oven. Cook, covered, for 5 to 7 minutes or until vegetables are tender.

3 Cut chicken into ½-inch pieces. Return chicken to Dutch oven. Add broth, thyme, and bay leaf. Bring to boiling; reduce heat. Simmer, uncovered, for 15 minutes.

4 Meanwhile, for dumplings, in a medium bowl stir together flour, chives, baking powder, and 1 teaspoon salt. Using a pastry blender, cut in butter until mixture resembles coarse crumbs. Stir in milk just until combined.

5 Remove thyme and bay leaf from soup. Stir in parsley; season to taste with additional salt and pepper. Bring to boiling. Drop dumpling dough in mounds onto hot bubbling soup. Cook, uncovered, for 10 minutes. Reduce heat to medium-low. Cook, covered, about 10 minutes more or until a wooden toothpick inserted in the centers of dumplings comes out clean.

NUTRITION FACTS PER SERVING:
334 cal., 12 g total fat (5 g sat. fat), 62 mg chol., 1260 mg sodium, 30 g carb., 2 g fiber, 24 g pro.

tip

To vary the flavor, add fresh mushrooms with the carrots, celery, and leek and substitute dill for chives in the dumplings.

Chicken Noodle Soup

START TO FINISH 35 minutes   MAKES 4 servings

4½   cups chicken broth
1   cup chopped onion (1 large)
1   cup sliced carrots (2 medium)
1   cup sliced celery (2 stalks)
1   bay leaf
1   teaspoon dried basil, crushed
1   teaspoon dried oregano, crushed
¼   teaspoon ground black pepper
1½   cups dried medium egg noodles
2   cups cubed cooked chicken or turkey

1 In a large saucepan combine broth, onion, carrots, celery, bay leaf, basil, oregano, and pepper. Bring to boiling; reduce heat. Simmer, covered, for 5 minutes.

2 Stir in noodles. Return to boiling; reduce heat. Simmer, covered, for 8 to 10 minutes or until noodles are tender but still firm and vegetables are just tender. Remove and discard bay leaf. Stir in chicken; heat through.

NUTRITION FACTS PER SERVING:
241 cal., 7 g total fat (2 g sat. fat), 77 mg chol., 1190 mg sodium, 20 g carb., 3 g fiber, 24 g pro.

Chicken Posole Soup

Photo on page 143

PREP 30 minutes COOK 30 minutes MAKES 8 servings

2   teaspoons vegetable oil
¾   cup chopped onion
2   teaspoons ground cumin
1   teaspoon hot chili powder
4   cups chopped cooked chicken
2   14.5-ounce cans reduced-sodium chicken broth
1   28-ounce can whole peeled plum tomatoes in puree, undrained and cut up
1   15.5-ounce can golden or white hominy, drained
1   10-ounce package frozen whole kernel corn
2   4-ounce cans diced green chile peppers, drained
    Lime wedges (optional)
1   cup shredded Mexican cheese blend (4 ounces)
    Halved grape tomatoes, snipped fresh cilantro, sliced avocado, and/or corn tortilla chips

1 In a 4-quart Dutch oven heat oil over medium heat. Add onion, cumin, and chili powder; cook until onion is tender, stirring occasionally. Add chicken, broth, tomatoes, hominy, corn, and chile peppers. Bring to boiling; reduce heat. Simmer, uncovered, for 30 minutes, stirring occasionally.

2 To serve, ladle soup into bowls. If desired, squeeze a lime wedge over each serving. Sprinkle with cheese. Top with grape tomatoes, cilantro, avocado, and/or tortilla chips.

NUTRITION FACTS PER SERVING:
392 cal., 21 g total fat (7 g sat. fat), 75 mg chol., 1191 mg sodium, 32 g carb., 7 g fiber, 22 g pro.

Chicken and Sausage Gumbo

PREP 45 minutes COOK 1 hour MAKES 10 servings

- 1 cup all-purpose flour
- 2/3 cup vegetable oil
- 1 cup sliced celery (2 stalks)
- 1 cup chopped green sweet pepper (1 medium)
- 1/2 cup chopped onion (1 medium)
- 2 cloves garlic, minced
- 8 ounces cooked smoked sausage links, cut into 1-inch pieces
- 8 ounces cooked andouille sausage links, cut into 1/2-inch pieces
- 2 pounds meaty chicken pieces (breast halves, thighs, and drumsticks), skinned if desired
- 5 cups water
- 1 teaspoon salt
- 1/4 to 1/2 teaspoon cayenne pepper
- 1/4 teaspoon ground black pepper
- 5 cups hot cooked rice (optional)

1 For roux, in a large heavy Dutch oven stir together flour and oil until smooth. Cook over medium-high heat for 5 minutes. Reduce heat to medium. Cook and stir for 10 to 15 minutes or until roux is reddish brown in color (the deeper the color, the richer and more flavorful the gumbo). Stir in celery, sweet pepper, onion, and garlic; cook for 5 minutes more, stirring occasionally. Add sausages; cook until sausages are light brown, stirring occasionally.

2 Add chicken, the water, salt, cayenne pepper, and black pepper. Bring to boiling; reduce heat. Simmer, covered, about 1 hour or until chicken is no longer pink (170°F for breasts; 180°F for thighs and drumsticks). Skim off fat.

3 Remove chicken from Dutch oven. When chicken is cool enough to handle, remove meat from bones; discard skin (if present) and bones. Coarsely chop chicken and return to sausage mixture. Cook for 2 to 3 minutes or until chicken is heated through. If desired, serve with hot rice.

NUTRITION FACTS PER SERVING:
460 cal., 34 g total fat (9 g sat. fat), 72 mg chol., 961 mg sodium, 12 g carb., 1 g fiber, 25 g pro.

189

Caribbean Chicken Stew

PREP 50 minutes   COOK 40 minutes   MAKES 8 servings

- 1 tablespoon vegetable oil
- 2 onions, cut into 1-inch pieces
- 3 to 3½ pounds meaty chicken pieces (breast halves, thighs, and drumsticks)
- 2 14.5-ounce cans chicken broth
- 2½ pounds sweet potatoes, peeled and cut into 1-inch pieces
- 1 14.5-ounce can diced tomatoes, undrained
- 1 10-ounce package frozen whole kernel corn
- ½ to 1 teaspoon crushed red pepper
- ½ teaspoon salt
- 2 tablespoons grated fresh ginger or 1 teaspoon ground ginger
- 1 cup canned unsweetened coconut milk
- 4 cups hot cooked rice

1 In a 4- to 5-quart Dutch oven heat oil over medium-high heat. Add onions; cook about 5 minutes or until tender, stirring occasionally. Add chicken and broth. Bring to boiling; reduce heat. Simmer, covered, about 30 minutes or until chicken is no longer pink (170°F for breasts; 180°F for thighs and drumsticks). Remove chicken from Dutch oven. Skim fat from broth.

2 Add sweet potatoes, tomatoes, corn, crushed red pepper, and salt to Dutch oven. Return to boiling; reduce heat. Simmer, covered, for 10 to 15 minutes or until vegetables are tender.

3 Meanwhile, when chicken is cool enough to handle, remove meat from bones; discard skin and bones. Chop chicken.

4 Using a slotted spoon, remove 1½ cups of the vegetables from Dutch oven. Remove 1 cup of the broth from Dutch oven. Cool slightly. Transfer vegetables and broth to a food processor or blender. Cover and process or blend until smooth. Return pureed mixture to Dutch oven. Add chopped chicken and ginger; heat through. Stir in coconut milk. Serve over hot rice.

NUTRITION FACTS PER SERVING:
587 cal., 26 g total fat (10 g sat. fat), 86 mg chol., 731 mg sodium, 60 g carb., 5 g fiber, 28 g pro.

Alphabet Soup with Turkey Meatballs

PREP 35 minutes BAKE 12 minutes (meatballs) at 350°F MAKES 6 servings

- 2 teaspoons olive oil
- 1 medium onion, sliced
- 3 cloves garlic, minced
- 1 cup dry white wine or reduced-sodium chicken broth
- 1 32-ounce carton reduced-sodium chicken broth
- 1½ cups water
- 1 recipe Turkey Meatballs
- 1 pound fresh asparagus, trimmed and cut into bite-size pieces (about 2 cups)
- 1 medium yellow or red sweet pepper, seeded and cut into bite-size pieces
- 1 cup dried alphabet-shape pasta
- 2 tablespoons snipped fresh basil or 1 teaspoon dried Italian seasoning, crushed

  Salt

  Cracked black pepper

  Finely shredded Parmesan cheese (optional)

1 In a 4-quart Dutch oven heat oil over medium-high heat. Add onion and garlic; cook about 5 minutes or until tender, stirring occasionally. Remove from heat. Add wine; return to heat. Bring to boiling; reduce heat. Simmer, uncovered, about 5 minutes or until wine is reduced by half.

2 Add broth and the water. Return to boiling. Stir in Turkey Meatballs, asparagus, sweet pepper, pasta, and, if using, Italian seasoning. Reduce heat. Simmer, covered, about 8 minutes or until pasta is tender but still firm. Stir in basil, if using. Season to taste with salt and black pepper.

3 Ladle soup into bowls. If desired, sprinkle with cheese.

NUTRITION FACTS PER SERVING:
268 cal., 5 g total fat (1 g sat. fat), 27 mg chol., 565 mg sodium, 33 g carb., 3 g fiber, 16 g pro.

Turkey Meatballs

Preheat oven to 350°F. Line a 15×10×1-inch baking pan with foil. Coat foil with nonstick cooking spray. In a medium bowl combine ⅓ cup seasoned fine dry bread crumbs, 1 teaspoon grated Parmesan cheese or reduced-sodium Worcestershire sauce (optional), and pinch cayenne pepper. Add 8 ounces uncooked lean ground turkey; mix well. On a cutting board, pat mixture into a 6×4-inch rectangle. Cut into twenty-four 1-inch squares. Shape each square into a meatball. Arrange meatballs in the prepared baking pan. Bake for 12 to 15 minutes until no longer pink (165°F). Drain off any fat.

To Store Soups or Stews:
Let cool by placing the pot in a sink of ice water; stir so it cools quickly. Once cool, to refrigerate, divide the soup or stew among shallow containers. Cover and refrigerate up to 3 days. To freeze, divide soup or stew among shallow freezer-safe containers. Leave about ½-inch space between the top of the soup or stew and the rim of the container. Cover and freeze for up to 3 months. Avoid freezing soups or stews thickened with cornstarch or flour; freezing causes them to lose their thickening capacity.

Clam Chowder *Photo on page 144*

PREP 50 minutes COOK 15 minutes MAKES 8 servings

- 1½ pints shucked clams or three 6.5-ounce cans minced clams, undrained
- 6 slices bacon, halved crosswise
- 1½ cups chopped onions (3 medium)
- ¾ cup finely chopped celery
- ½ cup dry white wine
- 3 cups peeled and chopped potatoes (3 medium)
- 2 teaspoons instant chicken bouillon granules
- 1½ teaspoons snipped fresh thyme
- ¼ teaspoon ground black pepper
- ¼ teaspoon crushed red pepper
- 3 cups milk
- 1½ cups whipping cream
- 3 tablespoons all-purpose flour
- ¾ cup shredded Parmigiano-Reggiano or Parmesan cheese (3 ounces)
- Snipped fresh Italian (flat-leaf) parsley (optional)
- Shredded Parmigiano-Reggiano or Parmesan cheese (optional)

1. If using, chop fresh clams, reserving juice; set clams aside. Strain clam juice to remove bits of shell. (Or drain canned clams, reserving juice.) If necessary, add enough water to the reserved clam juice to measure 1½ cups liquid; set aside.

2. In a 4-quart Dutch oven cook bacon over medium heat until crisp. Remove bacon and drain on paper towels, reserving 2 tablespoons drippings in skillet. Crumble bacon; set aside. Add onions and celery to the reserved drippings; cook over medium heat until tender, stirring occasionally. Remove from heat.

3. Add wine; return to heat. Bring to boiling; reduce heat. Boil gently, uncovered, for 2 to 3 minutes. Stir in the reserved clam liquid, potatoes, bouillon granules, thyme, black pepper, and crushed red pepper. Return to boiling; reduce heat. Simmer, covered, about 15 minutes or until potatoes are tender. Using the back of a fork, mash potatoes slightly against sides of pan.

4. In a medium bowl stir together milk, whipping cream, and flour; stir into potato mixture. Bring to simmering. Cook and stir until slightly thickened. Stir in clams and ¾ cup cheese; reduce heat. Cook and stir for 1 to 2 minutes more or until heated through and cheese is melted. Sprinkle each serving with crumbled bacon and, if desired, parsley and additional cheese.

NUTRITION FACTS PER SERVING:
438 cal., 27 g total fat (15 g sat. fat), 113 mg chol., 583 mg sodium, 24 g carb., 2 g fiber, 22 g pro.

Easy Maryland Crab Bisque

START TO FINISH **20 minutes** MAKES **6 servings**

2¾ cups milk

1 **10.75-ounce can condensed cream of asparagus soup**

1 **10.75-ounce can condensed cream of mushroom soup**

1 **cup half-and-half or light cream**

1 **cup cooked lump crabmeat, cartilage removed, or one 6-ounce can crabmeat, drained, flaked, and cartilage removed**

3 **tablespoons dry sherry or milk**

Fresh chives (optional)

In a 3-quart saucepan combine milk, asparagus soup, mushroom soup, and half-and-half. Bring just to boiling over medium heat, stirring frequently. Stir in crabmeat and dry sherry; heat through. If desired, garnish each serving with chives.

NUTRITION FACTS PER SERVING: *225 cal., 12 g total fat (5 g sat. fat), 51 mg chol., 882 mg sodium, 15 g carb., 0 g fiber, 12 g pro.*

Easy Shrimp Bisque

Prepare as directed, except substitute cream of shrimp soup for the cream of mushroom soup and 8 ounces peeled and deveined cooked small shrimp for the crabmeat.

Easy Mushroom Bisque

Prepare as directed, except cook 2 cups sliced fresh button, stemmed shiitake, and/or portobello mushrooms in 2 tablespoons hot butter until tender, stirring occasionally. Continue as directed, omitting crabmeat and chives. If desired, garnish each serving with additional sautéed mushrooms and caramelized onions.

Oyster Stew

START TO FINISH 25 minutes   MAKES 6 servings

- 1 pint (about 3 dozen) shucked oysters, undrained (about 1 pound)
- ¼ cup butter
- 1 cup finely chopped onion (1 large)
- ½ cup finely chopped celery (1 stalk)
- 2 tablespoons all-purpose flour
- ½ teaspoon salt
- ¼ teaspoon ground black pepper
- ⅛ teaspoon cayenne pepper
- 2 cups whole milk
- 2 cups half-and-half or light cream
- Cream sherry (optional)
- Freshly ground nutmeg (optional)
- Snipped fresh Italian (flat-leaf) parsley (optional)

1 Drain oysters, reserving liquor. Strain liquor to remove any shell pieces. Set oysters and liquor aside.

2 In a large saucepan heat butter over medium heat until melted. Add onion and celery; cook about 10 minutes or until onion is very tender, stirring occasionally. Sprinkle onion mixture with flour, salt, black pepper, and cayenne pepper; cook and stir for 2 minutes more. Gradually stir in milk and half-and-half. Bring to simmering.

3 Stir in drained oysters. Cook for 3 to 5 minutes or until oysters curl around the edges. Stir in oyster liquor; heat through. If desired, add a splash of sherry, nutmeg, and/or parsley.

NUTRITION FACTS PER SERVING:
294 cal., 21 g total fat (13 g sat. fat), 98 mg chol., 481 mg sodium, 15 g carb., 1 g fiber, 11 g pro.

194

Caramelized Onion Soup

PREP 25 minutes COOK 30 minutes MAKES 6 servings

3   tablespoons olive oil or butter

3   pounds sweet onions, such as Vidalia, Walla Walla, or Maui, halved and thinly sliced

1½ cups sliced shallots (12 medium)

4   cups vegetable broth

2   tablespoons dry white wine (optional)

    Salt

    Ground black pepper

6   ½-inch slices sourdough or French bread

1½ cups shredded Gouda or Edam cheese (6 ounces)

    Sliced green onions (optional)

1 In a 4- or 4½-quart Dutch oven heat 1 tablespoon of the oil over medium heat. Add ½ cup of the sweet onions, spreading in a single layer. Cook for 5 to 7 minutes or until brown, stirring occasionally. Remove onions; drain on paper towels and set aside.

2 Add the remaining 2 tablespoons oil to Dutch oven. Stir in the remaining sweet onions and shallots. Cook over medium heat for 20 to 25 minutes or until onions are tender, stirring occasionally. Increase heat to medium-high; cook about 5 minutes more or until onions are golden, stirring occasionally. Stir in broth and, if desired, wine; heat through. Season to taste with salt and pepper.

3 Meanwhile, for cheese toast, preheat broiler. Place bread slices on the unheated rack of a broiler pan. Broil about 4 inches from the heat about 1 minute or until light brown. Turn bread over; top with cheese. Broil for 1 to 2 minutes more or until cheese begins to melt.

4 To serve, ladle soup into bowls; add cheese toast. Top with the reserved ½ cup sweet onions and, if desired, green onions.

NUTRITION FACTS PER SERVING:
339 cal., 15 g total fat (6 g sat. fat),
32 mg chol., 1201 mg sodium, 40 g carb.,
3 g fiber, 13 g pro.

195

Three-Mushroom Soup

PREP 25 minutes   COOK 20 minutes   MAKES 6 servings

1   tablespoon olive oil

8   ounces fresh cremini, oyster, button, and/or stemmed shiitake mushrooms, sliced

2   ounces fresh portobello mushrooms, stemmed and sliced $\frac{1}{2}$ inch thick

2   ounces fresh porcini mushrooms, sliced $\frac{1}{2}$ inch thick

$\frac{1}{2}$ cup chopped onion (1 medium)

3   cloves garlic, minced

3   14.5-ounce cans reduced-sodium chicken broth

1   tablespoon snipped fresh thyme or $\frac{1}{2}$ teaspoon dried thyme, crushed

1 In a large saucepan heat oil over medium heat. Add mushrooms, onion, and garlic. Cook about 10 minutes or until mushrooms are tender and most of the liquid is evaporated, stirring occasionally.

2 Add broth and dried thyme (if using). Bring to boiling; reduce heat. Simmer, covered, for 20 minutes. Stir in fresh thyme (if using).

NUTRITION FACTS PER SERVING:
58 cal., 3 g total fat (0 g sat. fat), 0 mg chol., 474 mg sodium, 5 g carb., 1 g fiber, 4 g pro.

Butternut Squash and Carrot Soup

PREP 30 minutes   COOK 25 minutes   MAKES 6 servings

1 tablespoon butter

3 cups chopped, peeled butternut squash

2 cups thinly sliced carrots (4 medium)

¾ cup thinly sliced leeks or chopped onion (about 3 leeks)

2 14.5-ounce cans reduced-sodium chicken broth

¼ teaspoon ground white pepper

¼ teaspoon ground nutmeg

¼ cup half-and-half or light cream

Crème fraîche or sour cream (optional)

Pumpkin seeds (pepitas), toasted (optional)

Fresh tarragon sprigs (optional)

1 In a large saucepan heat butter over medium heat until melted. Add squash, carrots, and leeks. Cook, covered, for 8 minutes, stirring occasionally. Add broth, pepper, and nutmeg. Bring to boiling; reduce heat. Simmer, covered, for 25 to 35 minutes or until vegetables are very tender. Cool slightly.

2 Transfer one-third of the squash mixture to a food processor or blender. Cover and process or blend until nearly smooth. Transfer to a bowl. Repeat two more times with the remaining squash mixture. Return all of the squash mixture to saucepan.

3 Bring just to boiling. Stir in half-and-half; heat through. If desired, garnish each serving with crème fraîche, pumpkin seeds, and tarragon sprigs.

NUTRITION FACTS PER SERVING:
82 cal., 3 g total fat (2 g sat. fat), 9 mg chol., 364 mg sodium, 12 g carb., 2 g fiber, 3 g pro.

197

tip
To peel uncooked butternut squash (or any winter squash), start with a seeded half placed on a cutting surface. Use a sturdy vegetable peeler to cut off long strips of the peel, cutting away from yourself.

Creamy and Comforting Corn Chowder *Photo on page 144*

PREP 40 minutes   ROAST 20 minutes at 450°F   COOK 17 minutes   MAKES 8 servings

- 1   16-ounce package frozen whole kernel corn
- 1   pound Yukon gold potatoes, peeled and cut into ½-inch pieces
- 2   tablespoons olive oil
- ½   cup thinly sliced leeks (about 2 leeks)
- 2   tablespoons finely chopped shallot (1 medium)
- 4   cups chicken broth
- 1   teaspoon dried marjoram, crushed
- ½   teaspoon salt
- ½   teaspoon ground ginger
- ½   teaspoon ground white pepper
- 3   cups half-and-half or light cream
  Salt
  Ground white pepper

1 Thaw frozen corn; pat dry with paper towels. Preheat oven to 450°F. Line a 15×10×1-inch baking pan with foil; lightly grease foil. Spread corn on half of the prepared baking pan. In a resealable plastic bag combine potatoes and 1 tablespoon of the oil. Seal bag; shake to coat potatoes. Spread potatoes on the other half of the prepared baking pan. Roast, uncovered, for 10 minutes. Stir, keeping corn and potatoes separate. Roast for 10 minutes more, stirring once or twice. Remove from oven.

2 Transfer half of the roasted corn (about ¾ cup) to a food processor or blender. Cover and process or blend until corn is pureed (if necessary, add a small amount of chicken broth to help blend corn).

3 In a 4-quart Dutch oven heat the remaining 1 tablespoon oil over medium heat. Add leeks and shallot; cook and stir for 6 to 8 minutes or until leeks are very soft and golden. Add whole corn and pureed corn; cook and stir for 1 minute. Stir in roasted potatoes, 4 cups broth, marjoram, ½ teaspoon salt, ginger, and ½ teaspoon white pepper.

4 Bring to boiling; reduce heat. Simmer, covered, for 10 to 12 minutes or until potatoes are tender. Add half-and-half. Cook and stir until heated through. Season to taste with additional salt and white pepper.

NUTRITION FACTS PER SERVING: *253 cal., 15 g total fat (7 g sat. fat), 36 mg chol., 692 mg sodium, 28 g carb., 2 g fiber, 6 g pro.*

Fresh Tomato Soup

6   medium or 4 large tomatoes*
    (2 pounds total), cored and
    seeded

1½   cups coarsely chopped red
     sweet peppers (2 medium)

½   of a sweet onion, such as
    Vidalia, Walla Walla, or Maui,
    chopped (about ¼ cup)

¼   cup snipped fresh basil

1   cup reduced-sodium vegetable
    or chicken broth

2   tablespoons whipping cream

1   tablespoon honey

1 In a blender or food processor combine half of the tomatoes, half of the sweet peppers, half of the onion, and half of the basil; add half of the broth. Cover and blend or process until smooth. Transfer pureed mixture to a large saucepan. Repeat with the remaining tomatoes, sweet peppers, onion, basil, and broth.

2 Cook over medium heat until heated through. Stir in whipping cream and honey. Serve warm.

NUTRITION FACTS PER SERVING:
69 cal., 2 g total fat (1 g sat. fat), 7 mg chol., 105 mg sodium, 11 g carb., 3 g fiber, 2 g pro.

199

*tip
If tomatoes are out of season, substitute two 14.5-ounce cans whole tomatoes for the fresh tomatoes.

tip
This soup is also delicious and refreshing when served cold. Cover and chill for 2 to 24 hours before serving.

Soups and Stews

Sweet Potato–Black Bean Stew

PREP 25 minutes   COOK 15 minutes   MAKES 6 servings

- 1   tablespoon canola oil
- 2   medium sweet potatoes, peeled and cut into 1-inch pieces
- 1   medium red sweet pepper, seeded and cut into ½-inch pieces
- ½   cup coarsely chopped onion (1 medium)
- 1   fresh jalapeño chile pepper, seeded and chopped*
- 1   clove garlic, minced
- 1   tablespoon chili powder
- 1   teaspoon ground cumin
- 1   teaspoon cayenne pepper
- 3   cups vegetable broth
- 1   14.5-ounce can black beans, rinsed and drained
- 1   14.5-ounce can diced tomatoes, undrained
- 1   cup frozen whole kernel corn
- ¼   cup snipped fresh cilantro
- ¼   cup lime juice
-     Salt
-     Ground black pepper
-     Shredded cheddar cheese
-     Snipped fresh cilantro (optional)

1 In a large Dutch oven heat oil over medium-high heat. Add sweet potatoes, sweet pepper, onion, jalapeño pepper, and garlic. Cook about 4 minutes or until peppers and onion are tender, stirring occasionally.

2 Stir in chili powder, cumin, and cayenne pepper; reduce heat to medium. Cook, covered, for 7 to 8 minutes or until sweet potatoes are tender, stirring occasionally.

3 Add broth, beans, and tomatoes. Bring to boiling, stirring occasionally. Stir in corn; reduce heat. Simmer, uncovered, for 15 minutes.

4 Stir in ¼ cup cilantro and lime juice. Season to taste with salt and black pepper. Top each serving with cheese and, if desired, additional cilantro.

NUTRITION FACTS PER SERVING:
231 cal., 8 g total fat (3 g sat. fat), 15 mg chol., 708 mg sodium, 34 g carb., 7 g fiber, 11 g pro.

*tip

Because chile peppers contain volatile oils that can burn your skin and eyes, avoid direct contact with them as much as possible. When working with chile peppers, wear plastic or rubber gloves. If your bare hands do touch the peppers, wash your hands and nails well with soap and warm water.

Slow Cooker Favorites

Hearty dishes from the slow cooker just might be the ultimate in comfort food—they are easy on the cook and universally adored.

6

Saucy Pot Roast
with Whole Wheat Noodles

PREP **30 minutes** SLOW COOK **10 to 12 hours (low) or 4 to 5 hours (high)** MAKES **6 servings**

1   2- to 2½-pound boneless beef
     chuck arm pot roast

1   tablespoon vegetable oil

1   cup sliced carrots (2 medium)

1   cup sliced celery (2 stalks)

1   medium onion, sliced

2   cloves garlic, minced

1   tablespoon quick-cooking
     tapioca

1   14.5-ounce can Italian-style
     stewed tomatoes, undrained

1   6-ounce can tomato paste
     with garlic, basil, and oregano

1   tablespoon packed brown
     sugar

1   bay leaf

½   teaspoon salt

¼   teaspoon ground black pepper

3   to 4 cups hot cooked whole
     wheat egg noodles

     Celery leaves (optional)

1 Trim fat from meat. If necessary, cut meat to fit into a 3½- or 4-quart slow cooker. In a large skillet cook meat in hot oil over medium-high heat until brown on all sides. Drain off fat.

2 In the cooker combine carrots, sliced celery, onion, and garlic. Sprinkle with tapioca. Place meat on top of vegetables. In a medium bowl combine tomatoes, tomato paste, brown sugar, bay leaf, salt, and pepper. Pour mixture over meat.

3 Cover and cook on low-heat setting for 10 to 12 hours or on high-heat setting for 4 to 5 hours. Remove and discard bay leaf.

4 Using a slotted spoon, remove meat from cooker. Thinly slice meat. Skim fat from tomato mixture. Serve meat and tomato mixture with hot cooked noodles. If desired, garnish with celery leaves.

NUTRITION FACTS PER SERVING:
569 cal., 27 g total fat (10 g sat. fat), 127 mg chol., 693 mg sodium, 48 g carb., 4 g fiber, 32 g pro.

Fork-Tender Pot Roast

PREP 25 minutes SLOW COOK 10 to 12 hours (low) or 5 to 6 hours (high) MAKES 6 servings

1   2$\frac{1}{2}$- to 3-pound boneless beef chuck pot roast

1   tablespoon olive oil

1   cup coarsely chopped carrots (2 medium)

2   stalks celery, cut into 1-inch pieces

1   cup coarsely chopped onion (1 large)

1   bay leaf

1   clove garlic, minced

$\frac{3}{4}$ cup beef broth

$\frac{1}{4}$ cup dry red wine

2   tablespoons quick-cooking tapioca, crushed

1   tablespoon dried Italian seasoning, crushed

1   tablespoon tomato paste

1   teaspoon garlic powder

$\frac{3}{4}$ teaspoon ground black pepper

$\frac{1}{2}$ teaspoon dry mustard

$\frac{1}{2}$ teaspoon paprika

$\frac{1}{8}$ teaspoon salt

3   to 4 cups hot mashed potatoes (optional)

1 Trim fat from meat. In a large skillet cook meat in hot oil over medium-high heat until brown on all sides. Drain off fat.

2 In a 3$\frac{1}{2}$- or 4-quart slow cooker combine carrots, celery, onion, bay leaf, and garlic. Top with meat. In a small bowl combine broth, wine, tapioca, Italian seasoning, tomato paste, garlic powder, pepper, dry mustard, paprika, and salt. Pour over meat.

3 Cover and cook on low-heat setting for 10 to 12 hours or on high-heat setting for 5 to 6 hours.

4 Transfer meat to a serving platter. Using a slotted spoon, transfer vegetables to platter. Remove and discard bay leaf. Skim fat from cooking liquid. Drizzle cooking liquid over meat and vegetables. If desired, serve with mashed potatoes.

NUTRITION FACTS PER SERVING:
322 cal., 10 g total fat (3 g sat. fat), 83 mg chol., 349 mg sodium, 10 g carb., 2 g fiber, 43 g pro.

203

Pot Roast Paprikash

PREP 25 minutes SLOW COOK 10 to 12 hours (low) or 5 to 6 hours (high) + 30 minutes (high) MAKES 8 servings

1   2½-pound boneless beef round rump roast

2   tablespoons Hungarian paprika

½   teaspoon smoked paprika

1   14.5-ounce can diced tomatoes, undrained

1   14.5-ounce can beef broth

3   medium onions, halved and cut into ½-inch slices

3   large carrots, coarsely chopped

1   12-ounce jar roasted red sweet peppers, drained and cut into ½-inch strips

¼   cup water

2   tablespoons cornstarch

1   8-ounce carton sour cream

   Salt

   Ground black pepper

4   ounces dried medium egg noodles

¼   cup butter

⅓   cup snipped fresh Italian (flat-leaf) parsley

1 Trim fat from meat; cut meat into four pieces. Place meat in a 4- to 5-quart slow cooker. Sprinkle with paprika and smoked paprika. Top with tomatoes, broth, onions, carrots, and roasted peppers.

2 Cover and cook on low-heat setting for 10 to 12 hours or on high-heat setting for 5 to 6 hours.

3 Transfer meat to a cutting board. Using two forks, pull meat apart into coarse shreds. Skim fat from cooking liquid. Return shredded meat to liquid in cooker.

4 If using low-heat setting, turn to high-heat setting. In a small bowl combine the water and cornstarch; stir into mixture in cooker. Cover and cook for 30 minutes more. Stir in sour cream. Season to taste with salt and black pepper.

5 Meanwhile, cook noodles according to package directions; drain. Toss with butter. Serve meat mixture over noodles. Sprinkle with parsley.

NUTRITION FACTS PER SERVING:
523 cal., 28 g total fat (13 g sat. fat), 136 mg chol., 590 mg sodium, 35 g carb., 4 g fiber, 34 g pro.

204

tip

Don't leave leftovers in the slow cooker to cool down; transfer warm leftovers to containers and refrigerate or freeze promptly. Also, never reheat leftovers in the slow cooker.

So-Easy Pepper Steak

PREP 15 minutes SLOW COOK 9 to 10 hours (low) or 4 hours 30 minutes to 5 hours (high) MAKES 6 servings

1   pound boneless beef round steak, cut ¾ to 1 inch thick

½   teaspoon salt

¼   teaspoon ground black pepper

1   14.5-ounce can Cajun-, Mexican-, or Italian-style stewed tomatoes, undrained

⅓   cup tomato paste

½   teaspoon bottled hot pepper sauce (optional)

1   16-ounce package frozen sweet pepper and onion stir-fry vegetables

4   cups hot cooked whole wheat pasta (optional)

1 Trim fat from meat. Cut meat into six serving-size pieces. Sprinkle meat with salt and black pepper. Place in a 3½- or 4-quart slow cooker. In a medium bowl combine tomatoes, tomato paste, and, if desired, hot pepper sauce. Pour mixture over meat. Top with frozen vegetables.

2 Cover and cook on low-heat setting for 9 to 10 hours or on high-heat setting for 4½ to 5 hours. If desired, serve with hot cooked pasta.

NUTRITION FACTS PER SERVING:
258 cal., 6 g total fat (2 g sat. fat), 83 mg chol., 644 mg sodium, 12 g carb., 2 g fiber, 37 g pro.

tip

Resist the urge to lift the lid on your slow cooker to check the progress of dinner. Every time you do, heat is released and you'll have to add an extra 30 minutes to the total cooking time. If you do need to remove the lid to stir in ingredients during cooking time, do so quickly.

Slow Cooker Favorites

Beer-Braised Beef Short Ribs   *Photo on page 274*

PREP 20 minutes   SLOW COOK 11 to 12 hours (low) or 5 hours 30 minutes to 6 hours (high)   MAKES 4 servings

5   pounds bone-in beef
    short ribs

1   14.5-ounce can beef broth

1   12-ounce can dark beer

1   medium onion, cut into
    thin wedges

¼   cup molasses

2   tablespoons balsamic vinegar

1   teaspoon dried thyme,
    crushed

1   teaspoon bottled hot pepper
    sauce

½   teaspoon salt

2   to 3 cups hot mashed potatoes
    or hot buttered noodles
    (optional)

    Fresh thyme leaves (optional)

1 Place ribs in a 5- to 6-quart slow cooker. Add broth, beer, onion, molasses, vinegar, dried thyme, hot pepper sauce, and salt.

2 Cover and cook on low-heat setting for 11 to 12 hours or on high-heat setting for 5½ to 6 hours.

3 Using a slotted spoon, transfer ribs to a serving platter. Skim fat from cooking liquid. If desired, serve ribs with hot mashed potatoes and garnish with fresh thyme leaves. Pass cooking liquid for dipping.

NUTRITION FACTS PER SERVING:
481 cal., 19 g total fat (8 g sat. fat), 132 mg chol., 821 mg sodium, 22 g carb., 0 g fiber, 46 g pro.

206

Corned Beef and Cabbage

PREP 15 minutes   SLOW COOK 10 to 12 hours (low) or 5 to 6 hours (high)   MAKES 6 servings

1   3- to 4-pound corned beef brisket with spice packet

½   of a small head green cabbage, cut into 3 wedges

4   medium carrots, halved lengthwise and cut into 2-inch pieces

2   medium Yukon gold or yellow Finn potatoes, cut into 2-inch pieces

1   medium onion, quartered

½   cup water

1 Trim fat from meat. If necessary, cut meat to fit into a 5- to 6-quart slow cooker. Sprinkle spices from packet evenly over meat; rub in with your fingers. Place cabbage, carrots, potatoes, and onion in cooker. Add the water. Place meat on top of vegetables.

2 Cover and cook on low-heat setting for 10 to 12 hours or on high-heat setting for 5 to 6 hours.

3 Transfer meat to a serving platter; thinly slice across the grain. Using a slotted spoon, transfer vegetables to platter.

NUTRITION FACTS PER SERVING:
457 cal., 27 g total fat (7 g sat. fat), 115 mg chol., 1543 mg sodium, 16 g carb., 3 g fiber, 35 g pro.

207

Brisket Ciabatta Sandwiches

PREP 30 minutes   SLOW COOK 9 to 10 hours (low) or 4 hours 30 minutes to 5 hours (high)   MAKES 12 servings

- 1   3-pound fresh beef brisket
- 1   cup sliced fresh cremini or button mushrooms
- ½   cup chopped onion (1 medium)
- 2   cloves garlic, minced
- 1   14.5-ounce can fire-roasted crushed tomatoes or diced tomatoes, undrained
- ⅓   cup tomato paste with garlic, basil, and oregano, or plain tomato paste
- ¼   cup dry red wine or beef broth
- 1½ teaspoons Worcestershire sauce
- 1   teaspoon dried Italian seasoning, crushed
- ½   teaspoon salt
- ¼   teaspoon ground black pepper
- 12 ciabatta buns, split and toasted
  Shredded Italian cheese blend or Parmesan cheese (optional)
  Arugula (optional)

1 Trim fat from meat. If necessary, cut meat to fit into a 4- to 5-quart slow cooker. In the cooker combine mushrooms, onion, and garlic. Place meat on top of vegetables.

2 For sauce, in a medium bowl combine tomatoes, tomato paste, wine, Worcestershire sauce, Italian seasoning, salt, and pepper. Pour mixture over meat.

3 Cover and cook on low-heat setting for 9 to 10 hours or on high-heat setting for 4½ to 5 hours or until meat is tender. Transfer meat to a cutting board; cover with foil and keep warm. Skim fat from sauce.

4 If sauce is thin, transfer to a medium saucepan. Bring to boiling; reduce heat. Boil gently, uncovered, for 5 to 10 minutes or until slightly thickened.

5 Coarsely chop meat. Place meat on bottoms of buns. Spoon some of the sauce over meat. If desired, top with cheese and arugula. Replace tops of buns. Pass any remaining sauce.

NUTRITION FACTS PER SERVING:
596 cal., 26 g total fat (10 g sat. fat), 81 mg chol., 809 mg sodium, 60 g carb., 3 g fiber, 30 g pro.

All-American Sloppy Joes

PREP 40 minutes SLOW COOK 6 to 8 hours (low) or 3 to 4 hours (high) MAKES 16 servings

- 3 pounds lean ground beef or ground pork
- 2 cups chopped onions (2 large)
- 4 cloves garlic, minced
- 2½ cups chopped red sweet peppers (about 2 large)
- 2 cups chopped celery (4 stalks)
- 1 12-ounce can beer
- 1 cup ketchup
- 2 tablespoons molasses
- 2 tablespoons yellow mustard
- 4 teaspoons chili powder
- 2 teaspoons cider vinegar
  Dash bottled hot pepper sauce
- 16 whole grain hamburger buns or kaiser rolls, split and toasted
  Dill pickle slices and/or pickled jalapeño pepper slices (optional)

1 In an extra-large skillet cook ground beef, onions, and garlic over medium-high heat until meat is brown and onions are tender, using a wooden spoon to break up meat as it cooks. Drain off fat.

2 In a 3½- or 4-quart slow cooker combine meat mixture, sweet peppers, celery, beer, ketchup, molasses, mustard, chili powder, vinegar, and hot pepper sauce.

3 Cover and cook on low-heat setting for 6 to 8 hours or on high-heat setting for 3 to 4 hours.

4 Using a slotted spoon, spoon meat mixture onto bottoms of buns. If desired, add dill pickle and/ or pickled pepper slices. Replace tops of buns.

NUTRITION FACTS PER SERVING:
403 cal., 16 g total fat (5 g sat. fat), 58 mg chol., 575 mg sodium, 41 g carb., 3 g fiber, 23 g pro.

Bolognese Sauce

PREP 35 minutes   SLOW COOK 8 to 9 hours (low) or 4 hours to 4 hours 30 minutes (high)   MAKES 8 servings

1 pound ground beef, pork, and/or turkey

1 cup chopped carrots (2 medium)

½ cup chopped onion (1 medium)

½ cup chopped celery (1 stalk)

6 cloves garlic, minced

1 28-ounce can crushed tomatoes

1 15-ounce can tomato sauce

1 14.5-ounce can diced tomatoes, undrained

2 4-ounce cans (drained weight) sliced mushrooms, drained

¾ cup dry white wine

¼ cup water

1 tablespoon quick-cooking tapioca, crushed

1 teaspoon dried rosemary, crushed

½ teaspoon salt

½ teaspoon crushed red pepper

¼ teaspoon ground black pepper

⅛ teaspoon fennel seeds, crushed

½ cup whipping cream

8 cups hot cooked pasta

Grated Romano or Parmesan cheese (optional)

1 In a large skillet cook ground beef, carrots, onion, celery, and garlic over medium-high heat until meat is brown and vegetables are tender, using a wooden spoon to break up meat as it cooks. Drain off fat.

2 In a 4- to 5-quart slow cooker combine meat mixture, crushed tomatoes, tomato sauce, diced tomatoes, mushrooms, wine, the water, tapioca, rosemary, salt, crushed red pepper, black pepper, and fennel seeds.

3 Cover and cook on low-heat setting for 8 to 9 hours or on high-heat setting for 4 to 4½ hours.

4 Before serving, stir in whipping cream. Serve sauce over hot cooked pasta. If desired, sprinkle each serving with cheese.

NUTRITION FACTS PER SERVING: *441 cal., 12 g total fat (6 g sat. fat), 56 mg chol., 876 mg sodium, 58 g carb., 6 g fiber, 20 g pro.*

Make-Ahead Directions: Prepare as directed through Step 3. Transfer sauce to a freezer container. Seal, label, and freeze for up to 3 months. To serve, thaw in the refrigerator overnight. Transfer to a saucepan; heat through. Stir in whipping cream; heat through. Serve as directed.

Slow Cooker Moroccan Lamb Tagine

PREP 35 minutes SLOW COOK 8 to 10 hours (low) or 4 to 5 hours (high) MAKES 6 servings

1½ to 2 pounds boneless lamb shoulder roast or lamb stew meat

½ teaspoon salt

½ teaspoon ground ginger

½ teaspoon ground cumin

¼ teaspoon ground turmeric

¼ teaspoon ground cinnamon

1½ cups coarsely chopped, peeled sweet potato

2 medium carrots, cut into 1-inch pieces

½ cup chopped onion (1 medium)

⅓ cup chopped roma tomato (1 medium)

⅓ cup pitted whole dates, quartered

¼ cup pitted green olives, halved

2 tablespoons quick-cooking tapioca

½ teaspoon finely shredded lemon peel

1 tablespoon lemon juice

1 tablespoon honey

2 cloves garlic, minced

1 14.5-ounce can chicken broth

1 teaspoon orange flower water

3 cups hot cooked couscous

Sliced almonds, toasted

1 Trim fat from meat. Cut meat into 1-inch pieces. Place meat in a large bowl. In a small bowl combine salt, ginger, cumin, turmeric, and cinnamon. Sprinkle mixture over meat; toss gently to coat.

2 Transfer meat to a 3½- or 4-quart slow cooker. Stir in sweet potato, carrots, onion, tomato, dates, olives, tapioca, lemon peel, lemon juice, honey, and garlic. Pour broth over mixture in cooker.

3 Cover and cook on low-heat setting for 8 to 10 hours or on high-heat setting for 4 to 5 hours. Stir in orange flower water.

4 Serve in shallow bowls over hot cooked couscous. Sprinkle with almonds.

NUTRITION FACTS PER SERVING:
368 cal., 8 g total fat (2 g sat. fat), 70 mg chol., 674 mg sodium, 45 g carb., 5 g fiber, 28 g pro.

tip

Tagine *(tay-jean)* is the name of savory Moroccan meat or poultry stews as well as the ceramic vessel in which they are cooked. A slow cooker creates the same kind of moist, gentle cooking as the ceramic tagine.

Lamb Shanks with Polenta

PREP 15 minutes   SLOW COOK 11 to 12 hours (low) or 5 hours 30 minutes to 6 hours (high)   MAKES 4 servings

1	**pound boiling onions, peeled**
½	**cup pitted Greek black olives**
4	**pounds meaty lamb shanks**
4	**cloves garlic, minced**
2	**teaspoons dried rosemary, crushed**
½	**teaspoon salt**
¼	**teaspoon ground black pepper**
1	**cup chicken broth**
1¼	**cups quick-cooking polenta**
	Snipped fresh Italian (flat-leaf) parsley (optional)

1 In a 5- to 6-quart slow cooker combine onions and olives. Top with lamb shanks. Sprinkle with garlic, rosemary, salt, and pepper. Pour broth over mixture in cooker.

2 Cover and cook on low-heat setting for 11 to 12 hours or on high-heat setting for 5½ to 6 hours.

3 Before serving, prepare polenta according to package directions and set aside. Using a slotted spoon, transfer lamb, onions, and olives to a serving dish. If desired, garnish with parsley. Serve lamb with cooked polenta. If desired, skim fat from cooking liquid. Strain liquid; drizzle over lamb and polenta.

NUTRITION FACTS PER SERVING:
701 cal., 21 g total fat (7 g sat. fat), 136 mg chol., 768 mg sodium, 79 g carb., 12 g fiber, 46 g pro.

tip
Lamb foreshanks are smaller than hind shanks, making them a perfect fit for the slow cooker. You may need to ask the butcher to order them.

Home-Style Pork Pot Roast

PREP **20 minutes** SLOW COOK **10 to 12 hours (low) or 5 to 6 hours (high)** MAKES **6 servings**

1 **3- to 3½-pound boneless pork shoulder roast**

1 **tablespoon vegetable oil**

3 **tablespoons Dijon-style mustard**

1 **teaspoon dried thyme, crushed**

½ **teaspoon salt**

½ **teaspoon dried rosemary, crushed**

¼ **teaspoon ground black pepper**

12 **ounces red-skinned potatoes, cut into 1-inch pieces**

3 **medium parsnips, peeled and cut into 1-inch pieces**

3 **medium carrots, cut into 1-inch pieces**

1 **large onion, cut into wedges**

¾ **cup canned chicken broth with roasted garlic**

3 **tablespoons quick-cooking tapioca**

1 Trim fat from meat. If necessary, cut meat to fit into a 4- to 6-quart slow cooker. In a large skillet cook meat in hot oil over medium-high heat until brown on all sides. Drain off fat. Brush meat with mustard; sprinkle with thyme, salt, rosemary, and pepper.

2 In the cooker combine potatoes, parsnips, carrots, and onion. Pour broth over vegetables. Sprinkle with tapioca. Place meat on top of vegetables.

3 Cover and cook on low-heat setting for 10 to 12 hours or on high-heat setting for 5 to 6 hours.

4 Transfer meat and vegetables to a serving platter. Strain cooking liquid; skim off fat. Drizzle meat and vegetables with some of the cooking liquid. Pass the remaining cooking liquid.

NUTRITION FACTS PER SERVING:
451 cal., 15 g total fat (5 g sat. fat), 136 mg chol., 671 mg sodium, 29 g carb., 5 g fiber, 45 g pro.

Easy Southern-Style Ribs

PREP 25 minutes SLOW COOK 8 to 10 hours (low) or 4 to 5 hours (high) BROIL 5 minutes MAKES 6 servings

- 4 to 5 pounds pork loin back ribs or meaty pork spareribs, cut into 2- or 3-rib portions
- 1 tablespoon smoked paprika or Hungarian paprika
- 1½ teaspoons packed brown sugar
- 1 teaspoon ground pasilla chile pepper or ancho chile pepper
- ½ teaspoon salt
- ½ teaspoon garlic powder
- ½ teaspoon ground coriander
- ½ teaspoon dry mustard
- ¼ teaspoon celery salt
- ¼ teaspoon coarsely ground black pepper
- ⅛ teaspoon cayenne pepper
- ¾ cup barbecue sauce
- ½ cup chicken broth

1 Trim fat from ribs. For rub, in a small bowl combine paprika, brown sugar, ground pasilla pepper, salt, garlic powder, coriander, dry mustard, celery salt, black pepper, and cayenne pepper. Generously sprinkle rub over both sides of ribs; rub in with your fingers. Place ribs in a 5- to 6-quart slow cooker, cutting to fit.

2 In a small bowl combine ¼ cup of the barbecue sauce and the broth; pour over ribs.

3 Cover and cook on low-heat setting for 8 to 10 hours or on high-heat setting for 4 to 5 hours.

4 Preheat broiler. Line a baking sheet with foil. Transfer ribs, meaty sides up, to the prepared baking sheet. Brush with the remaining ½ cup barbecue sauce. Broil 6 to 8 inches from the heat for 5 to 8 minutes or until sauce begins to brown.

NUTRITION FACTS PER SERVING:
584 cal., 44 g total fat (16 g sat. fat), 152 mg chol., 831 mg sodium, 13 g carb., 0 g fiber, 30 g pro.

BBQ Pulled Pork Sandwiches

Photo on page 274

PREP 20 minutes SLOW COOK 8 to 9 hours (low) or 4 hours to 4 hours 30 minutes (high) MAKES 10 servings

2 medium onions, cut into thin wedges

½ cup water

1 2- to 2½-pound boneless pork sirloin roast

½ teaspoon chili powder

½ teaspoon ground black pepper

¼ teaspoon garlic powder

½ teaspoon ground cumin

1 cup barbecue sauce

¼ cup cider vinegar

1 tablespoon honey

¼ teaspoon ground ginger

10 whole wheat hamburger buns, split and toasted

1 In a 3½- or 4-quart slow cooker combine onions and the water; set aside. Trim fat from meat. If necessary, cut meat to fit into cooker. In a small bowl combine chili powder, pepper, garlic powder, and ¼ teaspoon of the cumin. Sprinkle mixture evenly over all sides of meat; rub in with your fingers. Place meat in cooker.

2 Cover and cook on low-heat setting for 8 to 9 hours or on high-heat setting for 4 to 4½ hours.

3 Using a slotted spoon, remove meat and onions from cooker. Using two forks, pull meat apart into shreds.

4 In a large saucepan combine barbecue sauce, vinegar, honey, ginger, and the remaining ¼ teaspoon cumin; heat through. Stir in shredded meat. Fill each bun with about ⅓ cup of the meat mixture and some of the onions.

NUTRITION FACTS PER SERVING:
251 cal., 5 g total fat (1 g sat. fat), 57 mg chol., 587 mg sodium, 27 g carb., 3 g fiber, 23 g pro.

215

Red Beans and Rice

PREP 30 minutes STAND 1 hour SLOW COOK 9 to 10 hours (low) or 4 hours 30 minutes to 5 hours (high) + 30 minutes (high) MAKES 6 servings

1 cup dried red kidney beans

1 cooked smoked pork hock (about 1½ pounds)

12 ounces cooked andouille sausage or kielbasa, cut into ½-inch pieces

2½ cups reduced-sodium chicken broth

½ cup chopped onion (1 medium)

½ cup chopped celery (1 stalk)

1 tablespoon tomato paste

2 cloves garlic, minced

½ teaspoon dried thyme, crushed

½ teaspoon dried oregano, crushed

⅛ to ¼ teaspoon cayenne pepper

1 8.8-ounce pouch cooked long grain rice

½ cup chopped red or yellow sweet pepper (1 small)

1 Rinse beans; drain. In a large saucepan combine beans and enough water to cover beans by 2 inches. Bring to boiling; reduce heat. Simmer, uncovered, for 10 minutes. Remove from heat. Cover and let stand for 1 hour. Drain and rinse beans.

2 In a 3½- or 4-quart slow cooker combine beans, pork hock, sausage, broth, onion, celery, tomato paste, garlic, thyme, oregano, and cayenne pepper.

3 Cover and cook on low-heat setting for 9 to 10 hours or on high-heat setting for 4½ to 5 hours.

4 Remove pork hock. When cool enough to handle, remove meat from bone; discard bone. Cut meat into bite-size pieces. Return meat to cooker. Stir in rice and sweet pepper.

5 If using low-heat setting, turn to high-heat setting. Cover and cook for 30 minutes more or until heated through.

NUTRITION FACTS PER SERVING:
429 cal., 22 g total fat (9 g sat. fat), 40 mg chol., 766 mg sodium, 37 g carb., 6 g fiber, 21 g pro.

Sausage Sandwiches with Roasted Veggies

PREP 20 minutes SLOW COOK 6 hours 30 minutes to 7 hours (low) or 3 hours to 3 hours 30 minutes (high)

MAKES 4 servings

Nonstick cooking spray

2 teaspoons olive oil

2 cooked smoked chicken sausage links with apple or two 4-inch pieces smoked turkey sausage

1 cup grape tomatoes

1 medium green sweet pepper, seeded and cut into thin strips

1 medium onion, cut into 12 wedges

4 cloves garlic, minced

1 teaspoon dried oregano, crushed

3 tablespoons light mayonnaise or salad dressing

1½ teaspoons packed dark brown sugar

1½ teaspoons yellow mustard

4 whole wheat hot dog buns, split and lightly toasted

1 Lightly coat a 3½- or 4-quart slow cooker with cooking spray; set aside. In a medium nonstick skillet heat 1 teaspoon of the oil over medium-high heat. Add sausage; cook until brown on all sides, turning frequently.

2 In the prepared cooker combine tomatoes, sweet pepper, onion, garlic, oregano, and the remaining 1 teaspoon oil. Top with sausage.

3 Cover and cook on low-heat setting for 6½ to 7 hours or on high-heat setting for 3 to 3½ hours.

4 Meanwhile, for sauce, in a small bowl combine mayonnaise, brown sugar, and mustard. Cover and chill until ready to serve.

5 To serve, cut each sausage link in half lengthwise. Fill each bun with about ⅓ cup of the vegetable mixture and a sausage half. Spoon sauce over sausage.

NUTRITION FACTS PER SERVING:
308 cal., 12 g total fat (3 g sat. fat), 34 mg chol., 596 mg sodium, 36 g carb., 3 g fiber, 13 g pro.

217

Ham and Brie Bread Pudding

PREP 25 minutes SLOW COOK 3 hours 30 minutes to 4 hours (low) STAND 30 minutes MAKES 6 servings

Nonstick cooking spray

4   to 4½ ounces Brie cheese

4   eggs, lightly beaten

3   cups milk, half-and-half,
     or light cream

2   cloves garlic, minced

1   teaspoon dried thyme,
     crushed

¼   teaspoon ground black pepper

6   cups dry herbed Italian
     flatbread (focaccia) cubes*
     (12 ounces)

1½   cups diced cooked ham

⅓   cup snipped dried tomatoes
     (not oil-packed)

1 Lightly coat the inside of a 3½- or 4-quart slow cooker with cooking spray; set aside. If desired, remove rind from cheese. Cut cheese into ½-inch pieces; set aside.

2 In a large bowl combine eggs, milk, garlic, thyme, and pepper. Gently stir in bread cubes, ham, dried tomatoes, and cheese. Spoon bread mixture into the prepared cooker.

3 Cover and cook on low-heat setting for 3½ to 4 hours or until a knife inserted in the center of bread pudding comes out clean (pudding will puff), giving crockery liner a half turn halfway through cooking, if possible.

4 Turn off cooker. If possible, remove crockery liner from cooker. Let stand, covered, for 30 minutes before serving (pudding will fall slightly as it cools).

NUTRITION FACTS PER SERVING:
370 cal., 16 g total fat (7 g sat. fat), 172 mg chol., 966 mg sodium, 34 g carb., 2 g fiber, 23 g pro.

218

*tip
To make dry focaccia cubes, preheat oven to 300°F. Cut focaccia into ½-inch cubes. Spread in a single layer in a 15×10×1-inch baking pan. Bake for 10 to 15 minutes or until cubes are dry, stirring twice; cool. (Or let focaccia cubes stand, loosely covered, at room temperature for 8 to 12 hours.)

Cherry Cola Ham

Photo on page 273

PREP 15 minutes SLOW COOK 8 to 9 hours (low) MAKES 20 servings

1 cup packed brown sugar

$\frac{2}{3}$ cup cherry-flavor cola

2 tablespoons lemon juice

1 tablespoon dry mustard

1 5- to 5$\frac{1}{2}$-pound cooked boneless ham

$\frac{1}{4}$ cup cold water

2 tablespoons cornstarch

1 tablespoon prepared horseradish

Fresh sage leaves (optional)

1 In a 5$\frac{1}{2}$- or 6-quart slow cooker combine brown sugar, cola, lemon juice, and dry mustard. Add ham, turning to coat.

2 Cover and cook on low-heat setting for 8 to 9 hours. Transfer ham to a serving platter; cover and keep warm.

3 For sauce, in a small saucepan stir together the water and cornstarch. Add cooking liquid from cooker. Cook and stir over medium heat until thickened and bubbly. Cook and stir for 2 minutes more. Stir in horseradish. Slice ham and serve with sauce. If desired, garnish with sage leaves.

NUTRITION FACTS PER SERVING:
201 cal., 7 g total fat (2 g sat. fat), 81 mg chol., 1379 mg sodium, 13 g carb., 0 g fiber, 20 g pro.

219

Lemon-Herb Roasted Chicken

PREP 20 hours   SLOW COOK 6 to 7 hours (low) or 3 hours to 3 hours 30 minutes (high)   MAKES 4 servings

1   4- to 5-pound whole roasting chicken

½   teaspoon kosher salt

¼   teaspoon freshly ground black pepper

4   sprigs fresh rosemary

4   sprigs fresh thyme

4   cloves garlic, peeled

1   tablespoon snipped fresh rosemary

1   tablespoon snipped fresh thyme

1   tablespoon bottled minced roasted garlic

2   lemons, thinly sliced

¼   cup dry white wine

1 Rinse chicken body cavity; pat dry with paper towels. Rub inside and outside of chicken with salt and pepper. Place rosemary sprigs, thyme sprigs, and garlic cloves in body cavity. In a small bowl combine snipped rosemary, snipped thyme, and roasted garlic. Gently slide roasted garlic mixture under skin of chicken over breast and thighs without tearing the skin (make slits in the skin on either side of backbone to reach the thigh meat).

2 Place chicken in a 4-quart oval slow cooker. Top with lemon slices; drizzle with wine.

3 Cover and cook on low-heat setting for 6 to 7 hours or on high-heat setting for 3 to 3½ hours.

NUTRITION FACTS PER SERVING:
721 cal., 50 g total fat (14 g sat. fat), 237 mg chol., 428 mg sodium, 9 g carb., 3 g fiber, 57 g pro.

Chicken with Sourdough Stuffing

PREP 20 minutes SLOW COOK 6 hours to 6 hours 30 minutes (low) or 3 hours to 3 hours 30 minutes (high)

MAKES 6 servings

6 cups crusty country sourdough bread cut into 1-inch cubes (10 ounces)

1⅓ cups chopped tomatoes (2 medium)

1 cup finely chopped carrots (2 medium)

1½ teaspoons dried thyme, crushed

¼ teaspoon coarsely ground black pepper

½ cup reduced-sodium chicken broth

6 small whole chicken legs (drumstick and thigh), skinned

⅓ cup thinly sliced leek (1 medium) or chopped onion (1 small)

1 For stuffing, in a large bowl combine bread cubes, tomatoes, carrots, thyme, and pepper. Drizzle with broth, tossing gently to moisten. (Stuffing will not be completely moistened.)

2 Place chicken in a 4- to 5-quart slow cooker. Sprinkle with leek. Lightly pack stuffing on top of chicken.

3 Cover and cook on low-heat setting for 6 to 6½ hours or on high-heat setting for 3 to 3½ hours.

NUTRITION FACTS PER SERVING: *270 cal., 6 g total fat (1 g sat. fat), 104 mg chol., 379 mg sodium, 22 g carb., 2 g fiber, 30 g pro.*

221

tip
Never put frozen raw poultry or meat into the slow cooker. Because of the slow rate of cooking, frozen meat will hover in the food safety danger zone (40°F to 140°F) for too long. If you're in a rush, use your microwave to thaw these foods.

Chicken and Biscuits *Photo on page 274*

PREP 30 minutes SLOW COOK 6 to 7 hours (low) or 3 hours to 3 hours 30 minutes (high) + 10 minutes
(low or high) MAKES 6 servings

- 2 **cups chopped red-skinned potatoes (2 medium)**
- 1 **cup coarsely chopped carrots (2 medium)**
- ½ **cup coarsely chopped onion (1 medium)**
- ½ **cup coarsely chopped celery (1 stalk)**
- 1 **4-ounce can (drained weight) sliced mushrooms, drained**
- 2 **cloves garlic, minced**
- ½ **teaspoon dried thyme, crushed**
- ½ **teaspoon dried sage, crushed**
- ¼ **teaspoon salt**
- ¼ **teaspoon ground black pepper**
- 2 **tablespoons quick-cooking tapioca, crushed**
- 1 **pound bone-in chicken thighs, skinned**
- 1 **cup chicken broth**
- 1 **cup frozen peas**
- 1 **3-ounce package cream cheese, cut up**
- 1 **recipe Cheesy Biscuits**

1 In a 3½- or 4-quart slow cooker combine potatoes, carrots, onion, celery, mushrooms, garlic, thyme, sage, salt, and pepper. Sprinkle tapioca over potato mixture. Place chicken on top of vegetables. Pour broth over mixture in cooker.

2 Cover and cook on low-heat setting for 6 to 7 hours or on high-heat setting for 3 to 3½ hours.

3 Remove chicken from cooker. When cool enough to handle, remove meat from bones; discard bones. Coarsely chop chicken; return to cooker. Add peas and cream cheese. Cover and cook for 10 minutes more. Stir well; serve with Cheesy Biscuits.

NUTRITION FACTS PER SERVING:
369 cal., 15 g total fat (7 g sat. fat), 63 mg chol., 927 mg sodium, 41 g carb., 3 g fiber, 18 g pro.

222

Cheesy Biscuits

Preheat oven to 450°F. In a medium bowl combine 1⅔ cups packaged biscuit mix and ½ cup shredded cheddar cheese (2 ounces). Stir in ½ cup milk. Turn dough out onto a lightly floured surface. Knead dough by folding and gently pressing it just until dough holds together. Pat or lightly roll dough until ½ inch thick. Cut dough with a floured 3-inch round biscuit cutter; reroll scraps as necessary. Place dough circles on an ungreased baking sheet. Bake for 10 to 12 minutes or until golden.

Cacciatore-Style Chicken

PREP 25 minutes SLOW COOK 6 to 7 hours (low) or 3 hours to 3 hours 30 minutes (high) + 15 minutes (high)

MAKES 6 servings

- 2   cups sliced fresh mushrooms
- 1   cup chopped celery (2 stalks)
- 1   cup chopped carrots (2 medium)
- 2   medium onions, cut into wedges
- 1   medium yellow, green, or red sweet pepper, seeded and cut into thin bite-size strips
- 4   cloves garlic, minced
- 12 chicken drumsticks (about 3½ pounds total), skinned
- ½   cup chicken broth
- ¼   cup dry white wine
- 2   tablespoons quick-cooking tapioca
- 2   bay leaves
- 1   teaspoon sugar
- 1   teaspoon dried oregano, crushed
- ½   teaspoon salt
- ¼   teaspoon ground black pepper
- 1   14.5-ounce can diced tomatoes, undrained
- ⅓   cup tomato paste
- 3   cups hot cooked pasta or rice
      Shredded fresh basil (optional)

1 In a 5- to 6-quart slow cooker combine mushrooms, celery, carrots, onions, sweet pepper, and garlic. Place chicken on top of vegetables. In a small bowl combine broth, wine, tapioca, bay leaves, sugar, oregano, salt, and black pepper. Pour over mixture in cooker.

2 Cover and cook on low-heat setting for 6 to 7 hours or on high-heat setting for 3 to 3½ hours.

3 Transfer chicken to a serving platter; cover and keep warm. Remove and discard bay leaves. If using low-heat setting, turn to high-heat setting. Stir in tomatoes and tomato paste. Cover and cook for 15 minutes more.

4 To serve, spoon vegetable mixture over chicken. Serve with hot pasta. If desired, garnish with basil.

NUTRITION FACTS PER SERVING:
345 cal., 7 g total fat (2 g sat. fat), 81 mg chol., 606 mg sodium, 37 g carb., 4 g fiber, 32 g pro.

223

Creamy Tomato, Sausage, and Mushroom Pasta Sauce

PREP 15 minutes SLOW COOK 6 to 8 hours (low) or 3 to 4 hours (high) MAKES 8 servings

- 1 26-ounce jar marinara sauce
- 1 15-ounce jar Alfredo pasta sauce
- 1 teaspoon dried Italian seasoning, crushed
- ¼ teaspoon ground black pepper
- 1 to 1½ pounds cooked Italian-flavor chicken sausage, halved lengthwise and cut into 1-inch pieces
- 3 cups sliced fresh baby portobello, stemmed shiitake, and/or cremini mushrooms (8 ounces)
- 1 8- to 9-ounce package frozen artichoke hearts
- 1 medium red sweet pepper, seeded and cut into 1-inch pieces
- 12 to 16 ounces dried rigatoni or penne pasta
   Snipped fresh basil
   Shredded Asiago or Parmesan cheese

1 For sauce, in a 4- to 5-quart slow cooker combine marinara sauce, Alfredo sauce, Italian seasoning, and black pepper. Stir in sausage, mushrooms, artichoke hearts, and sweet pepper.

2 Cover and cook on low-heat setting for 6 to 8 hours or on high-heat setting for 3 to 4 hours.

3 Before serving, cook pasta according to package directions; drain. Serve sauce over pasta. Sprinkle each serving with basil and cheese.

NUTRITION FACTS PER SERVING:
489 cal., 20 g total fat (10 g sat. fat), 85 mg chol., 1123 mg sodium, 53 g carb., 6 g fiber, 23 g pro.

224

Spiced Barbecue Turkey Thighs

PREP 20 minutes SLOW COOK 9 to 10 hours (low) or 4 hours 30 minutes to 5 hours (high) MAKES 4 servings

½ cup ketchup

2 tablespoons sugar

1 tablespoon quick-cooking tapioca

1 tablespoon cider vinegar

1 teaspoon Worcestershire sauce

¼ teaspoon ground cinnamon

¼ teaspoon crushed red pepper

2 to 2½ pounds turkey thighs or meaty chicken pieces (breast halves, thighs, and drumsticks), skinned

2 cups hot cooked brown rice or whole wheat pasta (optional)

Fresh cilantro leaves (optional)

1 In a 3½- or 4-quart slow cooker combine ketchup, sugar, tapioca, vinegar, Worcestershire sauce, cinnamon, and crushed red pepper. Place turkey thighs, meaty sides down, on top of mixture in cooker.

2 Cover and cook on low-heat setting for 9 to 10 hours or on high-heat setting for 4½ to 5 hours.

3 Transfer turkey to a cutting board. When turkey is cool enough to handle, remove meat from bones; discard bones. Coarsely chop or shred turkey. Pour cooking juices into a large bowl; skim off fat. Stir turkey into cooking juices.

4 If desired, serve turkey over hot cooked rice. If desired, garnish with cilantro.

NUTRITION FACTS PER SERVING:
226 cal., 4 g total fat (1 g sat. fat), 116 mg chol., 447 mg sodium, 17 g carb., 0 g fiber, 30 g pro.

225

Turkey, Black Bean, and Mango Tacos

PREP 25 minutes SLOW COOK 6 to 7 hours (low) or 3 hours to 3 hours 30 minutes (high) MAKES 8 servings

1¾ **pounds turkey thighs, skinned**

1 **15-ounce can black beans, rinsed and drained**

1 **10-ounce can enchilada sauce**

1 **10-ounce can diced tomatoes and green chiles, undrained**

1 **tablespoon ground ancho chile pepper**

2 **teaspoons ground cumin**

2 **tablespoons lime juice**

   Salt

   Ground black pepper

16 **5- to 6-inch corn or flour tortillas, warmed***

1 **medium ripe mango, peeled, pitted, and chopped**

½ **cup refrigerated avocado dip (guacamole)**

   Assorted fillings, such as shredded lettuce, crumbled Cotija or shredded Monterey Jack cheese, and/or sour cream (optional)

1 Place turkey thighs, bone sides down, in a 3½- or 4-quart slow cooker. In a medium bowl combine beans, enchilada sauce, tomatoes and chiles, ground ancho pepper, and cumin. Pour mixture over turkey.

2 Cover and cook on low-heat setting for 6 to 7 hours or on high-heat setting for 3 to 3½ hours.

3 Transfer turkey to a cutting board. When turkey is cool enough to handle, remove meat from bones; discard bones. Using two forks, pull turkey apart into shreds. Return shredded turkey to cooker. Stir in lime juice. Season to taste with salt and black pepper.

4 Using a slotted spoon, spoon turkey mixture onto tortillas. Top with mango, guacamole, and, if desired, assorted fillings. Fold tortillas in half.

NUTRITION FACTS PER SERVING:
428 cal., 13 g total fat (4 g sat. fat), 86 mg chol., 1110 mg sodium, 53 g carb., 8 g fiber, 30 g pro.

*tip
To warm tortillas in the oven, preheat oven to 350°F. Stack tortillas and wrap tightly in foil. Bake about 10 minutes or until heated through. To warm tortillas in the microwave, stack tortillas and wrap in paper towels. Microwave on 100 percent power (high) for 30 seconds.

Slow Cooker Marinara Sauce

PREP **20 minutes** SLOW COOK **8 to 10 hours (low) or 4 to 5 hours (high)** MAKES **6 servings**

1   28-ounce can Italian-style whole peeled tomatoes in puree, undrained and cut up

2   cups coarsely chopped carrots (4 medium)

1½ cups sliced celery (3 stalks)

1   cup chopped onion (1 large)

1   cup chopped green sweet pepper (1 large)

1   6-ounce can tomato paste

½   cup water

2   teaspoons sugar

2   teaspoons dried Italian seasoning, crushed

3   cloves garlic, minced

1   bay leaf

1   teaspoon salt

¼   teaspoon ground black pepper

12 ounces hot cooked whole grain spaghetti

Shredded Parmesan cheese

1 For sauce, in a 3½- or 4-quart slow cooker combine tomatoes, carrots, celery, onion, sweet pepper, tomato paste, the water, sugar, Italian seasoning, garlic, bay leaf, salt, and black pepper.

2 Cover and cook on low-heat setting for 8 to 10 hours or on high-heat setting for 4 to 5 hours.

3 Remove and discard bay leaf. In a large serving bowl pour sauce over hot cooked spaghetti; toss gently to coat. Sprinkle with cheese.

NUTRITION FACTS PER SERVING:
308 cal., 1 g total fat (0 g sat. fat), 0 mg chol., 636 mg sodium, 64 g carb., 6 g fiber, 11 g pro.

227

tip
Always fill your slow cooker at least half full but no more than two-thirds full.

Double-Cheese Macaroni and Cheese

PREP 25 minutes   SLOW COOK 3 hours (low)   MAKES 4 servings

10   ounces dried elbow macaroni
     Nonstick cooking spray
 1   12-ounce can evaporated milk
 2   cups milk
 6   1-ounce slices American
     cheese, torn
½   cup finely chopped celery
     (1 stalk)
⅓   cup finely chopped red onion
     (1 small)
½   teaspoon salt
½   teaspoon ground white
     pepper
½   cup shredded cheddar or
     Gruyère cheese (2 ounces)

1 In a large saucepan cook macaroni in a large amount of boiling water for 2 minutes; drain.

2 Coat the inside of a 3½- or 4-quart slow cooker with cooking spray. Add cooked macaroni, evaporated milk, 1½ cups of the milk, the American cheese, celery, onion, salt, and pepper. Stir well to combine.

3 Cover and cook on low-heat setting for 3 hours, giving the crockery liner a half turn after 1½ hours of cooking, if possible. Add remaining ½ cup milk and the cheddar cheese; stir until cheese is melted and mixture is creamy.

NUTRITION FACTS PER SERVING:
665 cal., 28 g total fat (17 g sat. fat), 89 mg chol., 1072 mg sodium, 71 g carb., 3 g fiber, 32 g pro.

Hearty Mushrooms and Polenta

PREP 25 minutes   SLOW COOK 6 to 7 hours (low)   MAKES 6 servings

2   tablespoons butter

3   cups sliced fresh cremini or stemmed shiitake mushrooms (8 ounces)

1   cup fresh or frozen whole kernel corn

7   cups vegetable broth or chicken broth

2   cups yellow cornmeal

1   tablespoon snipped fresh sage

4   cloves garlic, minced

1   teaspoon salt

1   teaspoon freshly ground black pepper

1   cup shredded Gruyère cheese (4 ounces)

½   cup halved or quartered yellow and/or red cherry tomatoes

    Fresh sage leaves (optional)

1 In a large skillet heat butter over medium heat until melted. Add mushrooms; cook until brown and liquid is evaporated. Stir in corn.

2 In a 4- to 5-quart slow cooker combine mushroom mixture, broth, cornmeal, snipped sage, garlic, salt, and pepper.

3 Cover and cook on low-heat setting for 6 to 7 hours. Stir until smooth. Stir in cheese until melted. Serve with tomatoes. If desired, garnish with sage leaves.

NUTRITION FACTS PER SERVING:
339 cal., 11 g total fat (6 g sat. fat), 31 mg chol., 1530 mg sodium, 49 g carb., 3 g fiber, 11 g pro.

229

Cheesy Mushroom and Pepper Grits

PREP 25 minutes   SLOW COOK 7 to 8 hours (low) or 3 hours 30 minutes to 4 hours (high)   MAKES 6 servings

- 9 cups vegetable broth
- 2 cups uncooked grits
- 3 cups torn fresh kale
- 2 cups sliced fresh cremini mushrooms (6 ounces)
- 2 fresh poblano chile peppers* or red sweet peppers, seeded and chopped
- ½ cup chopped onion (1 medium)
- 4 cloves garlic, minced
- 1 teaspoon salt
- 1 to 1½ cups shredded Monterey Jack cheese with jalapeño peppers or sharp cheddar cheese (4 to 6 ounces)
- ¼ cup butter
- 1 cup quartered or halved cherry tomatoes
- 1 cup chopped pecans, toasted
   Bottled hot pepper sauce

1 In a 5- to 6-quart slow cooker stir together broth and grits. Stir in kale, mushrooms, poblano peppers, onion, garlic, and salt.

2 Cover and cook on low-heat setting for 7 to 8 hours or on high-heat setting for 3½ to 4 hours or until grits are tender and mixture is starting to thicken.

3 Add cheese and butter, stirring until smooth. Serve with tomatoes, pecans, and hot pepper sauce.

NUTRITION FACTS PER SERVING:
539 cal., 28 g total fat (10 g sat. fat), 40 mg chol., 2009 mg sodium, 59 g carb., 6 g fiber, 14 g pro.

230

*tip
Because chile peppers contain volatile oils that can burn your skin and eyes, avoid direct contact with them as much as possible. When working with chile peppers, wear plastic or rubber gloves. If your bare hands do touch the peppers, wash your hands and nails well with soap and warm water.

Loaded Creamed Corn with Tomato and Bacon

PREP 25 minutes SLOW COOK 3 to 4 hours (low) or 1 hour 30 minutes to 2 hours (high) STAND 5 minutes

MAKES 16 servings

4 12-ounce packages frozen whole kernel corn, thawed

1½ cups half-and-half or light cream

1 cup chopped onion (1 large)

½ cup grated Parmesan cheese

¼ cup butter, cut up

1 teaspoon sugar

½ teaspoon salt

¼ teaspoon ground black pepper

5 thick slices bacon

¾ cup shredded Monterey Jack cheese with jalapeño peppers or Monterey Jack cheese (3 ounces)

½ cup chopped tomato (1 medium)

2 tablespoons snipped fresh Italian (flat-leaf) parsley

1 teaspoon red wine vinegar

⅛ teaspoon sugar

1 In a blender combine one of the packages of corn and the half-and-half. Cover and blend until smooth. In a 3½- or 4-quart slow cooker combine pureed corn, the remaining corn, onion, Parmesan cheese, butter, 1 teaspoon sugar, salt, and pepper.

2 Cover and cook on low-heat setting for 3 to 4 hours or on high-heat setting for 1½ to 2 hours.

3 In a large skillet cook bacon over medium heat until crisp. Remove bacon and drain on paper towels. Cut bacon into 1-inch pieces.

4 Sprinkle bacon and Monterey Jack cheese over corn mixture in cooker. Cover and let stand about 5 minutes or until cheese is melted.

5 In a small bowl stir together tomato, parsley, vinegar, and ⅛ teaspoon sugar. Before serving, spoon tomato mixture over corn mixture in cooker.

NUTRITION FACTS PER SERVING:
186 cal., 10 g total fat (6 g sat. fat), 27 mg chol., 258 mg sodium, 20 g carb., 2 g fiber, 7 g pro.

231

tip
When purchasing bacon for this recipe, avoid maple-flavor varieties.

Spanish Rice

PREP **25 minutes** SLOW COOK **4 hours to 4 hours 30 minutes (low)** MAKES **10 servings**

- 1 **28-ounce can diced tomatoes, undrained**
- 1 **cup uncooked converted rice (do not substitute long grain rice)**
- 1 **cup chopped onion (1 large)**
- 1 **cup chopped green sweet pepper (1 large)**
- 1 **cup chicken broth**
- 1 **8-ounce can tomato sauce**
- 1 **4-ounce can diced green chile peppers, undrained**
- 1 **tablespoon chili powder**
- 1 **tablespoon Worcestershire sauce**
- 2 **teaspoons packed brown sugar**
- 2 **cloves garlic, minced**
- ½ **teaspoon bottled hot pepper sauce**
- ¼ **teaspoon salt**
- ¼ **teaspoon ground black pepper**

1 Line a 3½- or 4-quart slow cooker with a disposable slow cooker liner. In the prepared cooker combine tomatoes, rice, onion, sweet pepper, broth, tomato sauce, chile peppers, chili powder, Worcestershire sauce, brown sugar, garlic, hot pepper sauce, salt, and black pepper.

2 Cover and cook on low-heat setting for 4 to 4½ hours.

NUTRITION FACTS PER SERVING:
110 cal., 0 g total fat (0 g sat. fat), 0 mg chol., 489 mg sodium, 25 g carb., 3 g fiber, 3 g pro.

232

Orange-Glazed Carrots and Parsnips

PREP 25 minutes   SLOW COOK 8 to 10 hours (low) or 4 to 5 hours (high)   MAKES 10 servings

2   pounds carrots, cut into
    2-inch chunks

1   pound parsnips, peeled and
    cut into 2-inch chunks

1   cup orange juice

½   cup orange marmalade

½   cup vegetable broth

¼   cup dry white wine

1   tablespoon quick-cooking
    tapioca, crushed

½   teaspoon salt

¼   teaspoon ground black pepper

2   tablespoons finely shredded
    orange peel

¼   cup snipped fresh parsley

3   tablespoons butter

1 In a 3½- or 4-quart slow cooker combine carrots and parsnips. In a small bowl combine orange juice, marmalade, broth, wine, tapioca, salt, and pepper. Pour juice mixture over carrot mixture; toss to coat.

2 Cover and cook on low-heat setting for 8 to 10 hours or on high-heat setting for 4 to 5 hours or until vegetables are tender, stirring in orange peel, parsley, and butter for the last 30 minutes of cooking.

NUTRITION FACTS PER SERVING:
159 cal., 4 g total fat (2 g sat. fat), 9 mg chol., 265 mg sodium, 31 g carb., 5 g fiber, 2 g pro.

233

tip

Quick-cooking tapioca is an ideal thickener for slow-cooked sauces, soups, and stews because it doesn't break down during long cooking times. Most recipes will call for tapioca to be crushed. The easiest way to crush tapioca is to use a mortar and pestle. If you don't have one, place tapioca in a small resealable plastic bag and crush it with a rolling pin.

Apple-Buttered Sweet Potatoes

PREP 15 minutes   SLOW COOK 6 to 7 hours (low) or 3 hours to 3 hours 30 minutes (high)   MAKES 10 servings

3 pounds sweet potatoes, peeled and cut into 1-inch pieces (about 8 cups)

2 medium Granny Smith or other tart cooking apples, peeled, cored, and cut into wedges

$\frac{1}{2}$ cup dried cherries or dried cranberries (optional)

1 cup whipping cream

1 cup apple butter

$1\frac{1}{2}$ teaspoons pumpkin pie spice

1 In a $3\frac{1}{2}$- or 4-quart slow cooker combine sweet potatoes, apples, and, if desired, dried cherries. In a medium bowl combine whipping cream, apple butter, and pumpkin pie spice. Pour over mixture in cooker; stir gently to combine.

2 Cover and cook on low-heat setting for 6 to 7 hours or on high-heat setting for 3 to $3\frac{1}{2}$ hours.

NUTRITION FACTS PER SERVING: *351 cal., 9 g total fat (6 g sat. fat), 33 mg chol., 25 mg sodium, 65 g carb., 5 g fiber, 2 g pro.*

Rustic Garlic Mashed Potatoes

Photo on page 274

PREP 25 minutes   SLOW COOK 6 to 8 hours (low) or 3 to 4 hours (high)   MAKES 12 servings

3   pounds russet potatoes, peeled and cut into 2-inch pieces

6   cloves garlic, halved

1   bay leaf

2   14.5-ounce cans chicken broth with roasted garlic

1   cup whole milk

¼   cup butter

1   teaspoon salt

   Ground black pepper

   Fresh bay leaves (optional)

1 In a 3½- or 4-quart slow cooker combine potatoes, garlic, and dried bay leaf. Pour broth over mixture in cooker.

2 Cover and cook on low-heat setting for 6 to 8 hours or on high-heat setting for 3 to 4 hours.

3 Drain potatoes in a colander set over a bowl to catch the cooking liquid; set liquid aside. Remove and discard bay leaf. Return potatoes to slow cooker. Using a potato masher, mash potatoes to desired consistency.

4 In a small saucepan heat milk and butter until milk is steaming and butter is almost melted. Add milk mixture and salt to mashed potatoes. Stir in enough of the reserved cooking liquid to make mashed potatoes light and fluffy.

5 Transfer mashed potatoes to a serving bowl. Sprinkle potatoes with pepper. If desired, garnish with fresh bay leaves.

NUTRITION FACTS PER SERVING:
135 cal., 5 g total fat (3 g sat. fat), 13 mg chol., 496 mg sodium, 21 g carb., 1 g fiber, 3 g pro.

235

Make-Ahead Directions: Prepare as directed, except leave mashed potatoes in slow cooker. Cover and keep warm on warm setting or low-heat setting for up to 2 hours. Reserve cooking liquid. If potatoes thicken, stir in enough of the reserved cooking liquid to make mashed potatoes light and fluffy. Serve as directed.

Pumpernickel-Cherry Stuffing

PREP 20 minutes BAKE 10 minutes at 350°F SLOW COOK 4 to 6 hours (low) or 2 hours 30 minutes to 3 hours (high)
MAKES 18 servings

6   cups pumpernickel bread cut into ³⁄₄-inch cubes (12 ounces)
6   cups rye bread cut into ³⁄₄-inch cubes
¼   cup butter
2   cups chopped onions (2 large)
1   cup chopped celery (2 stalks)
3   cloves garlic, minced
2   eggs, lightly beaten
1   14.5-ounce can chicken broth
2   cups dried cherries
1   cup chopped pear (1 medium)
1   cup chopped Granny Smith apple (1 medium)
¼   cup snipped fresh parsley
1   tablespoon snipped fresh sage
½   teaspoon ground black pepper
     Nonstick cooking spray

1 Preheat oven to 350°F. Spread pumpernickel and rye bread cubes in two 15×10×1-inch baking pans. Bake for 10 to 15 minutes or until cubes are dry and lightly toasted. Cool completely.

2 In a large skillet heat butter over medium-high heat until melted. Add onions and celery; cook about 5 minutes or until tender, stirring occasionally. Add garlic; cook and for 1 minute more.

3 In a large bowl combine eggs and broth. Add onion mixture, cherries, pear, apple, parsley, sage, and pepper. Fold in bread cubes until moistened.

4 Lightly coat the inside of a 5- to 6-quart slow cooker with cooking spray. Add bread mixture to cooker, spreading into an even layer.

5 Cover and cook on low-heat setting for 4 to 6 hours or on high-heat setting for 2½ to 3 hours. Serve immediately or keep warm, covered, on warm setting or low-heat setting for up to 2 hours.

NUTRITION FACTS PER SERVING:
160 cal., 4 g total fat (2 g sat. fat), 31 mg chol., 292 mg sodium, 30 g carb., 3 g fiber, 4 g pro.

Main Dish Meats, Poultry, and Seafood

These Sunday-dinner-worthy main dishes are satisfying, delicious, and will keep everyone coming back for more.

7

Sunday Oven Pot Roast

Photo on page 276

PREP 30 minutes BAKE 2 hours 5 minutes at 325°F MAKES 6 servings

1 2½- to 3-pound boneless beef chuck pot roast

Salt

Ground black pepper

2 tablespoons olive oil or vegetable oil

1 14.5-ounce can beef broth

1 cup chopped onion (1 large)

2 stalks celery, cut into 2-inch pieces

5 cups assorted vegetables, such as peeled Yukon gold or sweet potatoes, cut into 2-inch chunks; parsnips, peeled and cut into 2-inch chunks; whole shallots or garlic bulb, peeled and halved horizontally; and/or small carrots, cut into 1½-inch pieces

¼ cup cold water

3 tablespoons all-purpose flour

1 Preheat oven to 325°F. Trim fat from meat. Sprinkle meat with salt and pepper. In a roasting pan or large oven-going Dutch oven heat oil over medium heat. Add meat; cook until brown on all sides. Carefully drain off fat. Add broth, onion, and celery to pan.

2 Transfer roasting pan to oven. Bake, covered, for 1¼ hours. Remove celery with a slotted spoon; discard. Place 5 cups assorted vegetables around meat. Bake, uncovered, for 50 to 60 minutes more or until meat and vegetables are tender, spooning juices over meat and vegetables twice during baking. Using a slotted spoon, transfer meat and vegetables to a serving platter; keep warm.

3 For gravy, transfer cooking liquid to a glass measuring cup; skim off any fat. Discard enough cooking liquid or add enough water to measure 1½ cups. In a medium saucepan stir the cold water into flour until smooth; stir in the 1½ cups cooking liquid. Cook and stir until over medium heat until thickened and bubbly. Cook and stir for 1 minute more. Season to taste with salt and pepper. Serve meat and vegetables with gravy.

NUTRITION FACTS PER SERVING:
419 cal., 14 g total fat (4 g sat. fat), 112 mg chol., 584 mg sodium, 29 g carb., 4 g fiber, 43 g pro.

Boeuf Bourguignon

PREP 25 minutes   COOK 10 minutes   MAKES 4 servings

12   ounces boneless beef sirloin
      steak
1   tablespoon olive oil
1   cup thinly sliced carrots
      (2 medium)
½   cup thinly sliced celery
      (1 stalk)
2   cloves garlic, minced
1   cup frozen small whole onions
1   ounce dried chanterelle
      mushrooms, rinsed and
      chopped
2¾   cups lower-sodium beef broth
¾   cup dry red wine
⅓   cup tomato paste
1   teaspoon dried herbes de
      Provence, crushed
¼   teaspoon ground black pepper

1 Trim fat from meat. Cut meat into thin bite-size strips. In a 4-quart nonstick Dutch oven heat 2 teaspoons of the oil over medium-high heat. Add meat; cook and stir until brown. Remove meat from Dutch oven.

2 Add the remaining 1 teaspoon oil to Dutch oven. Add carrots, celery, and garlic; cook for 8 to 10 minutes or until vegetables are tender, stirring occasionally. Return meat to Dutch oven; add onions and mushrooms.

3 In a medium bowl whisk together broth, wine, tomato paste, herbes de Provence, and pepper. Stir broth mixture into meat mixture. Bring to boiling; reduce heat. Simmer, covered, for 10 minutes to blend flavors.

NUTRITION FACTS PER SERVING:
265 cal., 8 g total fat (2 g sat. fat), 52 mg chol., 525 mg sodium, 17 g carb., 3 g fiber, 22 g pro.

239

Main Dish Meats, Poultry, and Seafood

Braised Beef with Red Wine Sauce

PREP 40 minutes COOK 1 hour 30 minutes MAKES 6 servings

1 2½- to 3-pound boneless beef sirloin tip or round roast

4 ounces pancetta, chopped

2 tablespoons olive oil

½ teaspoon salt

¼ teaspoon freshly ground black pepper

1 cup chopped carrots (2 medium)

1 cup chopped onion (1 large)

¾ cup chopped red sweet pepper (1 medium)

½ cup chopped celery (1 stalk)

2 cloves garlic, minced

¾ cup dry red wine

1 28-ounce can Italian-style whole peeled tomatoes in puree, undrained and cut up

2 tablespoons snipped fresh basil or 1 teaspoon dried basil, crushed

1 tablespoon tomato paste

1 teaspoon snipped fresh oregano or ¼ teaspoon dried oregano, crushed

1 bay leaf

¼ cup whipping cream

1 Trim fat from roast; set aside. In a 4- to 6-quart Dutch oven cook pancetta over medium heat until crisp. Using a slotted spoon, remove pancetta and drain on paper towels, reserving drippings in Dutch oven. Add oil to Dutch oven. Add roast; cook over medium-high heat until brown on all sides. Sprinkle with salt and pepper. Transfer roast to a plate, reserving drippings in Dutch oven.

2 Add carrots, onion, sweet pepper, celery, and garlic to the reserved drippings. Cook about 10 minutes or until light brown, stirring occasionally. Remove from heat. Add wine; return to heat, stirring to scrape up crusty brown bits in bottom of pan. Simmer, uncovered, for 1 minute. Stir in tomatoes, basil, tomato paste, oregano, and bay leaf. Return roast to Dutch oven.

3 Bring to boiling; reduce heat. Simmer, covered, about 1½ hours or until roast is tender. Transfer roast to a serving platter; keep warm.

4 For sauce, simmer tomato mixture, uncovered, about 12 minutes or until reduced to about 4½ cups. Remove and discard bay leaf. Stir in whipping cream. Serve roast with sauce. Sprinkle with crisped pancetta.

NUTRITION FACTS PER SERVING:
425 cal., 16 g total fat (7 g sat. fat), 117 mg chol., 703 mg sodium, 16 g carb., 3 g fiber, 47 g pro.

Slow Cooker Directions: Use the ingredients as directed, except omit oil, reduce wine to ½ cup, and use dried basil and oregano. Cook pancetta as directed. In a 4- to 5-quart slow cooker combine carrots, onion, sweet pepper, celery, and garlic. Place roast on top of vegetables, trimming to fit if necessary. In a medium bowl combine the ½ cup wine, dried basil and oregano, tomatoes, tomato paste, bay leaf, salt, and pepper. Stir in 2 tablespoons quick-cooking tapioca, crushed. Pour tomato mixture over roast in cooker. Cover and cook on low-heat setting for 9 to 10 hours or on high-heat setting for 4½ to 5 hours. Remove and discard bay leaf. Transfer roast to a serving platter. For sauce, stir whipping cream and cooked pancetta into tomato mixture. Serve roast with sauce.

New England Boiled Dinner

PREP 25 minutes COOK 2 hours 25 minutes MAKES 6 servings

1   2- to 2½-pound corned beef brisket

1   teaspoon black peppercorns, if needed

2   bay leaves, if needed

2   medium red potatoes, peeled and quartered

3   medium carrots, quartered

2   medium parsnips or 1 medium rutabaga, peeled and cut into chunks

1   medium onion, cut into 6 wedges

1   small head green cabbage, cut into 6 wedges

Salt (optional)

Ground black pepper (optional)

Prepared horseradish or mustard (optional)

1   Trim fat from meat. Place meat in a 4- to 6-quart Dutch oven; add juices and spices from package of corned beef. (Add peppercorns and bay leaves if your brisket doesn't come with a packet of spices.) Add enough water to cover meat. Bring to boiling; reduce heat. Simmer, covered, about 2 hours or until meat is nearly tender.

2   Add potatoes, carrots, parsnips, and onion to Dutch oven. Return to boiling; reduce heat. Simmer, covered, for 10 minutes. Add cabbage. Simmer, covered, for 15 to 20 minutes more or until meat and vegetables are tender. If using, remove and discard bay leaves.

3   Thinly slice meat across the grain. Transfer meat and vegetables to a serving platter. If desired, season to taste with salt and ground pepper. If desired, serve with horseradish.

NUTRITION FACTS PER SERVING:
357 cal., 18 g total fat (5 g sat. fat), 77 mg chol., 131 mg sodium, 23 g carb., 5 g fiber, 25 g pro.

Swiss Steak

PREP 25 minutes COOK 1 hour 15 minutes MAKES 4 servings

- 2 tablespoons all-purpose flour
- 1 teaspoon smoked paprika or Hungarian paprika
- ¼ teaspoon salt
- ¼ teaspoon ground black pepper
- 4 5-ounce beef cubed steaks or two 10-ounce beef cubed steaks
- 1 tablespoon vegetable oil
- 1 14.5-ounce can diced tomatoes with basil, garlic, and oregano, undrained
- ½ cup sliced celery (1 stalk)
- ½ cup sliced carrot (1 medium)
- 1 small onion, sliced and separated into rings
- ¼ cup water
- 2 cups hot mashed potatoes

1 In a shallow dish stir together flour, paprika, salt, and pepper. If using 10-ounce steaks, cut each steak in half. Dip meat into flour mixture, turning to coat.

2 In a large skillet heat oil over medium-high heat. Add meat; cook until brown on both sides. Drain off fat. Add tomatoes, celery, carrot, onion, and the water. Bring to boiling; reduce heat. Simmer, covered, about 1¼ hours or until meat is tender. Serve meat and vegetable mixture with mashed potatoes.

NUTRITION FACTS PER SERVING:
421 cal., 15 g total fat (5 g sat. fat), 59 mg chol., 1099 mg sodium, 33 g carb., 3 g fiber, 36 g pro.

Oven Directions: Preheat oven to 350°F. Prepare and brown meat in skillet as directed. Transfer meat to a 2-quart square baking dish. In the same skillet combine tomatoes, celery, carrot, onion, and the water. Bring to boiling, scraping up crusty brown bits. Pour over meat. Bake, covered, about 1 hour or until tender.

Steak with Creamy Onion Sauce

START TO FINISH **30 minutes** MAKES **4 servings**

1 tablespoon butter

1 cup coarsely chopped sweet onion, such as Maui, Vidalia, or Walla Walla (1 large)

½ cup light sour cream

1 tablespoon capers, drained

2 teaspoons Montreal steak seasoning

4 beef rib-eye steaks, cut 1 inch thick

1 For sauce, in a large skillet heat butter over medium-low heat until melted. Add onion; cook, covered, for 13 to 15 minutes or until onion is very tender, stirring occasionally. Increase heat to medium-high. Cook, uncovered, for 3 to 5 minutes or until onion is golden, stirring frequently. Reduce heat to medium-low. Stir in sour cream, capers, and ½ teaspoon of the steak seasoning. Cook until heated through (do not boil).

2 Meanwhile, preheat broiler. Trim fat from steaks. Sprinkle steaks with the remaining 1½ teaspoons steak seasoning. Place steaks on the unheated rack of a broiler pan. Broil 3 to 4 inches from the heat for 12 to 14 minutes for medium-rare (145°F) or 15 to 18 minutes for medium (160°F), turning once halfway through broiling. Cover steaks with foil; let stand for 5 minutes before serving.

3 Transfer steaks to serving plates. Spoon some of the sauce over steaks. Pass the remaining sauce.

NUTRITION FACTS PER SERVING:
348 cal., 20 g total fat (9 g sat. fat), 116 mg chol., 550 mg sodium, 6 g carb., 1 g fiber, 36 g pro.

243

Chipotle Braised Short Ribs and Cheesy Polenta

PREP 50 minutes COOK 3 hours MAKES 6 servings

- 3 **pounds boneless beef short ribs or 12 bone-in beef short ribs**
- ¾ **teaspoon salt**
- ½ **teaspoon ground black pepper**
- ⅓ **cup all-purpose flour**
- 1 **tablespoon vegetable oil**
- 2 **cups dry red wine or cranberry juice**
- 1 **14.5-ounce can beef broth**
- 1 **tablespoon snipped fresh thyme or 1 teaspoon dried thyme, crushed**
- 3 **cloves garlic, peeled**
- 1 **bay leaf**
- 6 **cups water**
- 2 **tablespoons sugar**
- 8 **ounces baby carrots with tops, trimmed, or regular carrots, sliced**
- 2 **small parsnips, peeled and sliced**
- 1 **10-ounce package (15 to 20) red pearl onions, peeled***
- 1 **cup chopped, seeded tomatoes (2 medium)**
- 1 **or 2 canned chipotle peppers in adobo sauce, drained and chopped**
- 1 **recipe Cheesy Polenta**

1 Sprinkle ribs with salt and black pepper. Place flour in a shallow dish. Dip ribs into flour, turning to coat. In a 6- to 8-quart Dutch oven cook ribs, half at a time, in hot oil over medium-high heat until brown on all sides. Drain off fat. Add wine, broth, dried thyme (if using), garlic, and bay leaf. Bring to boiling; reduce heat. Simmer, covered, for 2 hours.

2 Meanwhile, in a large saucepan bring the water to boiling. Add sugar; stir until sugar is dissolved. Add carrots, parsnips, and onions. Cook for 5 to 7 minutes or just until vegetables are tender; drain. Submerge vegetables in a large bowl of ice water; cool for 5 minutes. Drain; cover and chill until needed.

3 Add tomatoes, chipotle peppers, and fresh thyme (if using) to rib mixture. Simmer, covered, for 30 minutes. Stir in chilled vegetables. Simmer, covered, about 30 minutes more or until ribs are very tender. Remove and discard bay leaf.

4 To serve, use a slotted spoon to transfer ribs and vegetables to shallow bowls. Spoon Cheesy Polenta alongside the ribs and vegetables. Skim fat from cooking liquid; spoon some of the liquid over ribs and vegetables.

NUTRITION FACTS PER SERVING:
463 cal., 15 g total fat (6 g sat. fat), 60 mg chol., 1100 mg sodium, 43 g carb., 5 g fiber, 25 g pro.

Cheesy Polenta

In a large saucepan bring 2½ cups water to boiling. Meanwhile, in a medium bowl combine 1 cup yellow cornmeal, 1 cup cold water, and ½ teaspoon salt. Slowly add cornmeal mixture to boiling water, stirring constantly. Cook and stir until mixture returns to boiling. Reduce heat to low. Cook, uncovered, for 10 to 15 minutes or until mixture is very thick, stirring occasionally. Stir in ¼ cup milk. Gently stir in ½ cup finely shredded Parmesan cheese (2 ounces) until melted.

244

***tip**
To peel pearl onions easily, cook in boiling water for 30 seconds. Drain and cool. Cut a thin slice off each root end and squeeze from the other end to remove the peel.

Beef Short Ribs with Smashed Horseradish Parsnips

PREP 25 minutes BAKE 2 hours at 350°F MAKES 4 servings

3   pounds bone-in beef short ribs

½   teaspoon salt

¼   teaspoon ground black pepper

1   tablespoon olive oil

1   14.5-ounce can lower-sodium beef broth

½   cup water

1½   pounds parsnips, peeled and cut into 1½-inch chunks

½   cup chopped onion (1 medium)

8   cloves garlic, peeled

1   teaspoon snipped fresh rosemary

¼   cup half-and-half or light cream

2   tablespoons butter

1   tablespoon prepared horseradish

    Salt

    Ground black pepper

    Snipped fresh rosemary (optional)

1 Preheat oven to 350°F. Sprinkle ribs with ½ teaspoon salt and ¼ teaspoon pepper. In a Dutch oven heat oil over medium-high heat. Add ribs; cook until brown on all sides. Remove ribs from Dutch oven. Drain off fat.

2 Add broth and the water to Dutch oven, stirring to scrape up crusty brown bits in bottom of pan. Bring to boiling. Return ribs to Dutch oven. Add parsnips, onion, garlic, and 1 teaspoon rosemary. Return to boiling. Cover Dutch oven and transfer to oven. Bake about 2 hours or until ribs are very tender.

3 Transfer ribs to a serving platter. Using a slotted spoon, transfer parsnips and garlic to a medium bowl. Coarsely mash parsnips with a potato masher. Stir in half-and-half, butter, and horseradish. Season to taste with additional salt and pepper.

4 Skim fat from cooking liquid. Serve ribs and mashed parsnips with some of the cooking liquid. If desired, sprinkle with additional rosemary.

NUTRITION FACTS PER SERVING:
761 cal., 63 g total fat (28 g sat. fat), 135 mg chol., 435 mg sodium, 21 g carb., 5 g fiber, 26 g pro.

German Meatballs with Spaetzle

PREP 25 minutes   COOK 25 minutes   MAKES 4 servings

1   egg, lightly beaten
¼   cup milk
¼   cup fine dry bread crumbs
1   tablespoon snipped fresh parsley
½   teaspoon salt
    Pinch ground black pepper
1   pound ground beef
1⅓ cups beef broth
1   4-ounce can (drained weight) mushroom stems and pieces, drained
½   cup chopped onion (1 medium)
1   8-ounce carton sour cream
2   tablespoons all-purpose flour
½   to 1 teaspoon caraway seeds
2   cups all-purpose flour
1   teaspoon salt
2   eggs, lightly beaten
1   cup milk
    Snipped fresh parsley (optional)

1 For meatballs, in a large bowl combine 1 egg and ¼ cup milk. Stir in bread crumbs, 1 tablespoon parsley, ½ teaspoon salt, and pepper. Add ground beef; mix well. Shape mixture into twenty-four 1½-inch meatballs.

2 In a large nonstick skillet cook meatballs over medium-high heat until brown. Drain off fat. Add broth, mushrooms, and onion. Bring to boiling; reduce heat. Simmer, covered, about 20 minutes or until meatballs are done (160°F). In a small bowl combine sour cream, 2 tablespoons flour, and caraway seeds; stir into broth mixture. Cook and stir until thickened and bubbly. Cook and stir for 1 minute more.

3 Meanwhile, for spaetzle, in a medium bowl stir together 2 cups flour and 1 teaspoon salt. Stir in 2 eggs and 1 cup milk. Let rest for 5 to 10 minutes. Bring a large saucepan of salted water to boiling. Holding a coarse-sieved colander or the basket for a deep-fat fryer over the pan of rapidly boiling water, pour batter into colander. Press batter through colander with the back of wooden spoon. Cook and stir for 5 minutes; drain. Serve meatballs with spaetzle. If desired, sprinkle with additional parsley.

NUTRITION FACTS PER SERVING:
733 cal., 35 g total fat (15 g sat. fat), 271 mg chol., 1675 mg sodium, 64 g carb., 3 g fiber, 39 g pro.

Chicken Fried Steak

PREP 35 minutes COOK 45 minutes MAKES 4 servings

- 1 pound boneless beef top round steak, cut ½ inch thick
- ¾ cup fine dry bread crumbs
- 1½ teaspoons snipped fresh basil or oregano or ½ teaspoon dried basil or oregano, crushed
- ½ teaspoon salt
- ¼ teaspoon ground black pepper
- 1 egg, lightly beaten
- 1 tablespoon milk
- 2 tablespoons vegetable oil
- 1 medium onion, sliced and separated into rings
- 2 tablespoons all-purpose flour
- 1⅓ cups milk
- Salt
- Ground black pepper

1 Trim fat from meat. Cut meat into four serving-size pieces. Place each piece between two pieces of plastic wrap. Using the flat side of a meat mallet, pound meat lightly until about ¼ inch thick. Remove plastic wrap.

2 In a shallow dish combine bread crumbs, basil, ½ teaspoon salt, and ¼ teaspoon pepper. In another shallow dish combine egg and 1 tablespoon milk. Dip meat pieces into egg mixture, then into bread crumb mixture, turning to coat.

3 In an extra-large skillet cook meat, half at time, in hot oil over medium heat until brown on both sides. (Add more oil, if necessary.) Return all of the meat to skillet. Reduce heat to medium-low. Cook, covered, for 45 to 60 minutes or until meat is tender. Transfer meat to a serving platter, reserving drippings in skillet. Keep meat warm.

4 For gravy, cook onion in the reserved drippings over medium heat until tender, stirring occasionally. (Add more oil, if necessary.) Stir in flour. Gradually stir in 1⅓ cups milk. Cook and stir until thickened and bubbly. Cook and stir for 1 minute more. If desired, season to taste with additional salt and pepper. Serve meat with gravy.

NUTRITION FACTS PER SERVING:
351 cal., 13 g total fat (3 g sat. fat), 108 mg chol., 578 mg sodium, 23 g carb., 1 g fiber, 34 g pro.

Steak au Poivre

START TO FINISH **30 minutes**   MAKES **4 servings**

- **4   beef tenderloin steaks or 2 boneless beef top loin steaks, cut 1 inch thick (about 1 pound total)**
- **1   tablespoon cracked black pepper**
- **2   tablespoons butter**
- **¼   cup brandy or beef broth**
- **¼   cup beef broth**
- **½   cup whipping cream**
- **2   teaspoons Dijon-style mustard**

1 Trim fat from steaks. Sprinkle pepper evenly over both sides of steaks; press in with your fingers. If using top loin steaks, cut each steak in half crosswise. In a large skillet cook steaks in hot butter over medium heat to desired doneness, turning once. For tenderloin steaks, allow 10 to 13 minutes for medium-rare (145°F) to medium (160°F). For top loin steaks, allow 12 to 15 minutes for medium-rare (145°F) to medium (160°F). Remove from heat.

2 Transfer steaks to a serving platter, reserving drippings in skillet. Keep steaks warm. Let skillet cool for 1 minute.

3 For sauce, in a small bowl combine brandy and broth; add to the reserved drippings, stirring to scrape up crusty brown bits in bottom of pan. Stir in whipping cream and mustard. Bring to boiling; reduce heat. Boil gently, uncovered, for 5 to 6 minutes or until mixture is reduced to ½ cup, stirring occasionally. Serve steaks with sauce.

NUTRITION FACTS PER SERVING:
370 cal., 25 g total fat (13 g sat. fat), 114 mg chol., 192 mg sodium, 2 g carb., 0 g fiber, 25 g pro.

tip
When buying meat for this recipe, you may see top loin steaks called strip steaks, New York strip, or Kansas City steaks.

Veal Chops with Tomato Cream Sauce

START TO FINISH **30 minutes** MAKES **4 servings**

4 veal loin chops, cut ½ to ¾ inch thick (about 1¾ pounds total)

¼ teaspoon salt

¼ teaspoon ground black pepper

1 tablespoon olive oil

¼ cup chicken broth

¼ cup dry white wine or chicken broth

1 14.5-ounce can diced tomatoes, undrained

2 tablespoons whipping cream

2 teaspoons snipped fresh thyme

1 teaspoon finely shredded lemon peel

1 Trim fat from chops. Sprinkle with salt and pepper. In an extra-large skillet cook chops in hot oil over medium heat, uncovered, for 10 to 14 minutes or until done (160°F), turning once. Transfer to a serving platter; keep warm.

2 For sauce, add broth and wine to skillet, stirring to scrape up crusty brown bits in bottom of skillet. Bring to boiling; reduce heat. Boil gently, uncovered, about 3 minutes or until liquid is reduced by half. Stir in tomatoes. Return to boiling; reduce heat. Boil gently, uncovered, for 5 minutes. Stir in whipping cream, thyme, and lemon peel; heat through. Serve chops with sauce.

NUTRITION FACTS PER SERVING:
320 cal., 13 g total fat (4 g sat. fat), 169 mg chol., 594 mg sodium, 6 g carb., 2 g fiber, 41 g pro.

249

Main Dish Meats, Poultry, and Seafood

Lamb Shanks with Beans

PREP 30 minutes STAND 1 hour COOK 2 hours 10 minutes MAKES 6 servings

1¼ cups dried navy beans

1 tablespoon vegetable oil

4 meaty lamb shanks (about 4 pounds total), cut into 3- to 4-inch pieces, or meaty veal shank cross cuts (about 3 pounds total)

1 medium onion, sliced and separated into rings

2 cloves garlic, minced

2 cups chicken broth

1 teaspoon dried thyme, crushed

½ teaspoon salt

¼ teaspoon ground black pepper

1 14.5-ounce can diced tomatoes, undrained

1 Rinse beans; drain. In a 4- to 6-quart Dutch oven combine beans and 4 cups water. Bring to boiling; reduce heat. Simmer, uncovered, for 2 minutes. Remove from heat. Cover and let stand for 1 hour. (Or place beans in water in Dutch oven. Cover and let soak in a cool place overnight.)

2 Drain and rinse beans and set aside. In the same Dutch oven heat oil over medium heat. Add lamb shanks; cook until brown on all sides. Remove from pan and set aside. Add onion and garlic to the same Dutch oven; cook until tender, stirring occasionally. Add beans, lamb shanks, broth, thyme, salt, and pepper. Bring to boiling; reduce heat. Simmer, covered, for 2 to 2½ hours or until meat and beans are tender. (If necessary, add more broth to keep mixture moist.)

3 Remove lamb shanks from Dutch oven. When cool enough to handle, cut meat off bones; discard bones. Coarsely chop meat. Skim fat from bean mixture. Stir meat and tomatoes into bean mixture. Bring to boiling; reduce heat. Simmer, covered, for 10 to 15 minutes or until heated through and flavors are blended.

NUTRITION FACTS PER SERVING:
430 cal., 10 g total fat (2 g sat. fat), 132 mg chol., 785 mg sodium, 31 g carb., 12 g fiber, 53 g pro.

Pork Pot Roast in Cider

PREP 15 minutes COOK 1 hour 30 minutes MAKES 4 servings

1 1½ to 2-pound boneless pork blade roast or sirloin roast

2 tablespoons vegetable oil

1¼ cups apple cider or apple juice

2 teaspoons instant beef bouillon granules

½ teaspoon dry mustard

¼ teaspoon ground black pepper

3 medium red-skinned or round white potatoes, peeled (if desired) and quartered

3 medium carrots, cut into 2-inch pieces

3 medium parsnips, peeled and cut into 2-inch pieces

1 large onion, cut into wedges

⅓ cup cold water

¼ cup all-purpose flour

1 Trim fat from meat. In a 4- to 6-quart Dutch oven heat oil over medium-high heat. Add meat; cook until brown on all sides. Drain off fat. In a medium bowl stir together apple cider, bouillon granules, dry mustard, and pepper. Pour mixture over meat. Bring to boiling; reduce heat. Simmer, covered, for 1 hour.

2 Add potatoes, carrots, parsnips, and onion. Simmer, covered, for 30 to 40 minutes more or until meat and vegetables are tender. Transfer meat and vegetables to a serving platter, reserving cooking liquid in Dutch oven. Keep meat and vegetables warm.

3 For gravy, measure cooking liquid; skim off fat. If necessary, add enough water to cooking liquid to measure 1½ cups. Return liquid to Dutch oven. In a small bowl stir ⅓ cup cold water into flour until smooth; stir into liquid in pan. Cook and stir over medium heat until thickened and bubbly. Cook and stir for 1 minute more.

4 To serve, remove string from meat, if present. Slice meat; serve with vegetables and gravy.

NUTRITION FACTS PER SERVING:
765 cal., 49 g total fat (15 g sat. fat), 123 mg chol., 573 mg sodium, 50 g carb., 6 g fiber, 32 g pro.

251

Slow Cooker Directions: Prepare and brown meat as directed. In a 3½- or 4-quart slow cooker combine potatoes, carrots, parsnips, and onion. Place meat on top of vegetables, cutting to fit if necessary. Stir together apple cider, bouillon granules, dry mustard, and pepper; pour over meat and vegetables. Cover and cook on low-heat setting for 8 to 10 hours or on high-heat setting for 4 to 5 hours or until tender. Transfer meat and vegetables to a serving platter; keep warm. Prepare gravy in a medium saucepan on the range top as directed in Step 3. Serve as directed.

Rosemary-Roasted Loin of Pork

PREP 30 minutes ROAST 1 hour at 375°F STAND 15 minutes MAKES 8 servings

- 1   cup sliced leeks (3 medium)
- 2   tablespoons snipped fresh basil
- 3   to 4 teaspoons snipped fresh rosemary
- 2   cloves garlic, minced
- ½   teaspoon salt
- ¼   teaspoon freshly ground black pepper
- 2   tablespoons olive oil
- 1   2½-pound boneless pork top loin roast (single loin)
- 2   sprigs fresh rosemary

1 Preheat oven to 375°F. In a food processor combine leeks, basil, snipped rosemary, garlic, salt, and pepper. Add 1 tablespoon of the oil. Cover and process until mixture forms a chunky paste.

2 Trim fat from meat. Cut meat in half lengthwise. Spread half of the leek mixture on cut sides of meat. Place cut sides together and tie tightly with 100-percent-cotton kitchen string. Thread rosemary sprigs through string on meat. Using a skewer, poke holes in the top and sides of meat; brush with the remaining 1 tablespoon oil. Spread the remaining leek mixture over meat. Place meat on a rack in a shallow roasting pan.

3 Roast, uncovered, for 1 to 1½ hours or until juices run clear (150°F). Transfer meat to a serving platter. Cover with foil; let stand for 15 minutes before carving. (Temperature of meat after standing should be 160°F.)

NUTRITION FACTS PER SERVING: *239 cal., 11 g total fat (3 g sat. fat), 83 mg chol., 206 mg sodium, 2 g carb., 0 g fiber, 31 g pro.*

Make-Ahead Directions: Prepare as directed through Step 2. Cover and chill for up to 24 hours. To serve, let stand at room temperature for 30 minutes. Roast as directed.

tip
It is essential to let cooked meat or poultry rest for 10 to 15 minutes before you serve it. The resting time allows the flavorful juices to be absorbed back into the meat rather than spilling out when you cut into it.

Pecan-Crusted Pork Tenderloin with Sautéed Apples and Sweet Potatoes

START TO FINISH **50 minutes** MAKES **4 servings**

- 2 tablespoons vegetable oil
- 1 medium onion, thinly sliced
- 2 medium sweet potatoes, peeled and thinly sliced
- 1 large Granny Smith apple, peeled, cored, and cut into 8 wedges
- ½ teaspoon salt
- ¼ teaspoon ground cinnamon
- 1 cup apple juice or apple cider
- 1 tablespoon coarse grain Dijon-style mustard
- 1 teaspoon packed brown sugar
- 1 12-ounce pork tenderloin
- ½ cup all-purpose flour
- 2 eggs, lightly beaten
- ⅓ cup ground pecans
- ¼ teaspoon ground black pepper
- 2 tablespoons snipped fresh chives
- 4 teaspoons finely chopped toasted pecans

1 In a large skillet heat 2 teaspoons of the oil over medium heat. Add onion; cook until tender, stirring occasionally. Add sweet potatoes, apple, ¼ teaspoon of the salt, and the cinnamon. Cook for 2 minutes, turning occasionally. Add ⅔ cup of the apple juice. Bring to boiling; reduce heat. Simmer, covered, for 10 to 12 minutes or until sweet potatoes are tender. Using a slotted spoon, transfer sweet potato mixture to a large bowl; cover and keep warm.

2 For sauce, add the remaining ⅓ cup apple juice, the mustard, and brown sugar to skillet; cook and stir for 1 minute. Remove from heat; cover and keep warm.

3 Trim fat from meat. Cut meat crosswise into eight slices. Place each slice between two pieces of plastic wrap. Using the flat side of a meat mallet, pound meat lightly until about ½ inch thick. Remove plastic wrap. Place ¼ cup of the flour in a shallow dish. Place eggs in a second shallow dish. In a third shallow dish combine the remaining ¼ cup flour, the ground pecans, the remaining ¼ teaspoon salt, and the pepper. Dip meat into flour, shaking off excess. Dip into eggs, then into pecan mixture, turning to coat.

4 In a 12-inch skillet heat 2 teaspoons of the remaining oil over medium-high heat. Add meat; cook for 3 minutes. Turn meat; add the remaining 2 teaspoons oil. Cook about 3 minutes more or just until meat is slightly pink in center (160°F). If meat browns too quickly, reduce heat to medium.

5 Divide meat and sweet potato mixture among serving plates. Stir chives into sauce; drizzle sauce over meat and sweet potato mixture. Sprinkle with chopped pecans.

NUTRITION FACTS PER SERVING:
455 cal., 20 g total fat (3 g sat. fat), 161 mg chol., 499 mg sodium, 40 g carb., 6 g fiber, 25 g pro.

253

Apricot-Stuffed Pork Tenderloin

PREP 45 minutes ROAST 50 minutes at 375°F STAND 15 minutes MAKES 12 servings

- 4   slices white bread, torn
- 3   tablespoons butter, melted
-     Nonstick cooking spray
- 1   cup dried apricots
- ½   cup fresh Italian (flat-leaf) parsley leaves
- 2   teaspoons fresh thyme leaves
- 1   medium onion, cut up
- 1   stalk celery, cut up
- 2   tablespoons olive oil
- ½   cup chicken broth
- ½   teaspoon salt
- ¼   teaspoon ground black pepper
- 2   1½-pound pork tenderloins
-     Salt
-     Ground black pepper
- ½   cup apricot preserves, melted

1 Preheat oven to 375°F. Line a 15x10x1-inch baking pan with foil; set aside. For stuffing, place bread in a food processor. Cover and process until coarse crumbs form. Transfer to a large bowl. Drizzle with melted butter; toss to coat.

2 Spread crumbs evenly in the prepared baking pan. Bake for 6 to 8 minutes or until golden, stirring once. Return bread crumbs to the large bowl. Place a rack in the foil-lined baking pan and coat with cooking spray; set pan aside.

3 In the food processor combine dried apricots, parsley, and thyme. Cover and process with on/off pulses until finely chopped. Stir mixture into bread crumbs.

4 In the food processor combine onion and celery. Cover and process until finely chopped. In a small skillet cook onion and celery in hot oil over medium heat about 5 minutes or until tender. Stir in broth; cook for 1 minute. Add onion mixture, ½ teaspoon salt, and ¼ teaspoon pepper to bread mixture, stirring to moisten.

5 Trim fat from meat. Using a sharp knife, make a lengthwise cut down the center of each tenderloin, cutting to, but not through, the opposite side. Cut horizontally into the meat, slicing away from the center cut. Repeat on the opposite side. Place each tenderloin between two pieces of plastic wrap. Using the flat side of a meat mallet, pound meat lightly from center to edges into a 12×8-inch rectangle.

6 Spread stuffing over meat to within 1 inch of the edges. Roll up each rectangle, starting from a short side. Tie with 100-percent-cotton kitchen string. Place stuffed tenderloins, seam sides down, on the rack in the prepared baking pan. Sprinkle with additional salt and pepper.

7 Roast, uncovered, for 50 to 55 minutes or until an instant-read thermometer inserted in the stuffing registers 145°F, brushing meat with some of the preserves during the last 5 minutes of roasting. Remove from oven. Cover meat with foil; let stand for 15 minutes. Remove string from meat. Slice meat; serve with the remaining preserves.

NUTRITION FACTS PER SERVING:
247 cal., 7 g total fat (3 g sat. fat), 77 mg chol., 289 mg sodium, 21 g carb., 1 g fiber, 24 g pro.

Apple-Stuffed Pork Chops

Photo on page 277

PREP 40 minutes BAKE 40 minutes at 375°F MAKES 4 servings

1 tablespoon butter

$\frac{2}{3}$ cup chopped, peeled (if desired) cooking apple (1 medium)

$\frac{1}{3}$ cup chopped onion (1 small)

2 teaspoons snipped fresh sage or $\frac{1}{2}$ teaspoon dried sage, crushed

2 tablespoons shredded white cheddar cheese

4 pork rib chops, loin chops, or boneless loin chops, cut $1\frac{1}{4}$ inches thick (about 3 pounds total)

Salt

Ground black pepper

1 cup coarse soft bread crumbs from crusty country bread (about 2 slices)

2 tablespoons chopped walnuts

2 tablespoons butter, melted

1 tablespoon snipped fresh Italian (flat-leaf) parsley

2 teaspoons finely shredded lemon peel

2 tablespoons butter

2 tablespoons all-purpose flour

$\frac{1}{4}$ teaspoon salt

Pinch ground black pepper

1 cup chicken broth

$\frac{1}{2}$ cup whipping cream

2 tablespoons Calvados or apple juice

$\frac{1}{2}$ cup shredded white cheddar cheese (2 ounces)

1 Preheat oven to 375°F. For stuffing, in a medium skillet heat 1 tablespoon butter over medium heat until melted. Add apple, onion, and sage; cook until tender, stirring occasionally. Remove from heat. Stir in 2 tablespoons cheese; set aside.

2 Trim fat from chops. Make a pocket in each chop by cutting horizontally from the fat side almost to the bone or the opposite side. Divide stuffing among pockets in chops. If necessary, secure the openings with wooden toothpicks. Sprinkle chops with salt and pepper.

3 In a small bowl combine bread crumbs, walnuts, 2 tablespoons melted butter, parsley, and lemon peel. Place chops on a rack in a shallow roasting pan. Top with bread crumb mixture. Bake, uncovered, for 40 to 50 minutes or until juices run clear (160°F).

4 For sauce, in a medium saucepan heat 2 tablespoons butter over medium heat until melted. Stir in flour, $\frac{1}{4}$ teaspoon salt, and pinch pepper. Gradually stir in broth, whipping cream, and Calvados. Cook and stir until thickened and bubbly. Cook and stir for 1 minute more. Stir in $\frac{1}{2}$ cup cheese until melted. Serve chops with sauce.

NUTRITION FACTS PER SERVING:
702 cal., 49 g total fat (25 g sat. fat), 157 mg chol., 995 mg sodium, 32 g carb., 3 g fiber, 30 g pro.

255

Main Dish Meats, Poultry, and Seafood

Mustard-Glazed Pork Chops

START TO FINISH 25 minutes MAKES 4 servings

4   **pork loin or rib chops, cut ½ inch thick**

     Salt

     Ground black pepper

2   **teaspoons olive oil**

1   **large onion, cut into thin wedges**

½   **cup apricot preserves**

¼   **cup water**

1   **tablespoon Dijon-style or spicy mustard**

1   **teaspoon paprika**

½   **teaspoon ground nutmeg**

     Fresh sage leaves (optional)

1   Trim fat from chops. Sprinkle chops with salt and pepper. In a 12-inch skillet heat oil over medium-high heat. Add chops and onion; cook for 6 minutes, turning chops and onion once halfway through cooking.

2   Meanwhile, for glaze, in a small microwave-safe bowl combine preserves, the water, mustard, paprika, and nutmeg. Microwave on 100 percent power (high) for 1 to 2 minutes or until preserves are melted. Pour glaze over chops; reduce heat to medium. Cook, covered, about 10 minutes or until juices run clear (160°F).

3   Divide chops and onion mixture among serving plates. If desired, garnish with sage.

NUTRITION FACTS PER SERVING:
503 cal., 32 g total fat (11 g sat. fat), 89 mg chol., 313 mg sodium, 31 g carb., 1 g fiber, 20 g pro.

Honey-and-Apple Ribs

PREP 30 minutes BAKE 1 hour 45 minutes at 350°F MAKES 4 servings

3   pounds bone-in pork
    country-style ribs
1   tablespoon vegetable oil
½   cup chopped onion
    (1 medium)
2   cloves garlic, minced
¾   cup chili sauce
½   cup apple juice or apple cider
¼   cup honey
2   tablespoons Worcestershire
    sauce
½   teaspoon dry mustard

1 Preheat oven to 350°F. Place ribs in a shallow roasting pan. Bake, uncovered, for 1 hour. Drain off fat.

2 Meanwhile, for sauce, in a medium saucepan heat oil over medium heat. Add onion and garlic; cook until tender, stirring occasionally. Stir in chili sauce, apple juice, honey, Worcestershire sauce, and dry mustard. Bring to boiling; reduce heat. Simmer, uncovered, for 20 minutes. (You should have about 1½ cups sauce.)

3 Spoon ⅓ cup of the sauce over ribs. Bake, covered, for 45 to 60 minutes more or until tender, turning ribs and spooning ⅓ cup additional sauce over ribs after 25 minutes. Heat the remaining sauce until warm; serve with ribs.

NUTRITION FACTS PER SERVING:
590 cal., 30 g total fat (10 g sat. fat), 163 mg chol., 828 mg sodium, 34 g carb., 3 g fiber, 44 g pro.

257

Main Dish Meats, Poultry, and Seafood

Ham Balls in Barbecue Sauce

Photo on page 276

PREP 20 minutes BAKE 45 minutes at 350°F MAKES 6 servings

2 eggs, lightly beaten

1½ cups soft bread crumbs (about 2 slices)

½ cup finely chopped onion (1 medium)

2 tablespoons milk

2 teaspoons dry mustard

¼ teaspoon ground black pepper

12 ounces ground cooked ham

12 ounces ground pork or beef

¾ cup packed brown sugar

½ cup ketchup

2 tablespoons cider vinegar

1 Preheat oven to 350°F. Lightly grease a 3-quart rectangular baking dish; set aside. In a large bowl combine eggs, bread crumbs, onion, milk, 1 teaspoon of the dry mustard, and the pepper. Add ground ham and ground pork; mix well. Shape meat mixture into 12 balls, using about ⅓ cup of the mixture for each ball. Place ham balls in the prepared baking dish.

2 For sauce, in a small bowl combine brown sugar, ketchup, vinegar, and remaining 1 teaspoon dry mustard, stirring until sugar is dissolved. Pour over ham balls.

3 Bake, uncovered, about 45 minutes or until ham balls are done (160°F).*

NUTRITION FACTS PER SERVING:
428 cal., 19 g total fat (7 g sat. fat), 144 mg chol., 1107 mg sodium, 42 g carb., 1 g fiber, 23 g pro.

258

*tip
The internal color of a meatball is not a reliable doneness indicator. A ham, pork, or beef meatball cooked to 160°F is safe, regardless of color. To measure the doneness of a meatball, insert an instant-read thermometer into the center of the meatball.

Brown Sugar–Glazed Ham

PREP 10 minutes BAKE 1 hour 35 minutes at 325°F STAND 15 minutes MAKES 16 servings

1   5- to 6-pound cooked ham
    (rump half or shank portion)
1½ cups packed brown sugar
1½ cups red wine vinegar
4   sprigs fresh mint

1 Preheat oven to 325°F. If desired, score ham in a diamond pattern by making shallow diagonal cuts at 1-inch intervals. Place ham on a rack in a shallow roasting pan. Insert an oven-going meat thermometer into ham so it does not touch bone. Bake, uncovered, for 1¼ to 1½ hours for rump, 1¾ to 2 hours for shank, or until thermometer registers 125°F.

2 Meanwhile, for glaze, in a medium saucepan stir together brown sugar, vinegar, and mint. Bring to boiling; reduce heat. Boil gently, uncovered, about 30 minutes or until glaze is reduced to 1 cup. Remove from heat. Remove and discard mint. Brush ham with some of the glaze.

3 Bake, uncovered, for 20 to 30 minutes more or until thermometer registers 135°F, brushing three more times with additional glaze. Remove from oven. Cover with foil; let stand for 15 minutes before carving. (Temperature of the meat after standing should be 140°F.) Heat any remaining glaze in saucepan until warm; serve with ham.

NUTRITION FACTS PER SERVING:
232 cal., 8 g total fat (3 g sat. fat), 51 mg chol., 1305 mg sodium, 22 g carb., 0 g fiber, 20 g pro.

259

Main Dish Meats, Poultry, and Seafood

Maple-Brined Chicken with Roasted Vegetables

PREP 1 hour CHILL 12 hours ROAST 1 hour 45 minutes at 400°F STAND 15 minutes MAKES 6 servings

1   cup kosher salt
½   cup packed brown sugar
4   cups apple juice or apple cider
4   cups water
1   cup maple syrup
2   tablespoons stone-ground Dijon-style mustard
1   5- to 6-pound roasting chicken
6   large carrots, cut into 2-inch chunks
2   large onions, cut into ½-inch slices
2   fennel bulbs, trimmed and cut into wedges
6   sprigs fresh thyme
4   cloves garlic, halved
3   tablespoons olive oil
    Salt
    Ground black pepper
1   medium orange, halved

1 For brine, in an extra-large stainless-steel stockpot combine 1 cup kosher salt and brown sugar; stir in apple juice, the water, maple syrup, and mustard. Cook and stir over medium-high heat until salt and sugar are completely dissolved. Remove from heat; cool to room temperature.

2 Remove giblets from chicken, if present; discard or reserve for another use. Rinse chicken inside and out with cool water. Place chicken in stockpot, making sure it is immersed in brine. Cover and chill for 12 hours.

3 In a resealable plastic bag combine carrots, onions, fennel, 2 of the thyme sprigs, and the garlic; drizzle oil over vegetables. Seal bag; massage vegetables to evenly coat with oil. Chill for up to 12 hours.

4 Preheat oven to 400°F. Remove chicken from brine; discard brine. Pat chicken dry inside and out with paper towels. Sprinkle chicken cavity with salt and pepper. Place orange halves and the remaining 4 thyme sprigs in cavity. Skewer neck skin to back. Tie drumsticks to tail. Twist wing tips under back. Spread vegetables evenly in an ungreased 13×9×2-inch baking pan. Place chicken, breast side up, on top of vegetables.

5 Roast, uncovered, for 1¾ to 2¼ hours or until an instant-read thermometer inserted in the center of an inside thigh muscle registers 180°F. Remove chicken and vegetables from oven. Tent chicken loosely with foil; let stand for 15 minutes before carving. Serve chicken with roasted vegetables.

NUTRITION FACTS PER SERVING:
692 cal., 44 g total fat (12 g sat. fat), 191 mg chol., 405 mg sodium, 22 g carb., 6 g fiber, 50 g pro.

Chicken and Potatoes with Lemon

PREP 20 minutes BAKE 30 minutes at 450°F MAKES 4 servings

4   bone-in chicken breast halves (about 1½ pounds total)
1   pound fingerling or baby Yukon gold potatoes
3   lemons, halved crosswise
⅓   cup pitted green and/or black olives
6   tablespoons olive oil
    Salt
    Ground black pepper
1   tablespoon honey
6   cups arugula and/or mixed salad greens

1 Preheat oven to 450°F. Place chicken, potatoes, lemons, and olives in an ungreased 3-quart rectangular baking dish. Drizzle with 2 tablespoons of the oil; toss to coat. Spread mixture in a single layer, arranging chicken skin sides up and lemons cut sides up. Sprinkle with salt and pepper.

2 Bake, uncovered, about 30 minutes or until chicken is no longer pink (170°F), potatoes are tender, and lemons are brown at the edges and soft throughout. Remove from oven.

3 Remove lemons from baking dish. Keep chicken, potatoes, and olives warm. When lemons are cool enough to handle, squeeze juice and pulp into a small bowl; discard any seeds. Whisk in the remaining 4 tablespoons oil and the honey. Season to taste with salt and pepper.

4 To serve, divide arugula and/or mixed greens among serving plates. Top with chicken, potatoes, and olives. Drizzle with lemon mixture. Sprinkle with additional pepper.

NUTRITION FACTS PER SERVING:
573 cal., 40 g total fat (8 g sat. fat), 87 mg chol., 435 mg sodium, 34 g carb., 7 g fiber, 26 g pro.

Oven-Barbecued Chicken

PREP 15 minutes BAKE 45 minutes at 375°F MAKES 4 servings

2   to 2½ pounds meaty chicken pieces (breast halves, thighs, and drumsticks), skinned
1   tablespoon vegetable oil
½   cup chopped onion (1 medium)
1   clove garlic, minced
¾   cup chili sauce
2   tablespoons honey
2   tablespoons soy sauce
1   tablespoon yellow mustard
½   teaspoon prepared horseradish
¼   teaspoon crushed red pepper

1   Preheat oven to 375°F. Arrange chicken pieces, bone side up, in an ungreased 13×9×2-inch baking pan or 3-quart rectangular baking dish. Bake, uncovered, for 25 minutes.

2   Meanwhile, for sauce, in a small saucepan heat oil over medium heat. Add onion and garlic; cook until tender, stirring occasionally. Stir in chili sauce, honey, soy sauce, mustard, horseradish, and crushed red pepper; heat through.

3   Turn chicken bone side down. Brush half of the sauce over the chicken. Bake, uncovered, for 20 to 30 minutes more or until chicken is no longer pink (170°F for breasts; 180°F for thighs and drumsticks).

4   Bring the remaining sauce to boiling. Serve chicken with sauce.

NUTRITION FACTS PER SERVING:
320 cal., 11 g total fat (3 g sat. fat), 92 mg chol., 1191 mg sodium, 20 g carb., 3 g fiber, 32 g pro.

262

Buttermilk-Brined Fried Chicken

Photo on page 275

PREP 30 minutes   CHILL 2 to 4 hours   COOK 12 minutes per batch   MAKES 6 servings

3   cups buttermilk

⅓   cup kosher salt

2   tablespoons sugar

2½   to 3 pounds meaty chicken pieces (breast halves, thighs, and drumsticks)

2   cups all-purpose flour

¼   teaspoon salt

¼   teaspoon ground black pepper

¾   cup buttermilk

Vegetable oil for deep-fat frying

1 For brine, in a resealable plastic bag set in a bowl combine 3 cups buttermilk, ⅓ cup kosher salt, and sugar. Using a chef's knife, cut chicken breasts in half crosswise. Add all of the chicken pieces to brine; seal bag. Chill for 2 to 4 hours. Drain chicken, discarding brine. Pat chicken dry with paper towels.

2 In a large bowl stir together flour, ¼ teaspoon salt, and pepper. Place ¾ cup buttermilk in a shallow dish. Dip chicken into flour mixture, then into buttermilk, turning to coat. Dip again into flour mixture.

3 Meanwhile, in a heavy Dutch oven or a deep-fat fryer heat 1½ inches oil to 350°F. Fry chicken, a few pieces at a time, in hot oil for 12 to 15 minutes or until chicken is no longer pink (170°F for breasts; 180°F for thighs and drumsticks) and coating is golden, turning once. (Oil temperature will drop; maintain temperature at 325°F.) Drain on a wire rack or paper towels. If desired, keep fried chicken warm in a 300°F oven while frying the remaining chicken pieces.

NUTRITION FACTS PER SERVING:
618 cal., 36 g total fat (7 g sat. fat), 110 mg chol., 1701 mg sodium, 37 g carb., 1 g fiber, 36 g pro.

263

Spicy Buttermilk-Brined Fried Chicken

Prepare as directed, except add 1½ teaspoons cayenne pepper to the flour mixture.

Pan-Fried Italian Chicken Parmesan

START TO FINISH **25 minutes** MAKES **4 servings**

8   **ounces dried linguine or fettuccine**

1   **egg, lightly beaten**

3   **tablespoons vegetable oil**

½   **teaspoon salt**

¼   **teaspoon coarsely ground black pepper**

½   **cup panko (Japanese-style bread crumbs)**

¼   **cup grated Parmesan cheese**

1   **teaspoon dried Italian seasoning, crushed**

4   **skinless, boneless chicken breast halves (about 1¼ pounds total)**

   Salt

   Coarsely ground black pepper

1   **cup marinara sauce**

   Grated Parmesan cheese (optional)

1 Cook pasta according to package directions; drain. Return pasta to pan; cover and keep warm.

2 Meanwhile, in a shallow dish combine egg, 1 tablespoon of the oil, ½ teaspoon salt, and ¼ teaspoon pepper. In another shallow dish combine panko, ¼ cup cheese, and Italian seasoning. Sprinkle chicken lightly with additional salt and pepper. Dip each chicken breast half into egg mixture, then into bread crumb mixture, turning to coat.

3 In a large skillet heat the remaining 2 tablespoons oil over medium-high heat. Add chicken; cook for 8 to 12 minutes or until no longer pink (170°F), turning once. (If chicken browns too quickly, reduce heat to medium.)

4 Meanwhile, place marinara sauce in a microwave-safe dish. Microwave on 100 percent power (high) about 1 minute or until heated through. Spoon about ¼ cup of the sauce over each chicken breast half. If desired, sprinkle with additional cheese. Serve with cooked pasta.

NUTRITION FACTS PER SERVING:
456 cal., 17 g total fat (4 g sat. fat), 175 mg chol., 807 mg sodium, 31 g carb., 1 g fiber, 42 g pro.

264

tip
Other good choices for oil to use in pan frying include corn, canola, peanut, sunflower, or safflower.

Classic Chicken and Dumplings

PREP 50 minutes CHILL 2 to 24 hours COOK 1 hour 5 minutes STAND 10 minutes MAKES 8 servings

1   egg, lightly beaten

3   tablespoons water

2   tablespoons peanut oil
    or vegetable oil

½   teaspoon salt

1   cup all-purpose flour

1   4- to 4½-pound broiler-fryer
    chicken, quartered

1   teaspoon kosher salt

5   cups chicken broth

2   cups water

2   stalks celery, halved

1   onion, halved

    Salt

    Ground black pepper

¼   cup whipping cream

2   tablespoons butter, cut up

3   hard-cooked eggs, sliced

1 For dumplings, in a medium bowl combine egg, 3 tablespoons water, oil, and ½ teaspoon salt. Stir in flour until smooth. Cover and chill for 2 to 24 hours.

2 Sprinkle chicken, including back and neck, with 1 teaspoon kosher salt; set aside. In a 6-quart Dutch oven combine broth, 2 cups water, celery, and onion. Bring to boiling. Add chicken pieces, placing legs, back, and neck in Dutch oven first and placing breast pieces, skin sides down, on top. Return to boiling; reduce heat. Simmer, covered, for 30 to 45 minutes or until breast pieces are no longer pink (170°F); remove breast pieces. Simmer, covered, for 30 to 40 minutes more or until legs are tender and no longer pink (180°F).

3 Remove chicken from Dutch oven. Remove and discard vegetables, reserving broth. When chicken is cool enough to handle, remove skin. Using two forks, pull meat apart into coarse shreds. Discard skin and bones.

4 On a well-floured surface, roll chilled dumpling dough until about 1/16 inch thick; cut into 2½×1½-inch pieces. Return broth to boiling. Season to taste with salt and pepper. Add dough pieces to broth. Cook, uncovered, for 3 to 5 minutes, shaking pan occasionally (do not stir). Return chicken to Dutch oven; reduce heat. Stir in whipping cream and butter. Gently place egg slices on top of mixture. Simmer, uncovered, for 2 minutes. Remove from heat. Cover and let stand for 10 minutes before serving.

NUTRITION FACTS PER SERVING:
655 cal., 35 g total fat (12 g sat. fat), 309 mg chol., 955 mg sodium, 26 g carb., 1 g fiber, 56 g pro.

265

Coq au Vin

PREP 45 minutes   COOK 35 minutes   MAKES 6 servings

$2\frac{1}{2}$ to 3 pounds meaty chicken pieces (breast halves, thighs, and drumsticks), skinned

2 tablespoons vegetable oil

Salt

Ground black pepper

12 to 18 pearl onions or shallots, peeled

$1\frac{1}{4}$ cups Pinot Noir or Burgundy

1 cup whole fresh button mushrooms

1 cup thinly sliced carrots (2 medium)

$\frac{1}{4}$ cup chicken broth or water

1 tablespoon snipped fresh parsley

$1\frac{1}{2}$ teaspoons snipped fresh marjoram or $\frac{1}{2}$ teaspoon dried marjoram, crushed

$1\frac{1}{2}$ teaspoons snipped fresh thyme or $\frac{1}{2}$ teaspoon dried thyme, crushed

1 bay leaf

2 cloves garlic, minced

2 tablespoons all-purpose flour

2 tablespoons butter, softened

2 slices bacon, crisp-cooked, drained, and crumbled

Snipped fresh parsley (optional)

Hot cooked noodles (optional)

1 In a large skillet cook chicken in hot oil over medium heat about 15 minutes or until chicken is brown, turning to cook evenly. Drain off fat. Sprinkle chicken with salt and pepper. Add onions, Pinot Noir, mushrooms, carrots, broth, 1 tablespoon parsley, dried marjoram (if using), dried thyme (if using), bay leaf, and garlic. Bring to boiling; reduce heat. Simmer, covered, for 35 to 40 minutes or until chicken is no longer pink (170°F for breasts; 180°F for thighs and drumsticks). If using, add fresh marjoram and thyme. Discard bay leaf. Transfer chicken and vegetables to a serving platter; keep warm.

2 For sauce, in a small bowl stir together flour and softened butter to make a smooth paste. Stir into wine mixture in skillet. Cook and stir until thickened and bubbly. Cook and stir for 1 minute more. Season to taste with additional salt and pepper.

3 Pour sauce over chicken and vegetables. Sprinkle with bacon. If desired, top with additional parsley and serve with hot cooked noodles.

NUTRITION FACTS PER SERVING:
288 cal., 12 g total fat (4 g sat. fat), 92 mg chol., 311 mg sodium, 7 g carb., 1 g fiber, 28 g pro.

266

Cheese-Stuffed Chicken Breasts

PREP 20 minutes   COOK 18 minutes   MAKES 4 servings

- 4 skinless, boneless chicken breast halves (about 1¼ pounds total)
- ½ of an 8-ounce tub cream cheese spread
- 2 tablespoons dried tomato pesto
- ¾ cup panko (Japanese-style bread crumbs)*
- 1 tablespoon grated Parmesan cheese
- ½ teaspoon dried basil, crushed
- ⅛ teaspoon garlic powder
- ⅛ teaspoon ground black pepper
- ¼ cup milk
- 1 tablespoon olive oil or vegetable oil
- 1 tablespoon butter

1 Using a sharp knife, cut a pocket in each chicken breast half by cutting horizontally through the thickest portion to, but not through, the opposite side. In a small bowl combine cream cheese and pesto. Spoon a well-rounded tablespoon of the cheese mixture into each pocket.

2 In a shallow bowl combine panko, Parmesan cheese, basil, garlic powder, and pepper. Place milk in a second shallow bowl. Dip stuffed chicken into milk to moisten, then into panko mixture, turning to coat.

3 In a large skillet heat oil and butter over medium heat. Add chicken. Cook for 18 to 20 minutes or until chicken is no longer pink (170°F), turning once halfway through cooking.

NUTRITION FACTS PER SERVING:
389 cal., 21 g total fat (9 g sat. fat), 124 mg chol., 299 mg sodium, 11 g carb., 1 g fiber, 38 g pro.

*tip
Panko are Japanese-style bread crumbs that add a light crispy coating to foods, such as the breading on this chicken. Look for panko at most grocery stores near the bread crumbs.

Main Dish Meats, Poultry, and Seafood

Herb-Roasted Turkey and Vegetables

PREP 30 minutes ROAST 20 minutes at 400°F + 1 hour 15 minutes at 350°F STAND 10 minutes MAKES 8 servings

- 2   tablespoons snipped fresh parsley
- 4   cloves garlic, minced
- 1   teaspoon snipped fresh rosemary
- 1   teaspoon snipped fresh thyme
- 1/2 teaspoon salt
- 1/2 teaspoon ground black pepper
- 1   2¾- to 3½-pound turkey breast portion with bone, skinned
     Nonstick cooking spray
- 3   cups tiny red-skinned potatoes (about 1 pound), quartered
- 2   cups baby carrots with tops (about 8 ounces), trimmed and halved lengthwise
- 2   cups white and/or red pearl onions (about 8 ounces), peeled and halved
- 1   tablespoon olive oil

1 Preheat oven to 400°F. In a small bowl combine parsley, garlic, rosemary, thyme, salt, and pepper. Set aside 1 tablespoon of the herb mixture.

2 Place turkey breast portion, bone side down, on a rack in a shallow roasting pan. Lightly coat with cooking spray. Sprinkle the remaining herb mixture evenly over turkey; rub in with your fingers. Roast, uncovered, for 20 minutes.

3 Meanwhile, in a large bowl combine potatoes, carrots, and pearl onions. Add the reserved 1 tablespoon herb mixture and the oil; toss to coat. Arrange vegetables around turkey in roasting pan.

4 Reduce oven temperature to 350°F. Roast, uncovered, for 1¼ to 1½ hours more or until juices run clear, turkey is no longer pink (170°F), and vegetables are tender, stirring vegetables once.

5 Transfer turkey to a cutting board. Cover loosely with foil; let stand for 10 minutes before carving. Serve turkey with vegetables.

NUTRITION FACTS PER SERVING:
231 cal., 3 g total fat (1 g sat. fat), 69 mg chol., 219 mg sodium, 21 g carb., 3 g fiber, 30 g pro.

Sausage-Stuffed Turkey Breast

Photo on page 276

PREP 20 minutes ROAST 1 hour 15 minutes at 325°F STAND 10 minutes MAKES 8 servings

- 1 2- to 3-pound boneless turkey breast with skin*
- ¾ teaspoon salt
- ¾ teaspoon ground black pepper
- 8 ounces bulk sweet Italian sausage
- ½ cup thinly sliced green onions (4)
- ⅓ cup snipped dried figs
- ¾ teaspoon fennel seeds
- 1 tablespoon olive oil

1 Preheat oven to 325°F. Place turkey, skin side down, between two pieces of plastic wrap. Using the flat side of a meat mallet, pound turkey lightly into a square of even thickness. Remove plastic wrap. Sprinkle turkey with ½ teaspoon of the salt and ½ teaspoon of the pepper.

2 For stuffing, in a medium skillet cook sausage over medium-high heat until brown, using a wooden spoon to break up meat as it cooks. Drain off fat. In a medium bowl combine sausage, green onions, figs, and fennel seeds.

3 Spoon stuffing onto turkey. Roll up turkey and stuffing. Tie at 2-inch intervals with 100-percent-cotton kitchen string. Sprinkle with remaining ¼ teaspoon salt and ¼ teaspoon pepper.

4 Place turkey in a shallow roasting pan. Rub skin with oil. Roast, uncovered, for 1¼ to 1¾ hours or until turkey is no longer pink (170°F) and an instant-read thermometer inserted into the center of stuffing registers 165°F.

5 Transfer turkey to a cutting board. Cover loosely with foil; let stand for 10 minutes. Remove and discard string before slicing.

NUTRITION FACTS PER SERVING:
287 cal., 17 g total fat (5 g sat. fat), 87 mg chol., 472 mg sodium, 5 g carb., 1 g fiber, 27 g pro.

269

Make-Ahead Directions: Prepare as directed through Step 3. Wrap stuffed turkey breast in plastic wrap and chill for up to 12 hours. Continue as directed in Step 4.

*tip
If you can't find boneless turkey breast with the skin on, purchase a 4- to 5-pound bone-in turkey breast and remove the bone (or ask your butcher to remove it for you).

BBQ Spice–Rubbed Turkey Breast

PREP 30 minutes ROAST 20 minutes at 400°F + 1 hour at 350°F STAND 10 minutes MAKES 10 servings

2   3- to 3½-pound fresh or
     frozen bone-in turkey breast
     halves
     Nonstick cooking spray
2   tablespoons packed dark
     brown sugar
2   teaspoons garlic powder
2   teaspoons paprika
1½   teaspoons salt
1   teaspoon ground cumin
1   teaspoon chili powder
¾   teaspoon ground black pepper
1   recipe Cranberry Barbecue
     Sauce

1 Thaw turkey, if frozen. Preheat oven to 400°F. Coat a large shallow roasting pan and rack with cooking spray. In a small bowl combine brown sugar, garlic powder, paprika, salt, cumin, chili powder, and pepper. Set aside.

2 Place turkey breast halves on parchment paper or waxed paper. Starting at breast bone of each turkey half, slip fingers between skin and meat to loosen skin, leaving skin partially attached at edges. Lift skin and spread spice mixture evenly under skin over breast meat. Insert an oven-going meat thermometer into thickest part of breast halves without touching bone. Place turkey breast halves, bone side down, on roasting rack in the prepared pan.

3 Roast, uncovered, on lower rack of oven for 20 minutes. Reduce oven temperature to 350°F. Roast, uncovered, for 1 to 1½ hours more or until thermometer registers 165°F, occasionally spooning pan juices over turkey.

4 Remove turkey from oven. Cover with foil; let stand for 10 minutes before slicing. Serve with Cranberry Barbecue Sauce.

NUTRITION FACTS PER SERVING:
406 cal., 7 g total fat (2 g sat. fat), 167 mg chol., 724 mg sodium, 25 g carb., 1 g fiber, 57 g pro.

270

Cranberry Barbecue Sauce

In a medium saucepan heat 1 tablespoon vegetable oil over medium heat. Add 1 cup chopped onion (1 large); cook about 5 minutes or until tender. Stir in one 16-ounce can whole cranberry sauce, ⅓ cup chili sauce, 1 tablespoon cider vinegar, 1 teaspoon Worcestershire sauce, and ¼ teaspoon ground black pepper. Bring to boiling; reduce heat. Simmer, uncovered, about 5 minutes or until thickened, stirring occasionally.

tip
To simplify the preparation, you can rub the spice mixture onto the outside of each turkey breast for a crusty appearance. To prevent overbrowning, cover turkey breasts with foil for the last 30 minutes of roasting.

Turkey Meat Loaf

PREP 30 minutes BAKE 1 hour at 350°F STAND 10 minutes MAKES 6 servings

1   tablespoon olive oil

1   cup finely chopped fresh
     mushrooms

¾   cup finely chopped onion

½   cup finely chopped green
     sweet pepper (1 small)

3   cloves garlic, minced

1   cup soft bread crumbs
     (from about 2 slices bread)

¾   cup ketchup

1   egg, lightly beaten

½   teaspoon salt

¼   teaspoon ground black pepper

1½   pounds uncooked ground
     turkey or chicken

2   tablespoons apricot preserves

1 Preheat oven to 350°F. Line a 13×9×2-inch baking pan with foil; set aside. In a large skillet heat oil over medium heat. Add mushrooms, onion, sweet pepper, and garlic; cook about 5 minutes or until tender, stirring occasionally.

2 In a large bowl combine the cooked vegetables, bread crumbs, ¼ cup of the ketchup, the egg, salt, and black pepper. Add ground turkey; mix well. Shape turkey mixture into a 9×5-inch loaf. Place in the prepared baking pan. Bake, uncovered, for 45 minutes.

3 Meanwhile, in a small bowl stir together the remaining ½ cup ketchup and the preserves. Spoon mixture over turkey loaf. Bake, uncovered, for 15 to 25 minutes more or until juices run clear (165°F).

4 Let meat loaf stand for 10 minutes. Using two spatulas, transfer loaf to a serving platter. Slice to serve.

NUTRITION FACTS PER SERVING:
279 cal., 13 g total fat (3 g sat. fat), 125 mg chol., 686 mg sodium, 18 g carb., 1 g fiber, 23 g pro.

271

Main Dish Meats, Poultry, and Seafood

Oven-Roasted Fish
with Peas and Tomatoes

PREP 20 minutes ROAST 22 minutes at 425°F MAKES 4 servings

1¼ pounds fresh or frozen skinless cod or ocean perch fillets

Nonstick cooking spray

2 cups frozen peas, thawed

1 cup fresh button mushrooms, halved

¾ cup grape tomatoes

1 medium onion, cut into very thin wedges

4 teaspoons olive oil

¼ teaspoon salt

¼ teaspoon ground black pepper

2 teaspoons snipped fresh dill or ½ teaspoon dried dill

1 Thaw fish, if frozen. Preheat oven to 425°F. Rinse fish; pat dry with paper towels. If necessary, cut fish into four serving-size pieces; set aside.

2 Lightly coat a 15×10×1-inch baking pan with cooking spray. In a medium bowl combine peas, mushrooms, tomatoes, and onion. Drizzle with 3 teaspoons of the oil and sprinkle with ⅛ teaspoon of the salt and ⅛ teaspoon of the pepper; toss gently to coat. Spoon vegetables onto one side of the prepared baking pan. Roast, uncovered, for 10 minutes.

3 Arrange fish fillets beside vegetable mixture in pan, tucking under any thin edges. Brush fish with the remaining 1 teaspoon oil and sprinkle with the remaining ⅛ teaspoon salt and ⅛ teaspoon pepper. Stir vegetable mixture. Roast, uncovered, about 12 minutes more or until fish flakes easily when tested with a fork and vegetables are tender.

4 To serve, transfer fish and vegetables to serving plates. Sprinkle with dill.

NUTRITION FACTS PER SERVING:
228 cal., 6 g total fat (1 g sat. fat), 60 mg chol., 306 mg sodium, 13 g carb., 4 g fiber, 30 g pro.

tip
To test fish for doneness, gently place the tines of a fork into the fish and twist the fork slightly. If ready, the fish should flake and easily pull apart.

Cherry Cola Ham

page 219

273

Rustic Garlic Mashed Potatoes
page 235

Chicken and Biscuits
page 222

BBQ Pulled Pork Sandwiches
page 215

Beer Braised Beef Short Ribs
page 206

Buttermilk-Brined
Fried Chicken
page 263

275

Ham Balls in Barbecue Sauce
page 258

Sausage-Stuffed
Turkey Breast
page 269

Sunday Oven Pot Roast
page 238

Pan Fried Fish
page 290

Apple-Stuffed Pork Chops
page 255

277

Poached Egg Salad
page 325

Fettuccine
alla Carbonara
page 307

Fish Tacos
with Lime
Sauce
page 321

Mexican Skillet Dinner
page 308

Saucy
Meatball
Subs
page 299

279

Fried Green
Tomatoes
page 335

280

Caesar Salad
with Parmesan
Croutons
page 357

281

Skillet
White Beans
page 352

Creamed Spinach page 337

Walnut-Sage
Potatoes au Gratin
page 346

Rosemary Satin Dinner Rolls
page 362

Oven-Fried
Veggies
page 340

283

Rhubarb Crisp
page 380

284

Best-Ever Chocolate Cake
page 367

Sour Cream
Pound Cake
page 369

Maple Pumpkin
Crème Brûlées page 382

Strawberry Ice Cream page 389

Banana-Butterscotch Cream Pie
page 375

Brownie Waffles
à la Mode
page 384

Fish and Sweet Potato Chips

PREP 30 minutes BAKE 55 minutes at 350°F FRY 4 to 6 minutes per batch MAKES 4 servings

1   recipe Sweet Potato Chips

4   4-ounce fresh or frozen cod
    or halibut fillets, about
    $1/2$ inch thick

$1/2$ cup all-purpose flour

$1/4$ cup fat-free milk

$1/4$ cup ale or nonalcoholic beer

1   egg

$1/2$ teaspoon salt

$1/4$ teaspoon ground black pepper

$1/2$ cup canola oil

    Malt vinegar

    Fresh parsley sprigs
    (optional)

1 Prepare Sweet Potato Chips. Meanwhile, thaw fish, if frozen. For batter, in a medium bowl combine flour, milk, ale, egg, salt, and pepper until smooth. Cover and chill for 30 minutes.

2 Reduce oven temperature to 250°F. Rinse fish; pat dry with paper towels. Cut fish crosswise into eight pieces.

3 In an 8-inch skillet heat oil over medium-high heat for 2 minutes. Dip half of the fish into batter, turning to coat and letting excess batter drip off. Fry fish in hot oil for 4 to 6 minutes or until coating is golden and fish flakes easily when tested with a fork, turning once. Drain on paper towels. Keep warm on a baking sheet in oven while frying the remaining fish.

4 Serve fish with vinegar and Sweet Potato Chips. If desired, garnish with parsley sprigs.

NUTRITION FACTS PER SERVING:
372 cal., 22 g total fat (3 g sat. fat), 72 mg chol., 837 mg sodium, 20 g carb., 2 g fiber, 23 g pro.

Sweet Potato Chips

Preheat oven to 350°F. Using a mandoline, slice 2 medium peeled sweet potatoes $1/16$ inch thick. Transfer to a large bowl. Pour enough boiling water over potatoes to cover; let stand for 10 minutes. Drain potatoes; pat dry with paper towels. For each batch, brush the bottom of a 15×10×1-inch baking pan with 2 tablespoons olive oil. Add half of the potato slices; turn to coat. Sprinkle with $1/4$ teaspoon salt, $1/8$ teaspoon paprika, and pinch ground black pepper. Bake, uncovered, for 20 minutes. Turn potato slices; sprinkle with additional salt. Bake, uncovered, for 20 minutes more. Turn slices again, removing any that are crisp on the edges and firm in the center, or are starting to brown throughout, and transferring to a wire rack. Continue baking, uncovered, for 15 minutes more, removing pan from oven every 5 minutes to remove chips that are done. Transfer all of the chips to wire racks; cool. Serve chips the same day as prepared.

Pan-Fried Fish *Photo on page 276*

PREP 10 minutes COOK 6 minutes per batch MAKES 4 servings

- 1 pound fresh or frozen fish fillets, $\frac{1}{2}$ to $\frac{3}{4}$ inch thick
- 1 egg, lightly beaten
- 2 tablespoons water
- $\frac{2}{3}$ cup cornmeal or fine dry bread crumbs
- $\frac{1}{2}$ teaspoon salt
  Pinch ground black pepper
  Vegetable oil or shortening for frying

1 Thaw fish, if frozen. Preheat oven to 300°F. Rinse fish; pat dry with paper towels. If necessary, cut into four serving-size pieces. In a shallow dish combine egg and the water. In another shallow dish stir together cornmeal, salt, and pepper. Dip fish into egg mixture, then into cornmeal mixture, turning to coat.

2 In a large skillet heat $\frac{1}{4}$ inch oil or melted shortening over medium-high heat. Add half of the fish in a single layer; fry on one side for 3 to 4 minutes or until golden. (If fillets have skin, fry skin side last.) Turn carefully. Fry for 3 to 4 minutes more or until second side is golden and fish flakes easily when tested with a fork. Drain on paper towels. Keep warm in oven while frying the remaining fish.

NUTRITION FACTS PER SERVING:
255 cal., 13 g total fat (2 g sat. fat), 101 mg chol., 230 mg sodium, 12 g carb., 1 g fiber, 23 g pro.

Spicy Hot Pan-Fried Fish

Prepare as directed, except omit black pepper. Reduce cornmeal to $\frac{1}{4}$ cup and combine with $\frac{1}{4}$ cup all-purpose flour, $\frac{3}{4}$ teaspoon cayenne pepper, $\frac{1}{2}$ teaspoon chili powder, $\frac{1}{2}$ teaspoon garlic powder, and $\frac{1}{2}$ teaspoon paprika.

tip

When pan-frying fish, it is very important to dry the fish thoroughly after rinsing. The drier the fish, the better the egg wash and crispy coating will cling to it.

Trout Almondine

4   fresh or frozen rainbow trout fillets with skin

¼   teaspoon salt

¼   teaspoon ground black pepper

1½   tablespoons all-purpose flour

1   tablespoon olive oil

2   tablespoons butter

2   tablespoons lemon juice

1   tablespoon snipped fresh Italian (flat-leaf) parsley

1   teaspoon snipped fresh thyme

¼   cup sliced almonds, toasted

1 Thaw fish, if frozen. Rinse fish; pat dry with paper towels. Sprinkle with salt and pepper. Coat fish lightly with flour.

2 In an extra-large skillet heat oil over medium-high heat. Add fish, skin sides up; cook for 3 minutes. Turn fish; cook about 2 minutes more or until fish flakes easily when tested with a fork. Transfer fish to a serving platter; keep warm.

3 In the same skillet heat butter over medium heat until it begins to brown, being careful not to burn. Remove from heat. Stir in lemon juice, parsley, and thyme. Drizzle lemon mixture over fish; sprinkle with toasted almonds.

NUTRITION FACTS PER SERVING:
247 cal., 17 g total fat (6 g sat. fat), 65 mg chol., 240 mg sodium, 4 g carb., 1 g fiber, 19 g pro.

tip
If trout isn't available, use flounder, sole, or tilapia.

Main Dish Meats, Poultry, and Seafood

Crispy Almond Fish with Potato Crisps

START TO FINISH **30 minutes at 450°F** MAKES **4 servings**

1 **pound fresh or frozen skinless cod or other fish fillets, about ³⁄₄ inch thick**

Nonstick cooking spray

2 **medium white- or yellow-flesh potatoes or sweet potatoes,* sliced ¹⁄₈ inch thick**

¹⁄₄ **teaspoon garlic salt**

¹⁄₄ **cup all-purpose flour**

2 **egg whites, lightly beaten**

2 **tablespoons fat-free milk**

¹⁄₄ **cup fine dry bread crumbs**

¹⁄₄ **cup finely chopped almonds**

1 **teaspoon snipped fresh thyme**

2 **tablespoons canola oil**

Snipped fresh chives (optional)

1 Thaw fish, if frozen. Preheat oven to 450°F. Line a large baking sheet with foil; coat foil with cooking spray. Coat a 9×9×2-inch baking pan with cooking spray; set aside.

2 For potato crisps, arrange potato slices in a single layer on the prepared baking sheet. Coat potato slices with cooking spray; sprinkle with garlic salt. Bake for 15 to 20 minutes or until brown and crisp. (If any slices brown more quickly than others, remove from baking sheet and keep warm.)

3 Meanwhile, rinse fish; pat dry with paper towels. If necessary, cut into four serving-size pieces. Place flour in a shallow dish. In a second shallow dish combine egg whites and milk. In a third shallow dish stir together bread crumbs, almonds, and thyme. Dip fish into flour, shaking off excess. Dip into egg mixture, then into bread crumb mixture, turning to coat.

4 Place fish in the prepared baking pan; drizzle with oil. Bake for 6 to 9 minutes or until fish flakes easily when tested with a fork. Serve fish with potato crisps. If desired, sprinkle with chives.

NUTRITION FACTS PER SERVING: *300 cal., 11 g total fat (1 g sat. fat), 49 mg chol., 237 mg sodium, 23 g carb., 3 g fiber, 26 g pro.*

292

*tip For two-color potato crisps, use one white-flesh potato and one yellow-flesh potato or sweet potato.

Coconut Shrimp with Mango Sauce

PREP **30 minutes**   BAKE **8 minutes at 425°F**   MAKES **4 servings**

- 12 **ounces fresh or frozen large shrimp in shells**
- 2 **medium mangoes, seeded, peeled, and chopped**
- ¼ **cup honey**
- 2 **tablespoons lime juice**
- ⅛ **teaspoon cayenne pepper**
- 1 **teaspoon finely shredded lime peel**
- 1 **tablespoon snipped fresh cilantro**
  Nonstick cooking spray
  Salt
- 1 **cup unsweetened flaked coconut**
  Fresh cilantro sprigs (optional)
  Lime wedges

1 Thaw shrimp, if frozen. Preheat oven to 425°F. In a blender combine 1 cup of the mango, the honey, lime juice, and cayenne pepper. Cover and blend until smooth. Remove ¼ cup of the mixture and pour into a shallow dish. Transfer the remaining mixture to a serving bowl for dipping sauce. Sprinkle with lime peel and 1 tablespoon cilantro.

2 Line a baking sheet with foil; lightly coat foil with cooking spray. Peel and devein shrimp, leaving tails intact if desired. Rinse shrimp; pat dry with paper towels. Sprinkle with salt. Place coconut in a shallow dish. Dip shrimp into the reserved ¼ cup mango mixture, then into coconut, turning and pressing shrimp to coat. Place on the prepared baking sheet. Bake, uncovered, for 8 to 10 minutes or until shrimp are opaque and coconut is golden.

3 Garnish shrimp with the remaining chopped mango and, if desired, cilantro sprigs. Serve with dipping sauce and lime wedges.

NUTRITION FACTS PER SERVING:
414 cal., 20 g total fat (17 g sat. fat), 129 mg chol., 285 mg sodium, 44 g carb., 7 g fiber, 20 g pro.

293

tip
To thaw shrimp quickly, place them in a bowl of cool water and let them soak for about 15 minutes or until no longer icy.

Main Dish Meats, Poultry, and Seafood

Beer-Steamed Mussels with Sausage and Fennel

PREP 35 minutes   SOAK 45 minutes   COOK 15 minutes   MAKES 4 servings

- 2 pounds fresh mussels
- 9 quarts water
- 9 tablespoons salt
- 4 ounces uncooked hot Italian turkey sausage links, casing removed
- 2 teaspoons olive oil
- 6 cloves garlic, thinly sliced
- 1 cup onion, chopped (1 large)
- ½ cup thinly sliced fennel (one small)
- 1 teaspoon fennel seeds
- ½ teaspoon salt
- ½ teaspoon crushed red pepper
- 1 cup seeded and chopped tomatoes (2 medium)
- 1 12-ounce bottle mild beer, such as Anchor Steam
- 1 cup chicken broth
- 1 lemon, cut into 6 wedges
- ⅓ cup snipped fresh Italian (flat-leaf) parsley

   Sliced crusty bread (optional)

1 Scrub mussels under cold running water. Using your fingers, pull out any beards visible between mussel shells; discard. In an extra-large bowl combine 3 quarts of the water and 3 tablespoons of the salt. Add mussels; soak for 15 minutes. Drain and rinse thoroughly; drain. Repeat two more times with remaining 6 quarts water and 6 tablespoons salt. Drain and rinse mussels thoroughly.

2 In an extra-large skillet with a tight-fitting lid, cook sausage in hot oil over medium heat until brown, using a wooden spoon to break up meat as it cooks. Remove sausage from skillet and drain on paper towels.

3 Add garlic to skillet; cook and stir about 2 minutes or just until golden. Stir in onion, fennel, fennel seeds, ½ teaspoon salt, and crushed red pepper. Cook, covered, about 5 minutes or until vegetables are tender. Stir in sausage and tomatoes.

4 Add beer and broth to skillet; bring to boiling. Stir in mussels and lemon wedges. Cook, covered, for 2 to 3 minutes or just until mussels open. Discard any mussels that do not open. Sprinkle with parsley. Serve mussels in bowls with broth and, if desired, crusty bread.

NUTRITION FACTS PER SERVING:
342 cal., 10 g total fat (2 g sat. fat), 82 mg chol., 1266 mg sodium, 23 g carb., 3 g fiber, 34 g pro.

30-Minute Meals

It's easy to put a comforting meal on the

table any night of the week with these

quick-to-fix, family-pleasing recipes.

Italian Fried Steak
with Roasted Pepper Pesto

START TO FINISH 30 minutes MAKES 4 servings

½ cup seasoned fine dry bread crumbs

½ cup grated Romano or Parmesan cheese

1 egg, lightly beaten

2 tablespoons water

1½ pounds beef cubed steaks

Salt

Ground black pepper

1 tablespoon olive oil

1 12-ounce jar roasted red sweet peppers, drained

⅔ cup fresh basil leaves

1 In a shallow dish combine bread crumbs and ¼ cup of the cheese. In another shallow dish combine egg and the water. Cut meat into eight portions; sprinkle lightly with salt and black pepper. Dip meat into egg mixture, then into crumb mixture, turning and pressing lightly to coat.

2 In a 12-inch skillet heat oil over medium-high heat. Cook meat, half at a time, in hot oil for 10 minutes, turning once and adding more oil as necessary during cooking. Transfer to a serving platter; cover and keep warm. Carefully wipe skillet clean.

3 Meanwhile, for sauce, in a blender or food processor combine roasted peppers and the remaining ¼ cup cheese. Cover and blend or process until nearly smooth. Finely snip ½ cup of the basil. Transfer pepper mixture to the skillet; heat through. Remove from heat. Stir in snipped basil. Serve sauce over meat. Sprinkle with the remaining basil.

NUTRITION FACTS PER SERVING:
425 cal., 21 g total fat (8 g sat. fat), 130 mg chol., 645 mg sodium, 15 g carb., 2 g fiber, 43 g pro.

Steak with Pan Sauce

START TO FINISH **25 minutes**   MAKES **2 servings**

2   beef steaks, such as top loin, rib-eye, or tenderloin, cut about ¾ inch thick

5   tablespoons cold unsalted butter

⅓   cup dry red wine or apple juice

¼   cup reduced-sodium beef broth

2   tablespoons finely chopped shallot or 1 clove garlic, minced

1   tablespoon whipping cream (no substitutes)

Salt

Ground white pepper

1 Trim fat from steaks. Heat a large skillet over medium-high heat (if possible do not use a nonstick skillet). Add 1 tablespoon of the butter; reduce heat to medium. Add steaks; cook about 6 minutes or until medium-rare (145°F), turning once. Transfer steaks to a serving platter. Cover with foil; let stand for 5 minutes while preparing sauce.

2 Drain fat from skillet. Add wine, broth, and shallot to skillet. Cook over medium heat, stirring to scrape up any crusty brown bits in bottom of skillet. Cook over medium heat for 3 to 4 minutes or until liquid is reduced to about 2 tablespoons. Reduce heat to medium-low.

3 Stir in whipping cream. Stir in the remaining 4 tablespoons butter, 1 tablespoon at a time, whisking until butter is melted and sauce is slightly thickened. Season to taste with salt and white pepper. Serve steaks with sauce.

NUTRITION FACTS PER SERVING:
668 cal., 57 g total fat (30 g sat. fat), 182 mg chol., 283 mg sodium, 3 g carb., 0 g fiber, 28 g pro.

297

tip

To vary the flavor of the sauce, stir in one of the following:

- 1 teaspoon snipped fresh thyme, tarragon, or oregano with the shallot
- ½ teaspoon Dijon-style mustard with the shallot
- ½ teaspoon balsamic vinegar into the finished sauce
- ½ teaspoon capers into the finished sauce

Mini Italian Meat Loaves with Green Beans

START TO FINISH 25 minutes at 450°F   MAKES 4 servings

1   egg, lightly beaten

1   cup tomato-base pasta sauce

½   cup fine dry bread crumbs

¼   cup fresh basil leaves,
     coarsely snipped if large

¼   teaspoon salt

1   pound lean ground beef

1   cup shredded mozzarella
     cheese (4 ounces)

12   ounces fresh green beans,
     trimmed

1   tablespoon olive oil

     Crushed red pepper
     (optional)

1 Preheat oven to 450°F. In a large bowl combine egg, ½ cup of the pasta sauce, the bread crumbs, 2 tablespoons of the basil, and the salt. Add ground beef and ½ cup of the cheese; mix well.

2 Divide meat mixture into four portions. Shape each portion into a 5½×2-inch oval loaf. Place in an ungreased 15×10×1-inch baking pan. Top with the remaining ½ cup pasta sauce and the remaining ½ cup cheese. Bake, uncovered, about 15 minutes or until done (160°F).

3 Meanwhile, in a medium saucepan cook green beans in a small amount of salted boiling water for 8 to 10 minutes or until crisp-tender; drain. Return beans to saucepan. Add oil and, if desired, crushed red pepper; toss gently to coat. Serve meat loaves with green beans. Sprinkle with the remaining 2 tablespoons basil.

NUTRITION FACTS PER SERVING: *496 cal., 29 g total fat (12 g sat. fat), 145 mg chol., 742 mg sodium, 25 g carb., 5 g fiber, 34 g pro.*

Saucy Meatball Subs

Photo on page 279

START TO FINISH **20 minutes** MAKES **4 servings**

2 eggs, lightly beaten

1½ cups soft whole wheat bread crumbs (2 slices)

½ cup finely chopped onion (1 medium)

½ teaspoon salt

½ teaspoon dried Italian seasoning, crushed

2 pounds lean ground beef

2 26- to 28-ounce jars tomato-base pasta sauce

12 hoagie buns or bratwurst buns

½ cup grated Parmesan cheese

1 Preheat oven to 350°F. In a large bowl combine eggs, bread crumbs, onion, salt, and Italian seasoning. Add ground beef; mix well. Shape into 48 meatballs. Arrange meatballs in a large roasting pan or 15×10×1-inch baking pan. Bake for 15 to 20 minutes or until done (160°F).* Drain well.

2 In a 4-quart Dutch oven combine the pasta sauce and meatballs. Heat through. Split buns or hollow out tops of unsplit buns. Spoon hot meatball mixture into buns. Spoon any remaining sauce over the meatballs. Sprinkle cheese over meatballs. If buns are split, top with bun halves. Let stand for 1 to 2 minutes before serving.

NUTRITION FACTS PER SERVING:
599 cal., 18 g total fat (6 g sat. fat), 86 mg chol., 1351 mg sodium, 83 g carb., 6 g fiber, 29 g pro.

299

tip
The internal color of a meatball is not a reliable doneness indicator. A beef, veal, lamb, or pork meatball cooked to 160°F is safe, regardless of color. To measure the doneness of a meatball, insert an instant-read thermometer into the center of the meatball.

Chili Burgers

START TO FINISH **30 minutes** MAKES **4 servings**

4 **4-ounce purchased uncooked ground beef or turkey patties**

½ **teaspoon salt**

   Pinch ground black pepper

1 **tablespoon vegetable oil**

¼ **cup chopped onion**

1 **clove garlic, minced**

1 **15-ounce can chili with beans**

1 **14.5-ounce can diced tomatoes, undrained**

4 **slices Texas toast, toasted**

½ **cup shredded cheddar cheese (2 ounces)**

1 Sprinkle patties with salt and pepper. Heat a 12-inch skillet over medium-high heat. Add patties; reduce heat to medium. Cook for 6 to 8 minutes or until done (160°F), turning once. Remove patties from skillet and keep warm. Drain off fat. Carefully wipe out skillet.

2 Add oil to skillet. Add onion and garlic; cook and stir over medium heat until tender. Stir in chili with beans and tomatoes. Bring to boiling; reduce heat. Simmer, uncovered, for 5 to 10 minutes or until desired consistency, stirring occasionally.

3 To serve, place burgers on top of toast. Spoon chili mixture over burgers. Sprinkle with cheese.

NUTRITION FACTS PER SERVING:
676 cal., 43 g total fat (16 g sat. fat), 172 mg chol., 1419 mg sodium, 39 g carb., 5 g fiber, 36 g pro.

Reuben Sandwiches

START TO FINISH **20 minutes** MAKES **4 servings**

3 tablespoons butter, softened

8 slices dark rye or pumpernickel bread

3 tablespoons bottled Thousand Island or Russian salad dressing

6 ounces thinly sliced cooked corned beef or pastrami

4 0.75-ounce slices Swiss cheese

1 cup sauerkraut, well drained

1 Spread softened butter on one side of each bread slice and salad dressing on the other side. With the buttered sides down, top four slices with meat, cheese, and sauerkraut. Add the remaining bread slices, dressing sides down.

2 Heat a large skillet over medium heat. Reduce heat to medium-low. Cook sandwiches, half at a time, in hot skillet for 4 to 6 minutes or until bread is toasted and cheese is melted, turning once.

NUTRITION FACTS PER SERVING:
487 cal., 29 g total fat (13 g sat. fat), 89 mg chol., 1509 mg sodium, 36 g carb., 5 g fiber, 20 g pro.

tip

Next time, instead of using corned beef and Swiss cheese, vary the flavor of this grilled meat and cheese sandwich. Leave off the sauerkraut and try one of these variations:

- Roast beef and provolone
- Turkey and Monterey Jack
- Ham and cheddar

Rosemary-Garlic Lamb Chops

START TO FINISH 20 minutes MAKES 4 servings

- 8 lamb rib chops, cut 1 inch thick (about 2 pounds total)
- 1 tablespoon snipped fresh rosemary
- 2 cloves garlic, minced
  Salt
  Ground black pepper
- 1 tablespoon olive oil
  Snipped fresh rosemary (optional)

1 Trim fat from chops. Sprinkle rosemary and garlic evenly over both sides of chops; rub in with your fingers. Sprinkle with salt and pepper. If desired, cover chops with plastic wrap and let stand for 15 minutes.

2 In a large nonstick skillet heat oil over medium-high heat. Add chops; reduce heat to medium. Cook for 9 to 11 minutes or until done (160°F), turning once. If chops brown too quickly, reduce heat to medium-low. Serve with additional snipped rosemary, if desired.

NUTRITION FACTS PER SERVING: 198 cal., 12 g total fat (4 g sat. fat), 64 mg chol., 216 mg sodium, 1 g carb., 0 g fiber, 20 g pro.

Oven-Fried Pork Chops

PREP 10 minutes BAKE 20 minutes at 425°F MAKES 4 servings

4 pork loin chops, cut ¾ inch thick
2 tablespoons butter, melted
1 egg, lightly beaten
2 tablespoons milk
¼ teaspoon ground black pepper
1 cup herb-seasoned stuffing mix, finely crushed

1 Preheat oven to 425°F. Trim fat from chops; set aside. Pour melted butter into a 13×9×2-inch baking pan, tilting pan to coat the bottom. In a shallow dish combine egg, milk, and pepper. Place stuffing mix in a second shallow dish. Dip chops into egg mixture, then into stuffing mix, turning to coat. Place chops in the prepared baking pan.

2 Bake, uncovered, for 10 minutes. Turn chops. Bake, uncovered, for 10 to 15 minutes more or until juices run clear (160°F).

NUTRITION FACTS PER SERVING:
327 cal., 14 g total fat (6 g sat. fat), 147 mg chol., 383 mg sodium, 13 g carb., 2 g fiber, 35 g pro.

303

Cornmeal-Crusted Pork

START TO FINISH **20 minutes** MAKES **4 servings**

- 1 **1-pound pork tenderloin**
- ½ **cup yellow cornmeal**
- ½ **teaspoon salt**
- ½ **teaspoon ground black pepper**
- 1 **egg, lightly beaten**
- 1 **tablespoon water**
- 2 **tablespoons olive oil or vegetable oil**
- 12 **ounces fresh green beans, trimmed**
- 2 **medium zucchini and/or yellow summer squash, thinly sliced diagonally**
  Salt
  Ground black pepper
- 2 **tablespoons small fresh oregano leaves (optional)**

1 Trim fat from meat. Cut meat into ½-inch slices. In a shallow dish stir together cornmeal, ½ teaspoon salt, and ½ teaspoon pepper. In another shallow dish combine egg and the water. Dip meat into egg mixture, then into cornmeal mixture, turning to coat.

2 In an extra-large skillet heat oil over medium-high heat. Add meat; cook about 4 minutes or until slightly pink in center (160°F), turning once. Transfer meat to a serving platter; keep warm.

3 Add green beans and zucchini and/or yellow squash to skillet. Cook and stir for 6 to 8 minutes or until crisp-tender. Season to taste with additional salt and pepper. Serve meat with vegetables. If desired, sprinkle with oregano leaves.

NUTRITION FACTS PER SERVING:
310 cal., 13 g total fat (3 g sat. fat), 127 mg chol., 385 mg sodium, 21 g carb., 5 g fiber, 29 g pro.

Pork Tenderloin Sandwiches

START TO FINISH **30 minutes** MAKES **4 servings**

1   1-pound pork tenderloin
¼   cup all-purpose flour
¼   teaspoon garlic salt
¼   teaspoon ground black pepper
1   egg, lightly beaten
1   tablespoon milk
½   cup seasoned fine dry bread crumbs
2   tablespoons vegetable oil
4   hamburger buns or kaiser rolls, split and toasted
    Ketchup, mustard, onion slices, and/or dill pickle slices

1 Trim fat from meat. Cut meat crosswise into four pieces. Place each piece between two pieces of plastic wrap. Using the flat side of a meat mallet, pound meat lightly until about ¼ inch thick. Remove plastic wrap.

2 In a shallow dish stir together flour, garlic salt, and pepper. In a second shallow dish combine egg and milk. Place bread crumbs in a third shallow dish. Dip meat into flour mixture, shaking off excess. Dip into egg mixture, then into bread crumbs, turning to coat.

3 In a large heavy skillet cook meat in hot oil over medium heat for 6 to 8 minutes or until meat is slightly pink in center, turning once.*

4 Serve meat in toasted buns with ketchup, mustard, onion, and/or pickle slices.

NUTRITION FACTS PER SERVING:
424 cal., 13 g total fat (3 g sat. fat), 127 mg chol., 776 mg sodium, 42 g carb., 2 g fiber, 33 g pro.

tip
If necessary, cook half the meat at a time. Keep warm on a baking sheet in a 300°F oven until the remaining meat is cooked. If necessary, add additional oil to pan.

Vermicelli with Sausage and Spinach

START TO FINISH **25 minutes** MAKES **4 servings**

1 **pound cooked smoked sausage, halved lengthwise and cut into $1/2$-inch slices**

$3/4$ **cup chopped onion**

2 **large cloves garlic, minced**

2 **teaspoons olive oil**

2 **14.5-ounce cans reduced-sodium chicken broth**

$1/4$ **cup water**

8 **ounces dried vermicelli or angel hair pasta (capellini), broken in half**

1 **9-ounce package fresh baby spinach**

$1/4$ **teaspoon ground black pepper**

$1/3$ **cup whipping cream**

1 In a 4-quart Dutch oven cook sausage, onion, and garlic in hot oil over medium-high heat until sausage is light brown and onion is tender.

2 Add broth and the water to Dutch oven; bring to boiling. Add pasta; cook for 3 minutes, stirring frequently. Add spinach and pepper; cook about 1 minute more or until spinach is wilted. Stir in whipping cream. Serve immediately.

NUTRITION FACTS PER SERVING:
689 cal., 43 g total fat (16 g sat. fat), 97 mg chol., 1470 mg sodium, 50 g carb., 4 g fiber, 26 g pro.

Fettuccine alla Carbonara

Photo on page 279

START TO FINISH **30 minutes**   MAKES **6 servings**

1   **pound dried fettuccine**

8   **slices bacon**

4   **ounces thinly sliced prosciutto**

2   **tablespoons finely chopped onion**

¾   **cup unsalted butter**

⅓   **cup dry white wine**

½   **cup whipping cream**

½   **cup milk**

½   **cup grated Parmesan cheese**

1   **tablespoon snipped fresh parsley**

Ground black pepper

1 Cook pasta according to package directions; drain. Return pasta to pan; cover and keep warm.

2 Meanwhile, for sauce, in a large skillet cook bacon over medium heat until crisp. Remove bacon and drain on paper towels. Coarsely crumble bacon. Cut prosciutto into ½-inch pieces. Set aside.

3 In a medium saucepan cook onion in hot butter over medium heat about 4 minutes or until tender, stirring occasionally. Add prosciutto. Cook and stir for 3 minutes. Remove from heat. Carefully add wine; return to heat. Bring to boiling; reduce heat. Boil gently, uncovered, for 5 minutes. Stir in cooked bacon, whipping cream, and milk. Return to boiling; reduce heat. Boil gently, uncovered, for 5 minutes. Stir in ¼ cup of the cheese and the parsley.

4 Immediately pour sauce over cooked pasta; stir gently to coat. Sprinkle each serving with some of the remaining ¼ cup cheese. Season to taste with pepper. Serve immediately.

NUTRITION FACTS PER SERVING:
722 cal., 43 g total fat (22 g sat. fat), 108 mg chol., 705 mg sodium, 59 g carb., 3 g fiber, 22 g pro.

307

tip

For best results, serve pasta immediately after cooking. If your noodles are done before the sauce, return the drained cooked pasta to the warm cooking pan. Stir in a little butter or olive oil to prevent them from sticking together. Cover and let the pasta stand no more than 15 minutes.

Mexican Skillet Dinner

Photo on page 279

START TO FINISH **25 minutes**   MAKES **6 servings**

12   ounces uncooked chorizo*
     or bulk pork sausage

2   cups frozen whole kernel corn

1   14.5-ounce can diced
    tomatoes, undrained

1   cup uncooked instant rice

½   cup water

2   teaspoons chili powder

½   teaspoon ground cumin

1   15-ounce can pinto beans,
    rinsed and drained

¾   cup shredded Mexican cheese
    blend or Colby and Monterey
    Jack cheese (3 ounces)

1 If present, remove casing from sausage. In a large skillet cook sausage over medium-high heat until brown, using a wooden spoon to break up meat as it cooks. Drain fat.

2 In the same skillet combine corn, tomatoes, rice, the water, chili powder, and cumin. Bring to boiling; reduce heat. Simmer, covered, about 5 minutes or until liquid is absorbed and rice is tender. Stir in beans and cooked sausage; heat through. Sprinkle with cheese. Cover and let stand for 2 to 3 minutes or until cheese is slightly melted.

NUTRITION FACTS PER SERVING:
230 cal., 27 g total fat (11 g sat. fat), 13 mg chol., 585 mg sodium, 38 g carb., 5 g fiber, 23 g pro.

*tip
Chorizo, a spicy sausage made of coarsely ground pork, can be found in stores specializing in Mexican foods. The Mexican version of the sausage, made of fresh pork, is what you want for this recipe; Spanish chorizo is made of smoked pork.

Apple-Glazed Pork Loaf

START TO FINISH 30 minutes at 425°F MAKES 4 servings

½   cup apple jelly

1   tablespoon Dijon-style mustard

2   medium apples

2   eggs, lightly beaten

½   teaspoon salt

½   teaspoon ground black pepper

1   pound ground pork

1   medium sweet potato, peeled and chopped

⅛   teaspoon cayenne pepper (optional)

1   tablespoon olive oil

2   ciabatta buns, split and toasted

1 Preheat oven to 425°F. Grease a 15×10×1-inch baking pan; set aside. For glaze, place jelly in a small microwave-safe bowl. Microwave on 100 percent power (high) about 20 seconds or until melted. Stir in mustard; set aside.

2 Core and chop 1 of the apples. In a large bowl combine half of the chopped apple, the eggs, salt, and black pepper. Add ground pork; mix well. Shape meat mixture into four 6×2-inch loaves. Place in the prepared baking pan. Spoon some of the glaze over loaves. Bake, uncovered, for 10 minutes. Core and thinly slice the remaining apple. Top loaves with apple slices; drizzle with the remaining glaze. Bake, uncovered, about 5 minutes more or until done (160°F).

3 Meanwhile, in another small microwave-safe bowl microwave sweet potato on high about 4 minutes or until nearly tender. In a medium skillet cook the remaining chopped apple, sweet potato, and, if desired, cayenne pepper in hot oil over medium-high heat about 3 minutes or until tender, stirring occasionally. To serve, place pork loaves on ciabatta bun halves. Top with sweet potato mixture.

NUTRITION FACTS PER SERVING:
697 cal., 32 g total fat (11 g sat. fat), 187 mg chol., 842 mg sodium, 74 g carb., 5 g fiber, 28 g pro.

Glazed Ham with Vegetables

START TO FINISH 20 minutes MAKES 4 servings

2 medium sweet potatoes, peeled and cut into 1-inch pieces

12 ounces Brussels sprouts, trimmed and halved lengthwise

2 tablespoons butter

1 to 1¼ pounds cooked boneless ham, cut into ¼-inch slices

½ cup apple butter

2 tablespoons cider vinegar

Salt

Ground black pepper

1 In a large saucepan cook sweet potatoes and Brussels sprouts in lightly salted boiling water for 8 or 10 minutes or just until tender; drain.

2 Meanwhile, in a 12-inch skillet heat butter over medium-high heat until melted. Add ham; cook for 4 to 5 minutes or until heated through, turning occasionally. Remove from heat.

3 Divide ham and vegetables among serving plates; cover and keep warm. Stir apple butter and vinegar into drippings in skillet; heat through. Drizzle mixture over ham and vegetables. Season to taste with salt and pepper.

NUTRITION FACTS PER SERVING:
513 cal., 16 g total fat (7 g sat. fat), 80 mg chol., 1664 mg sodium, 70 g carb., 8 g fiber, 23 g pro.

Barbecue Chicken Burgers and Waffle Fries

START TO FINISH 30 minutes MAKES 4 servings

⅓ cup grape jelly or **seedless raspberry jam**

⅓ cup **barbecue sauce**

3 cups frozen waffle-cut or thick-cut French-fried potatoes

4 slices packaged ready-to-serve cooked bacon, chopped

2 tablespoons fine dry bread crumbs

2 tablespoons finely chopped honey-roasted walnuts or almonds

1 tablespoon barbecue sauce

½ teaspoon poultry seasoning

¼ teaspoon salt

⅛ teaspoon ground black pepper

8 ounces uncooked ground chicken or turkey

½ cup shredded Italian cheese blend or Monterey Jack cheese with jalapeño peppers or crumbled Gorgonzola cheese (2 ounces)

Snipped fresh chives

8 dinner rolls or cocktail-size hamburger buns, split

Tomato slices and/or lettuce

1 Preheat oven to 425°F. In a small bowl whisk together jelly and ⅓ cup barbecue sauce until smooth; set aside.

2 Arrange fries in a single layer on an ungreased baking sheet. Sprinkle with bacon. Bake, uncovered, for 8 minutes.

3 Meanwhile, grease a shallow baking pan; set aside. In a medium bowl combine bread crumbs, nuts, 1 tablespoon barbecue sauce, poultry seasoning, salt, and pepper. Add ground chicken; mix well. Shape chicken mixture into eight balls. Place balls 2 inches apart in the prepared baking pan. Moisten the bottom of a glass and use the glass to press each ball until about ¼ inch thick.

4 Place pan with burgers in oven. Bake fries and burgers, uncovered, for 5 minutes. Stir fries; turn burgers. Bake, uncovered, for 5 minutes more.

5 Sprinkle fries with cheese. Brush some of the jelly mixture over burgers. Bake fries and burgers, uncovered, about 2 minutes more or until burgers are no longer pink in center (165°F) and cheese is melted on fries.

6 To serve, sprinkle fries with chives. Place burgers on bottoms of dinner rolls. Spoon the remaining jelly mixture over burgers. Top with tomato slices and/or lettuce; replace tops of rolls.

NUTRITION FACTS PER SERVING:
537 cal., 21 g total fat (7 g sat. fat), 20 mg chol., 902 mg sodium, 66 g carb., 4 g fiber, 22 g pro.

311

Baked Chicken Fingers with Dipping Sauces

PREP 20 minutes BAKE 8 minutes at 400°F MAKES 4 servings

1   egg, lightly beaten
¼   cup sour cream
¼   teaspoon salt
¼   teaspoon garlic powder
¼   teaspoon ground black pepper
1¼   to 1½ pounds skinless, boneless chicken breast halves
3   tablespoons vegetable oil
2   cups mini pretzel twists or 4 cups tortilla chips, crushed
1   recipe Honey Mustard Sauce, Sweet-and-Sour Apricot Sauce, or Cooled-Down Mexican Salsa

1 Preheat oven to 400°F. In a medium bowl combine egg, sour cream, salt, garlic powder, and pepper. Cut chicken lengthwise into ¾-inch-thick strips. Add chicken to egg mixture; stir to coat.

2 Brush a 15×10×1-inch baking pan with oil; set aside. Place crushed pretzels in a shallow dish. Dip chicken, a few pieces at a time, into pretzels, turning and pressing strips to coat. Arrange chicken in a single layer in the prepared baking pan, leaving space between each piece.

3 Bake, uncovered, for 8 to 10 minutes or until chicken is no longer pink (170°F), turning after 5 minutes. Serve with Honey Mustard Sauce.

NUTRITION FACTS PER SERVING:
505 cal., 29 g total fat (5 g sat. fat), 148 mg chol., 1053 mg sodium, 23 g carb., 1 g fiber, 35 g pro.

Honey Mustard Sauce
In a small bowl stir together ¼ cup mayonnaise or salad dressing and 1 tablespoon honey mustard. Cover and chill until ready to serve.

Sweet-and-Sour Apricot Sauce
In a small bowl stir together ½ cup apricot preserves (snip any large pieces of fruit), 2 tablespoons ketchup, 1 tablespoon rice vinegar, and 1 tablespoon soy sauce.

Cooled-Down Mexican Salsa
In a small bowl stir together ½ cup salsa, ¼ cup sour cream, and ¼ cup shredded Mexican cheese blend (1 ounce).

Chicken and Pasta Frittata

START TO FINISH **30 minutes** MAKES **4 servings**

4   **cups fresh baby spinach**

3   **tablespoons olive oil**

1   **tablespoon lemon juice**

1   **to 2 teaspoons honey**

    Salt

    Ground black pepper

1   **cup broccoli florets**

½   **cup chopped onion
    (1 medium)**

1¼ **cups cooked penne pasta**

1   **cup chopped cooked chicken
    (about 5 ounces)**

2   **tablespoons snipped fresh
    basil**

¼   **teaspoon salt**

¼   **teaspoon ground black pepper**

8   **eggs, lightly beaten**

½   **cup shredded mozzarella
    cheese (2 ounces)**

1 Preheat oven to 400°F. Place spinach in a large bowl. In a small bowl whisk together 1 tablespoon of the oil, lemon juice, and honey. Season to taste with salt and pepper. Drizzle lemon mixture over spinach; toss to coat. Set aside.

2 In a large oven-going skillet heat remaining 2 tablespoons oil over medium heat. Add broccoli and onion; cook about 5 minutes or until tender, stirring occasionally. Stir in pasta, chicken, basil, ¼ teaspoon salt, and ¼ teaspoon pepper.

3 Pour eggs over vegetable mixture in skillet. Cook over medium heat. As mixture sets, run a spatula around edges of skillet, lifting egg mixture so uncooked portion flows underneath. Continue cooking and lifting edges until egg mixture is almost set (surface will be moist). Sprinkle with cheese.

4 Transfer skillet to oven. Bake, uncovered, about 5 minutes or just until top is set. Sprinkle with additional pepper. Serve frittata with spinach mixture.

NUTRITION FACTS PER SERVING:
415 cal., 23 g total fat (7 g sat. fat), 462 mg chol., 421 mg sodium, 23 g carb., 2 g fiber, 30 g pro.

313

Thai Curried Noodle Bowl

START TO FINISH **30 minutes** MAKES **4 servings**

1	12- to 14-ounce package dried wide rice noodles
1	tablespoon vegetable oil
¾	cup coarsely chopped carrot
1	cup sliced fresh button or stemmed shiitake mushrooms
¾	cup coarsely chopped red sweet pepper (1 medium)
2	green onions, cut diagonally into ¼-inch slices
1	14-ounce can unsweetened regular or light coconut milk
3	to 4 teaspoons red curry paste
1	tablespoon lime juice
1½	teaspoons sugar
2	cups chopped or shredded cooked chicken (about 10 ounces)
¼	cup chopped dry-roasted peanuts
2	tablespoons snipped fresh cilantro

1 In a Dutch oven cook noodles in lightly salted boiling water for 5 minutes; drain.

2 Meanwhile, in a large skillet heat oil over medium-high heat. Add carrot; cook and stir for 3 minutes. Add mushrooms, sweet pepper, and green onions; cook and stir for 2 minutes more.

3 Stir in coconut milk, curry paste, lime juice, and sugar. Reduce heat to medium. Stir in chicken and cooked noodles; heat through. Remove from heat. Gently stir in peanuts and cilantro.

NUTRITION FACTS PER SERVING:
776 cal., 35 g total fat (21 g sat. fat), 62 mg chol., 411 mg sodium, 88 g carb., 5 g fiber, 29 g pro.

Layered Turkey Enchiladas

START TO FINISH **25 minutes** MAKES **4 servings**

1 tablespoon vegetable oil

1 pound turkey breast tenderloin, cut into bite-size strips

1 16-ounce package frozen sweet pepper and onion stir-fry vegetables

1 10-ounce can enchilada sauce

½ cup canned whole cranberry sauce

Salt

Ground black pepper

9 6-inch corn tortillas, halved

2 cups shredded Mexican cheese blend (8 ounces)

Fresh cilantro sprigs (optional)

Lime wedges (optional)

1 Position oven rack in the top third of the oven. Preheat oven to 450°F. In an extra-large skillet heat oil over medium heat. Add turkey; cook and stir about 4 minutes or until no longer pink. Add frozen vegetables, enchilada sauce, and cranberry sauce. Bring to boiling. Remove from heat. Sprinkle with salt and pepper.

2 In an ungreased 2-quart baking dish layer one-third of the tortillas and one-third of the cheese. Using a slotted spoon, top with half of the turkey mixture. Layer one-third of the tortillas, one-third of the cheese, and the remaining turkey mixture. Top with the remaining tortillas. Spoon the sauce remaining in skillet over layers in baking dish; sprinkle with the remaining cheese.

3 Bake, uncovered, about 5 minutes or until cheese is melted. Cut into squares. If desired, garnish with cilantro and serve with lime wedges.

NUTRITION FACTS PER SERVING:
615 cal., 25 g total fat (11 g sat. fat), 120 mg chol., 1171 mg sodium, 52 g carb., 6 g fiber, 45 g pro.

Turkey Salisbury Steaks

START TO FINISH **30 minutes**   MAKES **4 servings**

- 1 **pound uncooked ground turkey**
- 1 **envelope (half of a 2.2-ounce package) beefy onion soup mix**
- 2 **tablespoons Worcestershire sauce**
- 2 **teaspoons olive oil**
- 1 **clove garlic, minced**
- 1 **tablespoon butter**
- 2 **cups sliced fresh mushrooms**
- ½ **cup reduced-sodium chicken broth**
- ¼ **cup dry red wine or reduced-sodium chicken broth**
- ¼ **cup tomato paste**
  Fresh thyme leaves (optional)

1 In a large bowl combine ground turkey, 2 tablespoons of the dry soup mix, and 1 tablespoon of the Worcestershire sauce. Shape turkey mixture into four ½-inch-thick oval patties.

2 In a large skillet heat oil over medium-high heat. Add patties; cook about 3 minutes or until brown, turning once. Remove from skillet and set aside.

3 In the same skillet cook and stir garlic in hot butter over medium heat for 30 seconds. Add mushrooms; cook about 5 minutes or until tender, stirring occasionally. Add broth, wine, tomato paste, the remaining dry soup mix, and the remaining 1 tablespoon Worcestershire sauce. Stir to scrape up any crusty brown bits in bottom of skillet.

4 Return patties to skillet; spoon sauce over patties. Cook, covered, over medium-low heat about 8 minutes or until no longer pink in center (165°F), spooning sauce over patties halfway through cooking. If desired, sprinkle with thyme leaves.

NUTRITION FACTS PER SERVING:
285 cal., 15 g total fat (5 g sat. fat), 97 mg chol., 1008 mg sodium, 12 g carb., 1 g fiber, 23 g pro.

Cranberry-Sauced Hot Turkey Sandwiches

START TO FINISH **30 minutes**   MAKES **4 servings**

4   ¾-inch slices Italian bread or Texas toast, toasted

1   24-ounce package refrigerated garlic mashed potatoes or 2⅔ cups leftover mashed potatoes, reheated

2   tablespoons butter

12 ounces cooked turkey breast, sliced

3   tablespoons packed brown sugar

1   tablespoon cornstarch

1   16-ounce can whole cranberry sauce

¼   teaspoon finely shredded orange peel

⅓   cup dry red wine or orange juice

¼   cup orange juice

¼   teaspoon salt

⅛   teaspoon ground black pepper

1 Divide bread among serving plates. Prepare refrigerated mashed potatoes according to microwave package directions; set aside.

2 Meanwhile, in a large skillet heat butter over medium heat until melted. Add turkey; cook, covered, about 5 minutes or until heated through. Place turkey on top of toasted bread. Add a scoop of mashed potatoes next to sandwich on each plate. Cover and keep warm.

3 For sauce, stir brown sugar and cornstarch into drippings in skillet. Stir in cranberry sauce, orange peel, wine, orange juice, salt, and pepper. Cook and stir over medium-high heat until thickened and bubbly. Cook and stir for 1 minute more. Spoon sauce over turkey and mashed potatoes.

NUTRITION FACTS PER SERVING:
629 cal., 10 g total fat (4 g sat. fat), 86 mg chol., 682 mg sodium, 96 g carb., 4 g fiber, 32 g pro.

Sloppy Turkey and Veggie Sandwiches

START TO FINISH **25 minutes** MAKES **6 servings**

8 ounces uncooked ground turkey breast

2 cups chopped fresh cremini or button mushrooms

¾ cup chopped yellow or green sweet pepper (1 medium)

½ cup chopped onion (1 medium)

1 14.5-ounce can no-salt-added diced tomatoes with garlic, basil, and oregano, undrained

6 whole wheat hamburger buns, split and toasted

1 recipe Goat Cheese-Yogurt Sauce

1 In a large nonstick skillet cook ground turkey, mushrooms, sweet pepper, and onion over medium heat until turkey is brown and vegetables are tender, using a wooden spoon to break up meat as it cooks. Drain off any fat. Stir in tomatoes. Cook over medium-low heat for 5 minutes to blend flavors, stirring occasionally.

2 Fill buns with turkey mixture and Goat Cheese-Yogurt Sauce.

NUTRITION FACTS PER SERVING:
263 cal., 5 g total fat (3 g sat. fat), 27 mg chol., 392 mg sodium, 32 g carb., 7 g fiber, 21 g pro.

Goat Cheese-Yogurt Sauce

In a small microwave-safe bowl microwave 4 ounces soft goat cheese (chèvre) on 100 percent power (high) about 10 seconds or until softened. Stir in ¼ cup snipped fresh chives; 1 clove garlic, minced; ⅛ teaspoon salt; and ⅛ teaspoon ground black pepper. Gradually stir in one 6-ounce carton plain fat-free Greek yogurt until smooth.

Tuna Club Sandwiches

START TO FINISH 25 minutes MAKES 4 servings

½   cup roasted red sweet
     peppers
⅓   cup bottled ranch salad
     dressing
1   12-ounce can solid white
     tuna, drained and broken
     into chunks
1   8.75-ounce can whole kernel
     corn, drained
12   extra-thin slices sandwich
     bread, toasted
     Butterhead (Boston or Bibb)
     lettuce leaves (optional)

1 For sauce, in a blender combine half of the roasted peppers and the salad dressing. Cover and blend until nearly smooth.

2 Chop the remaining roasted peppers. In a medium bowl combine chopped peppers, tuna, and corn. Stir in ¼ cup of the sauce.

3 For each sandwich, spread 2 of the bread slices with tuna mixture and, if desired, top with lettuce; stack the 2 bread slices. Top with a third bread slice. Cut in half diagonally. Serve with the remaining sauce.

NUTRITION FACTS PER SERVING:
401 cal., 18 g total fat (2 g sat. fat), 45 mg chol., 895 mg sodium, 39 g carb., 3 g fiber, 23 g pro.

Salmon Burgers

START TO FINISH **30 minutes**   MAKES **4 servings**

1   **pound fresh or frozen skinless, boneless salmon fillets**

1   **cup broken herb-seasoned crackers**

1   **egg**

3   **tablespoons Dijon-style mustard**

Olive oil

4   **ciabatta buns, split**

Avocado slices (optional)

Sliced green onions (optional)

1 Thaw salmon, if frozen. Rinse salmon; pat dry with paper towels. Cut into 2-inch pieces; set aside.

2 Place crackers in a food processor. Cover and process until coarsely ground. Add half of the salmon, the egg, and 1 tablespoon of the mustard. Cover and process until salmon is ground and mixture is combined. Add the remaining salmon. Cover and process with several on/off pulses until salmon is coarsely chopped. Using damp hands, shape mixture into four ½-inch-thick patties. Brush patties lightly with oil.

3 For a charcoal or gas grill, grease grill rack. Place patties on the rack of a covered grill directly over medium heat. Grill for 4 to 6 minutes or until patties flake easily when tested with a fork, turning once halfway through grilling. While patties are grilling, add buns, cut sides down, to grill. Grill for 1 to 2 minutes or until toasted.

4 Spread the remaining 2 tablespoons mustard on cut sides of buns. Place salmon burgers on bottoms of buns. If desired, top with avocado slices and green onions. Replace tops of buns.

NUTRITION FACTS PER SERVING:
614 cal., 23 g total fat (5 g sat. fat), 120 mg chol., 968 mg sodium, 67 g carb., 3 g fiber, 36 g pro.

Fish Tacos with Lime Sauce

Photo on page 279

START TO FINISH **30 minutes** MAKES **4 servings**

- 1 **pound fresh or frozen skinless tilapia fillets**
- 2 **small carrots**
- 1 **cup packaged shredded cabbage with carrot (coleslaw mix)**
- ½ **cup mayonnaise**
- ¼ **cup lime juice**
- 1 **teaspoon chili powder**
- ⅓ **cup all-purpose flour**
- ½ **teaspoon salt**
- 2 **tablespoons vegetable oil**
- 1 **fresh jalapeño or serrano chile pepper, thinly sliced***
- 8 **6- to 7-inch flour tortillas, warmed****
  Lime wedges
  Bottled hot pepper sauce (optional)

1 Thaw fish, if frozen. Using a vegetable peeler, cut carrots lengthwise into ribbons. In a medium bowl combine carrots and coleslaw mix; set aside.

2 Rinse fish; pat dry with paper towels. Cut into 1-inch pieces. Place fish in another medium bowl.

3 In a small bowl combine mayonnaise, lime juice, and chili powder. Remove ⅓ cup of the mixture and pour over fish; toss gently to coat. Reserve the remaining mixture until ready to serve.

4 In a shallow dish stir together flour and salt. In a large skillet heat oil over medium heat. Working with one-third of the fish at a time, coat with flour mixture and add to hot oil. Cook for 2 to 4 minutes or until fish flakes easily when tested with a fork, turning to brown evenly. Drain on paper towels. (Add more oil as necessary during cooking.)

5 To serve, divide fish, coleslaw mixture, and jalapeño pepper among tortillas; top with the reserved lime mixture. Fold tortillas in half or roll up tortillas. Serve with lime wedges and, if desired, hot pepper sauce.

NUTRITION FACTS PER SERVING: *652 cal., 39 g total fat (5 g sat. fat), 67 mg chol., 557 mg sodium, 41 g carb., 2 g fiber, 31 g pro.*

*tip
Because chile peppers contain volatile oils that can burn your skin and eyes, avoid direct contact with them as much as possible. When working with chile peppers, wear plastic or rubber gloves. If your bare hands do touch the peppers, wash your hands and nails well with soap and warm water.

**tip
To warm tortillas in the oven, preheat oven to 350°F. Stack tortillas and wrap tightly in foil. Bake about 10 minutes or until heated through. To warm tortillas in the microwave, stack tortillas and wrap in paper towels. Microwave on 100 percent power (high) for 30 seconds.

321

Tilapia Vera Cruz

START TO FINISH 25 minutes   MAKES 4 servings

- 4   6- to 8-ounce fresh or frozen skinless tilapia, red snapper, mahi mahi, or other fish fillets
- 1   tablespoon olive oil
- 1   small onion, cut into thin wedges
- 1   fresh jalapeño chile pepper, seeded and finely chopped* (optional)
- 1   clove garlic, minced
- 1   14.5-ounce can diced tomatoes, undrained
- 1   cup sliced fresh cremini or button mushrooms
- ¾   cup pimiento-stuffed green olives, coarsely chopped
- 1   tablespoon snipped fresh oregano or ½ teaspoon dried oregano, crushed
- ¼   teaspoon salt
- ⅛   teaspoon ground black pepper
- 2   cups hot cooked rice and/or 8 crusty bread slices

1 Thaw fish, if frozen. Rinse fish; pat dry with paper towels. Set aside.

2 For sauce, in a 12-inch skillet heat oil over medium heat. Add onion, jalapeño pepper (if desired), and garlic; cook and stir for 2 to 3 minutes or until onion is tender. Stir in tomatoes, mushrooms, olives, oregano, salt, and black pepper. Bring to boiling.

3 Add fish to skillet; spoon sauce over fish. Return to boiling; reduce heat. Simmer, covered, for 8 to 10 minutes or until fish flakes easily when tested with a fork. Using a wide spatula, carefully transfer fish to a serving dish. Spoon sauce over fish. Serve with hot cooked rice and/or bread.

NUTRITION FACTS PER SERVING:
363 cal., 10 g total fat (2 g sat. fat), 84 mg chol., 1111 mg sodium, 31 g carb., 3 g fiber, 38 g pro.

Shrimp Vera Cruz

For a variation on this recipe, use shrimp. Prepare the sauce and substitute 1 pound cooked shelled and deveined shrimp for the fish; heat through.

*tip

Because chile peppers contain volatile oils that can burn your skin and eyes, avoid direct contact with them as much as possible. When working with chile peppers, wear plastic or rubber gloves. If your bare hands do touch the peppers, wash your hands and nails well with soap and warm water.

Pasta with White Clam Sauce

START TO FINISH **30 minutes**   MAKES **4 servings**

10   ounces dried linguine
     or fettuccine

 2   6.5-ounce cans chopped
     or minced clams

 2   cups half-and-half, light
     cream, or whole milk

½   cup chopped onion
     (1 medium)

 2   cloves garlic, minced

 2   tablespoons butter

¼   cup all-purpose flour

 2   teaspoons snipped fresh
     oregano or ½ teaspoon dried
     oregano, crushed

¼   teaspoon salt

⅛   teaspoon ground black pepper

¼   cup snipped fresh parsley

¼   cup dry white wine,
     nonalcoholic dry white wine,
     or chicken broth

¼   cup finely shredded or grated
     Parmesan cheese (1 ounce)

1 Cook pasta according to package directions; drain. Return pasta to pan; cover and keep warm.

2 Meanwhile, drain clams, reserving ½ cup of the juice. Add half-and-half to the reserved clam juice. Set clams and clam juice mixture aside.

3 In a medium saucepan cook onion and garlic in hot butter over medium heat until tender, stirring occasionally. Stir in flour, dried oregano (if using), salt, and pepper. Gradually stir in the reserved clam juice mixture. Cook and stir until thickened and bubbly. Cook and stir for 1 minute more. Stir in clams, fresh oregano (if using), parsley, and wine; heat through. Serve over cooked pasta. Sprinkle with cheese.

NUTRITION FACTS PER SERVING:
680 cal., 24 g total fat (14 g sat. fat), 125 mg chol., 430 mg sodium, 72 g carb., 3 g fiber, 40 g pro.

Skewered Shrimp Scampi

START TO FINISH 30 minutes MAKES 4 servings

1½ pounds fresh or frozen large shrimp in shells

3 tablespoons lemon juice

3 cloves garlic, minced

¼ teaspoon salt

¼ teaspoon ground black pepper

4 ounces dried regular or whole wheat vermicelli

Lemon wedges

1 tablespoon olive oil

2 tablespoons snipped fresh Italian (flat-leaf) parsley

1 Thaw shrimp, if frozen. Peel and devein shrimp, leaving tails intact if desired. Rinse shrimp; pat dry with paper towels. Thread shrimp onto four 10-inch skewers,* leaving ¼ inch between shrimp. Drizzle with lemon juice; sprinkle with garlic, salt, and pepper.

2 For a charcoal or gas grill, place shrimp on the rack of a covered grill directly over medium heat. Grill for 5 to 8 minutes or until shrimp are opaque, turning once halfway through grilling.

3 Meanwhile, cook pasta according to package directions; drain.

4 To serve, divide pasta among serving plates. Top with shrimp skewers. Squeeze lemon wedges over shrimp; drizzle with oil. Sprinkle with parsley.

NUTRITION FACTS PER SERVING:
314 cal., 6 g total fat (1 g sat. fat), 259 mg chol., 400 mg sodium, 28 g carb., 2 g fiber, 35 g pro.

Range-Top Directions: To cook in a skillet or grill pan, heat a lightly greased large skillet or grill pan over medium-high heat. Add shrimp skewers; cook for 6 to 10 minutes or until shrimp are opaque, turning once.

*tip
If using wooden skewers, soak in water for at least 30 minutes; drain before using.

Poached Egg Salad with Citrus Dressing

Photo on page 278

START TO FINISH **30 minutes** MAKES **4 servings**

¼ cup olive oil

3 tablespoons lemon juice

¼ teaspoon finely shredded orange peel*

2 tablespoons orange juice*

1 tablespoon finely snipped fresh tarragon

Salt

Ground black pepper

1 teaspoon cider vinegar

4 eggs

1 8-ounce log semisoft goat cheese (chèvre), chilled

2 eggs, lightly beaten

½ cup all-purpose flour

½ cup seasoned fine dry bread crumbs

4 cups fresh arugula, baby spinach, or mâche

1 cup watercress sprigs

¼ cup olive oil

1 For dressing, in a small bowl whisk together ¼ cup oil, lemon juice, orange peel, orange juice, and tarragon. Season to taste with salt and pepper. Set aside.

2 For poached eggs, line a dinner plate with paper towels; set aside. Fill a large skillet with 2 inches of water; add vinegar. Bring vinegar mixture to boiling; reduce heat to simmering (bubbles should begin to break the surface of the water). Break an egg into a cup and slip egg into the simmering water. Repeat with the remaining 3 eggs, allowing each egg an equal amount of space in the skillet. Simmer eggs, uncovered, for 3 to 5 minutes or until whites are completely set and yolks begin to thicken but are not hard. Using a slotted spoon, gently transfer eggs to the prepared plate.

3 Cut cheese into 12 slices. Place 2 beaten eggs in a shallow bowl. Place flour in a second shallow bowl. Place bread crumbs in a third shallow bowl. Dip each cheese slice into flour, shaking off excess. Dip into beaten eggs, then into bread crumbs, turning to coat. Chill for 10 minutes. Meanwhile, in a large bowl combine arugula and watercress. Drizzle with dressing; toss to coat.

4 In a medium skillet heat ¼ cup oil over medium heat. Add cheese slices; cook about 4 minutes or until golden, turning once.

5 To serve, divide arugula mixture among serving plates. Top with poached eggs and cheese slices. Sprinkle with additional salt and pepper.

NUTRITION FACTS PER SERVING:
205 cal., 19 g total fat (3 g sat. fat), 212 mg chol., 225 mg sodium, 3 g carb., 1 g fiber, 7 g pro.

325

*tip

For a tangier dressing, substitute lime peel and juice for the orange peel and juice.

Vegetable Egg Salad Wraps

START TO FINISH 30 minutes MAKES 6 servings

6   hard-cooked eggs, chopped

1/2   cup chopped cucumber

1/2   cup chopped yellow summer squash and/or zucchini

1/4   cup shredded carrot

2   tablespoons chopped red onion

1/4   cup mayonnaise

2   tablespoons Dijon-style mustard

1   tablespoon milk

1   teaspoon snipped fresh tarragon or basil or 1/4 teaspoon dried tarragon or basil, crushed

1/4   teaspoon salt

1/8   teaspoon paprika

6   leaf lettuce leaves

6   6- to 7-inch whole wheat flour tortillas

2   roma tomatoes, thinly sliced

1 In a large bowl combine eggs, cucumber, yellow squash and/or zucchini, carrot, and red onion. For dressing, in a small bowl stir together mayonnaise, mustard, milk, tarragon, salt, and paprika. Pour dressing over egg mixture; stir gently to combine.

2 For each sandwich, place a lettuce leaf on a tortilla. Arrange 3 or 4 tomato slices on top of lettuce, placing slices slightly off-center. Spoon about 1/2 cup of the egg mixture on top of tomato slices. Roll up tortilla; secure with a wooden pick, if necessary. Cut tortilla rolls in half crosswise.

NUTRITION FACTS PER SERVING: 244 cal., 15 g total fat (4 g sat. fat), 190 mg chol., 564 mg sodium, 16 g carb., 9 g fiber, 10 g pro.

326

Make-Ahead Directions: Prepare as directed in Step 1. Cover and chill for up to 24 hours. Assemble sandwiches as directed in Step 2.

Tomato-Avocado Grilled Cheese

START TO FINISH **25 minutes**   MAKES **4 servings**

1 ripe avocado, pitted and peeled

1 tablespoon lemon juice

½ teaspoon ground cumin

¼ teaspoon salt

2 tablespoons snipped fresh Italian (flat-leaf) parsley

8 slices whole grain bread

6 ounces reduced-fat Monterey Jack cheese, sliced

1 large tomato, thinly sliced

2 tablespoons butter, softened

1 In a small bowl use a fork to mash together avocado, lemon juice, cumin, and salt until smooth. Stir in parsley. Set aside.

2 Top 4 of the bread slices with cheese. Spread with avocado mixture and top with tomato slices. Place the remaining 4 bread slices on top of tomato slices. Spread outsides of sandwiches lightly with softened butter.

3 Heat a large nonstick griddle or 12-inch skillet over medium-high heat. Add sandwiches; cook for 4 to 6 minutes or until golden, turning once.

NUTRITION FACTS PER SERVING:
417 cal., 23 g total fat (10 g sat. fat), 45 mg chol., 772 mg sodium, 37 g carb., 11 g fiber, 22 g pro.

tip
Substitute any cheese that melts well for the Monterey Jack cheese. Options include cheddar, mozzarella, provolone, Muenster, or fontina. Try pepper Jack if you want to add a kick of heat.

30-Minute Meals

Falafel Pita Sandwiches

START TO FINISH 25 minutes MAKES 4 servings

1 15-ounce can garbanzo beans (chickpeas), rinsed and drained

¼ cup shredded carrot

2 tablespoons all-purpose flour

2 tablespoons snipped fresh parsley

3 tablespoons olive oil

3 cloves garlic, halved

1 teaspoon ground coriander

½ teaspoon salt

½ teaspoon ground cumin

⅛ teaspoon ground black pepper

½ cup mayonnaise

1 clove garlic, minced

¼ teaspoon cayenne pepper

4 pita bread rounds

1 cup fresh spinach leaves, coarsely shredded

1 In a food processor combine beans, carrot, flour, parsley, 1 tablespoon of the oil, the halved garlic cloves, coriander, salt, cumin, and black pepper. Cover and process until mixture is finely chopped and holds together (should have some visible pieces of garbanzo beans and carrot). Shape mixture into four 3-inch-diameter patties.

2 In a large skillet heat the remaining 2 tablespoons oil over medium-high heat. Add patties. Cook for 4 to 6 minutes or until brown and heated through, turning once.

3 Meanwhile, in a small bowl stir together mayonnaise, minced garlic, and cayenne pepper. Spread mixture over pita rounds. Top with spinach and bean patties.

NUTRITION FACTS PER SERVING:
607 cal., 34 g total fat (6 g sat. fat), 10 mg chol., 1093 mg sodium, 63 g carb., 7 g fiber, 12 g pro.

Fettuccine Alfredo

START TO FINISH 30 minutes MAKES 4 servings

8 ounces dried fettuccine
2 cloves garlic, minced
2 tablespoons butter
1 cup whipping cream
1/2 teaspoon salt
1/8 teaspoon ground black pepper
1/2 cup grated Parmesan cheese
Grated or finely shredded
Parmesan cheese (optional)

1 In a large saucepan cook fettuccine according to package directions; drain and keep warm.

2 Meanwhile, for sauce, in a large saucepan cook and stir garlic in hot butter over medium-high heat for 1 minute. Add whipping cream, salt, and pepper. Bring to boiling; reduce heat. Boil gently, uncovered, about 3 minutes or until mixture begins to thicken. Remove from heat. Stir in 1/2 cup cheese.

3 Add cooked fettuccine to sauce; stir gently to coat. If desired, sprinkle each serving with additional cheese.

NUTRITION FACTS PER SERVING: *514 cal., 32 g total fat (19 g sat. fat), 107 mg chol., 511 mg sodium, 45 g carb., 2 g fiber, 13 g pro.*

Lemony Fettuccine Alfredo with Shrimp and Peas

Prepare as directed, except add 8 ounces peeled and deveined uncooked shrimp and 1 cup frozen peas to fettuccine for the last 1 minute of cooking. Stir 1 teaspoon finely shredded lemon peel and 1 tablespoon lemon juice into sauce before adding fettuccine mixture.

NUTRITION FACTS PER SERVING: *603 cal., 33 g total fat (20 g sat. fat), 192 mg chol., 634 mg sodium, 51 g carb., 4 g fiber, 26 g pro.*

Shiitake Fettuccine Alfredo

Prepare as directed, except cook 1 1/2 cups sliced, stemmed fresh shiitake or button mushrooms in the butter for 4 to 5 minutes or until tender before adding the whipping cream, salt, and pepper.

NUTRITION FACTS PER SERVING: *544 cal., 32 g total fat (19 g sat. fat), 106 mg chol., 513 mg sodium, 53 g carb., 3 g fiber, 13 g pro.*

Angel Hair with Walnut Pesto

START TO FINISH 30 minutes MAKES 6 servings

4 cups lightly packed fresh basil leaves

2/3 cup olive oil

2 cloves garlic, quartered

1/2 teaspoon salt

1/2 cup broken walnuts, toasted, or pine nuts

1/2 cup freshly grated Parmigiano-Reggiano cheese

Salt

Ground black pepper

1 pound dried angel hair pasta (capellini)

1 For pesto, in a food processor combine basil, oil, garlic, and 1/2 teaspoon salt. Cover and process with several on/off pulses until basil is finely chopped.

2 Stop the machine and scrape down sides. Add walnuts and cheese. Cover and process about 30 seconds more or until mixture is smooth. Season to taste with additional salt and pepper.

3 Meanwhile, cook pasta in lightly salted boiling water according to package directions. Drain, reserving 1/4 cup of the cooking water. Return pasta and the reserved cooking water to pan. Add pesto to cooked pasta; toss gently to coat.

NUTRITION FACTS PER SERVING: *593 cal., 34 g total fat (5 g sat. fat), 6 mg chol., 397 mg sodium, 59 g carb., 4 g fiber, 15 g pro.*

Make-Ahead Directions: The pesto can be made ahead and kept tightly covered in the refrigerator for up to 1 week.

On the Side

Sometimes the most comforting part of a
meal comes from the side of the plate and
not the center. Count on any of these
veggie, rice, or pasta dishes to provide a
perfect accompaniment to any main dish.

Smoky Gouda-Sauced Broccoli

PREP 20 minutes BAKE 15 minutes at 425°F MAKES 6 servings

1¼   pounds broccoli, cut into
     spears
1   tablespoon butter
½   cup chopped onion
     (1 medium)
2   cloves garlic, minced
2   tablespoons all-purpose flour
¼   teaspoon salt
⅛   teaspoon ground black pepper
1½   cups milk
¾   cup shredded smoked Gouda
     cheese (3 ounces)
¾   cup soft bread crumbs
     (1 slice)
2   teaspoons butter, melted

1 Preheat oven to 425°F. Place broccoli in a steamer basket. Place basket in a large saucepan over 1 inch of boiling water. Steam, covered, for 6 to 8 minutes or until broccoli is crisp-tender.

2 Meanwhile, for sauce, in a medium saucepan heat 1 tablespoon butter over medium heat until melted. Add onion and garlic; cook until tender, stirring occasionally. Stir in flour, salt, and pepper. Gradually stir in milk. Cook and stir until thickened and bubbly. Gradually add cheese, stirring until melted.

3 Transfer broccoli to an ungreased 1½-quart au gratin dish or 2-quart square baking dish. Pour sauce over broccoli. In a small bowl combine bread crumbs and 2 teaspoons melted butter; sprinkle over sauce. Bake, uncovered, about 15 minutes or until crumbs are light brown.

NUTRITION FACTS PER SERVING:
145 cal., 8 g total fat (5 g sat. fat), 23 mg chol., 429 mg sodium, 13 g carb., 2 g fiber, 7 g pro.

Scalloped Corn

PREP 20 minutes BAKE 35 minutes at 325°F STAND 10 minutes MAKES 6 servings

1   10-ounce package frozen whole kernel corn

½   cup chopped onion (1 medium)

½   cup chopped green or red sweet pepper (1 small) (optional)

¼   cup water

¼   teaspoon salt

2   eggs, lightly beaten

1   14.75-ounce can cream-style corn

1½ cups coarsely crushed saltine crackers

1   cup milk

2   tablespoons butter, melted

¼   cup shredded cheddar cheese (1 ounce) (optional)

1 Preheat oven to 325°F. Grease a 2-quart square baking dish; set aside. In a medium saucepan combine frozen corn, onion, sweet pepper (if desired), the water, and salt. Bring to boiling; reduce heat. Simmer, covered, about 5 minutes or until vegetables are crisp-tender; drain.

2 Meanwhile, in a large bowl combine eggs, cream-style corn, 1 cup of the crushed crackers, and the milk. Stir in cooked vegetables. Transfer mixture to the prepared baking dish. In a small bowl combine the remaining ½ cup crushed crackers and melted butter; sprinkle over corn mixture.

3 Bake, uncovered, for 35 to 40 minutes or until a knife inserted near the center comes out clean. If desired, sprinkle with cheese. Let stand for 10 minutes before serving.

NUTRITION FACTS PER SERVING:
243 cal., 9 g total fat (4 g sat. fat), 85 mg chol., 531 mg sodium, 37 g carb., 2 g fiber, 8 g pro.

333

On the Side

Smothered Okra

PREP 20 minutes COOK 20 minutes MAKES 4 servings

2 tablespoons butter

½ cup chopped onion
(1 medium)

½ cup chopped green sweet
pepper (1 small)

2 cloves garlic, minced

8 ounces whole okra, cut into
½-inch pieces (2 cups),
or 2 cups frozen cut okra,
thawed

2 cups chopped, peeled
tomatoes (4 medium)

½ teaspoon salt

⅛ teaspoon ground black pepper

⅛ teaspoon cayenne pepper
(optional)

2 slices bacon, crisp-cooked,
drained, and crumbled
(optional)

1 In a large skillet heat butter over medium heat until melted. Add onion, sweet pepper, and garlic; cook about 5 minutes or until tender, stirring occasionally. Stir in okra, tomatoes, salt, black pepper, and, if desired, cayenne pepper.

2 Bring to boiling; reduce heat. Simmer, covered, about 20 minutes for fresh okra, 10 minutes for frozen okra, or until okra is tender. If desired, sprinkle with bacon.

NUTRITION FACTS PER SERVING:
99 cal., 6 g total fat (4 g sat. fat), 15 mg chol., 342 mg sodium, 11 g carb., 4 g fiber, 2 g pro.

Fried Green Tomatoes

Photo on page 280

PREP 25 minutes · COOK 8 minutes per batch · MAKES 6 servings

- 3 firm green tomatoes*
- ½ teaspoon salt
- ¼ teaspoon ground black pepper
- ⅔ cup fine dry bread crumbs or cornmeal
- 2 eggs, lightly beaten
- ½ cup all-purpose flour
- ¼ cup milk
- ¼ cup vegetable oil
- Salt
- Ground black pepper

1 Remove stem end from each tomato. Cut tomatoes into ½-inch slices; sprinkle with ½ teaspoon salt and ¼ teaspoon pepper. Let tomato slices stand at room temperature for 15 minutes.

2 Meanwhile, place bread crumbs, eggs, flour, and milk in separate shallow dishes.

3 Dip each tomato slice into milk, then into flour. Continue dipping into eggs, then into bread crumbs, turning to coat.

4 In a large skillet heat oil over medium heat. Cook tomato slices, half at a time, in hot oil for 8 to 12 minutes or until brown, turning once. (If tomatoes brown too quickly, reduce heat to medium-low. If necessary, add additional oil.) Season to taste with additional salt and additional pepper.

NUTRITION FACTS PER SERVING:
194 cal., 12 g total fat (2 g sat. fat), 72 mg chol., 465 mg sodium, 18 g carb., 1 g fiber, 5 g pro.

*tip
Only underripe tomatoes are firm enough to hold up to frying, so pick green tomatoes from the garden or look for them at farmers' markets.

Collard Greens

PREP 15 minutes COOK 1 hour MAKES 6 servings

2 pounds collard greens
1 teaspoon olive oil
1 medium onion, sliced and separated into rings
1 14.5-ounce can reduced-sodium chicken broth
1 smoked turkey neck bone or drumstick bone*
¼ teaspoon ground black pepper

1 Remove and discard stems from collard greens. Coarsely chop greens (you should have about 9 cups packed); set aside. In a 4-quart Dutch oven heat oil over medium heat. Add onion; cook about 5 minutes or until tender, stirring occasionally.

2 Add collard greens, broth, turkey bone, and pepper. Bring to boiling; reduce heat. Simmer, covered, about 1 hour or until collard greens are tender. Remove and discard turkey bone. Use a slotted spoon to serve warm greens.

NUTRITION FACTS PER SERVING:
39 cal., 1 g total fat (0 g sat. fat), 0 mg chol., 137 mg sodium, 6 g carb., 3 g fiber, 2 g pro.

*tip
If using a turkey drumstick, remove meat and reserve for another use; use only the bone for this recipe.

Creamed Spinach

Photo on page 282

2 9-ounce packages fresh spinach, large stems removed, or two 10-ounce packages frozen chopped spinach, thawed

2 tablespoons butter

½ cup chopped onion (1 medium)

2 or 3 cloves garlic, minced

1 cup whipping cream

½ teaspoon ground black pepper

¼ teaspoon salt

¼ teaspoon ground nutmeg

1 In a large Dutch oven cook fresh spinach (if using) in salted rapidly boiling water for 1 minute. Drain well, squeezing out excess liquid. Pat dry with paper towels. Using kitchen scissors, coarsely snip spinach; set aside. (If using frozen spinach, drain well after thawing, squeezing out excess liquid.)

2 In a large skillet heat butter over medium heat until melted. Add onion and garlic; cook about 5 minutes or until onion is tender, stirring occasionally. Stir in whipping cream, pepper, salt, and nutmeg. Bring to boiling; cook, uncovered, for 3 to 5 minutes or until cream starts to thicken. Stir in spinach. Simmer, uncovered, about 2 minutes more or until mixture reaches desired consistency, stirring occasionally.

NUTRITION FACTS PER SERVING:
312 cal., 29 g total fat (17 g sat. fat), 98 mg chol., 347 mg sodium, 11 g carb., 4 g fiber, 6 g pro.

Mushroom Medley au Gratin

PREP 35 minutes   BAKE 15 minutes at 350°F   MAKES 6 servings

- 2 tablespoons grated Parmesan cheese
- 2 tablespoons fine dry bread crumbs
- 2 teaspoons butter, melted
- 8 ounces fresh shiitake mushrooms
- 4 ounces fresh oyster mushrooms
- 2 tablespoons butter
- 1 pound fresh button mushrooms, sliced
- 1 clove garlic, minced
- 2 tablespoons all-purpose flour
- 2 teaspoons Dijon-style mustard
- 1½ teaspoons snipped fresh thyme or ½ teaspoon dried thyme, crushed
- ¼ teaspoon salt
- ⅔ cup milk

1 Preheat oven to 350°F. In a small bowl stir together cheese, bread crumbs, and 2 teaspoons melted butter; set aside.

2 Remove stems from shiitake and oyster mushrooms. Reserve stems for another use or discard. Slice mushroom caps.

3 In a large skillet heat 2 tablespoons butter over medium-high heat until melted. Add button mushrooms and garlic; cook about 5 minutes or until tender and most of the liquid is evaporated, stirring occasionally. Remove mushrooms, reserving drippings in skillet.

4 Add shiitake and oyster mushrooms to the reserved drippings. Cook over medium heat for 7 to 8 minutes or until tender and most of the liquid is evaporated, stirring occasionally. Stir in flour, mustard, thyme, and salt. Gradually stir in milk. Cook and stir until thickened and bubbly. Stir in button mushroom mixture.

5 Transfer mixture to an ungreased 1-quart au gratin dish or casserole. Sprinkle with bread crumb mixture. Bake, uncovered, about 15 minutes or until heated through.

NUTRITION FACTS PER SERVING:
120 cal., 7 g total fat (4 g sat. fat), 17 mg chol., 237 mg sodium, 10 g carb., 2 g fiber, 6 g pro.

338

tip
Mushrooms are like sponges and soak up water very quickly when they are rinsed off, so the best way to clean them is to simply wipe them with a slightly damp paper towel.

Rosemary-Roasted Vegetables

PREP 30 minutes ROAST 20 minutes at 425°F MAKES 12 servings

1 pound fresh Brussels sprouts

12 ounces fresh green beans, trimmed if desired

1 bunch green onions, trimmed and cut up

12 sprigs fresh rosemary

8 slices pancetta or bacon, partially cooked, drained, and cut up

2 tablespoons olive oil

Salt

Freshly ground black pepper

1 lemon, halved

1 Preheat oven to 425°F. Trim Brussels sprouts; cut any large sprouts in half. In a covered large saucepan cook Brussels sprouts in a small amount of lightly salted boiling water for 3 minutes. Add green beans; cook for 5 minutes more; drain.

2 Transfer Brussels sprouts and beans to an ungreased 13×9×2-inch baking pan. Add green onions and rosemary sprigs; toss to combine. Top with pancetta. Drizzle oil over vegetable mixture. Sprinkle with salt and pepper.

3 Roast, uncovered, about 20 minutes or until vegetables are crisp-tender and pancetta is crisp. Remove rosemary sprigs and transfer to a serving platter. Squeeze juice from lemon over vegetables.

NUTRITION FACTS PER SERVING:
143 cal., 10 g total fat (4 g sat. fat), 10 mg chol., 275 mg sodium, 6 g carb., 3 g fiber, 4 g pro.

339

On the Side

Oven-Fried Veggies
Photo on page 283

PREP 25 minutes BAKE 20 minutes at 400°F MAKES 6 servings

1   cup panko (Japanese-style bread crumbs)

½   cup grated Parmesan cheese

1   teaspoon dried oregano, basil, or thyme, crushed

½   teaspoon garlic powder

½   teaspoon ground black pepper

1   egg, lightly beaten

1   tablespoon milk

4   cups cauliflower florets, broccoli florets, whole fresh button mushrooms, and/or halved baby carrots

¼   cup butter, melted

1   recipe Easy Aïoli or bottled ranch salad dressing (optional)

1 Preheat oven to 400°F. Line a 15×10×1-inch baking pan with parchment paper; set aside. In a plastic bag combine panko, cheese, oregano, garlic powder, and pepper. In a small bowl combine egg and milk.

2 Add 1 cup of the vegetables to egg mixture; toss to coat. Using a slotted spoon, transfer vegetables to panko mixture. Close bag and shake to coat well. Place coated vegetables in the prepared baking pan. Repeat with the remaining vegetables. Drizzle melted butter over vegetables.

3 Bake, uncovered, for 20 to 25 minutes or until golden, stirring twice. If desired, serve with Easy Aïoli.

NUTRITION FACTS PER SERVING:
169 cal., 11 g total fat (6 g sat. fat), 62 mg chol., 222 mg sodium, 12 g carb., 2 g fiber, 7 g pro.

Easy Aïoli
In a medium bowl combine ⅓ cup mayonnaise and 3 cloves garlic, minced. Whisk in 1 teaspoon water, ½ teaspoon lemon juice, and ⅛ teaspoon kosher salt. Gradually whisk in ¼ cup olive oil until smooth. Cover and chill for at least 1 hour before serving.

Hush Puppies

1   cup cornmeal
¼   cup all-purpose flour
2   teaspoons sugar
¾   teaspoon baking powder
½   teaspoon salt
¼   teaspoon baking soda
1   egg, lightly beaten
½   cup buttermilk or sour milk*
¼   cup sliced green onions (2)
     Vegetable oil or shortening
     for deep-fat frying

1 In a medium bowl stir together cornmeal, flour, sugar, baking powder, salt, and baking soda. Make a well in the center of flour mixture; set aside.

2 In a small bowl combine egg, buttermilk, and green onions. Add egg mixture all at once to flour mixture. Stir just until moistened (batter should be lumpy).

3 In a 3-quart saucepan or deep-fat fryer heat 2 inches oil to 375°F. For each hush puppy, drop a slightly rounded tablespoon batter into the hot oil. Fry, a few at a time, about 3 minutes or until golden, turning once. Remove with a slotted spoon and drain on paper towels. Serve warm.

NUTRITION FACTS PER SERVING:
85 cal., 5 g total fat (1 g sat. fat), 15 mg chol., 136 mg sodium, 10 g carb., 1 g fiber, 2 g pro.

341

*tip
To make ½ cup sour milk, place 2 teaspoons lemon juice or vinegar in a glass measuring cup. Add enough milk to make ½ cup total liquid; stir. Let stand for 5 minutes before using.

Onion Rings

PREP 15 minutes COOK 2 minutes per batch MAKES 6 servings

¾ cup all-purpose flour

⅔ cup milk

1 egg

1 tablespoon vegetable oil

¼ teaspoon salt

Vegetable oil for deep-fat frying

4 mild yellow or white onions (1¼ pounds total), sliced ¼ inch thick and separated into rings

Salt

1 recipe Chipotle Ketchup or Curried Aïoli

1 In a medium bowl whisk together flour, milk, egg, 1 tablespoon oil, and ¼ teaspoon salt just until smooth.

2 In a deep-fat fryer or large deep skillet heat 1 inch oil to 365°F. Using a fork, dip onion rings into batter; allow excess to drip off.* Fry onion rings, a few at a time, in hot oil for 2 to 3 minutes or until golden, stirring once or twice with the fork to separate rings. Remove onion rings from oil and drain on paper towels. Sprinkle with additional salt. Serve with Chipotle Ketchup.

NUTRITION FACTS PER SERVING:
657 cal., 58 g total fat (5 g sat. fat), 37 mg chol., 771 mg sodium, 31 g carb., 2 g fiber, 5 g pro.

Chipotle Ketchup

In a small bowl combine 1 cup ketchup and 2 teaspoons finely chopped canned chipotle peppers in adobo sauce.

Curried Aïoli

In a medium bowl combine ½ cup mayonnaise; 2 cloves garlic, minced; 1 teaspoon lemon juice; and ½ teaspoon curry powder. Gradually whisk in ⅓ cup olive oil until smooth.

*tip

You may need to stir the last few onion rings into the batter to coat them well.

Ranch Fries

PREP 25 minutes BAKE 40 minutes at 400°F MAKES 6 servings

Nonstick cooking spray

3 **pounds russet potatoes, cut into 2¼-inch pieces**

1 **2-ounce envelope ranch salad dressing mix**

1 Preheat oven to 400°F. Lightly coat two baking sheets with cooking spray; set aside. In a large bowl toss together potatoes and salad dressing mix. Spread potatoes in a single layer on the prepared baking sheets; lightly coat potatoes with cooking spray.

2 Bake for 20 minutes. Toss potatoes; lightly coat potatoes again with cooking spray. Switch positions of baking sheets in oven. Bake about 20 minutes more or until potatoes are golden and crisp.

NUTRITION FACTS PER SERVING:
191 cal., 0 g total fat (0 g sat. fat), 0 mg chol., 678 mg sodium, 42 g carb., 4 g fiber, 5 g pro.

Spicy Baked Sweet Potato Fries

PREP 15 minutes BAKE 20 minutes at 425°F MAKES 4 servings

Nonstick cooking spray

2 medium sweet potatoes (about 1 pound total)

½ teaspoon sea salt

½ teaspoon ground cumin

½ teaspoon chili powder

½ teaspoon paprika

¼ teaspoon ground black pepper

Sea salt or coarse salt (optional)

1 recipe Horseradish Mayonnaise (optional)

1 Preheat oven to 425°F. Lightly coat a 15×10×1-inch baking pan with cooking spray; set aside. Scrub potatoes thoroughly with a brush; pat dry. Cut lengthwise into quarters. Cut each quarter lengthwise into four wedges. Arrange potatoes in a single layer in the prepared baking pan. Lightly coat potatoes with cooking spray.

2 In a small bowl combine ½ teaspoon salt, cumin, chili powder, paprika, and pepper. Sprinkle mixture evenly over potatoes.

3 Bake about 20 minutes or until potatoes are brown and tender, turning once. If desired, sprinkle with additional salt and serve with Horseradish Mayonnaise.

NUTRITION FACTS PER SERVING:
76 cal., 0 g total fat (0 g sat. fat), 0 mg chol., 340 mg sodium, 17 g carb., 3 g fiber, 2 g pro.

Horseradish Mayonnaise

In a small bowl stir together ½ cup mayonnaise or salad dressing, 1 tablespoon prepared horseradish, and 1 teaspoon snipped fresh chives.

Twice-Baked Potatoes

PREP 30 minutes BAKE 1 hour 2 minutes at 425°F MAKES 4 servings

4   **medium baking potatoes (6 to 8 ounces each)**

½   **cup sour cream or plain yogurt**

¼   **teaspoon garlic salt**

⅛   **teaspoon ground black pepper**

    Milk (optional)

    Salt

    Ground black pepper

¾   **cup finely shredded cheddar cheese (3 ounces)**

1   **tablespoon snipped fresh chives (optional)**

1 Preheat oven to 425°F. Scrub potatoes thoroughly with a brush; pat dry. Prick potatoes several times with a fork. Bake for 40 to 60 minutes or until tender. Cool slightly. Cut a lengthwise slice off the top of each baked potato; discard skin from slice and place pulp in a bowl. Scoop out potato pulp from baked potatoes, leaving ¼-inch-thick shells; add potato pulp to bowl.

2 Mash potato pulp with a potato masher or an electric mixer on low speed. Add sour cream, garlic salt, and ⅛ teaspoon pepper; beat until smooth. If necessary, stir in 1 to 2 tablespoons milk to reach desired consistency. Season to taste with salt and additional pepper. Stir in ½ cup of the cheese and, if desired, chives. Spoon mashed potato mixture into potato shells. Place in a 2-quart shallow baking dish.

3 Bake, uncovered, for 20 to 25 minutes or until light brown. Sprinkle with the remaining ¼ cup cheese. Bake for 2 to 3 minutes more or until cheese is melted.

NUTRITION FACTS PER SERVING:
277 cal., 13 g total fat (8 g sat. fat), 37 mg chol., 238 mg sodium, 30 g carb., 3 g fiber, 11 g pro.

345

tip

If you like, stir a little crumbled cooked bacon, finely chopped cooked ham, or sliced prosciutto into the potato mixture.

Walnut-Sage Potatoes au Gratin *Photo on page 282*

PREP 25 minutes BAKE 1 hour 10 minutes at 350°F STAND 10 minutes MAKES 8 servings

2 pounds potatoes (6 medium)

3 tablespoons walnut oil
or canola oil

½ cup chopped onion
(1 medium)

2 cloves garlic, minced

3 tablespoons all-purpose flour

½ teaspoon salt

¼ teaspoon ground black pepper

2½ cups milk

3 tablespoons snipped fresh
sage

1 cup shredded Gruyère cheese
(4 ounces)

⅓ cup broken walnuts

Fresh sage leaves (optional)

1 If desired, peel potatoes. Thinly slice potatoes (you should have 6 cups). Place potato slices in a colander. Rinse with cool water; set aside to drain.

2 Preheat oven to 350°F. Grease a 2-quart casserole; set aside. For sauce, in a medium saucepan heat oil over medium heat. Add onion and garlic; cook until tender, stirring occasionally. Stir in flour, salt, and pepper. Gradually stir in milk. Cook and stir until thickened and bubbly. Remove from heat; stir in snipped sage.

3 In the prepared casserole layer half of the potatoes, half of the sauce, and half of the cheese. Repeat with the remaining potatoes and the remaining sauce.

4 Bake, covered, for 40 minutes. Bake, uncovered, about 25 minutes or just until potatoes are tender. Sprinkle with the remaining cheese and the nuts. Bake, uncovered, for 5 minutes more. Let stand for 10 minutes before serving. If desired, garnish with sage leaves.

NUTRITION FACTS PER SERVING:
217 cal., 12 g total fat (3 g sat. fat), 17 mg chol., 187 mg sodium, 20 g carb., 2 g fiber, 9 g pro.

tip
Walnut oil, which perfumes this dish with a lovely aroma and infuses it with flavor, must be stored in the refrigerator. Drizzle extra walnut oil on salad greens or steamed vegetables.

Apple, Bacon, and Leek Stuffing

PREP 45 minutes   BAKE 30 minutes at 350°F   MAKES 12 servings

Nonstick cooking spray

9 slices bacon

¼ cup butter

2 cups sliced fresh button mushrooms

1½ cups coarsely chopped leeks (about 5)

1½ cups chopped celery (3 stalks)

3 cups coarsely chopped, peeled (if desired) Fuji or Granny Smith apples (3 medium)

6 cloves garlic, minced

½ cup whipping cream

12 cups dry country-style bread cubes*

1 tablespoon fresh snipped sage or 1 teaspoon dried sage, crushed

1 tablespoon fresh thyme leaves or 1 teaspoon dried thyme, crushed

¼ teaspoon ground black pepper

1¼ to 1¾ cups chicken broth

Fresh sage leaves (optional)

1. Preheat oven to 350°F. Coat a 3-quart rectangular baking dish with cooking spray; set aside. In an extra-large skillet cook bacon over medium heat until crisp. Remove bacon and drain on paper towels, reserving 3 tablespoons drippings in skillet. Crumble bacon; set aside. Add butter to the reserved drippings. Add mushrooms, leeks, and celery. Cook over medium heat for 7 to 10 minutes or until vegetables are tender, stirring occasionally. Add apples and garlic. Cook and stir for 2 to 4 minutes or just until apples are softened. Stir in whipping cream.

2. In an extra large bowl combine apple mixture, crumbled bacon, bread cubes, snipped or dried sage, thyme, and pepper. Drizzle with enough of the broth to moisten, tossing gently to combine. Transfer mixture to the prepared baking dish.

3. Bake, uncovered, for 30 to 35 minutes or until heated through and top is light brown. If desired, garnish with sage leaves.

NUTRITION FACTS PER SERVING:
268 cal., 15 g total fat (7 g sat. fat), 34 mg chol., 507 mg sodium, 28 g carb., 3 g fiber, 7 g pro.

Make-Ahead Directions: Prepare as directed through Step 2. Cover with foil and chill for 2 to 24 hours. To serve, preheat oven to 375°F. Bake, covered, for 40 minutes. Bake, uncovered, about 15 minutes more or until heated through and top is light brown.

*tip

To make dry bread cubes, preheat oven to 300°F. Cut 18 to 21 fresh bread slices into ½-inch cubes to yield 12 cups bread cubes. Spread cubes in two 15×10×1-inch baking pans. Bake for 10 to 15 minutes or until cubes are dry, stirring twice; cool. (Cubes will continue to dry and crisp as they cool.) Or let bread cubes stand, loosely covered, at room temperature for 8 to 12 hours.

On the Side

Perfect Mashed Potatoes

PREP 15 minutes COOK 20 minutes MAKES 10 servings

- 3 pounds Yukon gold or red-skinned potatoes (9 medium), peeled (if desired) and cut into 2-inch pieces
- ¼ cup butter
- 1 teaspoon salt
- ½ teaspoon ground black pepper
- ⅔ to ¾ cup milk, whipping cream, half-and-half, or light cream

    Butter (optional)

    Snipped fresh chives (optional)

1 In a large covered saucepan cook potatoes in enough lightly salted boiling water to cover for 20 to 25 minutes or until tender; drain.

2 Mash with a potato masher, press through a ricer, or beat with an electric mixer on low speed.* Add ¼ cup butter, salt, and pepper. Gradually beat in enough milk to make mashed potatoes light and fluffy. If desired, top with additional butter and chives.

NUTRITION FACTS PER SERVING:
154 cal., 5 g total fat (3 g sat. fat), 14 mg chol., 280 mg sodium, 25 g carb., 3 g fiber, 3 g pro.

*tip
If you leave the peel on the potatoes, use a potato masher rather than the mixer to mash the potatoes.

**tip
To make ⅔ to ¾ cup sour milk, place 2 teaspoons lemon juice or vinegar in a glass measuring cup. Add enough milk to make ⅔ to ¾ cup total liquid; stir. Let stand for 5 minutes before using.

Make-Ahead Directions: Prepare Perfect Mashed Potatoes (or Boursin Mashed Potatoes, Blue Cheese–Rosemary Mashed Potatoes, or Buttermilk-Bacon Mashed Potatoes) as directed. Transfer to a bowl; cool slightly. Cover and chill for 24 to 48 hours. To serve, transfer mashed potatoes to a 4- to 5-quart slow cooker. Cover and cook on low-heat setting for 3½ to 4 hours or until heated through. Stir before serving. Or transfer slightly cooled mashed potatoes to an ungreased 3-quart rectangular baking dish. Cover and chill for 24 to 48 hours. To serve, preheat oven to 350°F. Bake, uncovered, about 1¼ hours or until heated through.

Prepare Duchess Potatoes as directed, except do not drizzle with butter or bake. Cover and chill for 2 to 4 hours. To serve, preheat oven to 450°F. Drizzle potatoes with butter. Bake about 20 minutes or until light brown.

Boursin Mashed Potatoes
Prepare as directed, except beat in two 5.2-ounce packages semisoft cheese with garlic and fines herbes with the milk. If desired, beat in ¼ cup snipped fresh Italian (flat-leaf) parsley.

NUTRITION FACTS PER SERVING: *270 cal., 18 g total fat (12 g sat. fat), 15 mg chol., 455 mg sodium, 26 g carb., 3 g fiber, 5 g pro.*

Blue Cheese–Rosemary Mashed Potatoes

Prepare as directed, except beat in one 3-ounce package softened cream cheese and ⅔ cup additional milk with the ⅔ to ¾ cup milk. Beat in ⅔ cup crumbled blue cheese and 2 teaspoons snipped fresh rosemary.

NUTRITION FACTS PER SERVING: *215 cal., 11 g total fat (6 g sat. fat), 30 mg chol., 433 mg sodium, 25 g carb., 3 g fiber, 6 g pro.*

Buttermilk-Bacon Mashed Potatoes

Prepare as directed, except replace milk with buttermilk or sour milk.** Stir in ½ cup crumbled, crisp-cooked bacon (about 8 slices) and ⅓ cup finely chopped green onions.

NUTRITION FACTS PER SERVING: *188 cal., 8 g total fat (4 g sat. fat), 20 mg chol., 439 mg sodium, 25 g carb., 3 g fiber, 6 g pro.*

Potato Pancakes

Cover and chill leftover mashed potatoes overnight or until thoroughly chilled. In a medium bowl combine 1 lightly beaten egg and 2 tablespoons chopped green onion (1); stir in 1½ cups mashed potatoes. Place ½ cup flour in a shallow dish. Shape ¼ cup of the potato mixture into a ½-inch-thick patty. Dip both sides of patty into flour. Repeat with the remaining potato mixture. In a large skillet heat 3 tablespoons vegetable oil over medium heat. Add patties; cook about 8 minutes or until golden, turning patties once (if necessary, work in batches). Makes 6 servings.

NUTRITION FACTS PER SERVING: *162 cal., 9 g total fat (2 g sat. fat), 40 mg chol., 106 mg sodium, 16 g carb., 1 g fiber, 3 g pro.*

Duchess Potatoes

Prepare Perfect Mashed Potatoes as directed, except cook 3 cloves garlic, halved, with the potatoes. Add ¼ to ½ teaspoon freshly grated nutmeg with the butter. Reduce milk to 2 to 4 tablespoons and add salt and ground white pepper to taste. Cool slightly. Beat in 2 eggs and ½ cup grated Romano cheese on low speed. Preheat oven to 450°F. Grease a 15×10×1-inch baking pan. Using a pastry bag fitted with a large star tip, pipe potatoes into eight mounds in the prepared baking pan. (Or spoon eight mounds into baking pan.) Drizzle mounds with 2 tablespoons melted butter. If desired, sprinkle with additional freshly grated nutmeg. Bake for 10 to 12 minutes or until light brown. Makes 8 servings.

NUTRITION FACTS PER SERVING: *249 cal., 11 g total fat (7 g sat. fat), 81 mg chol., 224 mg sodium, 31 g carb., 4 g fiber, 7 g pro.*

349

Baked Cheese Grits

PREP 15 minutes BAKE 25 minutes at 325°F STAND 5 minutes MAKES 4 servings

2   cups chicken broth
½   cup quick-cooking grits
1   egg, lightly beaten
1   cup shredded cheddar cheese
     (4 ounces)
2   tablespoons sliced green
     onion (1)
1   tablespoon butter
½   cup chopped tomato
     (optional)
     Sliced green onion (optional)

1 Preheat oven to 325°F. In a medium saucepan bring broth to boiling. Slowly add grits, stirring constantly. Gradually stir about ½ cup of the hot mixture into egg. Return egg mixture to saucepan. Remove from heat. Stir in cheese, 2 tablespoons green onion, and butter until cheese and butter are melted.

2 Pour grits mixture into an ungreased 1-quart casserole. Bake for 25 to 30 minutes or until a knife inserted near the center comes out clean. Let stand for 5 minutes before serving. If desired, top with tomato and additional green onion.

NUTRITION FACTS PER SERVING:
238 cal., 14 g total fat (8 g sat. fat), 91 mg chol., 694 mg sodium, 17 g carb., 0 g fiber, 11 g pro.

Sweet-Spicy Baked Beans

PREP 15 minutes   BAKE 1 hour 45 minutes at 325°F   MAKES 10 servings

½ cup packed brown sugar

½ cup ketchup

¼ cup salsa

¼ cup barbecue sauce

¼ cup yellow mustard or spicy brown mustard

1½ teaspoons steak seasoning

1 31-ounce can pork and beans in tomato sauce, undrained

1 15-ounce can butter beans, black beans, or pinto beans, rinsed and drained

1 15-ounce can dark red kidney beans, rinsed and drained

½ cup chopped onion (1 medium)

1 Preheat oven to 325°F. Lightly grease a 2½- to 3-quart casserole; set aside. In a large bowl combine brown sugar, ketchup, salsa, barbecue sauce, mustard, and steak seasoning. Stir in pork and beans, butter beans, kidney beans, and onion.

2 Transfer bean mixture to the prepared casserole. Bake, covered, for 1 hour. Stir beans. Bake, uncovered, about 45 minutes more or until desired consistency, stirring occasionally. Beans will thicken slightly as they cool.

NUTRITION FACTS PER SERVING:
229 cal., 1 g total fat (0 g sat. fat), 6 mg chol., 1095 mg sodium, 47 g carb., 8 g fiber, 10 g pro.

Skillet White Beans

Photo on page 282

PREP 20 minutes   COOK 25 minutes   MAKES 12 servings

3 tablespoons butter

1 large sweet onion, such as Vidalia, Maui, or Walla Walla, halved and thinly sliced

½ cup maple syrup

⅓ cup white balsamic vinegar or lemon juice

2 tablespoons packed brown sugar

2 tablespoons snipped fresh sage

2 tablespoons tomato paste

1 teaspoon salt

½ teaspoon freshly ground black pepper

2 15-ounce cans navy beans, rinsed and drained

2 15-ounce cans butter beans, rinsed and drained

1 15-ounce can garbanzo beans (chickpeas), rinsed and drained

Sour cream

Yellow, red, and/or green tomatoes, chopped (optional)

Fresh sage leaves (optional)

1 In a 12-inch skillet heat butter over medium heat until melted. Add onion; cook about 15 minutes or until very tender and brown, stirring occasionally. Stir in maple syrup, vinegar, brown sugar, snipped sage, tomato paste, salt, and pepper. Stir in navy beans, butter beans, and garbanzo beans.

2 Cook, covered, over medium heat for 10 to 15 minutes or until heated through, stirring occasionally. Transfer to a serving bowl. Top with sour cream. If desired, garnish with tomatoes and sage leaves.

NUTRITION FACTS PER SERVING:
246 cal., 7 g total fat (4 g sat. fat), 21 mg chol., 570 mg sodium, 43 g carb., 9 g fiber, 10 g pro.

Creamy Coleslaw

PREP 30 minutes   CHILL 2 hours   MAKES 22 servings

- 1 medium head green cabbage, cut into $\frac{1}{4}$- to $\frac{1}{2}$-inch strips (about 9 cups)
- $\frac{1}{2}$ of a small head red cabbage, cut into $\frac{1}{4}$- to $\frac{1}{2}$-inch strips (about 3 cups)
- 1 cup shredded carrots (2 medium)
- $\frac{3}{4}$ cup mayonnaise
- $\frac{1}{2}$ cup sour cream
- 2 tablespoons sugar
- 1 tablespoon cider vinegar
- 1 tablespoon Dijon-style mustard
- $\frac{1}{2}$ teaspoon salt
- $\frac{1}{2}$ teaspoon ground black pepper

In an extra-large bowl combine green cabbage, red cabbage, and carrots. In a small bowl combine mayonnaise, sour cream, sugar, vinegar, mustard, salt, and pepper. Stir mayonnaise mixture into cabbage mixture. Cover and chill for 2 hours before serving.

NUTRITION FACTS PER SERVING:
84 cal., 7 g total fat (2 g sat. fat), 5 mg chol., 128 mg sodium, 5 g carb., 1 g fiber, 1 g pro.

Summer Vegetable Potato Salad

START TO FINISH 35 minutes MAKES 8 servings

1 pound yellow or red tiny
   new potatoes, sliced

2 ears of corn, cooked, or 1 cup
   frozen whole kernel corn,
   thawed

4 roma tomatoes, sliced or
   cut into thin wedges

¼ cup fresh basil leaves, torn

¼ cup olive oil

3 tablespoons balsamic vinegar

1 tablespoon finely chopped
   shallot or red onion

½ teaspoon Dijon-style mustard

¼ teaspoon sugar

¼ teaspoon salt

¼ teaspoon ground black pepper

½ cup crumbled goat cheese
   (chèvre) or feta cheese
   (2 ounces)

   Fresh basil leaves

1 In a covered medium saucepan cook potatoes in enough salted boiling water to cover about 5 minutes or just until tender; drain and cool. Cut corn kernels from cobs. On a large serving platter arrange potatoes and tomatoes. Sprinkle with corn and ¼ cup basil.

2 For dressing, in a screw-top jar combine oil, vinegar, shallot, mustard, sugar, salt, and pepper. Cover and shake well. Pour dressing over salad. Sprinkle with cheese and additional basil leaves.

NUTRITION FACTS PER SERVING:
164 cal., 9 g total fat (2 g sat. fat), 6 mg chol., 127 mg sodium, 17 g carb., 2 g fiber, 4 g pro.

Roasted Vegetable Pasta Salad with Walnut Pesto

PREP 40 minutes ROAST 45 minutes at 400°F MAKES 16 servings

1 small eggplant (about 10 ounces), coarsely chopped

1½ cups coarsely chopped zucchini

1½ cups coarsely chopped yellow summer squash

1 cup coarsely chopped red onion (1 large)

1 cup coarsely chopped fennel (1 medium)

¾ cup coarsely chopped green sweet pepper (1 medium)

¾ cup coarsely chopped red sweet pepper (1 medium)

3 tablespoons olive oil

12 ounces dried whole wheat penne pasta

1 cup torn fresh basil

⅓ cup grated Pecorino Romano cheese

¼ cup broken walnuts, toasted

2 cloves garlic, minced

½ teaspoon salt

½ cup olive oil

2 tablespoons lemon juice

2 cups cherry tomatoes, halved

Salt

Ground black pepper

Snipped fresh basil (optional)

1 Preheat oven to 400°F. In a shallow roasting pan combine eggplant, zucchini, yellow squash, onion, fennel, and sweet peppers. Drizzle with 3 tablespoons oil; toss to coat. Roast, uncovered, for 45 to 50 minutes or until vegetables are tender, stirring twice. Transfer to an extra-large bowl; cool.

2 Meanwhile, cook pasta according to package directions; drain. Rinse with cold water; drain again. Stir cooked pasta into roasted vegetables.

3 For pesto, in a blender combine 1 cup basil, cheese, walnuts, garlic, and ½ teaspoon salt. Cover and blend with several on/off pulses until basil is chopped. With blender running, gradually add ½ cup oil and lemon juice.

4 Add pesto to pasta mixture; stir gently to coat. Stir in tomatoes. Season to taste with additional salt and black pepper. Serve at room temperature. If desired, sprinkle with additional basil.

NUTRITION FACTS PER SERVING:
203 cal., 12 g total fat (2 g sat. fat), 2 mg chol., 177 mg sodium, 21 g carb., 2 g fiber, 5 g pro.

tip
Walnuts are an inexpensive (and heart-healthy) alternative to using pine nuts in pesto.

Creamy Broccoli Salad

PREP 20 minutes CHILL 2 to 24 hours MAKES 12 servings

1 cup mayonnaise, light mayonnaise, or salad dressing
½ cup raisins
¼ cup finely chopped red onion
3 tablespoons sugar
2 tablespoons cider vinegar
7 cups chopped broccoli florets
½ cup sunflower kernels
8 slices bacon, crisp-cooked, drained, and crumbled

In a large bowl combine mayonnaise, raisins, onion, sugar, and vinegar. Stir in broccoli. Cover and chill for 2 to 24 hours. Before serving, stir in sunflower kernels and bacon.

NUTRITION FACTS PER SERVING:
247 cal., 20 g total fat (4 g sat. fat), 13 mg chol., 242 mg sodium, 13 g carb., 2 g fiber, 5 g pro.

Caesar Salad with Parmesan Croutons

Photo on page 281

START TO FINISH **30 minutes**   MAKES **6 servings**

2   tablespoons lemon juice

3   oil-packed anchovy fillets

3   cloves garlic

¼   cup olive oil

1   hard-cooked egg yolk

1   teaspoon Dijon-style mustard

½   teaspoon sugar

1   clove garlic, halved

10   cups torn romaine lettuce

1   recipe Parmesan Croutons or 2 cups purchased garlic-Parmesan croutons

¼   cup grated Parmesan cheese or ½ cup Parmesan cheese curls

Anchovy fillets, halved lengthwise (optional)

Ground black pepper

1 For dressing, in a blender combine lemon juice, 3 anchovy fillets, and 3 garlic cloves. Cover and blend until mixture is nearly smooth, stopping to scrape down sides as needed. Add oil, cooked egg yolk, mustard, and sugar. Cover and blend until smooth. If desired, cover and chill for up to 24 hours.

2 To serve, rub the inside of a wooden salad bowl with cut sides of halved garlic clove; discard garlic clove. Add lettuce and Parmesan Croutons to bowl. Pour dressing over lettuce mixture; toss gently to coat. Sprinkle with cheese and, if desired, add additional anchovy fillets. Sprinkle each serving with pepper.

NUTRITION FACTS PER SERVING: *261 cal., 20 g total fat (8 g sat. fat), 62 mg chol., 362 mg sodium, 15 g carb., 2 g fiber, 6 g pro.*

Parmesan Croutons

Preheat oven to 300°F. Cut four ¾-inch slices Italian or French bread into 1-inch pieces (you should have about 3½ cups); set aside. In a small saucepan heat ¼ cup butter over medium heat until melted. Transfer to a large bowl. Stir in 3 tablespoons grated Parmesan cheese and 2 cloves garlic, minced. Add bread pieces, stirring to coat. Spread bread in a single layer in a shallow baking pan. Bake about 20 minutes or until bread is crisp and golden, stirring once. Cool completely. Store in an airtight container at room temperature for up to 24 hours.

Chicken Caesar Salad

Prepare as directed, except add 2 cups chopped cooked chicken with the romaine lettuce. Makes 6 main-dish servings.

NUTRITION FACTS PER SERVING: *350 cal., 15 g total fat (9 g sat. fat), 104 mg chol., 402 mg sodium, 15 g carb., 2 g fiber, 20 g pro.*

357

BLT Salad with Buttermilk Dressing

START TO FINISH 30 minutes MAKES 4 servings

4 slices bacon
2 tablespoons crème fraîche or sour cream
2 tablespoons mayonnaise or salad dressing
1 tablespoon snipped fresh dill
1 tablespoon cider vinegar
1 clove garlic, minced
¼ cup buttermilk or sour milk*
   Salt
   Freshly ground black pepper
2 heads romaine lettuce
   Olive oil
1 cup cherry tomatoes, halved
½ cup shaved Parmesan cheese (2 ounces)

1 Preheat oven to 375°F. Arrange bacon in a shallow baking pan. Bake about 15 minutes or until crisp. Remove bacon and drain on paper towels. Crumble bacon; set aside.

2 Meanwhile, for dressing, in a small bowl whisk together crème fraîche, mayonnaise, dill, vinegar, and garlic. Whisk in buttermilk. Season to taste with salt and pepper.

3 Cut each head of lettuce in half lengthwise. Brush lettuce with oil and sprinkle with additional salt and pepper. For a charcoal or gas grill, place lettuce on the rack of a covered grill directly over medium heat. Grill about 2 minutes or until lightly charred, turning once halfway through grilling. (For a grill pan, preheat pan. Add lettuce, in batches if necessary, and cook as above.)

4 Divide lettuce, bacon, and cherry tomatoes among serving plates.** Drizzle with dressing and sprinkle with cheese.

NUTRITION FACTS PER SERVING:
223 cal., 19 g total fat (7 g sat. fat), 32 mg chol., 516 mg sodium, 4 g carb., 1 g fiber, 9 g pro.

*tip
To make ¼ cup sour milk, place 1 teaspoon lemon juice or vinegar in a glass measuring cup. Add enough milk to make ¼ cup total liquid; stir. Let stand for 5 minutes before using.

**tip
You can vary this salad by serving it in pita bread rounds or on grilled slices of ciabatta bread. If you like, substitute sautéed pancetta for the bacon. Or to make a Cobb salad, add avocado slices, grilled chicken, and crumbled blue cheese.

Corn Bread

PREP **10 minutes** BAKE **35 minutes at 350°F** MAKES **24 servings**

Nonstick cooking spray

2½ cups all-purpose flour

2 cups cornmeal

½ cup sugar

4 teaspoons baking powder

1 teaspoon salt

3 eggs, lightly beaten

2¼ cups milk

½ cup butter, melted

1 Preheat oven to 350°F. Coat a 13×9×2-inch baking pan with cooking spray; set aside.

2 In a large bowl stir together flour, cornmeal, sugar, baking powder, and salt. In a medium bowl combine eggs, milk, and melted butter. Add egg mixture all at once to flour mixture. Stir just until moistened. Do not overmix.

3 Pour batter into the prepared baking pan, spreading evenly. Bake for 35 to 40 minutes or until a wooden toothpick inserted in the center comes out clean. Serve warm.

NUTRITION FACTS PER SERVING: *163 cal., 5 g total fat (3 g sat. fat), 38 mg chol., 203 mg sodium, 28 g carb., 1 g fiber, 3 g pro.*

Old-Fashioned Yeast Biscuits

PREP 40 minutes   RISE 30 minutes   BAKE 10 minutes at 450°F   MAKES 18 to 26 servings

- 1 package active dry yeast
- ¼ cup warm water (105°F to 115°F)
- 5 cups all-purpose flour
- ¼ cup sugar
- 1 tablespoon baking powder
- 1 tablespoon kosher salt
- 1 teaspoon baking soda
- ¾ cup lard, chilled, or ½ cup shortening and ¼ cup butter, chilled
- 2 cups buttermilk or sour milk*
- 3 tablespoons butter, melted

1 In a small bowl dissolve yeast in the warm water; let stand for 5 minutes. Meanwhile, grease two large baking sheets; set aside.

2 In a large bowl stir together flour, sugar, baking powder, salt, and baking soda. Using a pastry blender, cut in lard until mixture resembles large peas. Stir in yeast mixture and buttermilk just until combined.

3 Turn dough out onto a lightly floured surface. Knead dough by folding and gently pressing it just until dough holds together. (Dough will be slightly sticky.)

4 Lightly roll dough until ½ inch thick. Using a floured fork, prick dough completely through at ½-inch intervals. Cut dough with a floured 2½- to 3-inch round cutter. Dip cutter into flour between cuts and reroll scraps as necessary. Place dough circles ½ inch apart on the prepared baking sheets. Cover and let rise in a warm place until nearly double in size (30 to 45 minutes).

5 Preheat oven to 450°F. Bake for 10 to 12 minutes or until golden, rotating baking sheets halfway through baking. Brush generously with melted butter. Serve hot.

NUTRITION FACTS PER SERVING:
232 cal., 11 g total fat (5 g sat. fat), 14 mg chol., 475 mg sodium, 28 g carb., 1 g fiber, 2 g pro.

Make-Ahead Directions: Prepare as directed through Step 3. Cover and chill for up to 3 days. To serve, continue as directed in Step 4. You don't need to wait for the biscuits to rise until nearly double, but you should allow them to come to room temperature before baking.

tip
To make 2 cups sour milk, place 2 tablespoons lemon juice or vinegar in a glass measuring cup. Add enough milk to make 2 cups total liquid; stir. Let stand for 5 minutes before using.

Multigrain Rolls

PREP 45 minutes RISE 1 hour 30 minutes BAKE 12 minutes at 375°F MAKES 18 servings

3¾ to 4 cups all-purpose flour
2 packages active dry yeast
1½ cups milk
⅓ cup honey
¼ cup butter
2 teaspoons salt
2 eggs
⅔ cup whole wheat flour
½ cup rye flour
½ cup quick-cooking rolled oats
⅓ cup toasted wheat germ
1 tablespoon cornmeal
Cornmeal or quick-cooking rolled oats
1 egg, lightly beaten
1 tablespoon water
Sesame seeds, poppy seeds, and/or cornmeal

1 In a large mixing bowl combine 2 cups of the all-purpose flour and the yeast; set aside. In a medium saucepan heat and stir milk, honey, butter, and salt just until warm (120°F to 130°F) and butter is almost melted. Add butter mixture to flour mixture; add 2 eggs. Beat with an electric mixer on low to medium speed for 30 seconds, scraping sides of bowl constantly. Beat on high speed for 3 minutes. Using a wooden spoon, stir in whole wheat flour, rye flour, ½ cup oats, wheat germ, and 1 tablespoon cornmeal. Stir in as much of the remaining all-purpose flour as you can.

2 Turn dough out onto a lightly floured surface. Knead in enough of the remaining all-purpose flour to make a moderately stiff dough that is smooth and elastic (6 to 8 minutes total). Shape dough into a ball. Place in a lightly greased bowl, turning once to grease surface of dough. Cover and let rise in a warm place until double in size (1 to 1½ hours).

3 Punch dough down. Turn dough out onto a lightly floured surface. Divide dough into six portions. Cover and let rest for 10 minutes. Meanwhile, lightly grease two large baking sheets; sprinkle with additional cornmeal.

4 Divide each portion of dough into thirds. Shape each third into a ball by pulling dough and pinching underneath. Flatten and pull each ball to form a 4×2-inch oval. Place on the prepared baking sheets. Using kitchen scissors, make three slanted cuts about ¾ inch deep on both long sides of each oval, creating a feathered look. Cover and let rise in a warm place until nearly double in size (30 to 45 minutes).

5 Preheat oven to 375°F. In a small bowl combine beaten egg and the water. Brush rolls with egg mixture. Sprinkle with sesame seeds, poppy seeds, and/or additional cornmeal. Bake for 12 to 15 minutes or until golden. Transfer to wire racks; cool.

NUTRITION FACTS PER SERVING:
212 cal., 5 g total fat (2 g sat. fat), 44 mg chol., 298 mg sodium, 36 g carb., 2 g fiber, 7 g pro.

361

Rosemary Satin Dinner Rolls *Photo on page 282*

PREP 40 minutes   RISE 1 hour 30 minutes   BAKE 12 minutes at 400°F   MAKES 12 servings

2½ to 3 cups all-purpose flour
1 package active dry yeast
⅔ cup cream-style cottage cheese
¼ cup water
¼ cup butter
2 tablespoons finely chopped onion
½ teaspoon salt
½ teaspoon dried rosemary, crushed
1 egg
1 egg yolk
1 tablespoon water

1 In a large mixing bowl stir together ¾ cup of the flour and the yeast; set aside. In a small saucepan heat and stir cottage cheese, ¼ cup water, ¼ cup butter, onion, salt, and rosemary just until warm (120°F to 130°F) and butter is almost melted. Add cottage cheese mixture to flour mixture; add egg. Beat with an electric mixer on low to medium speed for 30 seconds, scraping sides of bowl constantly. Beat on high speed for 3 minutes. Using a wooden spoon, stir in as much of the remaining flour as you can.

2 Turn dough out onto a lightly floured surface. Knead in enough of the remaining flour to make a moderately stiff dough that is smooth and elastic (6 to 8 minutes total). Shape dough into a ball. Place in a lightly greased bowl, turning once to grease surface of dough. Cover and let rise in a warm place until double in size (about 1 hour).

3 Punch dough down. Turn dough out onto a lightly floured surface. Divide dough in half. Cover and let rest for 10 minutes. Meanwhile, lightly grease two large baking sheets; set aside.

4 Shape dough into desired rolls and place on the prepared baking sheets. In a small bowl combine egg yolk and 1 tablespoon water; brush over rolls. Cover and let rise in a warm place until nearly double in size (about 30 minutes). Preheat oven to 400°F. Bake for 12 to 15 minutes or until golden. Serve warm.

Make-Ahead Directions: Prepare as directed through Step 2, but do not let rise. Cover and chill for 12 to 24 hours. To serve, let dough stand at room temperature for 30 minutes. Continue as directed in Step 3.

Parker House Rolls

Roll each dough half until ¼ inch thick. Cut dough with a floured 2½-inch round cutter. Brush with ¼ cup melted butter. Using the dull edge of a table knife, make an off-center crease in each round. Fold each round along the crease. Press folded edge firmly. Place, larger section up, 2 to 3 inches apart on the prepared baking sheets. Makes 12 rolls.

Butterhorn Rolls

Roll each dough half into a 10-inch circle. Brush with ¼ cup melted butter. Cut each dough circle into eight wedges. To shape rolls, begin at wide end of each wedge and loosely roll toward the point. Place, point side down, 2 to 3 inches apart on the prepared baking sheets. Makes 16 rolls.

NUTRITION FACTS PER SERVING:
187 cal., 9 g total fat (5 g sat. fat), 57 mg chol., 201 mg sodium, 21 g carb., 1 g fiber, 5 g pro.

Sage and Pepper Popovers

PREP 15 minutes BAKE 40 minutes at 400°F MAKES 6 servings

1 tablespoon shortening or nonstick cooking spray

2 eggs, lightly beaten

1 cup milk

1 tablespoon olive oil

1 cup all-purpose flour

2 tablespoons grated Parmesan cheese

2 teaspoons finely snipped fresh sage or thyme or ½ teaspoon dried sage or thyme, crushed

½ teaspoon salt

½ teaspoon freshly ground black pepper

1 Preheat oven to 400°F. Using ½ teaspoon shortening for each cup, grease the bottoms and sides of six popover pan cups or 6-ounce custard cups. (Or lightly coat with cooking spray.) If using custard cups, place cups in a 15×10×1-inch baking pan; set aside.

2 In a medium bowl combine eggs, milk, and oil. Stir in flour until smooth. Stir in cheese, sage, salt, and pepper.

3 Fill the prepared cups half full with batter. Bake about 40 minutes or until very firm.

4 Immediately after removing from oven, prick each popover with a fork to let steam escape. Turn off oven. For crisper popovers, return to oven for 5 to 10 minutes or until popovers reach desired crispness. Remove popovers from cups. Serve immediately.

NUTRITION FACTS PER SERVING:
153 cal., 7 g total fat (2 g sat. fat), 74 mg chol., 237 mg sodium, 17 g carb., 1 g fiber, 5 g pro.

Oatmeal Batter Bread

PREP 20 minutes RISE 45 minutes BAKE 40 minutes at 350°F MAKES 12 servings

1	cup warm milk (105°F to 115°F)
¼	cup honey or packed brown sugar
1	package active dry yeast
1¾	cups all-purpose flour
1	egg, lightly beaten
1	tablespoon vegetable oil
½	teaspoon salt
¾	cup whole wheat flour
½	cup rolled oats

1 In a large mixing bowl combine milk, honey, and yeast, stirring until yeast is dissolved. Let stand for 5 minutes. Meanwhile, grease an 8×4×2-inch loaf pan; set aside.

2 Add all-purpose flour, egg, oil, and salt to yeast mixture. Beat with an electric mixer on low speed until combined, scraping sides of bowl constantly. Beat on high speed for 3 minutes. Using a wooden spoon, stir in whole wheat flour and oats until combined. Transfer batter to the prepared loaf pan, spreading evenly. Cover and let rise in a warm place until double in size (about 45 minutes).

3 Preheat oven to 350°F. Bake about 40 minutes or until bread sounds hollow when lightly tapped. If necessary to prevent overbrowning, cover loosely with foil for the last 10 to 15 minutes of baking. Immediately remove bread from pan. Cool on a wire rack.

NUTRITION FACTS PER SERVING:
166 cal., 3 g total fat (1 g sat. fat), 19 mg chol., 113 mg sodium, 31 g carb., 2 g fiber, 5 g pro.

Desserts

Go ahead and give into your cravings for something sweet with one of these scrumptious homespun cakes, cookies, puddings, candies, and more!

10

Chocolate Flourless Torte

PREP 20 minutes BAKE 45 minutes at 350°F COOL 1 hour CHILL 4 hours MAKES 16 servings

1 **pound semisweet chocolate, cut up**

1 **pound unsalted butter or regular butter**

1 **cup sugar**

1 **cup whipping cream**

½ **teaspoon salt***

9 **eggs**

4 **teaspoons vanilla**

Unsweetened cocoa powder

Whipped cream

1 Preheat oven to 350°F. Grease the bottom and sides of a 10-inch springform pan that has a removable bottom. Line a baking sheet with foil. Set aside.

2 In large heavy saucepan combine chocolate, butter, sugar, whipping cream, and, if necessary, salt. Cook over medium-low heat until chocolate and butter are melted, stirring frequently. Remove from heat.

3 In a large bowl whisk together eggs and vanilla. Gradually stir half of the hot chocolate mixture into egg mixture. Return egg mixture to saucepan, stirring to combine. Pour batter into the prepared springform pan, spreading evenly.

4 Place springform pan on the prepared baking sheet. Bake for 45 to 50 minutes or until center is set and a knife inserted near the center comes out clean.

5 Cool in pan on a wire rack for 1 hour. Cover and chill about 4 hours or until firm. Using a small sharp knife, loosen torte from sides of pan; remove sides of pan. Sprinkle torte with cocoa powder and serve with whipped cream.

NUTRITION FACTS PER SERVING: *517 cal., 45 g total fat (27 g sat. fat), 211 mg chol., 124 mg sodium, 29 g carb., 2 g fiber, 6 g pro.*

*tip
Omit the salt if using regular butter.

Best-Ever Chocolate Cake

Photo on page 285

PREP 30 minutes   STAND 30 minutes   BAKE 30 minutes at 350°F   COOL 1 hour   MAKES 12 servings

¾	cup butter
3	eggs
2	cups all-purpose flour
¾	cup unsweetened cocoa powder
1	teaspoon baking soda
¾	teaspoon baking powder
½	teaspoon salt
2	cups sugar
2	teaspoons vanilla
1½	cups milk
1	recipe Chocolate–Sour Cream Frosting
	White and dark chocolate curls (optional)
1	recipe Candied Nuts (optional)

1 Allow butter and eggs to stand at room temperature for 30 minutes. Meanwhile, preheat oven to 350°F. Lightly grease the bottoms of three 8×1½-inch round cake pans, two 9×1½-inch round cake pans, two 8×8×2-inch square cake pans, or one 13×9×2-inch baking pan. Line bottoms of pan(s) with waxed paper; grease and lightly flour pan(s). Set aside. In a medium bowl stir together flour, cocoa powder, baking soda, baking powder, and salt; set aside.

2 In a large mixing bowl beat butter with an electric mixer on medium to high speed for 30 seconds. Gradually add sugar, about ¼ cup at a time, beating on medium speed for 3 to 4 minutes or until well mixed. Scrape sides of bowl; beat on medium speed for 2 minutes more. Add eggs, one at a time, beating well after each addition. Beat in vanilla.

3 Alternately add flour mixture and milk to butter mixture, beating on low speed after each addition just until combined. Beat on medium to high speed for 20 seconds more. Spread batter evenly in the prepared pan(s).

4 Bake for 30 to 35 minutes for round cake pans, 35 to 40 minutes for square pans or 13×9-inch pan, or until a wooden toothpick inserted in the center(s) comes out clean.

5 Cool layers in pans on wire racks for 10 minutes. Remove layers from pans; peel off waxed paper. Cool completely on wire racks. Or place 8-inch square cakes or 13×9-inch cake in pan(s) on a wire rack(s); cool completely. Frost with Chocolate–Sour Cream Frosting. If desired, top with chocolate curls and Candied Nuts. Store, covered, in the refrigerator.

Candied Nuts

Preheat oven to 325°F. Line a baking sheet with foil. Butter foil; set baking sheet aside. Spread 3 cups pecan halves or whole almonds in a shallow baking pan. Bake for 10 minutes, stirring once. Meanwhile, in a medium heavy skillet heat ½ cup sugar over medium-high heat, shaking skillet occasionally to heat sugar evenly. Do not stir. Heat until some of the sugar is melted (it should look syrupy); begin to stir only the melted sugar to keep it from overbrowning. Stir in the remaining sugar as it melts. Reduce heat to medium-low; cook about 5 minutes or until all the sugar is melted and golden. Stir in 2 tablespoons butter. Remove from heat. Stir in ½ teaspoon vanilla. Add warm nuts to skillet, stirring to coat. Pour nut mixture onto the prepared baking sheet; cool completely. Break apart.

Chocolate–Sour Cream Frosting

In a large saucepan cook and stir one 12-ounce package (2 cups) semisweet chocolate pieces and ½ cup butter over low heat until melted. Cool for 5 minutes. Stir in one 8-ounce carton sour cream. Gradually beat in 4½ cups powdered sugar with a wooden spoon until smooth. (This frosts tops and sides of two or three 8- or 9-inch cake layers. Halve the recipe for two 8-inch square cakes or one 13×9-inch cake.)

NUTRITION FACTS PER SERVING:
760 cal., 35 g total fat (20 g sat. fat), 118 mg chol., 475 mg sodium, 99 g carb., 5 g fiber, 7 g pro.

Apple Cake with Buttery Caramel Sauce

PREP 35 minutes BAKE 45 minutes at 350°F COOL 45 minutes MAKES 16 servings

- 2   **cups all-purpose flour**
- 1   **teaspoon baking powder**
- ½   **teaspoon salt**
- ½   **teaspoon ground nutmeg**
- ½   **teaspoon ground cinnamon**
- ¼   **teaspoon baking soda**
- ½   **cup butter, softened**
- 2   **cups sugar**
- 2   **eggs**
- 6   **cups coarsely chopped, unpeeled cooking apples (9 medium)**
- 1   **cup chopped walnuts**
- 1   **recipe Buttery Caramel Sauce**

1 Preheat oven to 350°F. Grease a 13×9×2-inch baking pan; set aside. In a medium bowl stir together flour, baking powder, salt, nutmeg, cinnamon, and baking soda; set aside.

2 In a large mixing bowl beat butter with an electric mixer on medium to high speed for 30 seconds. Gradually add sugar, about ¼ cup at a time, beating on medium speed until well mixed. Scrape sides of bowl; beat on medium speed for 2 minutes more. Add eggs, one at a time, beating well after each addition. Add flour mixture to butter mixture, beating on low speed just until combined. Fold in apples and walnuts. (Batter will be thick.) Spread batter in the prepared baking pan.

3 Bake for 45 to 50 minutes or until a wooden toothpick inserted near the center comes out clean. Cool in pan on a wire rack for 45 minutes. Serve warm with Buttery Caramel Sauce.

NUTRITION FACTS PER SERVING:
369 cal., 17 g total fat (8 g sat. fat), 59 mg chol., 188 mg sodium, 23 g carb., 2 g fiber, 4 g pro.

Buttery Caramel Sauce

In a small saucepan heat ⅓ cup butter over medium heat until melted. Stir in ⅓ cup granulated sugar, ⅓ cup packed brown sugar, and ⅓ cup whipping cream. Bring to boiling, stirring constantly. Remove from heat; stir in ½ teaspoon vanilla. Serve warm.

Make-Ahead Directions: Cool cake completely in pan. Cover with foil and freeze for up to 1 month. Store sauce, covered, in the refrigerator for up to 1 week. To serve, thaw covered cake in the refrigerator overnight. Preheat oven to 325°F. Bake, covered, about 30 minutes or until warm. Reheat sauce in a saucepan over medium heat until warm.

Sour Cream Pound Cake

Photo on page 286

PREP 25 minutes STAND 30 minutes BAKE 1 hour at 325°F COOL 1 hour MAKES 10 servings

½ cup butter
3 eggs
½ cup sour cream
1½ cups all-purpose flour
¼ teaspoon baking powder
⅛ teaspoon baking soda
1 cup sugar
½ teaspoon vanilla

1 Allow butter, eggs, and sour cream to stand at room temperature for 30 minutes. Meanwhile, preheat oven to 325°F. Grease and lightly flour a 9×5×3-inch loaf pan; set aside. In a medium bowl stir together flour, baking powder, and baking soda; set aside.

2 In a large mixing bowl beat butter with an electric mixer on medium to high speed for 30 seconds. Gradually add sugar, beating about 10 minutes or until light and fluffy. Beat in vanilla. Add eggs, one at a time, beating for 1 minute after each addition and scraping bowl frequently. Alternately add flour mixture and sour cream to butter mixture, beating on low to medium speed after each addition just until combined. Pour batter into the prepared pan.

3 Bake for 60 to 75 minutes or until a wooden toothpick inserted near the center comes out clean. Cool cake in pan on a wire rack for 10 minutes. Remove from pan; cool completely on rack.

NUTRITION FACTS PER SERVING: *268 cal., 13 g total fat (7 g sat. fat), 93 mg chol., 116 mg sodium, 35 g carb., 1 g fiber, 4 g pro.*

Lemon–Poppy Seed Pound Cake

Prepare as directed, except substitute ½ cup lemon yogurt for sour cream. Gently stir 1 teaspoon finely shredded lemon peel, 2 tablespoons lemon juice, and 2 tablespoons poppy seeds into batter.

NUTRITION FACTS PER SERVING: *272 cal., 12 g total fat (6 g sat. fat), 88 mg chol., 116 mg sodium, 38 g carb., 1 g fiber, 5 g pro.*

Blueberry Pound Cake

Prepare as directed, except pour boiling water over ½ cup dried blueberries and let stand for 10 minutes. Drain well. Fold rehydrated berries into batter.

NUTRITION FACTS PER SERVING: *296 cal., 13 g total fat (7 g sat. fat), 93 mg chol., 116 mg sodium, 41 g carb., 1 g fiber, 4 g pro.*

Golden Layer Cake with Chocolate Icing

PREP 30 minutes   STAND 30 minutes   BAKE 15 minutes at 350°F   COOL 1 hour   MAKES 16 servings

1   cup unsalted butter
5   eggs
3   cups cake flour
2   teaspoons cream of tartar
1   teaspoon baking soda
½   teaspoon kosher salt
2   cups sugar
2   teaspoons vanilla
1   cup milk
1   recipe Chocolate Icing

1 Allow butter and eggs to stand at room temperature for 30 minutes. Meanwhile, preheat oven to 350°F. Lightly grease the bottoms of five 9×1½-inch round cake pans. Line bottoms of pans with waxed paper; grease and lightly flour pans. Set aside. In a medium bowl stir together cake flour, cream of tartar, baking soda, and salt; set aside.

2 In a large mixing bowl beat butter with an electric mixer on medium to high speed for 30 seconds. Gradually add sugar, about ¼ cup at a time, beating on medium speed until well mixed. Add eggs, one at a time, beating well after each addition. Beat in vanilla. Alternately add flour mixture and milk to butter mixture, beating on low speed after each addition just until combined. Spread about 1⅓ cups of the batter in each of the prepared cake pans.

3 Bake about 15 minutes or until tops spring back when lightly touched. Cool layers in pans on wire racks for 5 minutes. Remove layers from pans; peel off waxed paper. Cool completely on wire racks. Frost generously with Chocolate Icing.

Chocolate Icing

In a 4- to 5-quart heavy Dutch oven stir together 5 cups sugar, ⅓ cup unsweetened cocoa powder, and ½ teaspoon kosher salt. Add one 12-ounce can evaporated milk, ½ cup whole milk, and ½ cup unsalted butter. Cook and stir over medium heat until mixture boils. Clip a candy thermometer to side of pan. Reduce heat to medium-low; continue boiling at a moderate, steady rate, stirring occasionally, until thermometer registers 230°F, thread stage (15 to 20 minutes). Adjust heat as necessary to maintain a steady boil. Remove Dutch oven from heat. Add 2 teaspoons vanilla, but do not stir. If necessary, tilt pan so the bulb of the thermometer is covered with chocolate mixture. Cool, without stirring, to 165°F to 170°F or until icing reaches pourable, but not runny, consistency (about 20 minutes). Stir before using.

NUTRITION FACTS PER SERVING:
657 cal., 21 g total fat (13 g sat. fat), 120 mg chol., 248 mg sodium, 113 g carb., 1 g fiber, 7 g pro.

tips

If you do not have five cake pans, bake in batches. Chill the remaining batter while the other cake layers bake.

It is important to let eggs come to room temperature before you use them in almost any kind of baking, especially cakes. Room-temperature eggs beat up fluffier and with more volume than cold eggs.

Red Velvet Cupcakes with White Chocolate Filling and Mascarpone Frosting

PREP 50 minutes BAKE 18 minutes at 350°F COOL 45 minutes MAKES 18 servings

2¼   cups all-purpose flour

1½   cups sugar

¼   cup unsweetened cocoa powder

1   teaspoon baking soda

1   teaspoon salt

1   cup vegetable oil

1   cup buttermilk or sour milk*

2   eggs

1   2-ounce bottle (¼ cup) red food coloring

1   teaspoon vinegar

1   teaspoon vanilla

1   recipe White Chocolate Whipped Cream

1   recipe Mascarpone Frosting

     Grated white chocolate and/or white chocolate curls (optional)

*tip

To make 1 cup sour milk, place 1 tablespoon lemon juice or vinegar in a glass measuring cup. Add enough milk to make 1 cup total liquid; stir. Let stand for 5 minutes before using.

1 Preheat oven to 350°F. Line eighteen 2½-inch muffin cups with paper bake cups; set aside.

2 In a large mixing bowl stir together flour, sugar, cocoa powder, baking soda, and salt. Add oil, buttermilk, eggs, food coloring, vinegar, and vanilla. Beat with an electric mixer on low to medium speed until combined. Spoon batter into the prepared muffin cups, filling each about three-fourths full.

3 Bake for 18 to 20 minutes or until a wooden toothpick inserted near the centers comes out clean. Cool cupcakes in muffin cups on wire racks for 5 minutes. Remove from muffin cups. Cool completely on wire racks.

4 Spoon White Chocolate Whipped Cream into a decorating bag fitted with a large round or star tip. Push tip into the top of each cupcake and force some of the whipped cream inside cake.

5 Generously pipe or spread Mascarpone Frosting onto tops of cupcakes. If desired, sprinkle with grated white chocolate and/or white chocolate curls.

NUTRITION FACTS PER SERVING:
449 cal., 22 g total fat (7 g sat. fat), 47 mg chol., 254 mg sodium, 60 g carb., 1 g fiber, 4 g pro.

White Chocolate Whipped Cream

In a small saucepan cook and stir 3 ounces chopped white baking chocolate with cocoa butter and ¼ cup whipping cream over low heat until chocolate is nearly melted. Remove from heat; stir until smooth. Cool for 15 minutes. In a chilled large mixing bowl beat ¾ cup whipping cream with an electric mixer on medium speed until soft peaks form (tips curl). Add cooled white chocolate mixture. Beat on medium to high speed just until stiff peaks form (tips stand straight). If desired, cover and chill for up to 24 hours before using.

Mascarpone Frosting

Allow ½ cup mascarpone cheese or cream cheese and 2 tablespoons butter to stand at room temperature for 30 minutes. In a large mixing bowl beat cheese and butter with an electric mixer on medium to high speed until smooth. Beat in ½ teaspoon vanilla. Gradually add 4 cups powdered sugar, beating well. Beat in 2 to 4 teaspoons milk, 1 teaspoon at a time, to reach spreading consistency. Use red food coloring to tint desired amount of frosting pink.

Desserts

Soda Fountain Ice Cream Pie

PREP 20 minutes FREEZE 9 hours 30 minutes STAND 15 minutes MAKES 10 servings

1½ cups crushed rolled sugar ice cream cones (12 cones)

¼ cup sugar

½ cup butter, melted

3 cups fresh strawberries, hulled

1 quart vanilla ice cream

⅓ cup malted milk powder

½ cup finely chopped fresh strawberries

1 recipe Sweetened Whipped Cream (optional)

Malted milk balls, coarsely chopped (optional)

Fresh strawberries (optional)

Hot fudge ice cream topping (optional)

1 For crust, in a medium bowl combine crushed cones and sugar. Drizzle with melted butter; toss gently to coat. Press mixture evenly onto the bottom of an 8- or 9-inch springform pan. Cover and freeze about 30 minutes or until firm.

2 Meanwhile, place 3 cups strawberries in a blender. Cover and blend until smooth.

3 In a chilled large bowl stir ice cream with a wooden spoon until softened. Stir in ½ cup of the pureed strawberries and the malted milk powder. Spoon half of the mixture over crust, spreading evenly. Cover and freeze for 30 minutes. (Cover and freeze the remaining ice cream mixture.)

4 Spoon the remaining pureed strawberries over ice cream layer. Cover and freeze for 30 minutes more. Stir the remaining ice cream mixture to soften. Spoon over strawberry layer, spreading evenly. Top with ½ cup chopped strawberries. Cover and freeze about 8 hours or until firm.

5 Let pie stand at room temperature for 15 minutes before serving. Remove sides of pan. Cut pie into wedges. If desired, top with Sweetened Whipped Cream, chopped malted milk balls, and additional strawberries. If desired, serve with hot fudge topping.

NUTRITION FACTS PER SERVING:
308 cal., 17 g total fat (10 g sat. fat), 52 mg chol., 178 mg sodium, 37 g carb., 2 g fiber, 4 g pro.

Sweetened Whipped Cream

In a chilled medium mixing bowl beat 1 cup whipping cream, 2 tablespoons sugar, and ½ teaspoon vanilla with an electric mixer on medium speed until soft peaks form (tips curl).

French Silk Pie

PREP 25 minutes BAKE 14 minutes at 450°F STAND 20 minutes CHILL 5 to 24 hours MAKES 8 servings

1 recipe Pastry for a Single-Crust Pie
1 cup whipping cream
1 cup semisweet chocolate pieces (6 ounces)
⅓ cup butter
⅓ cup sugar
2 egg yolks, lightly beaten
3 tablespoons crème de cacao or whipping cream
1 recipe Sweetened Whipped Cream
  Unsweetened cocoa powder

1 Preheat oven to 450°F. Prepare Pastry for a Single-Crust Pie. On a lightly floured surface, use your hands to slightly flatten pastry. Roll pastry from center to edges into a circle about 12 inches in diameter. Wrap pastry circle around the rolling pin. Unroll into a 9-inch pie plate. Ease pastry into pie plate without stretching it. Trim pastry to ½ inch beyond edge of pie plate. Fold under extra pastry even with the plate's edge. Crimp edge as desired. Generously prick bottom and sides of pastry with a fork. Line pastry with a double thickness of foil. Bake for 8 minutes. Remove foil. Bake for 6 to 8 minutes more or until golden. Cool on a wire rack.

2 Meanwhile, in a medium heavy saucepan combine whipping cream, chocolate pieces, butter, and sugar. Cook and stir over low heat about 10 minutes or until chocolate is melted. Remove from heat. Gradually stir about half of the hot mixture into egg yolks. Return egg yolk mixture to saucepan. Cook and stir over medium-low heat about 5 minutes or until mixture is slightly thickened and begins to bubble. Remove from heat. (Mixture may appear slightly curdled.) Stir in crème de cacao.

3 Place the saucepan in a bowl of ice water about 20 minutes or until mixture stiffens and becomes hard to stir, stirring occasionally.

4 Transfer chocolate mixture to a large mixing bowl. Beat with an electric mixer on medium to high speed for 2 to 3 minutes or until light and fluffy, scraping sides of bowl frequently. Spread mixture in the prepared pastry shell. Cover and chill for 5 to 24 hours. To serve, top with Sweetened Whipped Cream and sprinkle with cocoa powder.

Pastry for a Single-Crust Pie

In a medium bowl stir together 1½ cups all-purpose flour and ½ teaspoon salt. Using a pastry blender, cut in ¼ cup shortening and ¼ cup butter, cut up, or shortening until pieces are pea size. Sprinkle 1 tablespoon ice water over part of the flour mixture; toss gently with a fork. Push moistened pastry to side of bowl. Repeat moistening flour mixture, using 1 tablespoon ice water at a time, until all of the flour mixture is moistened (¼ to ⅓ cup ice water total). Gather flour mixture into a ball, kneading gently until it holds together.

Sweetened Whipped Cream

In a chilled medium mixing bowl beat 1 cup whipping cream, 2 tablespoons sugar, and ½ teaspoon vanilla with an electric mixer on medium speed until soft peaks form (tips curl).

NUTRITION FACTS PER SERVING:
583 cal., 44 g total fat (25 g sat. fat), 150 mg chol., 263 mg sodium, 44 g carb., 2 g fiber, 7 g pro.

Double-Coconut Cream Pie

PREP 50 minutes BAKE 14 minutes at 450°F + 15 minutes at 350°F COOL 1 hour CHILL 3 to 6 hours
MAKES 8 servings

  3   **eggs**
  1   **recipe Pastry for a
      Single-Crust Pie
      (recipe, page 373)**
 ⅔   **cup sugar**
 ¼   **cup cornstarch**
 ¼   **teaspoon salt**
  2   **cups milk**
 ¾   **cup cream of coconut***
  2   **tablespoons butter**
  1   **cup flaked coconut**
2½   **teaspoons vanilla**
 ¼   **teaspoon cream of tartar**
  2   **tablespoons flaked coconut**

1 Separate yolks from egg whites. Set egg yolks aside. In a large bowl allow egg whites to stand at room temperature for 30 minutes.

2 Meanwhile, preheat oven to 450°F. Prepare Pastry for a Single-Crust Pie. On a lightly floured surface, use your hands to slightly flatten pastry. Roll pastry from center to edges into a circle about 12 inches in diameter. Wrap pastry circle around the rolling pin. Unroll into a 9-inch pie plate. Ease pastry into pie plate without stretching it. Trim pastry to ½ inch beyond edge of pie plate. Fold under extra pastry even with the plate's edge. Crimp edge as desired. Generously prick bottom and sides of pastry with a fork. Line pastry with a double thickness of foil. Bake for 8 minutes. Remove foil. Bake for 6 to 8 minutes more or until golden. Cool on a wire rack. Reduce oven temperature to 350°F.

3 For filling, in a medium saucepan combine ⅓ cup of the sugar, the cornstarch, and salt. Stir in ¼ cup of the milk until smooth. Stir in the remaining 1¾ cups milk and cream of coconut. Cook and stir over medium heat until thickened. Cook and stir for 2 minutes more. Remove from heat. Gradually stir about 1 cup of the hot filling into egg

yolks. Return yolk mixture to saucepan. Bring to a gentle boil. Cook and stir for 2 minutes more. Remove from heat. Stir in butter until melted. Stir in 1 cup coconut and 2 teaspoons of the vanilla. Cover and keep warm.

4 For meringue, add the remaining ½ teaspoon vanilla and cream of tartar to egg whites. Beat with an electric mixer on medium speed about 1 minute or until soft peaks form (tips curl). Gradually add the remaining ⅓ cup sugar, 1 tablespoon at a time, beating on high speed about 4 minutes or until stiff glossy peaks form (tips stand straight) and sugar is dissolved (rub a small amount between two fingers; it should feel completely smooth).

5 Transfer warm filling to the prepared pastry shell. Immediately spread meringue over warm filling, sealing to edge of pastry. Sprinkle with 2 tablespoons coconut. Bake about 15 minutes or until top is golden. Cool on wire rack for at least 1 hour. Cover and chill within 2 hours. Chill for 3 to 6 hours before serving.

NUTRITION FACTS PER SERVING:
399 cal., 26 g total fat (15 g sat. fat), 92 mg chol., 229 mg sodium, 35 g carb., 2 g fiber, 7 g pro.

*tip
Look for cream of coconut with the drink mixers in the liquor section of supermarkets or at a liquor store.

Banana-Butterscotch Cream Pie

Photo on page 287

PREP 40 minutes BAKE 14 minutes at 450°F CHILL 4 to 24 hours MAKES 8 servings

1 recipe Pastry for a Single-Crust Pie (recipe, page 373)
1 teaspoon unflavored gelatin
1 tablespoon cold water
1½ cups packed dark brown sugar
¼ cup butter
1 cup whipping cream
1½ cups whole milk
¼ cup cornstarch
1 tablespoon all-purpose flour
   Pinch salt
3 egg yolks, lightly beaten
1 egg, lightly beaten
1 teaspoon vanilla
3 bananas
2 ounces white baking chocolate, melted and slightly cooled
2 ounces dark chocolate, melted and slightly cooled

1 Preheat oven to 450°F. If using, prepare Pastry for a Single-Crust Pie. On a lightly floured surface, use your hands to slightly flatten pastry. Roll pastry from center to edges into a circle about 12 inches in diameter. Wrap pastry circle around the rolling pin. Unroll into a 9-inch pie plate. Ease pastry into pie plate without stretching it. Trim pastry to ½ inch beyond edge of pie plate. Fold under extra pastry even with the plate's edge. Crimp edge as desired. Generously prick bottom and sides of pastry with a fork. Line pastry with a double thickness of foil. Bake for 8 minutes. Remove foil. Bake for 6 to 8 minutes more or until golden. Cool on a wire rack. (If using refrigerated piecrust, follow package directions.)

2 In a 6-ounce custard cup stir gelatin into the cold water; set aside to soften.

3 In a large saucepan combine 1 cup of the brown sugar and the butter. Cook and stir over medium heat for 10 to 12 minutes or until mixture is slightly dark brown in color and smells almost burnt. Immediately add whipping cream (mixture may sputter). Remove from heat.

4 In a small saucepan heat milk just until bubbly around the edges. Remove from heat.

5 In a medium bowl stir together the remaining ½ cup brown sugar, cornstarch, flour, and salt. Add egg yolks, egg, and vanilla. Whisk about 1 minute or until fluffy. Gradually stir hot milk into egg mixture. Add egg mixture to cream mixture in saucepan. Cook and stir over medium heat about 15 minutes or until thickened and bubbly. Remove from heat; stir in gelatin mixture.

6 Cut bananas into ½-inch slices; fold into cream mixture. Pour into the prepared pastry shell. Cover surface of filling with plastic wrap and chill pie for 4 to 24 hours.

7 Before serving, fill a small, heavy resealable plastic bag with melted white chocolate. Fill another bag with melted dark chocolate. Snip a small hole in one corner of each bag. Pipe chocolates over pie.

NUTRITION FACTS PER SERVING:
712 cal., 37 g total fat (20 g sat. fat), 184 mg chol., 309 mg sodium, 88 g carb., 3 g fiber, 8 g pro.

Buttermilk Pie

PREP 40 minutes   BAKE 12 minutes at 450°F and 45 minutes at 350°F   COOL 1 hour   CHILL 4 hours   MAKES 8 servings

1 **recipe Pastry for a Single-Crust Pie (recipe, page 373)***

½ **cup butter**

1 **cup sugar**

3 **tablespoons all-purpose flour**

3 **eggs**

1 **cup buttermilk**

1 **teaspoon vanilla**

Ground nutmeg (optional)

Whipped cream (optional)

1 Preheat oven to 450°F. Prepare Pastry for a Single-Crust Pie. On a lightly floured surface, use your hands to slightly flatten pastry. Roll pastry from center to edges into a circle about 12 inches in diameter. Wrap pastry circle around the rolling pin. Unroll into a 9-inch pie plate. Ease pastry into pie plate without stretching it. Trim pastry to ½ inch beyond edge of pie plate. Fold under extra pastry even with the plate's edge. Crimp edge as desired. Do not prick pastry. Line pastry with a double thickness of foil. Bake for 8 minutes. Remove foil. Bake for 4 to 5 minutes more or until set and dry. Remove from oven. Reduce oven temperature to 350°F.

2 Meanwhile, in a medium saucepan heat butter over medium-low heat until melted. Stir in sugar and flour. Remove from heat. In a medium mixing bowl beat eggs with an electric mixer on medium to high speed for 1 minute. Stir in buttermilk and vanilla. Gradually whisk egg mixture into butter mixture until smooth. Pour egg mixture into the prepared pastry shell.

3 Cover top of pie loosely with foil. Bake for 45 to 50 minutes or until center appears set when gently shaken. Cool on a wire rack for 1 hour. Cover and chill for at least 4 hours before serving. If desired, sprinkle with nutmeg and serve with whipped cream.

NUTRITION FACTS PER SERVING:
394 cal., 22 g total fat (10 g sat. fat), 111 mg chol., 214 mg sodium, 44 g carb., 1 g fiber, 6 g pro.

*tip
When there's no time to make pastry from scratch, substitute a rolled refrigerated unbaked piecrust or use piecrust mix. For a one-crust pie, you also can substitute a frozen deep-dish unbaked pastry shell.

Caramel Apple Pie

PREP 40 minutes BAKE 50 minutes at 375°F COOL 1 hour MAKES 8 servings

1 **recipe Pastry for a Single-Crust Pie (recipe, page 373)**

½ **cup sugar**

3 **tablespoons all-purpose flour**

1 **teaspoon ground cinnamon**

⅛ **teaspoon salt**

6 **cups thinly sliced, peeled cooking apples (6 medium)**

1 **recipe Brown Sugar Topping**

½ **cup chopped pecans (optional)**

¼ **cup caramel-flavor ice cream topping**

1 Preheat oven to 375°F. Prepare Pastry for a Single-Crust Pie. On a lightly floured surface, use your hands to slightly flatten pastry. Roll pastry from center to edges into a circle about 12 inches in diameter. Wrap pastry circle around the rolling pin. Unroll into a 9-inch pie plate. Ease pastry into pie plate without stretching it. Trim pastry to ½ inch beyond edge of pie plate. Fold under extra pastry even with the plate's edge. Crimp edge as desired. Do not prick pastry.

2 In a large bowl stir together sugar, flour, cinnamon, and salt. Add apples; toss gently to coat. Transfer apple mixture to pastry-lined pie plate. Sprinkle with Brown Sugar Topping.

3 Cover edge of pie loosely with foil. Bake for 25 minutes. Remove foil. Bake for 25 to 30 minutes more or until apples are tender and top is golden. Transfer to a wire rack. If desired, sprinkle pie with pecans. Drizzle with caramel topping; cool.

NUTRITION FACTS PER SERVING:
532 cal., 20 g total fat (9 g sat. fat), 31 mg chol., 223 mg sodium, 85 g carb., 3 g fiber, 5 g pro.

Brown Sugar Topping

In a medium bowl stir together 1 cup packed brown sugar, ½ cup all-purpose flour, and ½ cup quick-cooking rolled oats. Using a pastry blender, cut in ½ cup butter until mixture resembles coarse crumbs.

tip

To make the pie with a braided pastry edge, prepare Pastry for a Double-Crust Pie (see recipe, page 378). Line pie plate with half of the pastry. Trim pastry even with pie plate rim. Roll the remaining pastry ball until ⅛ to ¼ inch thick. Cut pastry into ¼-inch-wide strips. Braid three strips at a time. In a small bowl combine 1 lightly beaten egg white and 1 tablespoon water. Brush some of the egg white mixture over edge of pastry. Press on braided pastry until braids cover entire edge of pie. Brush braided pastry with egg white mixture. Bake as directed.

Desserts

Lattice Cherry Pie

PREP 40 minutes BAKE 55 minutes at 375°F COOL 1 hour MAKES 8 servings

1 recipe Pastry for a Double-Crust Pie

2 14.5-ounce cans pitted tart red cherries (water pack)

1½ cups sugar

¼ cup cornstarch

½ teaspoon ground cinnamon

1 tablespoon butter

½ teaspoon almond extract

1 Preheat oven to 375°F. Prepare Pastry for a Double-Crust Pie. On a lightly floured surface, use your hands to slightly flatten one pastry ball. Roll pastry from center to edges into a circle about 12 inches in diameter. Wrap pastry circle around the rolling pin. Unroll pastry into a 9-inch pie plate. Ease pastry into pie plate without stretching it.

2 Drain cherries, reserving liquid from one of the cans (discard liquid from the other can). In a medium saucepan combine sugar, cornstarch, and cinnamon. Gradually stir in the reserved cherry liquid. Cook and stir over medium-high heat just until bubbly. Remove from heat; stir in cherries, butter, and almond extract.

3 Transfer cherry mixture to pastry-lined pie plate. Trim pastry to ½ inch beyond edge of pie plate.

4 Roll the remaining pastry ball into a 12-inch-diameter circle; cut into ½-inch-wide strips. Place half of the pastry strips on filling 1 inch apart. Give pie a quarter turn; arrange the remaining strips perpendicular to the first half of strips on filling. Press strip ends into bottom pastry on rim. Fold bottom pastry over strip ends; seal and crimp edge.

5 Cover edge of pie loosely with foil. Bake for 35 minutes. Remove foil. Bake for 20 to 25 minutes more or until pastry is golden and filling is bubbly. Cool on a wire rack.

NUTRITION FACTS PER SERVING:
488 cal., 18 g total fat (5 g sat. fat), 4 mg chol., 237 mg sodium, 78 g carb., 2 g fiber, 2 g pro.

Pastry for a Double-Crust Pie

In a large bowl stir together 2½ cups all-purpose flour and 1 teaspoon salt. Using a pastry blender, cut in ½ cup shortening and ¼ cup butter, cut up, or shortening until pieces are pea size. Sprinkle 1 tablespoon ice water over part of the flour mixture; toss gently with a fork. Push moistened pastry to side of bowl. Repeat moistening flour mixture, using 1 tablespoon ice water at a time, until all of the flour mixture is moistened (½ to ⅔ cup ice water total). Gather flour mixture into a ball, kneading gently until it holds together. Divide pastry in half; form halves into balls.

tip
For an unconventional, yet delicious, topping, pair this pie with lemon or cheesecake frozen yogurt or ice cream.

Cherry-Berry Shortcakes

PREP 30 minutes   BAKE 10 minutes at 425°F   COOL 5 minutes   MAKES 6 servings

- 2 cups fresh blueberries or frozen unsweetened blueberries, thawed
- 1 cup fresh raspberries; frozen unsweetened raspberries, thawed; or sliced fresh strawberries
- 1 cup fresh pitted sweet cherries or frozen unsweetened pitted sweet cherries, thawed
- ¼ cup sugar
- 3 cups packaged biscuit mix
- ¼ teaspoon ground nutmeg or cinnamon
- ¼ cup butter
- ⅔ cup half-and-half, light cream, or whole milk
  Sugar
- 1 recipe Sweetened Whipped Cream

1. Preheat oven to 425°F. In a large bowl combine blueberries, raspberries, cherries, and ¼ cup sugar; set aside.

2. In another large bowl stir together biscuit mix and nutmeg. Using a pastry blender, cut in butter until mixture resembles coarse crumbs. Make a well in the center of mixture. Add half-and-half all at once. Stir with a fork just until moistened. Drop dough into six mounds onto an ungreased baking sheet; flatten each mound with the back of a spoon until about ¾ inch thick. Sprinkle lightly with additional sugar.

3. Bake for 10 to 12 minutes or until golden. Cool on a wire rack for 5 minutes.

4. Split warm shortcakes in half horizontally. Place bottom layers in shallow dessert dishes. Spoon whipped cream and fruit mixture onto bottom layers. Replace top layers.

NUTRITION FACTS PER SERVING:
604 cal., 35 g total fat (18 g sat. fat), 86 mg chol., 855 mg sodium, 67 g carb., 4 g fiber, 7 g pro.

Sweetened Whipped Cream

In a chilled medium mixing bowl beat 1 cup whipping cream, 2 tablespoons sugar, and ½ teaspoon vanilla with an electric mixer on medium speed until soft peaks form (tips curl).

Rhubarb Crisp   *Photo on page 284*

PREP 20 minutes   BAKE 30 minutes at 375°F   MAKES 6 servings

⅔ cup granulated sugar

2 or 3 teaspoons cornstarch*

¼ teaspoon ground cinnamon

2 cups sliced fresh rhubarb or frozen unsweetened sliced rhubarb, thawed

2 cups coarsely chopped fresh strawberries

2 tablespoons snipped fresh basil

½ cup all-purpose flour

½ cup quick-cooking rolled oats

⅓ cup packed brown sugar

¼ teaspoon salt

3 tablespoons butter, melted

1 recipe Sweetened Whipped Cream (optional)

1 Preheat oven to 375°F. In a large bowl stir together granulated sugar, cornstarch, and cinnamon. Stir in rhubarb, strawberries, and basil. Transfer mixture to an ungreased 2-quart square baking dish.

2 For topping, in a medium bowl stir together flour, oats, brown sugar, and salt. Stir in melted butter. Sprinkle topping over fruit mixture.

3 Bake, uncovered, for 30 to 35 minutes or until fruit is tender and topping is golden. Serve warm. If desired, top with Sweetened Whipped Cream.

NUTRITION FACTS PER SERVING: *281 cal., 7 g total fat (4 g sat. fat), 15 mg chol., 144 mg sodium, 54 g carb., 3 g fiber, 3 g pro.*

Sweetened Whipped Cream

In a chilled medium mixing bowl beat 1 cup whipping cream, 2 tablespoons sugar, and ½ teaspoon vanilla with an electric mixer on medium speed until soft peaks form (tips curl).

*tip
For fresh rhubarb, use 2 teaspoons cornstarch; for frozen rhubarb, use 3 teaspoons cornstarch.

Peach-Praline Cobbler

PREP 40 minutes BAKE 25 minutes at 400°F MAKES 12 servings

8   **cups sliced, peeled fresh peaches (8 medium) or frozen unsweetened peach slices**

¾   **cup packed brown sugar**

¼   **cup butter, melted**

1½   **cups chopped pecans**

1   **cup granulated sugar**

1   **cup water**

2   **tablespoons cornstarch**

1   **teaspoon ground cinnamon**

¾   **cup milk**

2   **teaspoons lemon juice**

2¼   **cups all-purpose flour**

2   **teaspoons granulated sugar**

2   **teaspoons baking powder**

½   **teaspoon baking soda**

½   **teaspoon salt**

½   **cup shortening**

   Half-and-half, light cream, or milk (optional)

1 Thaw frozen peach slices, if using; do not drain. For pecan filling, in a medium bowl stir together brown sugar and melted butter. Stir in pecans; set aside.

2 Preheat oven to 400°F. In a Dutch oven combine peaches, 1 cup granulated sugar, the water, cornstarch, and cinnamon. Cook and stir until thickened and bubbly. Cover and keep warm.

3 In a small bowl combine milk and lemon juice; set aside. In a large bowl stir together flour, 2 teaspoons granulated sugar, baking powder, baking soda, and salt. Using a pastry blender, cut in shortening until mixture resembles coarse crumbs. Make a well in the center of flour mixture. Add milk mixture all at once. Using a fork, stir just until moistened.

4 Turn dough out onto a lightly floured surface. Knead dough by folding and gently pressing it just until dough holds together. Roll dough into a 12×8-inch rectangle; spread with pecan filling. Roll up rectangle, starting from one of the long sides. Slice into 12 equal pieces.

5 Transfer hot peach mixture to an ungreased 3-quart rectangular baking dish. Place biscuit pieces on top of peach mixture. Bake, uncovered, about 25 minutes or until biscuits are golden. Serve warm. If desired, serve with half-and-half.

NUTRITION FACTS PER SERVING:
511 cal., 23 g total fat (6 g sat. fat), 12 mg chol., 272 mg sodium, 76 g carb., 7 g fiber, 6 g pro.

Maple-Pumpkin Crème Brûlées

Photo on page 286

PREP 25 minutes BAKE 40 minutes at 350°F CHILL 4 to 8 hours STAND 20 minutes MAKES 8 servings

- 8 **egg yolks**
- 2 **cups whipping cream**
- 1 **cup canned pumpkin**
- ½ **cup maple syrup**
- ¼ **cup packed brown sugar**
- 2 **teaspoons vanilla**
- ½ **teaspoon ground cinnamon**
- ½ **teaspoon freshly grated nutmeg**
- ⅓ **cup granulated sugar**

1 Preheat oven to 350°F. In a large bowl combine egg yolks, whipping cream, pumpkin, maple syrup, brown sugar, vanilla, cinnamon, and nutmeg; whisk until smooth. Spoon pumpkin mixture into eight 6-ounce ramekins or custard cups.

2 Place ramekins or custard cups in a shallow roasting pan. Place roasting pan on oven rack. Pour enough boiling water into roasting pan to reach halfway up sides of ramekins or custard cups.

3 Bake for 40 to 45 minutes or until edges are set (centers will shake slightly). Carefully remove ramekins or custard cups from water; cool completely on a wire rack. Cover and chill for 4 to 8 hours.

4 Before serving, let custards stand at room temperature for 20 minutes. Meanwhile, for caramelized sugar, in a medium heavy skillet heat granulated sugar over medium-high heat until sugar begins to melt, shaking skillet occasionally to heat sugar evenly. Do not stir. Once sugar starts to melt, reduce heat to low and cook about 5 minutes or until all of the sugar is melted and golden, stirring as needed with a wooden spoon. Quickly drizzle caramelized sugar over custards. (If sugar hardens in the skillet, return to heat; stir until melted.)

NUTRITION FACTS PER SERVING: *386 cal., 27 g total fat (16 g sat. fat), 292 mg chol., 36 mg sodium, 34 g carb., 1 g fiber, 4 g pro.*

tip

It can be a challenge to tell when crème brûlée is done. Check with the wobble test. Using tongs, gently shake a custard-filled ramekin. A perfectly cooked custard will jiggle slightly in the center when shaken.

S'mores Cheesecake

PREP 45 minutes BAKE 40 minutes at 375°F COOL 45 minutes CHILL 4 hours MAKES 12 servings

1½ **cups finely crushed graham crackers**

1 **tablespoon sugar**

⅓ **cup butter, melted**

4 **ounces semisweet chocolate, chopped**

3 **8-ounce packages cream cheese, softened**

¾ **cup sugar**

½ **cup sour cream**

2 **teaspoons vanilla**

2 **tablespoons all-purpose flour**

3 **eggs**

1 **recipe Chocolate Ganache**

3 **cups tiny marshmallows**

Broken graham crackers (optional)

Chopped semisweet chocolate (optional)

1 Preheat oven to 375°F. For crust, in a medium bowl stir together crushed graham crackers and 1 tablespoon sugar. Drizzle with melted butter; toss to coat. Press mixture evenly onto the bottom and about 1½ inches up the sides of a 9-inch springform pan that has a removable bottom.

2 For filling, in a small heavy saucepan cook and stir 4 ounces chocolate over low heat until melted; cool slightly. In a medium mixing bowl beat cream cheese, ¾ cup sugar, sour cream, and vanilla with an electric mixer on medium speed until smooth. Add flour; beat well. Add cooled chocolate. Add eggs; beat on low speed just until combined.

3 Pour filling into crust-lined pan. Place pan in a shallow baking pan. Bake for 40 to 45 minutes or until center appears nearly set when gently shaken (center may look soft but will set up as it cools).

4 Cool cheesecake in pan on a wire rack for 15 minutes. Using a small metal spatula, loosen crust from sides of pan. Cool for 30 minutes more. Remove sides of pan (leave cheesecake in shallow baking pan).

5 Preheat broiler. Spoon Chocolate Ganache over top of cheesecake, spreading evenly and allowing it to drip down sides (set any remaining ganache aside). Pile marshmallows in center of cheesecake.

6 Broil 4 to 5 inches from the heat for 30 to 60 seconds or just until marshmallows are golden (watch closely to prevent burning). Cover loosely; chill for at least 4 hours. Before serving, drizzle with any remaining ganache. If desired, top with broken graham crackers and additional chopped chocolate.

NUTRITION FACTS PER SERVING:
583 cal., 39 g total fat (22 g sat. fat), 147 mg chol., 366 mg sodium, 53 g carb., 2 g fiber, 8 g pro.

Chocolate Ganache

In a medium saucepan bring 1 cup whipping cream just to boiling over medium-high heat. Remove from heat. Add 12 ounces chopped milk, semisweet, or bittersweet chocolate (do not stir). Let stand for 5 minutes. Stir until smooth. Cool for 15 minutes.

Brownie Waffles à la Mode

Photo on page 288

PREP 40 minutes FREEZE 8 hours COOK 1 minute per waffle MAKES 10 servings

1   quart vanilla ice cream
½   cup crushed striped round peppermint candies
2   ounces unsweetened chocolate, chopped
¼   cup butter
½   cup all-purpose flour
¼   cup unsweetened cocoa powder
¼   teaspoon baking powder
¼   teaspoon baking soda
¼   teaspoon salt
2   eggs, lightly beaten
⅔   cup sugar
¼   cup half-and-half or light cream
1   teaspoon vanilla
½   teaspoon instant espresso coffee powder (optional)
    Nonstick cooking spray
    Chocolate fudge ice cream topping
    Crushed striped round peppermint candies (optional)

1 In a chilled large bowl combine ice cream and ½ cup crushed candies. Stir with a wooden spoon just until combined. Cover and freeze about 8 hours or until firm.

2 In a small saucepan cook and stir chocolate and butter over low heat until melted; cool.

3 In a medium bowl stir together flour, cocoa powder, baking powder, baking soda, and salt. Make a well in the center of flour mixture. In a small bowl combine eggs, sugar, half-and-half, vanilla, espresso powder (if desired), and melted chocolate mixture. Add egg mixture all at once to flour mixture. Stir just until moistened (batter should be slightly lumpy).

4 Preheat a 7½-inch round waffle baker; lightly coat surface with cooking spray. Spoon a scant ½ cup of the batter onto grids of preheated waffle baker. Close lid quickly; do not open until done. Bake about 1 minute or until waffle is cooked through. (Waffle will not be crisp; do not overcook.) When done, use a fork to lift waffle off grid. Cool on a wire rack. Repeat with the remaining batter.

5 Separate waffles into quarters. Serve waffle sections and ice cream in dessert bowls. Drizzle with fudge topping and, if desired, sprinkle with additional crushed candies.

NUTRITION FACTS PER SERVING: *396 cal., 21 g total fat (12 g sat. fat), 113 mg chol., 313 mg sodium, 49 g carb., 1 g fiber, 6 g pro.*

Make-Ahead Directions: Prepare as directed through Step 4, except freeze ice cream for up to 1 month. Place baked and cooled waffles in an airtight container; cover. Store at room temperature for up to 24 hours or freeze for up to 1 month. To serve, thaw waffles if frozen. Continue as directed in Step 5.

Toffee-Pear Sticky Pudding

PREP 30 minutes BAKE 43 minutes at 350°F COOL 10 minutes MAKES 9 servings

1¼ cups water

1¼ cups pitted whole Medjool or other dates

1 cup chopped, peeled pear (1 medium)

½ teaspoon baking soda

1 cup all-purpose flour

1 teaspoon baking powder

½ teaspoon salt

¼ teaspoon ground nutmeg

¾ cup packed dark brown sugar

⅓ cup butter, softened

2 eggs

½ teaspoon vanilla

1 recipe Toffee-Pear Sauce

1 In a large saucepan combine the water, dates, and pear. Bring to boiling; reduce heat. Cook, covered, about 15 minutes or until fruit is tender and most of the liquid is absorbed. Mash with a potato masher, fork, or immersion blender until as smooth as possible. Stir in baking soda; set aside.

2 Preheat oven to 350°F. Grease an 8×8×2-inch baking pan; set aside. In a small bowl stir together flour, baking powder, salt, and nutmeg; set aside. In a large mixing bowl beat brown sugar and butter with an electric mixer on medium speed about 1 minute or until combined. Beat in eggs, one at a time, and vanilla. Stir in date mixture. Stir in flour mixture just until combined. Pour batter into the prepared baking pan.

3 Bake for 40 to 45 minutes or until a wooden toothpick inserted near the center comes out clean. Place pan on a wire rack. Immediately use a long skewer to prick top of cake all over. Spoon the portion of Toffee-Pear Sauce without pears over cake. Bake for 3 minutes more. Cool on the wire rack for 10 minutes. Serve warm with the portion of Toffee-Pear Sauce with pear slices.

NUTRITION FACTS PER SERVING:
531 cal., 27 g total fat (17 g sat. fat), 123 mg chol., 405 mg sodium, 72 g carb., 4 g fiber, 4 g pro.

Toffee-Pear Sauce

Peel and core 1 medium pear; cut into thin slices. In a medium skillet heat 1 tablespoon butter over medium heat until melted. Add pear slices; cook for 2 to 3 minutes or until tender and light brown, turning pear slices occasionally and reducing heat to low if slices brown too quickly. Set aside. In a small saucepan heat ½ cup butter over medium heat until melted. Stir in brown sugar. Bring to boiling, stirring until sugar is dissolved. Reduce heat. Boil gently, uncovered, for 5 minutes, stirring occasionally. Carefully stir in ¾ cup whipping cream. Return to boiling. Remove from heat; stir in 1 teaspoon vanilla. Divide sauce in half. Stir pear slices into one portion.

White Chocolate Bread Pudding with Hard Sauce

PREP 30 minutes CHILL 1 to 8 hours BAKE 1 hour at 350°F MAKES 12 servings

- 2 cups milk, half-and-half, or light cream
- 10 ounces white baking chocolate with cocoa butter, coarsely chopped
- 1 vanilla bean or 1½ teaspoons vanilla
- 5 eggs, lightly beaten
- ⅔ cup sugar
- ½ teaspoon ground cinnamon
- 6 cups dry French bread cubes (from 12 ounces bread)*
- ⅓ cup dried tart cherries, dried cranberries, or raisins
- 1 recipe Hard Sauce

1 In a medium saucepan cook and stir milk, half of the white chocolate, and, if using, vanilla bean over low heat just until mixture is simmering and chocolate is melted. Remove from heat. Remove vanilla bean. Using a sharp paring knife, split vanilla bean in half lengthwise. Using the knife tip, scrape out seeds. Stir seeds (or 1½ teaspoons vanilla, if using) into milk mixture.

2 In a large bowl combine eggs, sugar, and cinnamon. Gradually add milk mixture, stirring constantly.

3 In an ungreased 2-quart square baking dish toss together bread cubes, dried cherries, and the remaining white chocolate. Pour milk mixture evenly over bread mixture. Press mixture lightly with the back of a large spoon to moisten all of the ingredients. Cover with foil and chill for 1 to 8 hours.

4 Preheat oven to 350°F. Place baking dish in another larger pan. Place pan on oven rack. Pour enough hot water into larger pan to reach halfway up sides of baking dish. Bake, covered, about 1 hour or until top appears evenly set. Serve warm with Hard Sauce.

NUTRITION FACTS PER SERVING:
703 cal., 39 g total fat (20 g sat. fat), 277 mg chol., 485 mg sodium, 69 g carb., 1 g fiber, 12 g pro.

Hard Sauce

In a small heavy saucepan combine 1 cup butter and ½ cup sugar. Cook and stir over medium heat until butter is melted and mixture is bubbly. Gradually stir hot butter mixture into 4 lightly beaten egg yolks. Return egg yolk mixture to saucepan. Cook and stir over medium-low heat about 15 minutes or until mixture reaches a temperature of 170°F. Remove from heat. Stir in ¼ cup whiskey or milk. If necessary, stir in enough hot water, 1 teaspoon at a time, to reach desired consistency. If desired, cover and let stand at room temperature for up to 1 hour (if sauce becomes too thick, stir in hot water, 1 teaspoon at a time, to thin sauce).

*tip
To dry fresh bread cubes, preheat oven to 350°F. Place bread cubes in a large shallow baking pan. Bake about 10 minutes or until bread cubes are dry, stirring twice.

Butterscotch Pudding

PREP 20 minutes   COOK 20 minutes   CHILL 4 to 5 hours   MAKES 8 servings

1   cup packed light brown sugar

¼   cup cornstarch

¼   teaspoon salt

4   cups half-and-half or light cream

5   egg yolks, lightly beaten

¼   cup butter, cut up

2   teaspoons vanilla

1 In a medium saucepan combine brown sugar, cornstarch, and salt. Stir in half-and-half. Cook and stir over medium heat until thickened and bubbly. Cook and stir for 2 minutes more. Remove from heat.

2 Gradually stir about 1 cup of the hot mixture into egg yolks. Return egg yolk mixture to saucepan. Bring to a gentle boil; reduce heat. Cook and stir for 2 minutes more. Remove from heat. Stir in butter and vanilla.

3 Pour into a large bowl. Cover surface of pudding with plastic wrap. Chill for 4 to 5 hours or until thoroughly chilled. Stir before serving.

NUTRITION FACTS PER SERVING:
373 cal., 23 g total fat (13 g sat. fat), 189 mg chol., 182 mg sodium, 38 g carb., 0 g fiber, 5 g pro.

tip

Top pudding with chopped chocolate-covered English toffee; or with homemade or purchased soft cookies, crumbled (such as oatmeal, chocolate chip, or molasses cookies), and dried cherries. Or top with a mixture of ⅓ cup goat cheese (chèvre), ¼ cup crème fraîche, and 1 tablespoon sugar; sprinkle with freshly grated nutmeg.

Chocolate Pudding

PREP 10 minutes   COOK 20 minutes   MAKES 4 servings

¾ cup sugar

⅓ cup unsweetened cocoa powder*

2 tablespoons cornstarch

2⅔ cups milk

4 egg yolks, lightly beaten

1 tablespoon butter

1½ teaspoons vanilla

1 In a medium heavy saucepan stir together sugar, cocoa powder, and cornstarch. Stir in milk. Cook and stir over medium heat until thickened and bubbly. Cook and stir for 2 minutes more. Remove from heat.

2 Gradually stir about 1 cup of the hot mixture into egg yolks. Return egg yolk mixture to saucepan. Bring to a gentle boil; reduce heat. Cook and stir for 2 minutes. Remove from heat. Stir in butter and vanilla.

3 Pour pudding into a bowl. Cover surface of pudding with plastic wrap. Cool slightly and serve warm, or chill. (Do not stir during chilling.)

NUTRITION FACTS PER SERVING:
359 cal., 14 g total fat (7 g sat. fat), 234 mg chol., 96 mg sodium, 54 g carb., 2 g fiber, 9 g pro.

*tip
For the most intense chocolate flavor, use unsweetened Dutch-process cocoa powder.

Strawberry Ice Cream

Photo on page 286

PREP 30 minutes FREEZE Per manufacturer's directions MAKES 24 servings

5 cups fresh **strawberries,** hulled

3 cups whipping cream

1½ cups sugar

1½ cups milk

1 12-ounce can evaporated milk

4 eggs* or pasteurized eggs, lightly beaten, or 1 cup refrigerated or frozen egg product, thawed

1½ to 2 teaspoons vanilla

1 In an extra-large bowl mash strawberries with a potato masher. Stir in whipping cream, sugar, milk, evaporated milk, eggs, and vanilla.

2 Freeze strawberry mixture in a 4- to 5-quart ice cream freezer according to the manufacturer's directions. If desired, ripen for at least 4 hours.**

NUTRITION FACTS PER SERVING:
402 cal., 27 g total fat (16 g sat. fat), 163 mg chol., 89 mg sodium, 36 g carb., 1 g fiber, 7 g pro.

*tip

Using raw eggs poses higher risk of foodborne illness, especially in people with weakened immune systems, children, and the elderly.

**tip

For a traditional ice cream freezer, after churning remove lid and dasher. Cover top with foil. Plug the lid hole with a cloth; replace lid on can and fill the outer freezer bucket with ice and rock salt (enough to cover top of the freezer can) in a ratio of 4 cups ice to 1 cup rock salt. Let stand at room temperature about 4 hours.

For an ice cream freezer with an insulated freezer bowl, transfer the ice cream to a freezer container. Cover and store in the freezer for at least 4 hours.

Desserts

Butter-Pecan Ice Cream

PREP 30 minutes CHILL 4 to 24 hours FREEZE Per manufacturer's directions + 6 hours MAKES 6 servings

4   egg yolks

¾   cup sugar

3   cups half-and-half
     or light cream

1   tablespoon vanilla

1   12-ounce jar caramel sauce

¼   cup maple syrup

1   cup coarsely chopped pecans,
     toasted

     Coarsely chopped pecans,
     toasted (optional)

1 In a medium mixing bowl beat egg yolks and sugar with an electric mixer on high speed about 5 minutes or until thick and lemon color. Stir in 2 cups of the half-and-half. Transfer mixture to a 2-quart saucepan. Cook and stir over medium heat just until mixture starts to bubble and coat a metal spoon. Remove from heat. Stir in the remaining 1 cup half-and-half and the vanilla. Transfer mixture to a large bowl. Cover and chill for 4 to 24 hours.

2 Freeze mixture in a 2-quart ice cream freezer according to the manufacturer's directions. Transfer to a chilled large bowl.

3 Meanwhile, in a small bowl combine caramel sauce and maple syrup. Gently fold ¾ cup of the caramel mixture and 1 cup pecans into the ice cream, leaving some swirls of caramel mixture. Cover and freeze about 6 hours or until firm. Serve with the remaining caramel mixture and, if desired, additional chopped pecans.

NUTRITION FACTS PER SERVING:
299 cal., 15 g total fat (5 g sat. fat), 92 mg chol., 127 mg sodium, 40 g carb., 1 g fiber, 4 g pro.

Homemade Oatmeal Cream Pies

PREP 40 minutes BAKE 8 minutes per batch at 350°F MAKES 13 servings

- ¾ cup all-purpose flour
- ½ teaspoon baking soda
- ½ teaspoon salt
- ¼ teaspoon baking powder
- ½ cup butter, softened
- ½ cup peanut butter
- ½ cup granulated sugar
- ½ cup packed brown sugar
- 1 egg
- 1 teaspoon vanilla
- 1 cup quick-cooking rolled oats
- 2 teaspoons hot water
- ¼ teaspoon salt
- 1 7-ounce jar marshmallow crème
- ½ cup shortening
- ⅓ cup powdered sugar

1 Preheat oven to 350°F. Grease a cookie sheet; set aside. In a small bowl stir together flour, baking soda, salt, and baking powder; set aside.

2 In a large mixing bowl beat softened butter and peanut butter with an electric mixer on medium speed until combined. Add granulated sugar and brown sugar. Beat until fluffy, scraping sides of bowl occasionally. Beat in egg and vanilla until combined. Using a wooden spoon, stir in flour mixture and oats just until combined.

3 Drop dough by rounded teaspoons 2 inches apart onto the prepared cookie sheet. Bake for 8 to 10 minutes or until edges are light brown and centers are set. Cool on cookie sheet for 1 minute. Transfer to a wire rack; cool.

4 For marshmallow filling, in a medium bowl combine the hot water and salt, stirring until salt is dissolved. Add marshmallow crème, shortening, and powdered sugar. Beat on medium speed until combined.

5 Spread marshmallow filling on bottoms of half of the cookies. Top with the remaining cookies, bottom side down.

NUTRITION FACTS PER SERVING:
367 cal., 20 g total fat (8 g sat. fat), 35 mg chol., 305 mg sodium, 43 g carb., 1 g fiber, 5 g pro.

Make-Ahead Directions: Layer unfilled cookies between sheets of waxed paper in an airtight container; cover. Store at room temperature for up to 3 days. Continue as directed in Step 4.

tip

For the best results, serve these sweet sandwich cookies the same day you fill them.

Desserts

Frosted Maple Drops

PREP 30 minutes   BAKE 8 minutes per batch at 350°F   MAKES 96 servings

1   cup butter, softened
1   cup packed brown sugar
1   teaspoon baking soda
⅛   teaspoon salt
1   cup maple syrup
1   egg
1   teaspoon vanilla
4   cups all-purpose flour
½   cup evaporated milk
6   tablespoons butter, melted
1   teaspoon maple flavoring
3   to 4 cups powdered sugar

1 Preheat oven to 350°F. Lightly grease a cookie sheet; set aside. In a large mixing bowl beat 1 cup softened butter with an electric mixer on medium to high speed for 30 seconds. Add brown sugar, baking soda, and salt. Beat until combined, scraping sides of bowl occasionally. Beat in maple syrup, egg, and vanilla until combined. Beat in as much of the flour as you can with the mixer. Using a wooden spoon, stir in any remaining flour.

2 Drop dough by rounded teaspoons 2 inches apart onto the prepared cookie sheet; flatten slightly. Bake for 8 to 10 minutes or until tops are set. Transfer cookies to a wire rack; cool.

3 For icing, in a medium bowl stir together evaporated milk, melted butter, and maple flavoring. Gradually stir in enough of the powdered sugar to reach spreading consistency. Spread tops of cookies with icing.

NUTRITION FACTS PER SERVING:
77 cal., 3 g total fat (2 g sat. fat), 10 mg chol., 38 mg sodium, 12 g carb., 0 g fiber, 1 g pro.

Praline Snickerdoodles

PREP 30 minutes CHILL 1 hour BAKE 10 minutes per batch at 375°F MAKES 48 servings

1	cup butter, softened
1¾	cups sugar
1	teaspoon cream of tartar
1	teaspoon baking soda
¼	teaspoon salt
2	eggs
1	teaspoon vanilla
3	cups all-purpose flour
1	cup toffee pieces
½	cup chopped pecans
2	teaspoons ground cinnamon

1 In a large mixing bowl beat softened butter with an electric mixer on medium to high speed for 30 seconds. Add 1½ cups of the sugar, the cream of tartar, baking soda, and salt. Beat until combined, scraping sides of bowl occasionally. Beat in eggs and vanilla until combined. Beat in as much of the flour as you can with the mixer. Using a wooden spoon, stir in any remaining flour, the toffee pieces, and pecans. Cover and chill about 1 hour or until dough is easy to handle.

2 Preheat oven to 375°F. In a small bowl stir together the remaining ¼ cup sugar and the cinnamon. Shape dough into 1½-inch balls. Roll balls in cinnamon-sugar to coat.

3 Place balls 2 inches apart on an ungreased cookie sheet. Bake for 10 to 12 minutes or until edges are golden. Transfer cookies to a wire rack; cool.

NUTRITION FACTS PER SERVING:
126 cal., 6 g total fat (3 g sat. fat), 22 mg chol., 89 mg sodium, 16 g carb., 0 g fiber, 1 g pro.

Big Soft Ginger Cookies

PREP 25 minutes   BAKE 10 minutes per batch at 350°F   MAKES 24 servings

2¼ cups all-purpose flour
2   teaspoons ground ginger
1   teaspoon baking soda
¾   teaspoon ground cinnamon
½   teaspoon ground cloves
¾   cup butter, softened
1   cup sugar
1   egg
¼   cup mild-flavor molasses
2   tablespoons sugar

1 Preheat oven to 350°F. In a medium bowl stir together flour, ginger, baking soda, cinnamon, and cloves; set aside.

2 In a large mixing bowl beat softened butter with an electric mixer on medium to high speed for 30 seconds. Add 1 cup sugar. Beat until combined, scraping sides of bowl occasionally. Beat in egg and molasses until combined. Beat in as much of the flour mixture as you can with the mixer. Using a wooden spoon, stir in any remaining flour mixture.

3 Place 2 tablespoons sugar in a small bowl. Shape dough into 1½-inch balls. Roll balls in sugar to coat. Place balls about 2½ inches apart on an ungreased cookie sheet. Bake about 10 minutes or until light brown but still puffed. Do not overbake. Cool on cookie sheet for 2 minutes. Transfer to a wire rack; cool.

NUTRITION FACTS PER SERVING:
141 cal., 6 g total fat (4 g sat. fat), 25 mg chol., 119 mg sodium, 20 g carb., 0 g fiber, 1 g pro.

Peanut Butter Cookies

PREP 40 minutes CHILL 1 hour BAKE 8 minutes per batch at 375°F MAKES 36 servings

½ cup peanut butter
½ cup butter, softened
½ cup granulated sugar
½ cup packed brown sugar
½ teaspoon baking soda
¼ teaspoon salt
1 egg
½ teaspoon vanilla
1¼ cups all-purpose flour
   Granulated sugar

1 In a large mixing bowl beat peanut butter and softened butter with an electric mixer on medium to high speed for 30 seconds. Add ½ cup granulated sugar, brown sugar, baking soda, and salt. Beat until combined, scraping sides of bowl occasionally. Beat in egg and vanilla until combined. Beat in as much of the flour as you can with the mixer. Using a wooden spoon, stir in any remaining flour. Cover and chill about 1 hour or until dough is easy to handle.

2 Preheat oven to 375°F. Shape dough into 1-inch balls. Place balls 2 inches apart on an ungreased cookie sheet. Flatten by making crisscross marks with the tines of a fork, dipping fork into additional granulated sugar before flattening each cookie.

3 Bake about 8 minutes or until edges are light brown. Transfer cookies to a wire rack; cool.

NUTRITION FACTS PER SERVING:
82 cal., 4 g total fat (2 g sat. fat), 13 mg chol., 71 mg sodium, 9 g carb., 0 g fiber, 2 g pro.

To Store: Layer cookies between sheets of waxed paper in an airtight container; cover. Store at room temperature for up to 3 days or freeze for up to 3 months.

Chocolate Chip Cookies

PREP 40 minutes BAKE 8 minutes per batch at 375°F MAKES 60 servings

½ cup butter, softened

½ cup shortening or vegetable oil

1 cup packed brown sugar

½ cup granulated sugar

½ teaspoon baking soda

½ teaspoon salt

2 eggs

1 teaspoon vanilla

2¾ cups all-purpose flour

1 12-ounce package (2 cups) semisweet chocolate pieces or miniature candy-coated semisweet chocolate pieces

1½ cups chopped walnuts, pecans, or hazelnuts (filberts), toasted if desired (optional)

1 Preheat oven to 375°F. In a large mixing bowl beat softened butter and shortening with an electric mixer on medium to high speed for 30 seconds. Add brown sugar, granulated sugar, baking soda, and salt. Beat until combined, scraping sides of bowl occasionally. Beat in eggs and vanilla until combined. Beat in as much of the flour as you can with the mixer. Using a wooden spoon, stir in any remaining flour. Stir in chocolate pieces and, if desired, nuts.

2 Drop dough by rounded teaspoons 2 inches apart onto an ungreased cookie sheet. Bake for 8 to 9 minutes or just until edges are light brown. Cool on cookie sheet for 2 minutes. Transfer to a wire rack; cool.

NUTRITION FACTS PER SERVING:
99 cal., 5 g total fat (2 g sat. fat), 11 mg chol., 45 mg sodium, 13 g carb., 0 g fiber, 1 g pro.

Macaroon Chocolate Bars

PREP 30 minutes BAKE 33 minutes at 350°F MAKES 48 servings

- 2 cups crushed chocolate sandwich cookies with white filling
- ½ cup sugar
- ⅓ cup unsweetened cocoa powder
- ½ cup butter, melted
- 1½ teaspoons vanilla
- ⅔ cup all-purpose flour
- ⅓ cup sugar
- ¼ teaspoon salt
- 2¾ cups flaked coconut
- 3 egg whites, lightly beaten
- ½ cup semisweet chocolate pieces
- 1 teaspoon shortening

1 Preheat oven to 350°F. Line a 13×9×2-inch baking pan with foil, extending the foil over edges of pan. Lightly grease foil; set pan aside.

2 In a large bowl stir together crushed cookies, ½ cup sugar, and cocoa powder. Drizzle with melted butter and 1 teaspoon of the vanilla; toss gently to coat. Press mixture evenly onto the bottom of the prepared baking pan. Bake for 8 minutes.

3 Meanwhile, for filling, in a large bowl stir together flour, ⅓ cup sugar, and salt. Stir in coconut. Add egg whites and the remaining ½ teaspoon vanilla, stirring until combined. Spoon filling over hot crust. Using wet hands, carefully press filling to edges of pan.

4 Bake for 25 to 28 minutes more or until filling is set and light brown. Cool in pan on a wire rack.

5 In a small saucepan cook and stir chocolate and shortening over low heat until melted. Drizzle over uncut bars. Chill until chocolate is set. Using the edges of the foil, lift uncut bars out of pan. Cut into bars.

NUTRITION FACTS PER SERVING:
85 cal., 5 g total fat (3 g sat. fat), 5 mg chol., 51 mg sodium, 10 g carb., 1 g fiber, 1 g pro.

To Store: Layer bars between sheets of waxed paper in an airtight container; cover. Store at room temperature for up to 3 days or freeze for up to 3 months.

tip
For a fancy presentation, arrange the bars on a serving plate, then drizzle the melted chocolate over both the bars and the plate.

Fudgy Brownies

PREP 25 minutes BAKE 30 minutes at 350°F MAKES 16 servings

½ cup butter

3 ounces unsweetened chocolate, coarsely chopped

1 cup sugar

2 eggs

1 teaspoon vanilla

⅔ cup all-purpose flour

¼ teaspoon baking soda

½ cup chopped nuts (optional)

1 recipe Chocolate–Cream Cheese Frosting (optional)

1 In a medium saucepan cook and stir butter and chocolate over low heat until melted; cool. Preheat oven to 350°F. Line an 8×8×2-inch baking pan with foil, extending the foil over edges of pan. Grease foil; set pan aside.

2 Stir sugar into cooled chocolate mixture. Add eggs, one at a time, beating with a wooden spoon after each addition just until combined. Stir in vanilla. In a small bowl stir together flour and baking soda. Add flour mixture to chocolate mixture; stir just until combined. If desired, stir in nuts. Spread batter in the prepared baking pan.

3 Bake for 30 minutes. Cool in pan on a wire rack. If desired, spread with Chocolate–Cream Cheese Frosting. Using the edges of the foil, lift uncut brownies out of pan. Cut into brownies.

NUTRITION FACTS PER SERVING:
157 cal., 10 g total fat (6 g sat. fat), 43 mg chol., 90 mg sodium, 18 g carb., 1 g fiber, 2 g pro.

Chocolate-Cream Cheese Frosting

In a small saucepan cook and stir 1 cup semisweet chocolate pieces over low heat until melted; cool. In a medium bowl stir together two 3-ounce packages softened cream cheese and ½ cup powdered sugar. Stir in melted chocolate until smooth.

tip

Lining your pan with foil lets you effortlessly lift your brownies or other bar cookies out of the pan. To line a pan, flip it over and shape foil around the outside, extending it about 1 inch past the edges. Place the foil lining inside the pan; grease foil if directed in the recipe. Bake and cool as directed. To remove, grasp the foil overhang and lift out the brownies in a block. Place on a cutting board and cut into bars.

Easy Chocolate Fudge

PREP 45 minutes   CHILL 2 to 3 hours   MAKES 96 servings

$4\frac{1}{2}$ cups sugar

1   12-ounce can evaporated milk

$\frac{1}{2}$ teaspoon salt

1   16-ounce bar milk chocolate, chopped

1   12-ounce package (2 cups) semisweet chocolate pieces

1   7-ounce jar marshmallow crème

1   cup chopped walnuts or pecans (optional)

1   teaspoon vanilla

1 Line a 13×9×2-inch baking pan with foil, extending the foil over edges of pan. Butter foil; set pan aside.

2 Butter the sides of a 3-quart heavy saucepan. In the saucepan combine sugar, evaporated milk, and salt. Cook and stir over medium-high heat until mixture comes to boiling. Reduce heat to medium; continue cooking and stirring for 10 minutes.

3 Remove saucepan from heat. Add milk chocolate, semisweet chocolate, marshmallow crème, nuts (if desired), and vanilla. Stir until chocolates are melted and mixture is combined. Using a wooden spoon, beat for 3 to 5 minutes or until mixture starts to become thicker.

4 Immediately pour fudge into the prepared pan; shake pan gently to spread fudge to edges of pan. Cover and chill for 2 to 3 hours or until firm.

5 Using the edges of the foil, lift uncut fudge out of pan. Cut into squares.

NUTRITION FACTS PER SERVING:
90 cal., 3 g total fat (2 g sat. fat), 2 mg chol., 22 mg sodium, 16 g carb., 1 g fiber, 1 g pro.

To Store: Layer fudge between sheets of waxed paper in an airtight container; cover. Store at room temperature for up to 2 days or chill for up to 1 month.

Easy Mocha Fudge

Prepare Easy Chocolate Fudge as directed, except stir 2 tablespoons instant espresso coffee powder or coffee crystals into mixture with the vanilla in Step 3.

Easy Chocolate–Peanut Butter Fudge

Prepare Easy Chocolate Fudge as directed, except stir $\frac{1}{2}$ cup peanut butter into mixture in saucepan before bringing to boiling in Step 2 and substitute 1 cup chopped peanuts for the walnuts.

Chocolate-Covered Cherries

PREP 1 hour 15 minutes   CHILL 1 to 4 hours   STAND 3 to 4 hours   MAKES 40 servings

- 2 **10-ounce jars (40 cherries) maraschino cherries with stems**
- 3 **tablespoons butter, softened**
- 3 **tablespoons light-color corn syrup**
- 2 **cups powdered sugar**
- 8 **ounces chocolate-flavor candy coating, cut up**
- 8 **ounces bittersweet or semisweet chocolate, cut up**

1 Let cherries stand on paper towels for 2 hours to drain. Line a baking sheet with waxed paper; set aside.

2 In a medium bowl combine butter and corn syrup; stir in powdered sugar. Knead mixture until smooth (chill if mixture is too soft to handle). Shape about ¾ teaspoon of the mixture around each cherry. Place coated cherries, stem sides up, on the prepared baking sheet. Chill for 1 to 4 hours or until firm.

3 In a medium heavy saucepan cook and stir candy coating and chocolate over low heat until melted and smooth. Line another baking sheet with waxed paper. Holding cherries by stems, dip one at a time into melted mixture. If necessary, spoon mixture over cherries to cover completely. (Be sure to completely seal cherries in melted mixture to prevent juice from leaking.) Let excess mixture drip off. Place coated cherries, stem side up, on the prepared baking sheet.

4 Let cherries stand for 1 to 2 hours or until coating is set. Store, tightly covered, in the refrigerator for up to 1 month. (The longer the cherries are stored, the more the mixture around the cherries will soften and liquefy.)

NUTRITION FACTS PER SERVING:
117 cal., 5 g total fat (3 g sat. fat), 2 mg chol., 7 mg sodium, 19 g carb., 1 g fiber, 0 g pro.

Caramels

PREP 20 minutes COOK 45 minutes STAND 2 hours MAKES 64 servings

1 cup chopped walnuts, toasted if desired (optional)*

1 cup butter

1 16-ounce package (2¼ cups packed) brown sugar

2 cups half-and-half or light cream

1 cup light-color corn syrup

1 teaspoon vanilla

1 Line an 8×8×2-inch or 9×9×2 inch baking pan with foil, extending the foil over edges of pan. Butter foil. If desired, sprinkle walnuts over bottom of pan. Set pan aside.

2 In a 3-quart heavy saucepan heat butter over low heat until melted. Stir in brown sugar, half-and-half, and corn syrup. Cook and stir over medium-high heat until mixture boils. Clip a candy thermometer to side of pan. Reduce heat to medium; continue boiling at a moderate, steady rate, stirring frequently, until the thermometer registers 248°F, firm-ball stage (45 to 60 minutes). Adjust heat as necessary to maintain a steady boil and watch temperature carefully during the last 10 to 15 minutes of cooking as temperature can increase quickly at the end.

3 Remove saucepan from heat; remove thermometer. Stir in vanilla. Quickly pour mixture into the prepared pan. Let stand about 2 hours or until firm. Using the edges of the foil, lift uncut caramels out of pan. Using a buttered knife, cut into 1-inch squares. Wrap each piece in waxed paper or plastic wrap. Store at room temperature for up to 2 weeks.

NUTRITION FACTS PER SERVING:
73 cal., 4 g total fat (2 g sat. fat), 10 mg chol., 27 mg sodium, 10 g carb., 0 g fiber, 0 g pro.

Shortcut Caramels

Prepare as directed, except substitute one 14-ounce can sweetened condensed milk for the half-and-half. Bring mixture to boiling over medium heat instead of medium-high heat. This mixture will take less time to reach 248°F (20 to 25 minutes instead of 45 to 60 minutes).

*tip

To toast nuts, preheat oven to 350°F. Spread nuts in a shallow baking pan. Bake for 5 to 10 minutes or until light brown, watching carefully and stirring once or twice.

401

Desserts

Index

Note: Page references in *italics* indicate photographs.

A

All-American Cheeseburger Soup, 172
All-American Sloppy Joes, 209
Almonds
    Candied Nuts, 367
    Chili Nuts, 60, 134
    Crispy Almond Fish with Potato
        Crisps, 292
    Rosemary-Roasted Nuts, 59
    Trout Almondine, 291
Alphabet Soup with Turkey
    Meatballs, 191
Angel Hair with Walnut Pesto, 330
Appetizers and snacks. *See also* Dips
    and spreads
    Avocado Deviled Eggs, 53
    Chili Nuts, 60, 134
    Fiery Chipotle Wings, 56
    Florida Crab Cakes, 57
    Fried Ravioli with Marinara Sauce,
        50, 132
    Homemade Kettle-Style Corn, 61
    Hot Wings, 56
    Marinated Shrimp Scampi, 58
    Olive Medley Pinwheels, 52
    Potato Skins, 49
    Ragin' Cajun Wings, 56
    Rosemary-Roasted Nuts, 59
    Saucy Spiced Apricot Meatballs, 54
    Soft Pretzels, 48, 133
    Stuffed Mushrooms, 51
    Sugared Bacon-Wrapped Smokies,
        55, 134
    Sweet-and-Savory Potato Chips, 47
    Sweet Potato Fritters with
        Yogurt-Chive Dipping
        Sauce, 46, 135

Apple cider
    Apple Cider Doughnuts, 32
    Hot Apple Cider, 65
Apples
    Apple, Bacon, and Leek Stuffing, 347
    Apple-Buttered Sweet Potatoes, 234
    Apple Cake with Buttery Caramel
        Sauce, 368
    Apple-Glazed Pork Loaf, 309
    Apple-Stuffed Pork Chops, 255, 277
    Baked Apples, 103
    Caramel Apple Pie, 377
    Cinnamon Rolls, 33, 129
    Pecan-Crusted Pork Tenderloin
        with Sautéed Apples and Sweet
        Potatoes, 253
    Pork and Ale Ragout, 82
Apricots
    Apricot Green Tea, 64
    Apricot-Stuffed Pork Tenderloin,
        254
    Fruit-and-Nut Baked Oatmeal, 36
    Saucy Spiced Apricot Meatballs, 54
    Spiced Apricot Sauce, 54
    Sweet-and-Sour Apricot Sauce, 312
Artichokes
    Baked Risotto with Sausage and
        Artichokes, 124
    Cheesy Artichoke and Spinach
        Dip, 40
    Creamy Artichoke Lasagna
        Bake, 162
    Smoky Salmon Casserole, 154
Arugula
    Chicken and Potatoes with
        Lemon, 261
    Poached Egg Salad with Citrus
        Dressing, *278*, 325

Skillet-Roasted Potatoes with
    Pork, 79
Asparagus, Zucchini, and Yellow
    Pepper Frittata with Fontina, 16
Avocados
    Avocado Deviled Eggs, 53
    Bacon-Biscuit Egg Sandwiches, 18
    Fresh Taco Salad, 101
    Fried Egg, Avocado, and Bacon
        Breakfast Sandwiches, 17, 131
    Guacamole, 44
    Mexican Seven-Layer Dip, 43
    Toasted Cumin Guacamole, 44
    Tomato-Avocado Grilled Cheese, 327

B

Bacon
    Apple, Bacon, and Leek Stuffing, 347
    Bacon-Biscuit Egg Sandwiches, 18
    Bacon-Cheddar Cheese Ball, 39
    Baked Potato Soup, *142*, 183
    BLT Salad with Buttermilk
        Dressing, 358
    Buttermilk-Bacon Mashed
        Potatoes, 349
    Creamy Broccoli Salad, 356
    Fettuccine alla Carbonara, *279*, 307
    Fried Egg, Avocado, and Bacon
        Breakfast Sandwiches, 17, 131
    Loaded Creamed Corn with Tomato
        and Bacon, 231
    Potato Skins, 49
    Quiche Lorraine, 6
    Rosemary-Roasted Vegetables, 339
    Sugared Bacon-Wrapped Smokies,
        55, 134
    Three-Cheese Beer Soup, 182
Baked Apples, 103

Baked Beef Ravioli, 117
Baked Brie Strata, 13
Baked Cheese Grits, 350
Baked Chicken Cordon Bleu, 145
Baked Chicken Fingers with Dipping
    Sauces, 312
Baked Denver Strata, 12
Baked Eggplant Parmesan, 99
Baked Eggs with Cheese and Basil
    Sauce, 10
Baked French Toast, 26
Baked Penne with Meat Sauce, 72
Baked Potato Soup, 142, 183
Baked Pumpkin Pudding, 107
Baked Risotto with Sausage and
    Artichokes, 124
Baked Ziti with Three Cheeses, 159
Banana Bread, 29
Banana-Butterscotch Cream Pie,
    287, 375
Barbecue Chicken Burgers and Waffle
    Fries, 311
Basil
    Angel Hair with Walnut Pesto, 330
    Baked Eggs with Cheese and Basil
        Sauce, 10
    Roasted Vegetable Pasta Salad with
        Walnut Pesto, 355
BBQ Pulled Pork Sandwiches, 215, 274
BBQ Spice-Rubbed Turkey Breast, 270
Beans. See also Green beans
    Bean-and-Beef Tortilla Casserole,
        119
    Black Bean and Corn Breakfast
        Burritos, 19
    Brazilian Pork and Black Bean
        Stew, 179
    Chili, 175
    Chili Burgers, 300
    Cincinnati-Style Chili Casserole,
        120
    Crispy Chipotle Bean Burritos, 102
    Easy Ham and Bean Soup, 181
    Falafel Pita Sandwiches, 328
    Flat-Iron Steak with BBQ Beans,
        71, 138
    Fresh Taco Salad, 101
    Ham and Bean Soup, 181
    Lamb Shanks with Beans, 250
    Meatball Tortilla Soup, 144, 174

Mexican Biscuit Casserole, 118
Mexican Seven-Layer Dip, 43
Mexican Skillet Dinner, 279, 308
Pasta Fagioli, 184
Red Beans and Rice, 216
Skillet White Beans, 282, 352
Southwest Pork Chops, 80
Sweet Potato–Black Bean Stew, 200
Sweet-Spicy Baked Beans, 351
Turkey, Black Bean, and Mango
    Tacos, 226
Veggie Burgers, 100
Beef. See also Veal
    All-American Cheeseburger Soup,
        172
    All-American Sloppy Joes, 209
    Baked Beef Ravioli, 117
    Baked Penne with Meat Sauce, 72
    Bean-and-Beef Tortilla Casserole,
        119
    Beef and Noodles, 76
    Beef Short Ribs with Smashed
        Horseradish Parsnips, 245
    Beef Stroganoff Casserole, 114
    Beef–Sweet Pepper Calzones,
        74, 138
    Beer-Braised Beef Short Ribs,
        206, 274
    Boeuf Bourguignon, 239
    Bolognese Sauce, 210
    Braised Beef with Red Wine
        Sauce, 240
    Brisket Ciabatta Sandwiches, 208
    Cheeseburger and Fries Casserole,
        112, 141
    Chicken Fried Steak, 247
    Chili, 175
    Chili Burgers, 300
    Chipotle Braised Short Ribs and
        Cheesy Polenta, 244
    Cincinnati-Style Chili Casserole, 120
    Corned Beef and Cabbage, 207
    Double-Crust Pizza Casserole, 113
    Easy Beef and Noodle Soup, 171
    Easy Shepherd's Pie, 115
    Flat-Iron Steak with BBQ Beans,
        71, 138
    Fork-Tender Pot Roast, 203
    German Meatballs with Spaetzle,
        246

Goulash, 173
Italian Fried Steak with Roasted
    Pepper Pesto, 296
Kansas City Steak Soup, 144, 170
Lasagna Panini, 73
Mexican Biscuit Casserole, 118
Mini Italian Meat Loaves with Green
    Beans, 298
Mustard-Herb Beef Stew, 176
New England Boiled Dinner, 241
Our Best Meat Loaf, 75
Pot Roast Paprikash, 204
Reuben Sandwiches, 301
Saucy Meatball Subs, 279, 299
Saucy Pot Roast with Whole Wheat
    Noodles, 202
So-Easy Pepper Steak, 205
Spiced Pot Roast with Root
    Vegetables, 70
Steak au Poivre, 248
Steak with Creamy Onion Sauce, 243
Steak with Pan Sauce, 297
Sunday Oven Pot Roast, 238, 276
Swiss Steak, 242
Tex-Mex Meatballs, 144, 174
Beer
    Beer-Braised Beef Short Ribs,
        206, 274
    Beer-Steamed Mussels with
        Sausage and Fennel, 294
    Three-Cheese Beer Soup, 182
Best-Ever Chocolate Cake, 285, 367
Big Soft Ginger Cookies, 394
Biscuits
    Cheesy Biscuits, 222, 274
    Flaky Buttermilk Biscuits with
        Sausage Gravy, 20
    Old-Fashioned Yeast Biscuits, 360
    One-Dish Turkey and Biscuits, 152
Black Bean and Corn Breakfast
    Burritos, 19
Blueberries
    Blueberry Muffins, 35
    Blueberry Pancakes, 24, 131
    Blueberry Pound Cake, 369
    Cherry-Berry Shortcakes, 379
Blue Cheese–Rosemary Mashed
    Potatoes, 349
Boeuf Bourguignon, 239
Bolognese Sauce, 210

Boursin Mashed Potatoes, 348
Braised Beef with Red Wine Sauce, 240
Brazilian Pork and Black Bean
      Stew, 179
Bread pudding
      Baked Brie Strata, 13
      Baked Denver Strata, 12
      Ham and Brie Bread Pudding, 218
      White Chocolate Bread Pudding
            with Hard Sauce, 386
Breads. *See also* Biscuits; Rolls;
      Tortillas
      Apple Cider Doughnuts, 32
      Baked French Toast, 26
      Banana Bread, 29
      Blueberry Muffins, 35
      Corn Bread, 359
      Ham-and-Cheese Stuffed French
            Toast, 27
      Oatmeal Batter Bread, 364
      Ooey-Gooey Monkey Bread, 31
      Orange-Raisin Brunch Bread, 30
      Parmesan Croutons, *281*, 357
      Peanut Butter–Streusel Muffins,
            34, *131*
      Sage and Pepper Popovers, 363
      Soft Pretzels, 48, *133*
Bread stuffings
      Apple, Bacon, and Leek Stuffing, 347
      Chicken with Sourdough
            Stuffing, 221
      Pumpernickel-Cherry Stuffing,
            236
      Turkey and Stuffing Bake, 90
Brisket Ciabatta Sandwiches, 208
Broccoli
      Broccoli-Cauliflower Bake, 164
      Creamy Broccoli Salad, 356
      Creamy Chicken-Broccoli
            Bake, 128
      Oven-Fried Veggies, *283*, 340
      Smoky Gouda-Sauced Broccoli, 332
Brownie Raspberry Tart, 109
Brownies, Fudgy, 398
Brownie Waffles à la Mode, *288*, 384
Brown Sugar–Glazed Ham, 259
Brown Sugar Topping, 377
Brussels sprouts
      Glazed Ham with Vegetables, 310
      Rosemary-Roasted Vegetables, 339

Burgers
      Barbecue Chicken Burgers and
            Waffle Fries, 311
      Chili Burgers, 300
      Salmon Burgers, 320
      Veggie Burgers, 100
Burritos
      Black Bean and Corn Breakfast
            Burritos, 19
      Crispy Chipotle Bean Burritos, 102
Butterhorn Rolls, 362
Buttermilk-Bacon Mashed Potatoes,
      349
Buttermilk-Brined Fried Chicken,
      263, *275*
Buttermilk Pie, 376
Butternut Squash and Carrot Soup, 197
Butter-Pecan Ice Cream, 390
Butterscotch Pudding, 387
Buttery Caramel Sauce, 368

C

Cabbage
      Corned Beef and Cabbage, 207
      Creamy Coleslaw, 353
      Fish Tacos with Lime Sauce, *279*, 321
      New England Boiled Dinner, 241
Cacciatore-Style Chicken, 223
Caesar Salad with Parmesan Croutons,
      281, 357
Cajun-Flavored Catfish, 92
Cajun Shrimp and Corn Bread
      Casserole, 155
Cakes
      Apple Cake with Buttery Caramel
            Sauce, 368
      Best-Ever Chocolate Cake, *285*, 367
      Blueberry Pound Cake, 369
      Chocolate Flourless Torte, 366
      Golden Layer Cake with Chocolate
            Icing, 370
      Lemon–Poppy Seed Pound Cake,
            369
      Marbled Angel Food Cake, 110
      Overnight Coffee Cake, 28
      Red Velvet Cupcakes with White
            Chocolate Filling and
            Mascarpone Frosting, 371
      Sour Cream Pound Cake, *286*, 369
      Upside-Down Pineapple-Ginger
            Carrot Cake, 106

Calzones, Beef–Sweet Pepper, 74, *138*
Candied Nuts, 367
Caramel Apple Pie, 377
Caramelized Onion Soup, 195
Caramels, 401
Caribbean Chicken Stew, 190
Carrots
      Butternut Squash and Carrot
            Soup, 197
      Cinnamon and Brown Sugar
            Custards, 108
      Herbed Root Vegetable Cobbler,
            141, 165
      Orange-Glazed Carrots and
            Parsnips, 233
      Oven-Fried Veggies, *283*, 340
      Upside-Down Pineapple-Ginger
            Carrot Cake, 106
Casserole-Style Chiles Rellenos, 158
Catfish, Cajun-Flavored, 92
Cauliflower
      Broccoli-Cauliflower Bake, 164
      Oven-Fried Veggies, *283*, 340
Chai, 67
Cheddar
      All-American Cheeseburger
            Soup, 172
      Bacon-Cheddar Cheese Ball, 39
      Baked Cheese Grits, 350
      Baked Denver Strata, 12
      Casserole-Style Chiles Rellenos, 158
      Cheese and Vegetable Rice
            Casserole, 157
      Cheesy Biscuits, 222, *274*
      Cheesy Potluck Potatoes, 168
      Double-Cheese Macaroni and
            Cheese, 228
      Loaded Macaroni and Cheese, 160
      Mexican Seven-Layer Dip, 43
      Potato Skins, 49
      Skillet Chicken, Macaroni, and
            Cheese, 89
      Three-Cheese Beer Soup, 182
      Twice-Baked Potatoes, 345
Cheese. *See also* Cheddar; Cream
      cheese; Monterey Jack;
      Mozzarella; Parmesan
      Asparagus, Zucchini, and Yellow
            Pepper Frittata with Fontina, 16
      Baked Brie Strata, 13

Baked Chicken Cordon Bleu, 145
Baked Denver Strata, 12
Baked Eggplant Parmesan, 99
Baked Potato Soup, 142, 183
Baked Ziti with Three Cheeses, 159
Blue Cheese–Rosemary Mashed
    Potatoes, 349
Caramelized Onion Soup, 195
Cheese-and-Onion Scrambled
    Eggs, 18
Cheese and Vegetable Rice
    Casserole, 157
Cheese-Stuffed Chicken Breasts,
    267
Classic Lasagna, 116
Crab and Spinach Pasta with
    Fontina, 156
Creamy Artichoke Lasagna
    Bake, 162
Creamy Blue Cheese Dip, 42
Crispy Chipotle Bean Burritos, 102
Double-Cheese Macaroni and
    Cheese, 228
Duchess Potatoes, 349
Goat Cheese–Yogurt Sauce, 318
Greek Vegetable and Feta Cheese
    Pie, 97
Ham and Brie Bread Pudding, 218
Ham-and-Cheese Stuffed French
    Toast, 27
Hash Brown–Crusted Quiche, 7
Hearty Mushrooms and Polenta,
    229
Layered Turkey Enchiladas, 315
Loaded Macaroni and Cheese, 160
Mascarpone Frosting, 371
Mexican Skillet Dinner, 279, 308
New Potato Bake, 167
Poached Egg Salad with Citrus
    Dressing, 278, 325
Quiche Lorraine, 6
Reuben Sandwiches, 301
Skillet Chicken, Macaroni, and
    Cheese, 89
Smoky Gouda-Sauced Broccoli, 332
Smoky Salmon Casserole, 154
Spinach and Mushroom Quiche, 6
Stuffed Mushrooms, 51
Three-Cheese Beer Soup, 182

Three-Cheese Ziti and Smoked
    Chicken Casserole, 147
Turkey Manicotti, 150
Walnut-Sage Potatoes au Gratin,
    282, 346
Cheeseburger and Fries Casserole,
    112, 141
Cheesecake, S'mores, 383
Cheesy Artichoke and Spinach
    Dip, 40
Cheesy Mushroom and Pepper
    Grits, 230
Cheesy Polenta, 244
Cheesy Potluck Potatoes, 168
Cherries
    Cherry-Berry Shortcakes, 379
    Chocolate-Covered Cherries, 400
    Fruit-and-Nut Baked Oatmeal, 36
    Lattice Cherry Pie, 378
    Pumpernickel-Cherry Stuffing, 236
    White Chocolate Bread Pudding
        with Hard Sauce, 386
Cherry Cola Ham, 219, 273
Chicken
    Baked Chicken Cordon Bleu, 145
    Baked Chicken Fingers with Dipping
        Sauces, 312
    Barbecue Chicken Burgers and
        Waffle Fries, 311
    Buttermilk-Brined Fried Chicken,
        263, 275
    Cacciatore-Style Chicken, 223
    Caribbean Chicken Stew, 190
    Cheese-Stuffed Chicken Breasts,
        267
    Chicken and Biscuits, 222, 274
    Chicken and Noodles, 87
    Chicken and Pasta Frittata, 313
    Chicken and Potatoes with
        Lemon, 261
    Chicken and Rice–Stuffed Peppers, 88
    Chicken and Sausage Gumbo, 189
    Chicken and Wild Rice Casserole,
        127
    Chicken and Wild Rice Soup, 185
    Chicken Caesar Salad, 357
    Chicken Enchilada Casserole,
        139, 148
    Chicken Noodle Soup, 187
    Chicken Piccata, 84

Chicken Posole Soup, 143, 188
Chicken Soup with Chive
    Dumplings, 186
Chicken with Marsala Risotto, 85
Chicken with Sourdough
    Stuffing, 221
Classic Chicken and Dumplings, 265
Coq au Vin, 266
Cornflake Chicken 'n' Waffles, 21
Creamy Chicken-Broccoli Bake, 128
Deep-Dish Chicken Potpie, 149
Fiery Chipotle Wings, 56
Hot Wings, 56
Lemon-Herb Roast Chicken, 220
Lightened-Up Chicken Enchiladas,
    148
Maple-Brined Chicken with Roasted
    Vegetables, 260
Oven-Barbecued Chicken, 262
Pan-Fried Italian Chicken
    Parmesan, 264
Potluck Chicken Tetrazzini, 146
Ragin' Cajun Wings, 56
Skillet Chicken, Macaroni, and
    Cheese, 89
Spicy Buttermilk-Brined Fried
    Chicken, 263
Sweet Herbed Oven-Fried Chicken,
    86, 137
Thai Curried Noodle Bowl, 314
Three-Cheese Ziti and Smoked
    Chicken Casserole, 147
Chicken Fried Steak, 247
Chicken sausages
    Creamy Tomato, Sausage, and
        Mushroom Pasta Sauce, 224
    Sausage Sandwiches with Roasted
        Veggies, 217
Chile peppers
    Casserole-Style Chiles Rellenos, 158
    Chili con Queso, 45
    Chipotle Braised Short Ribs and
        Cheesy Polenta, 244
    Chipotle Ketchup, 342
    Roasted Poblano Chili con Queso, 45
Chili, 175
Chili Burgers, 300
Chili con Queso, 45
Chili Nuts, 60, 134
Chipotle Ketchup, 342

Chocolate
  Best-Ever Chocolate Cake, *285, 367*
  Brownie Raspberry Tart, 109
  Brownie Waffles à la Mode, *288, 384*
  Chocolate Chip Cookies, 396
  Chocolate-Covered Cherries, 400
  Chocolate–Cream Cheese
      Frosting, 398
  Chocolate Flourless Torte, 366
  Chocolate Ganache, 383
  Chocolate Icing, 370
  Chocolate Pudding, 388
  Chocolate–Sour Cream Frosting, 367
  Cinnamon Rolls, 33, 129
  Easy Chocolate Fudge, 399
  Easy Chocolate–Peanut Butter
      Fudge, 399
  Easy Mocha Fudge, 399
  French Silk Pie, 373
  Fudgy Brownies, 398
  Macaroon Chocolate Bars, 397
  Marbled Angel Food Cake, 110
  Peanut Butter–Streusel Muffins,
      34, *131*
  Peppermint Hot Chocolate, 66
  Red Velvet Cupcakes with White
      Chocolate Filling and
      Mascarpone Frosting, 371
  S'mores Cheesecake, 383
  White Chocolate Whipped
      Cream, 371
Cilantro Ranch Dressing, 101
Cincinnati-Style Chili Casserole, 120
Cinnamon and Brown Sugar
    Custards, 108
Cinnamon Rolls, 33, *129*
Clams
  Clam Chowder, *144,* 192
  Pasta with White Clam Sauce,
      323
Classic Chicken and Dumplings, 265
Classic Lasagna, 116
Coconut
  Coconut Shrimp with Mango
      Sauce, 293
  Double-Coconut Cream Pie, 374
  Macaroon Chocolate Bars, 397
Coffee
  Easy Mocha Fudge, 399
  Vanilla Café Latte, 68

Coleslaw, Creamy, 353
Collard Greens, 336
Cookies and bars
  Big Soft Ginger Cookies, 394
  Chocolate Chip Cookies, 396
  Frosted Maple Drops, 392
  Fudgy Brownies, 398
  Homemade Oatmeal Cream Pies, 391
  Macaroon Chocolate Bars, 397
  Praline Snickerdoodles, 393
Cooled-Down Mexican Salsa, 312
Coq au Vin, 266
Corn
  Black Bean and Corn Breakfast
      Burritos, 19
  Creamed Corn Casserole, 166
  Creamy and Comforting Corn
      Chowder, *144,* 198
  Homemade Kettle-Style Corn, 61
  Loaded Creamed Corn with Tomato
      and Bacon, 231
  Roasted Corn and Crab Dip, 41, *134*
  Scalloped Corn, 333
Corn Bread, 359
Corn Bread Dumplings, 155
Corn Bread–Topped Sausage Bake, 125
Corned Beef and Cabbage, 207
Cornflake Chicken 'n' Waffles, 21
Cornmeal. *See also* Polenta
  Cheesy Polenta, 244
  Corn Bread, 359
  Corn Bread Dumplings, 155
  Cornmeal-Crusted Pork, 304
  Hearty Mushrooms and Polenta,
      229
  Hush Puppies, 341
  Overnight Three-Grain Waffles,
      22, *130*
  Pan-Fried Fish, *276,* 290
  Spicy Hot Pan-Fried Fish, 290
  Vegetable-Polenta Lasagna, 98
Crabmeat
  Crab and Spinach Pasta with
      Fontina, 156
  Easy Maryland Crab Bisque, 193
  Florida Crab Cakes, 57
  Roasted Corn and Crab Dip, 41, *134*
Cranberries
  Cranberry Barbecue Sauce, 270
  Cranberry-Sauced Hot Turkey
      Sandwiches, 317

Pear-Cranberry Deep-Dish Pie,
      104, *138*
Cream cheese
  Cheese-Stuffed Chicken Breasts,
      267
  Cheesy Artichoke and Spinach
      Dip, 40
  Chili con Queso, 45
  Chocolate–Cream Cheese
      Frosting, 398
  Creamed Corn Casserole, 166
  Dill Dip, 42
  Mascarpone Frosting, 371
  Olive Medley Pinwheels, 52
  Roasted Poblano Chili con Queso, 45
  S'mores Cheesecake, 383
  Spinach-Dill Dip, 42
Creamed Corn Casserole, 166
Creamed Spinach, *282,* 337
Creamy and Comforting Corn
    Chowder, *144,* 198
Creamy Artichoke Lasagna Bake, 162
Creamy Blue Cheese Dip, 42
Creamy Broccoli Salad, 356
Creamy Chicken-Broccoli Bake, 128
Creamy Coleslaw, 353
Creamy Marshmallow Dip for Fruit, 38
Creole-Style Shrimp and Grits, 95
Crispy Chipotle Bean Burritos, 102
Crispy Fish and Peppers, 93
Cupcakes, Red Velvet, with White
      Chocolate Filling and Mascarpone
      Frosting, 371
Curried Aïoli, 342
Curried Noodle Bowl, Thai, 314

D

Dates
  Baked Apples, 103
  Toffee-Pear Sticky Pudding, 385
Deep-Dish Chicken Potpie, 149
Desserts. *See also* Cakes; Cookies and
      bars
  Baked Apples, 103
  Baked Pumpkin Pudding, 107
  Banana-Butterscotch Cream Pie,
      287, 375
  Brownie Raspberry Tart, 109
  Brownie Waffles à la Mode, *288, 384*
  Buttermilk Pie, 376

Butter-Pecan Ice Cream, 390
Butterscotch Pudding, 387
Caramel Apple Pie, 377
Caramels, 401
Cherry-Berry Shortcakes, 379
Chocolate-Covered Cherries, 400
Chocolate Pudding, 388
Cinnamon and Brown Sugar
    Custards, 108
Double-Coconut Cream Pie, 374
Easy Chocolate Fudge, 399
Easy Chocolate–Peanut Butter
    Fudge, 399
Easy Mocha Fudge, 399
French Silk Pie, 373
Frosted Maple Drops, 392
Lattice Cherry Pie, 378
Maple-Pumpkin Crème Brûlées,
    286, 382
Peach-Praline Cobbler, 381
Pear-Cranberry Deep-Dish Pie,
    104, 138
Rhubarb Crisp, 284, 380
Shortcut Caramels, 401
S'mores Cheesecake, 383
Soda Fountain Ice Cream Pie, 372
Strawberry Cream Pie, 105
Strawberry Ice Cream, 286, 389
Toffee-Pear Sticky Pudding, 385
White Chocolate Bread Pudding
    with Hard Sauce, 386
Dill
    Dill Dip, 42
    Spinach-Dill Dip, 42
Dips and spreads
    Bacon-Cheddar Cheese Ball, 39
    Cheesy Artichoke and Spinach
        Dip, 40
    Chili con Queso, 45
    Chipotle Ketchup, 342
    Cooled-Down Mexican Salsa, 312
    Creamy Blue Cheese Dip, 42
    Creamy Marshmallow Dip for
        Fruit, 38
    Curried Aïoli, 342
    Dill Dip, 42
    Easy Aïoli, 340
    Guacamole, 44
    Honey Mustard Sauce, 312
    Horseradish Mayonnaise, 344

Lightened-Up Marshmallow Dip, 38
Mexican Seven-Layer Dip, 43
Roasted Corn and Crab Dip, 41, 134
Roasted Poblano Chili con Queso, 45
Spinach-Dill Dip, 42
Sweet-and-Sour Apricot Sauce, 312
Toasted Cumin Guacamole, 44
Tropical Salsa, 57
Yogurt-Chive Dipping Sauce, 46, 135
Double-Cheese Macaroni and
    Cheese, 228
Double-Coconut Cream Pie, 374
Double-Crust Pizza Casserole, 113
Doughnuts, Apple Cider, 32
Dressing, Cilantro Ranch, 101
Drinks
    Apricot Green Tea, 64
    Chai, 67
    Hot Apple Cider, 65
    Peppermint Hot Chocolate, 66
    Shirley Temple, 62
    Vanilla Café Latte, 68
    Watermelon and Strawberry
        Lemonade, 63
Duchess Potatoes, 349
Dumplings
    Chicken Soup with Chive
        Dumplings, 186
    Classic Chicken and Dumplings, 265
    Corn Bread Dumplings, 155
    Herbed Parmesan Dumplings, 165

E

Easy Aïoli, 340
Easy Beef and Noodle Soup, 171
Easy Chocolate Fudge, 399
Easy Chocolate–Peanut Butter
    Fudge, 399
Easy Ham and Bean Soup, 181
Easy Hash Brown Bake, 15, 140
Easy Maryland Crab Bisque, 193
Easy Mocha Fudge, 399
Easy Mushroom Bisque, 193
Easy Shepherd's Pie, 115
Easy Shrimp Bisque, 193
Easy Southern-Style Ribs, 214
Easy Tomato Sauce, 100
Eggplant
    Baked Eggplant Parmesan, 99
    Moussaka, 121

Roasted Vegetable Pasta Salad with
    Walnut Pesto, 355
Eggs
    Asparagus, Zucchini, and Yellow
        Pepper Frittata with Fontina, 16
    Avocado Deviled Eggs, 53
    Bacon-Biscuit Egg Sandwiches, 18
    Baked Eggs with Cheese and Basil
        Sauce, 10
    Black Bean and Corn Breakfast
        Burritos, 19
    Casserole-Style Chiles Rellenos, 158
    Cheese-and-Onion Scrambled
        Eggs, 18
    Chicken and Pasta Frittata, 313
    Fried Egg, Avocado, and Bacon
        Breakfast Sandwiches, 17, 131
    Hash Brown Omelet, 9
    Mushroom-Thyme Omelets, 8
    Poached Egg Salad with Citrus
        Dressing, 278, 325
    Smoked Salmon Eggs Benedict,
        11, 131
    Vegetable Egg Salad Wraps, 326
Enchiladas
    Chicken Enchilada Casserole,
        139, 148
    Layered Turkey Enchiladas, 315
    Lightened-Up Chicken Enchiladas,
        148

F

Falafel Pita Sandwiches, 328
Fennel
    Beer-Steamed Mussels with
        Sausage and Fennel, 294
    Maple-Brined Chicken with Roasted
        Vegetables, 260
Fettuccine Alfredo, 329
Fettuccine alla Carbonara, 279, 307
Fiery Chipotle Wings, 56
Fish. See also Salmon
    Cajun-Flavored Catfish, 92
    Crispy Almond Fish with Potato
        Crisps, 292
    Crispy Fish and Peppers, 93
    Fish and Sweet Potato Chips, 289
    Fish Tacos with Lime Sauce, 279, 321
    Oven-Roasted Fish with Peas and
        Tomatoes, 272

Fish (*continued*)
Pan-Fried Fish, *276, 290*
Spicy Hot Pan-Fried Fish, *290*
Tilapia Vera Cruz, *322*
Trout Almondine, *291*
Tuna Club Sandwiches, *319*
Tuna Noodle Casserole, *141, 153*
Flaky Buttermilk Biscuits with Sausage Gravy, *20*
Flat-Iron Steak with BBQ Beans, *71, 138*
Florida Crab Cakes, *57*
Fork-Tender Pot Roast, *203*
French Silk Pie, *373*
French toast
Baked French Toast, *26*
Ham-and-Cheese Stuffed French Toast, *27*
Fresh Taco Salad, *101*
Fresh Tomato Sauce, *78, 136*
Fresh Tomato Soup, *199*
Fried Egg, Avocado, and Bacon Breakfast Sandwiches, *17, 131*
Fried Green Tomatoes, *280, 335*
Fried Ravioli with Marinara Sauce, *50, 132*
Frittatas
Asparagus, Zucchini, and Yellow Pepper Frittata with Fontina, *16*
Chicken and Pasta Frittata, *313*
Fritters, Sweet Potato, with Yogurt-Chive Dipping Sauce, *46, 135*
Frosted Maple Drops, *392*
Frostings
Chocolate–Cream Cheese Frosting, *398*
Chocolate–Sour Cream Frosting, *367*
Mascarpone Frosting, *371*
Vanilla Frosting, *33*
Fruit. *See also specific fruits*
Creamy Marshmallow Dip for Fruit, *38*
Fruit-and-Nut Baked Oatmeal, *36*
Fudge
Easy Chocolate Fudge, *399*
Easy Chocolate–Peanut Butter Fudge, *399*
Easy Mocha Fudge, *399*
Fudgy Brownies, *398*

G

Garlic
Easy Aïoli, *340*
Rosemary-Garlic Lamb Chops, *302*
Rustic Garlic Mashed Potatoes, *235, 274*
German Meatballs with Spaetzle, *246*
Ginger
Big Soft Ginger Cookies, *394*
Upside-Down Pineapple-Ginger Carrot Cake, *106*
Glazed Ham with Vegetables, *310*
Glazes
Chocolate Ganache, *383*
Spiced Glaze, *32*
Goat Cheese–Yogurt Sauce, *318*
Golden Layer Cake with Chocolate Icing, *370*
Goulash, *173*
Grains. *See also* Cornmeal; Grits; Oats; Rice
Multigrain Rolls, *361*
Overnight Three-Grain Waffles, *22, 130*
Gravy, Sausage, *20*
Greek Vegetable and Feta Cheese Pie, *97*
Green beans
Cornmeal-Crusted Pork, *304*
Green Bean Casserole with Crispy Shallots, *163*
Mini Italian Meat Loaves with Green Beans, *298*
Rosemary-Roasted Vegetables, *339*
Vegetable-Pork Oven Stew, *178*
Greens. *See also* Spinach
BLT Salad with Buttermilk Dressing, *358*
Caesar Salad with Parmesan Croutons, *281, 357*
Chicken and Potatoes with Lemon, *261*
Chicken Caesar Salad, *357*
Collard Greens, *336*
Fresh Taco Salad, *101*
Poached Egg Salad with Citrus Dressing, *278, 325*
Skillet-Roasted Potatoes with Pork, *79*

Grits
Baked Cheese Grits, *350*
Cheesy Mushroom and Pepper Grits, *230*
Creole-Style Shrimp and Grits, *95*
Guacamole, *44*

H

Ham
Baked Chicken Cordon Bleu, *145*
Baked Denver Strata, *12*
Brown Sugar–Glazed Ham, *259*
Cherry Cola Ham, *219, 273*
Easy Ham and Bean Soup, *181*
Easy Hash Brown Bake, *15, 140*
Fettuccine alla Carbonara, *279, 307*
Glazed Ham with Vegetables, *310*
Ham and Bean Soup, *181*
Ham and Brie Bread Pudding, *218*
Ham-and-Cheese Stuffed French Toast, *27*
Ham Balls in Barbecue Sauce, *258, 276*
One-Step Ham Casserole, *123, 141*
Potato-Ham Bake, *14*
Saucy Bow-Tie Pasta Casserole, *126*
Hard Sauce, *386*
Hash Brown–Crusted Quiche, *7*
Hash Brown Omelet, *9*
Hearty Mushrooms and Polenta, *229*
Herbed Parmesan Dumplings, *165*
Herbed Root Vegetable Cobbler, *141, 165*
Herbs. *See also specific herbs*
Herb-Roasted Turkey and Vegetables, *268*
Lemon-Herb Roast Chicken, *220*
Homemade Kettle-Style Corn, *61*
Homemade Oatmeal Cream Pies, *391*
Home-Style Pork Pot Roast, *213*
Hominy
Chicken Posole Soup, *143, 188*
Honey-and-Apple Ribs, *257*
Honey Mustard Sauce, *312*
Horseradish
Beef Short Ribs with Smashed Horseradish Parsnips, *245*
Horseradish Mayonnaise, *344*
Hot Apple Cider, *65*
Hot Wings, *56*
Hush Puppies, *341*

I

Ice cream
    Brownie Waffles à la Mode, 288, 384
    Butter-Pecan Ice Cream, 390
    Soda Fountain Ice Cream Pie, 372
    Strawberry Ice Cream, 286, 389
Icing, Chocolate, 370
Italian Fried Steak with Roasted Pepper Pesto, 296

K

Kansas City Steak Soup, 144, 170
Ketchup, Chipotle, 342

L

Lamb
    Lamb Shanks with Beans, 250
    Lamb Shanks with Polenta, 212
    Luck o' the Irish Stew, 177
    Moussaka, 121
    Rosemary-Garlic Lamb Chops, 302
    Slow Cooker Moroccan Lamb Tagine, 211
    Tomato-Topped Lamb Chops and Rice, 77
Lasagna
    Classic Lasagna, 116
    Creamy Artichoke Lasagna Bake, 162
    Vegetable-Polenta Lasagna, 98
Lasagna Panini, 73
Lattice Cherry Pie, 378
Layered Turkey Enchiladas, 315
Lemons
    Chicken and Potatoes with Lemon, 261
    Chicken Piccata, 84
    Lemon-Herb Roast Chicken, 220
    Lemon–Poppy Seed Pound Cake, 369
    Lemony Fettuccine Alfredo with Shrimp and Peas, 329
    Watermelon and Strawberry Lemonade, 63
Lightened-Up Chicken Enchiladas, 148
Lightened-Up Marshmallow Dip, 38

Loaded Creamed Corn with Tomato and Bacon, 231
Loaded Macaroni and Cheese, 160
Luck o' the Irish Stew, 177

M

Macaroon Chocolate Bars, 397
Mama's Spicy Meatballs with Fresh Tomato Sauce, 78, 136
Mangoes
    Coconut Shrimp with Mango Sauce, 293
    Turkey, Black Bean, and Mango Tacos, 226
Maple syrup
    Frosted Maple Drops, 392
    Maple-Brined Chicken with Roasted Vegetables, 260
    Maple-Pumpkin Crème Brûlées, 286, 382
    Skillet White Beans, 282, 352
    Spiced Maple Syrup, 26
Marbled Angel Food Cake, 110
Marinated Shrimp Scampi, 58
Marshmallow crème
    Creamy Marshmallow Dip for Fruit, 38
    Easy Chocolate Fudge, 399
    Easy Chocolate–Peanut Butter Fudge, 399
    Easy Mocha Fudge, 399
    Homemade Oatmeal Cream Pies, 391
    Lightened-Up Marshmallow Dip, 38
Mascarpone Frosting, 371
Meat. See Beef; Lamb; Pork; Veal
Meatballs
    German Meatballs with Spaetzle, 246
    Ham Balls in Barbecue Sauce, 258, 276
    Mama's Spicy Meatballs with Fresh Tomato Sauce, 78, 136
    Meatball Tortilla Soup, 144, 174
    Saucy Meatball Subs, 279, 299
    Saucy Spiced Apricot Meatballs, 54
    Tex-Mex Meatballs, 144, 174
    Turkey Meatballs, 191

Meat loaf
    Apple-Glazed Pork Loaf, 309
    Mini Italian Meat Loaves with Green Beans, 298
    Our Best Meat Loaf, 75
    Turkey Meat Loaf, 271
Mexican Biscuit Casserole, 118
Mexican Seven-Layer Dip, 43
Mexican Skillet Dinner, 279, 308
Mini Italian Meat Loaves with Green Beans, 298
Monterey Jack
    Cheesy Mushroom and Pepper Grits, 230
    Cheesy Potluck Potatoes, 168
    Chicken Enchilada Casserole, 139, 148
    Chili con Queso, 45
    Lightened-Up Chicken Enchiladas, 148
    Loaded Creamed Corn with Tomato and Bacon, 231
    Nacho Turkey Casserole, 151
    Roasted Poblano Chili con Queso, 45
    Tomato-Avocado Grilled Cheese, 327
Moussaka, 121
Mozzarella
    Baked Beef Ravioli, 117
    Baked Eggs with Cheese and Basil Sauce, 10
    Beef–Sweet Pepper Calzones, 74, 138
    Classic Lasagna, 116
    Creamy Artichoke Lasagna Bake, 162
    Double-Crust Pizza Casserole, 113
    Lasagna Panini, 73
    Loaded Macaroni and Cheese, 160
    Mini Italian Meat Loaves with Green Beans, 298
    Saucy Bow-Tie Pasta Casserole, 126
    Turkey Manicotti, 150
    Vegetable-Polenta Lasagna, 98
Muffins
    Blueberry Muffins, 35
    Peanut Butter–Streusel Muffins, 34, 131
Multigrain Rolls, 361

Mushrooms
  Cheesy Mushroom and Pepper
    Grits, 230
  Creamy Tomato, Sausage,
    and Mushroom Pasta
    Sauce, 224
  Easy Mushroom Bisque, 193
  Green Bean Casserole with Crispy
    Shallots, 163
  Hearty Mushrooms and Polenta,
    229
  Mushroom Medley au Gratin, 338
  Mushroom-Thyme Omelets, 8
  Oven-Fried Veggies, 283, 340
  Shiitake Fettuccine Alfredo, 329
  Spinach and Mushroom Quiche, 6
  Stuffed Mushrooms, 51
  Three-Mushroom Soup, 196
Mussels, Beer-Steamed, with Sausage
  and Fennel, 294
Mustard
  Honey Mustard Sauce, 312
  Mustard-Glazed Pork Chops, 256
  Mustard-Herb Beef Stew, 176

N

Nacho Turkey Casserole, 151
New England Boiled Dinner, 241
New Potato Bake, 167
Noodles
  Beef and Noodles, 76
  Chicken and Noodles, 87
  Chicken Noodle Soup, 187
  Creamy Chicken-Broccoli
    Bake, 128
  Easy Beef and Noodle Soup, 171
  German Meatballs with Spaetzle,
    246
  Pork Chop Casserole, 122
  Pot Roast Paprikash, 204
  Saucy Pot Roast with Whole Wheat
    Noodles, 202
  Thai Curried Noodle Bowl, 314
  Tuna Noodle Casserole, 141, 153
Nuts. See also Almonds; Pecans;
  Walnuts
  Candied Nuts, 367
  Chili Nuts, 60, 134

Easy Chocolate–Peanut Butter
  Fudge, 399
Fudgy Brownies, 398
Rosemary-Roasted Nuts, 59

O

Oatmeal Batter Bread, 364
Oats
  Brown Sugar Topping, 377
  Fruit-and-Nut Baked Oatmeal, 36
  Homemade Oatmeal Cream
    Pies, 391
  Multigrain Rolls, 361
  Oatmeal Batter Bread, 364
  Overnight Three-Grain Waffles,
    22, 130
  Rhubarb Crisp, 284, 380
Okra, Smothered, 334
Old-Fashioned Yeast Biscuits, 360
Olives
  Lamb Shanks with Polenta, 212
  Olive Medley Pinwheels, 52
  Shrimp Vera Cruz, 322
  Tilapia Vera Cruz, 322
Omelets
  Hash Brown Omelet, 9
  Mushroom-Thyme Omelets, 8
One-Dish Turkey and Biscuits, 152
One-Step Ham Casserole, 123, 141
Onions
  Caramelized Onion Soup, 195
  Onion Rings, 342
  Steak with Creamy Onion
    Sauce, 243
Ooey-Gooey Monkey Bread, 31
Orange-Glazed Carrots and
  Parsnips, 233
Orange-Raisin Brunch Bread, 30
Our Best Meat Loaf, 75
Oven-Barbecued Chicken, 262
Oven-Fried Pork Chops, 303
Oven-Fried Veggies, 283, 340
Oven-Puffed Pancake with Caramelized
  Plums, 23
Oven-Roasted Fish with Peas and
  Tomatoes, 272
Overnight Coffee Cake, 28
Overnight Three-Grain Waffles, 22, 130
Oyster Stew, 194

P

Pacific Northwest Paella, 94
Paella, Pacific Northwest, 94
Pancakes
  Blueberry Pancakes, 24, 131
  Oven-Puffed Pancake with
    Caramelized Plums, 23
  Potato Pancakes, 349
  Pumpkin Pancakes, 25
Pan-Fried Fish, 276, 290
Pan-Fried Italian Chicken Parmesan,
  264
Parker House Rolls, 362
Parmesan
  Baked Ziti with Three Cheeses, 159
  Cheesy Artichoke and Spinach
    Dip, 40
  Cheesy Polenta, 244
  Chicken Caesar Salad, 357
  Creamy Artichoke Lasagna
    Bake, 162
  Fettuccine Alfredo, 329
  Fettuccine alla Carbonara, 279, 307
  Herbed Parmesan Dumplings, 165
  Lemony Fettuccine Alfredo with
    Shrimp and Peas, 329
  Pan-Fried Italian Chicken
    Parmesan, 264
  Parmesan Croutons, 281, 357
  Shiitake Fettuccine Alfredo, 329
Parsnips
  Beef Short Ribs with Smashed
    Horseradish Parsnips, 245
  Orange-Glazed Carrots and
    Parsnips, 233
Pasta. See also Noodles
  Alphabet Soup with Turkey
    Meatballs, 191
  Angel Hair with Walnut Pesto, 330
  Baked Beef Ravioli, 117
  Baked Penne with Meat Sauce, 72
  Baked Ziti with Three Cheeses, 159
  Beef Stroganoff Casserole, 114
  Chicken and Pasta Frittata, 313
  Cincinnati-Style Chili Casserole, 120
  Classic Lasagna, 116
  Crab and Spinach Pasta with
    Fontina, 156

Creamy Artichoke Lasagna
    Bake, 162
Creamy Tomato, Sausage, and
    Mushroom Pasta Sauce, 224
Double-Cheese Macaroni and
    Cheese, 228
Fettuccine Alfredo, 329
Fettuccine alla Carbonara,
    279, 307
Fried Ravioli with Marinara Sauce,
    50, 132
Lemony Fettuccine Alfredo with
    Shrimp and Peas, 329
Loaded Macaroni and Cheese, 160
One-Step Ham Casserole, 123, 141
Pan-Fried Italian Chicken
    Parmesan, 264
Pasta Fagioli, 184
Pasta with White Clam Sauce, 323
Potluck Chicken Tetrazzini, 146
Roasted Vegetable Pasta Salad with
    Walnut Pesto, 355
Saucy Bow-Tie Pasta Casserole, 126
Shiitake Fettuccine Alfredo, 329
Skewered Shrimp Scampi, 324
Skillet Chicken, Macaroni, and
    Cheese, 89
Slow Cooker Marinara Sauce, 227
Smoky Salmon Casserole, 154
Spicy Shrimp Pasta, 96
Teriyaki Pork Lo Mein, 81
Three-Cheese Ziti and Smoked
    Chicken Casserole, 147
Tortellini-Vegetable Bake, 161
Turkey Manicotti, 150
Vermicelli with Sausage and
    Spinach, 306
Pastry, 104
Pastry for a Double-Crust Pie, 378
Pastry for a Single-Crust Pie,
    6, 373
Pastry Topper, 149
Peach-Praline Cobbler, 381
Peanut butter
    Easy Chocolate–Peanut Butter
        Fudge, 399
    Peanut Butter Cookies, 395
    Peanut Butter–Streusel Muffins,
        34, 131

Peanuts
    Chili Nuts, 60, 134
    Easy Chocolate–Peanut Butter
        Fudge, 399
Pears
    Pear-Cranberry Deep-Dish Pie,
        104, 138
    Toffee-Pear Sauce, 385
    Toffee-Pear Sticky Pudding, 385
Peas
    Lemony Fettuccine Alfredo with
        Shrimp and Peas, 329
    Oven-Roasted Fish with Peas and
        Tomatoes, 272
    Pea Soup, 180
Pecans
    Butter-Pecan Ice Cream, 390
    Candied Nuts, 367
    Caramel Apple Pie, 377
    Overnight Coffee Cake, 28
    Peach-Praline Cobbler, 381
    Pecan-Crusted Pork Tenderloin
        with Sautéed Apples and Sweet
        Potatoes, 253
    Praline Snickerdoodles, 393
Peppercorns
    Sage and Pepper Popovers, 363
    Steak au Poivre, 248
Peppermint Hot Chocolate, 66
Peppers. See also Chile peppers
    Asparagus, Zucchini, and Yellow
        Pepper Frittata with Fontina, 16
    Baked Denver Strata, 12
    Beef–Sweet Pepper Calzones, 74, 138
    Cacciatore-Style Chicken, 223
    Cheesy Mushroom and Pepper
        Grits, 230
    Chicken and Rice–Stuffed Peppers, 88
    Crispy Fish and Peppers, 93
    Italian Fried Steak with Roasted
        Pepper Pesto, 296
    Pot Roast Paprikash, 204
    So-Easy Pepper Steak, 205
Perfect Mashed Potatoes, 348
Pies. See also Quiche
    Banana-Butterscotch Cream Pie,
        287, 375
    Buttermilk Pie, 376
    Double-Coconut Cream Pie, 374
    French Silk Pie, 373

Greek Vegetable and Feta Cheese
    Pie, 97
Lattice Cherry Pie, 378
Pastry for a Double-Crust Pie, 378
Pastry for a Single-Crust Pie, 6, 373
Pear-Cranberry Deep-Dish Pie,
    104, 138
Soda Fountain Ice Cream Pie, 372
Strawberry Cream Pie, 105
Pineapple-Ginger Carrot Cake,
    Upside-Down, 106
Pizza Stew with Biscuits, 83
Plums, Caramelized, Oven-Puffed
    Pancake with, 23
Poached Egg Salad with Citrus
    Dressing, 278, 325
Polenta, Lamb Shanks with, 212
Popcorn
    Homemade Kettle-Style Corn, 61
Popovers, Sage and Pepper, 363
Poppy Seed–Lemon Pound Cake, 369
Pork. See also Bacon; Ham; Sausages
    Apple-Glazed Pork Loaf, 309
    Apple-Stuffed Pork Chops, 255, 277
    Apricot-Stuffed Pork Tenderloin,
        254
    BBQ Pulled Pork Sandwiches,
        215, 274
    Brazilian Pork and Black Bean
        Stew, 179
    Cornmeal-Crusted Pork, 304
    Easy Southern-Style Ribs, 214
    Ham Balls in Barbecue Sauce,
        258, 276
    Home-Style Pork Pot Roast, 213
    Honey-and-Apple Ribs, 257
    Mama's Spicy Meatballs with Fresh
        Tomato Sauce, 78, 136
    Mustard-Glazed Pork Chops, 256
    Oven-Fried Pork Chops, 303
    Pea Soup, 180
    Pecan-Crusted Pork Tenderloin
        with Sautéed Apples and Sweet
        Potatoes, 253
    Pork and Ale Ragout, 82
    Pork Chop Casserole, 122
    Pork Pot Roast in Cider, 251
    Pork Tenderloin Sandwiches, 305
    Red Beans and Rice, 216
    Rosemary-Roasted Loin of Pork, 252

411

Pork (continued)
    Saucy Spiced Apricot Meatballs, 54
    Skillet-Roasted Potatoes with
        Pork, 79
    Southwest Pork Chops, 80
    Teriyaki Pork Lo Mein, 81
    Vegetable-Pork Oven Stew, 178
Potatoes. *See also* Sweet potatoes
    Baked Potato Soup, *142*, 183
    Barbecue Chicken Burgers and
        Waffle Fries, 311
    Blue Cheese–Rosemary Mashed
        Potatoes, 349
    Boursin Mashed Potatoes, 348
    Buttermilk-Bacon Mashed
        Potatoes, 349
    Cheeseburger and Fries Casserole,
        112, 141
    Cheesy Potluck Potatoes, 168
    Chicken and Biscuits, *222*, 274
    Chicken and Potatoes with
        Lemon, 261
    Cranberry-Sauced Hot Turkey
        Sandwiches, 317
    Crispy Almond Fish with Potato
        Crisps, 292
    Duchess Potatoes, 349
    Easy Hash Brown Bake, 15, *140*
    Easy Shepherd's Pie, 115
    Hash Brown–Crusted Quiche, 7
    Hash Brown Omelet, 9
    Herbed Root Vegetable Cobbler,
        141, 165
    Herb-Roasted Turkey and
        Vegetables, 268
    New Potato Bake, 167
    Perfect Mashed Potatoes, 348
    Potato-Ham Bake, 14
    Potato Pancakes, 349
    Potato Skins, 49
    Ranch Fries, 343
    Rustic Garlic Mashed Potatoes,
        235, *274*
    Skillet-Roasted Potatoes with
        Pork, 79
    Summer Vegetable Potato Salad, 354
    Sweet-and-Savory Potato Chips, 47
    Twice-Baked Potatoes, 345
    Walnut-Sage Potatoes au Gratin,
        282, 346
Potluck Chicken Tetrazzini, 146

Pot Roast Paprikash, 204
Poultry. *See* Chicken; Turkey
Praline Sauce, 22
Praline Snickerdoodles, 393
Pretzels, Soft, 48, *133*
Puddings. *See also* Bread pudding
    Baked Pumpkin Pudding, 107
    Butterscotch Pudding, 387
    Chocolate Pudding, 388
    Toffee-Pear Sticky Pudding, 385
Pumpernickel-Cherry Stuffing, 236
Pumpkin
    Baked Pumpkin Pudding, 107
    Maple-Pumpkin Crème Brûlées,
        286, 382
    Pumpkin Pancakes, 25

Q

Quiche
    Hash Brown–Crusted Quiche, 7
    Quiche Lorraine, 6
    Spinach and Mushroom Quiche, 6

R

Ragin' Cajun Wings, 56
Raisins
    Baked Apples, 103
    Cinnamon Rolls, 33, *129*
    Creamy Broccoli Salad, 356
    Fruit-and-Nut Baked Oatmeal, 36
    Orange-Raisin Brunch Bread, 30
Ranch Fries, 343
Raspberries
    Brownie Raspberry Tart, 109
    Cherry-Berry Shortcakes, 379
Ravioli, Fried, with Marinara Sauce,
    50, *132*
Red Beans and Rice, 216
Red Velvet Cupcakes with White
    Chocolate Filling and Mascarpone
    Frosting, 371
Reuben Sandwiches, 301
Rhubarb Crisp, *284*, 380
Rice
    Baked Chicken Cordon Bleu, 145
    Baked Risotto with Sausage and
        Artichokes, 124
    Cheese and Vegetable Rice
        Casserole, 157
    Chicken and Rice–Stuffed Peppers, 88

    Chicken and Wild Rice Casserole,
        127
    Chicken and Wild Rice Soup, 185
    Chicken with Marsala Risotto, 85
    Mexican Skillet Dinner, *279*, 308
    Pacific Northwest Paella, 94
    Red Beans and Rice, 216
    Spanish Rice, 232
    Tomato-Topped Lamb Chops and
        Rice, 77
    Turkey and Stuffing Bake, 90
Risotto
    Baked Risotto with Sausage and
        Artichokes, 124
    Chicken with Marsala Risotto, 85
Roasted Corn and Crab Dip, 41, *134*
Roasted Poblano Chili con Queso, 45
Roasted Salmon and Tomatoes, 91
Roasted Vegetable Pasta Salad with
    Walnut Pesto, 355
Rolls
    Butterhorn Rolls, 362
    Cinnamon Rolls, 33, *129*
    Multigrain Rolls, 361
    Parker House Rolls, 362
    Rosemary Satin Dinner Rolls,
        282, 362
Rosemary
    Blue Cheese–Rosemary Mashed
        Potatoes, 349
    Rosemary-Garlic Lamb Chops, 302
    Rosemary-Roasted Loin of Pork, 252
    Rosemary-Roasted Nuts, 59
    Rosemary-Roasted Vegetables, 339
    Rosemary Satin Dinner Rolls,
        282, 362
Rustic Garlic Mashed Potatoes,
    235, *274*

S

Sage and Pepper Popovers, 363
Salads
    BLT Salad with Buttermilk
        Dressing, 358
    Caesar Salad with Parmesan
        Croutons, *281*, 357
    Chicken Caesar Salad, 357
    Creamy Broccoli Salad, 356
    Creamy Coleslaw, 353
    Fresh Taco Salad, 101

Poached Egg Salad with Citrus Dressing, *278, 325*
Roasted Vegetable Pasta Salad with Walnut Pesto, 355
Summer Vegetable Potato Salad, 354
Salmon
Pacific Northwest Paella, 94
Roasted Salmon and Tomatoes, 91
Salmon Burgers, 320
Smoked Salmon Eggs Benedict, 11, 131
Smoky Salmon Casserole, 154
Salsa
Cooled-Down Mexican Salsa, 312
Tropical Salsa, 57
Sandwiches. *See also* Burgers
All-American Sloppy Joes, 209
Bacon-Biscuit Egg Sandwiches, 18
BBQ Pulled Pork Sandwiches, 215, *274*
Brisket Ciabatta Sandwiches, 208
Cranberry-Sauced Hot Turkey Sandwiches, 317
Falafel Pita Sandwiches, 328
Fried Egg, Avocado, and Bacon Breakfast Sandwiches, 17, 131
Lasagna Panini, 73
Pork Tenderloin Sandwiches, 305
Reuben Sandwiches, 301
Saucy Meatball Subs, *279*, 299
Sausage Sandwiches with Roasted Veggies, 217
Sloppy Turkey and Veggie Sandwiches, 318
Tomato-Avocado Grilled Cheese, 327
Tuna Club Sandwiches, 319
Vegetable Egg Salad Wraps, 326
Sauces
Bolognese Sauce, 210
Buttery Caramel Sauce, 368
Cranberry Barbecue Sauce, 270
Creamy Tomato, Sausage, and Mushroom Pasta Sauce, 224
Easy Tomato Sauce, 100
Fresh Tomato Sauce, 78, *136*
Goat Cheese–Yogurt Sauce, 318
Hard Sauce, 386
Honey Mustard Sauce, 312
Praline Sauce, 22

Sausage Gravy, 20
Slow Cooker Marinara Sauce, 227
Spiced Apricot Sauce, 54
Sweet-and-Sour Apricot Sauce, 312
Toffee-Pear Sauce, 385
Yogurt-Chive Dipping Sauce, 46, 135
Saucy Bow-Tie Pasta Casserole, 126
Saucy Meatball Subs, *279*, 299
Saucy Pot Roast with Whole Wheat Noodles, 202
Saucy Spiced Apricot Meatballs, 54
Sausages. *See also* Chicken sausages; Turkey sausages
Baked Risotto with Sausage and Artichokes, 124
Brazilian Pork and Black Bean Stew, 179
Chicken and Sausage Gumbo, 189
Classic Lasagna, 116
Corn Bread–Topped Sausage Bake, 125
Double-Crust Pizza Casserole, 113
Mexican Skillet Dinner, *279*, 308
Red Beans and Rice, 216
Sausage Gravy, 20
Sausage-Stuffed Turkey Breast, 269, *276*
Sugared Bacon-Wrapped Smokies, 55, *134*
Vermicelli with Sausage and Spinach, 306
Scalloped Corn, 333
Seafood. *See* Fish; Shellfish
Shallots
Caramelized Onion Soup, 195
Green Bean Casserole with Crispy Shallots, 163
Shellfish. *See also* Shrimp
Beer-Steamed Mussels with Sausage and Fennel, 294
Clam Chowder, *144*, 192
Crab and Spinach Pasta with Fontina, 156
Easy Maryland Crab Bisque, 193
Florida Crab Cakes, 57
Oyster Stew, 194
Pasta with White Clam Sauce, 323
Roasted Corn and Crab Dip, 41, *134*

Shiitake Fettuccine Alfredo, 329
Shirley Temple, 62
Shortcakes, Cherry-Berry, 379
Shortcut Caramels, 401
Shrimp
Cajun Shrimp and Corn Bread Casserole, 155
Coconut Shrimp with Mango Sauce, 293
Creole-Style Shrimp and Grits, 95
Easy Shrimp Bisque, 193
Lemony Fettuccine Alfredo with Shrimp and Peas, 329
Marinated Shrimp Scampi, 58
Shrimp Vera Cruz, 322
Skewered Shrimp Scampi, 324
Spicy Shrimp Pasta, 96
Skewered Shrimp Scampi, 324
Skillet Chicken, Macaroni, and Cheese, 89
Skillet-Roasted Potatoes with Pork, 79
Skillet White Beans, *282*, 352
Sloppy Turkey and Veggie Sandwiches, 318
Slow Cooker Marinara Sauce, 227
Slow Cooker Moroccan Lamb Tagine, 211
Smoked Salmon Eggs Benedict, 11, 131
Smoky Gouda-Sauced Broccoli, 332
Smoky Salmon Casserole, 154
S'mores Cheesecake, 383
Smothered Okra, 334
Soda Fountain Ice Cream Pie, 372
So-Easy Pepper Steak, 205
Soft Pretzels, 48, 133
Soups. *See also* Stews
All-American Cheeseburger Soup, 172
Alphabet Soup with Turkey Meatballs, 191
Baked Potato Soup, *142*, 183
Butternut Squash and Carrot Soup, 197
Caramelized Onion Soup, 195
Chicken and Sausage Gumbo, 189
Chicken and Wild Rice Soup, 185
Chicken Noodle Soup, 187
Chicken Posole Soup, *143*, 188
Chicken Soup with Chive Dumplings, 186

Soups (*continued*)
  Clam Chowder, *144*, 192
  Creamy and Comforting Corn Chowder, *144, 198*
  Easy Beef and Noodle Soup, 171
  Easy Ham and Bean Soup, 181
  Easy Maryland Crab Bisque, 193
  Easy Mushroom Bisque, 193
  Easy Shrimp Bisque, 193
  Fresh Tomato Soup, 199
  Ham and Bean Soup, 181
  Kansas City Steak Soup, *144*, 170
  Meatball Tortilla Soup, *144*, 174
  Pasta Fagioli, 184
  Pea Soup, 180
  Three-Cheese Beer Soup, 182
  Three-Mushroom Soup, 196
Sour Cream Pound Cake, *286, 369*
Southwest Pork Chops, 80
Spanish Rice, 232
Spiced Apricot Sauce, 54
Spiced Barbecue Turkey Thighs, 225
Spiced Glaze, 32
Spiced Maple Syrup, 26
Spiced Pot Roast with Root Vegetables, 70
Spicy Baked Sweet Potato Fries, 344
Spicy Buttermilk-Brined Fried Chicken, 263
Spicy Hot Pan-Fried Fish, 290
Spicy Shrimp Pasta, 96
Spinach
  Cheesy Artichoke and Spinach Dip, 40
  Crab and Spinach Pasta with Fontina, 156
  Creamed Spinach, *282*, 337
  Greek Vegetable and Feta Cheese Pie, 97
  Spinach and Mushroom Quiche, 6
  Spinach-Dill Dip, 42
  Vermicelli with Sausage and Spinach, 306
Squash. *See also* Pumpkin; Zucchini
  Butternut Squash and Carrot Soup, 197
  Roasted Vegetable Pasta Salad with Walnut Pesto, 355
Steak au Poivre, 248
Steak with Creamy Onion Sauce, 243

Steak with Pan Sauce, 297
Stews
  Boeuf Bourguignon, 239
  Brazilian Pork and Black Bean Stew, 179
  Caribbean Chicken Stew, 190
  Chili, 175
  Goulash, 173
  Luck o' the Irish Stew, 177
  Mustard-Herb Beef Stew, 176
  Oyster Stew, 194
  Pizza Stew with Biscuits, 83
  Slow Cooker Moroccan Lamb Tagine, 211
  Sweet Potato–Black Bean Stew, 200
  Vegetable-Pork Oven Stew, 178
Stratas
  Baked Brie Strata, 13
  Baked Denver Strata, 12
Strawberries
  Cherry-Berry Shortcakes, 379
  Rhubarb Crisp, *284*, 380
  Soda Fountain Ice Cream Pie, 372
  Strawberry Cream Pie, 105
  Strawberry Ice Cream, *286*, 389
  Watermelon and Strawberry Lemonade, 63
Streusel-Nut Topping, 29
Stuffed Mushrooms, 51
Stuffing. *See* Bread stuffings
Sugared Bacon-Wrapped Smokies, 55, 134
Summer Vegetable Potato Salad, 354
Sunday Oven Pot Roast, 238, *276*
Sweet-and-Savory Potato Chips, 47
Sweet-and-Sour Apricot Sauce, 312
Sweetened Whipped Cream, 372, 373, 379, 380
Sweet Herbed Oven-Fried Chicken, 86, 137
Sweet potatoes
  Apple-Buttered Sweet Potatoes, 234
  Pecan-Crusted Pork Tenderloin with Sautéed Apples and Sweet Potatoes, 253
  Spicy Baked Sweet Potato Fries, 344
  Sweet-and-Savory Potato Chips, 47
  Sweet Potato–Black Bean Stew, 200
  Sweet Potato Chips, 289
Sweet-Spicy Baked Beans, 351
Swiss Steak, 242

T

Tacos
  Fish Tacos with Lime Sauce, *279, 321*
  Turkey, Black Bean, and Mango Tacos, 226
Tart, Brownie Raspberry, 109
Tea
  Apricot Green Tea, 64
  Chai, 67
Teriyaki Pork Lo Mein, 81
Tex-Mex Meatballs, *144*, 174
Thai Curried Noodle Bowl, 314
Three-Cheese Beer Soup, 182
Three-Cheese Ziti and Smoked Chicken Casserole, 147
Three-Mushroom Soup, 196
Tilapia Vera Cruz, 322
Toasted Cumin Guacamole, 44
Toffee-Pear Sauce, 385
Toffee-Pear Sticky Pudding, 385
Tomatoes
  BLT Salad with Buttermilk Dressing, 358
  Bolognese Sauce, 210
  Creamy Tomato, Sausage, and Mushroom Pasta Sauce, 224
  Easy Tomato Sauce, 100
  Fresh Tomato Sauce, 78, *136*
  Fresh Tomato Soup, 199
  Fried Green Tomatoes, *280, 335*
  Loaded Creamed Corn with Tomato and Bacon, 231
  Oven-Roasted Fish with Peas and Tomatoes, 272
  Roasted Salmon and Tomatoes, 91
  Shrimp Vera Cruz, 322
  Slow Cooker Marinara Sauce, 227
  Smothered Okra, 334
  Spanish Rice, 232
  Swiss Steak, 242
  Tilapia Vera Cruz, 322
  Tomato-Avocado Grilled Cheese, 327
  Tomato-Topped Lamb Chops and Rice, 77
  Veal Chops with Tomato Cream Sauce, 249
Tortellini-Vegetable Bake, 161

Tortillas
    Bean-and-Beef Tortilla Casserole, 119
    Black Bean and Corn Breakfast
        Burritos, 19
    Chicken Enchilada Casserole,
        139, 148
    Fish Tacos with Lime Sauce,
        279, 321
    Fresh Taco Salad, 101
    Layered Turkey Enchiladas, 315
    Lightened Up Chicken Enchiladas,
        148
    Meatball Tortilla Soup, 144, 174
    Nacho Turkey Casserole, 151
    Olive Medley Pinwheels, 52
    Turkey, Black Bean, and Mango
        Tacos, 226
    Vegetable Egg Salad Wraps, 326
Tropical Salsa, 57
Trout Almondine, 291
Tuna Club Sandwiches, 319
Tuna Noodle Casserole, 141, 153
Turkey
    BBQ Spice–Rubbed Turkey
        Breast, 270
    Cranberry-Sauced Hot Turkey
        Sandwiches, 317
    Herb-Roasted Turkey and
        Vegetables, 268
    Layered Turkey Enchiladas, 315
    Nacho Turkey Casserole, 151
    One-Dish Turkey and Biscuits, 152
    Pizza Stew with Biscuits, 83
    Saucy Spiced Apricot Meatballs, 54
    Sausage-Stuffed Turkey Breast,
        269, 276
    Sloppy Turkey and Veggie
        Sandwiches, 318
    Spiced Barbecue Turkey Thighs, 225
    Turkey, Black Bean, and Mango
        Tacos, 226
    Turkey and Stuffing Bake, 90
    Turkey Manicotti, 150
    Turkey Meatballs, 191
    Turkey Meat Loaf, 271
    Turkey Salisbury Steaks, 316

Turkey sausages
    Beer-Steamed Mussels with
        Sausage and Fennel, 294
Twice-Baked Potatoes, 345

U

Upside-Down Pineapple-Ginger Carrot
    Cake, 106

V

Vanilla Café Latte, 68
Vanilla Frosting, 33
Veal Chops with Tomato Cream
    Sauce, 249
Vegetables. See also specific vegetables
    Cheese and Vegetable Rice
        Casserole, 157
    Glazed Ham with Vegetables, 310
    Herbed Root Vegetable Cobbler,
        141, 165
    Oven-Fried Veggies, 283, 340
    Roasted Vegetable Pasta Salad with
        Walnut Pesto, 355
    Rosemary-Roasted Vegetables, 339
    Spiced Pot Roast with Root
        Vegetables, 70
    Sunday Oven Pot Roast, 238, 276
    Tortellini-Vegetable Bake, 161
    Vegetable Egg Salad Wraps, 326
    Vegetable-Polenta Lasagna, 98
    Vegetable-Pork Oven Stew, 178
Veggie Burgers, 100
Vermicelli with Sausage and
    Spinach, 306

W

Waffles
    Brownie Waffles à la Mode,
        288, 384
    Cornflake Chicken 'n' Waffles, 21
    Overnight Three-Grain Waffles,
        22, 130
Walnuts
    Angel Hair with Walnut Pesto, 330
    Apple Cake with Buttery Caramel
        Sauce, 368

    Caramels, 401
    Chocolate Chip Cookies, 396
    Creamy Blue Cheese Dip, 42
    Easy Chocolate Fudge, 399
    Fruit-and-Nut Baked Oatmeal, 36
    Roasted Vegetable Pasta Salad with
        Walnut Pesto, 355
    Rosemary-Roasted Nuts, 59
    Shortcut Caramels, 401
    Streusel-Nut Topping, 29
    Walnut-Sage Potatoes au Gratin,
        282, 346
Watermelon and Strawberry
    Lemonade, 63
Whipped cream
    Sweetened Whipped Cream, 372,
        373, 379, 380
    White Chocolate Whipped
        Cream, 371
White Chocolate Bread Pudding with
    Hard Sauce, 386
White Chocolate Whipped Cream, 371
Wild rice
    Chicken and Wild Rice Casserole,
        127
    Chicken and Wild Rice Soup, 185

Y

Yogurt
    Goat Cheese–Yogurt Sauce, 318
    Yogurt-Chive Dipping Sauce,
        46, 135

Z

Zucchini
    Asparagus, Zucchini, and Yellow
        Pepper Frittata with Fontina, 16
    Baked Brie Strata, 13
    Cornmeal-Crusted Pork, 304
    Greek Vegetable and Feta Cheese
        Pie, 97
    Hash Brown–Crusted Quiche, 7
    Roasted Vegetable Pasta Salad with
        Walnut Pesto, 355

Metric Information

The charts on this page provide a guide for converting measurements from the U.S. customary system, which is used throughout this book, to the metric system.

PRODUCT DIFFERENCES

Most of the ingredients called for in the recipes in this book are available in most countries. However, some are known by different names. Here are some common American ingredients and their possible counterparts:

- All-purpose flour is enriched, bleached, or unbleached white household flour. When self-rising flour is used in place of all-purpose flour in a recipe that calls for leavening, omit the leavening agent (baking soda or baking powder) and salt.
- Baking soda is bicarbonate of soda.
- Cornstarch is cornflour.
- Golden raisins are sultanas.
- Light-color corn syrup is golden syrup.
- Powdered sugar is icing sugar.
- Sugar (white) is granulated, fine granulated, or castor sugar.
- Vanilla or vanilla extract is vanilla essence.

VOLUME AND WEIGHT

The United States traditionally uses cup measures for liquid and solid ingredients. The chart below shows the approximate imperial and metric equivalents. If you are accustomed to weighing solid ingredients, the following approximate equivalents will be helpful.

- 1 cup butter, castor sugar, or rice = 8 ounces = ½ pound = 250 grams
- 1 cup flour = 4 ounces = ¼ pound = 125 grams
- 1 cup icing sugar = 5 ounces = 150 grams

Canadian and U.S. volume for a cup measure is 8 fluid ounces (237 ml), but the standard metric equivalent is 250 ml.

1 British imperial cup is 10 fluid ounces.

In Australia, 1 tablespoon equals 20 ml, and there are 4 teaspoons in the Australian tablespoon.

Spoon measures are used for smaller amounts of ingredients. Although the size of the tablespoon varies slightly in different countries, for practical purposes and for recipes in this book, a straight substitution is all that's necessary. Measurements made using cups or spoons always should be level unless stated otherwise.

COMMON WEIGHT RANGE REPLACEMENTS

Imperial / U.S.	Metric
½ ounce	15 g
1 ounce	25 g or 30 g
4 ounces (¼ pound)	115 g or 125 g
8 ounces (½ pound)	225 g or 250 g
16 ounces (1 pound)	450 g or 500 g
1 ¼ pounds	625 g
1 ½ pounds	750 g
2 pounds or 2 ¼ pounds	1,000 g or 1 Kg

OVEN TEMPERATURE EQUIVALENTS

Fahrenheit Setting	Celsius Setting*	Gas Setting
300°F	150°C	Gas Mark 2 (very low)
325°F	160°C	Gas Mark 3 (low)
350°F	180°C	Gas Mark 4 (moderate)
375°F	190°C	Gas Mark 5 (moderate)
400°F	200°C	Gas Mark 6 (hot)
425°F	220°C	Gas Mark 7 (hot)
450°F	230°C	Gas Mark 8 (very hot)
475°F	240°C	Gas Mark 9 (very hot)
500°F	260°C	Gas Mark 10 (extremely hot)
Broil	Broil	Grill

Electric and gas ovens may be calibrated using Celsius. However, for an electric oven, increase Celsius setting 10 to 20 degrees when cooking above 160°C. For convection or forced air ovens (gas or electric), lower the temperature setting 25°F/10°C when cooking at all heat levels.

BAKING PAN SIZES

Imperial / U.S.	Metric
9×1½-inch round cake pan	22- or 23×4-cm (1.5 L)
9×1½-inch pie plate	22- or 23×4-cm (1 L)
8×8×2-inch square cake pan	20×5-cm (2 L)
9×9×2-inch square cake pan	22- or 23×4.5-cm (2.5 L)
11×7×1½-inch baking pan	28×17×4-cm (2 L)
2-quart rectangular baking pan	30×19×4.5-cm (3 L)
13×9×2-inch baking pan	34×22×4.5-cm (3.5 L)
15×10×1-inch jelly roll pan	40×25×2-cm
9×5×3-inch loaf pan	23×13×8-cm (2 L)
2-quart casserole	2 L

U.S./STANDARD METRIC EQUIVALENTS

⅛ teaspoon = 0.5 ml	
¼ teaspoon = 1 ml	
½ teaspoon = 2 ml	
1 teaspoon = 5 ml	
1 tablespoon = 15 ml	
2 tablespoons = 25 ml	
¼ cup = 2 fluid ounces = 50 ml	
⅓ cup = 3 fluid ounces = 75 ml	
½ cup = 4 fluid ounces = 125 ml	
⅔ cup = 5 fluid ounces = 150 ml	
¾ cup = 6 fluid ounces = 175 ml	
1 cup = 8 fluid ounces = 250 ml	
2 cups = 1 pint = 500 ml	
1 quart = 1 liter	